Rewriting the Renaissance

The Discourses of Sexual Difference in Early Modern Europe

Edited by
Margaret W. Ferguson,
Maureen Quilligan,
and Nancy J. Vickers

THE UNIVERSITY OF CHICAGO PRESS
Chicago and London

MARGARET W. FERGUSON is associate professor of English and comparative literature at Yale University. MAUREEN QUILLIGAN is associate professor of English at the University of Pennsylvania. NANCY J. VICKERS is associate professor and chairman of French and Italian at Dartmouth College.

The University of Chicago Press, Chicago 60637
The University of Chicago Press, Ltd., London
© 1986 by The University of Chicago
All rights reserved. Published 1986
Paperback edition 1987
Printed in the United States of America

98 97 96 95 94 93 92 91 90 89   7 6 5 4 3

LIBRARY OF CONGRESS CATALOGING-IN-PUBLICATION DATA
Main entry under title;

Rewriting the Renaissance.

  (Women in culture and society)
  Bibliography: p.
  Includes index.
  1. Sex role—Europe—History—Congresses.   2. Women—Europe—History—
Renaissance, 1450–1600—Congresses.   3. Patriarchy—Europe—History—Con-
gresses.   4. European literature—Renaissance, 1450–1600—History and criticism—
Congresses.   5. Sex role in literature—Congresses.   I. Ferguson, Margaret W.,
1948–.   II. Quilligan, Maureen, 1944–.   III. Vickers, Nancy J.
IV. Series.

HQ1075.5.E85R48   1986   305.3   85-28829
ISBN 0-226-24313-3
ISBN 0-226-24314-1 (pbk.)

Contents

Series Editor's Foreword

CATHARINE R. STIMPSON

The "Renaissance" shimmers in Western cultural history. The word haunts several imaginations, be they those of urban planners in Motor City or scholars in research universities. Like the phoenix, the "Renaissance" promises that time is renewable. In a fresh epoch, art, literature, and learning can be powerful; power can be artful, literate, and learned. Man is no ruined piece of nature, no poor forked creature, but golden, zestful, grand, human.

Recently, we have affixed the term "early modern period" to "Renaissance" as a supplementary name for those 250 or so years between 1450 and 1700 in Europe. "Early modern" is a far more sober, far less lyrical, set of phonemes than "Renaissance." Despite this, the phrase points to an ambitious, energetic, fruitful effort to resee the Renaissance and to see it wholly. This attempt involves both dispelling old illusions, no matter how glamorous they might be, and spelling out new perceptions, no matter how sacrilegious they might seem.

Rewriting the Renaissance is a dazzling array of such perceptions. They begin with feminist scholarship. As the editors of this volume tell us, such work foregrounds "phenomena" that we have ignored, distorted, or marginalized. Among them are patriarchy itself, the rule of the fathers; the marginalization of those whom the patriarchs would control; and the resistance of those on the margins. Significantly, some women, refusing to reduce their lives to the needle and the distaff, insisted that they, too, might enter public culture and wield the pen. Indeed, a woman, Elizabeth I, was the most formidable ruler Europe knew.

Today, feminist scholars argue about what the object of their inquiry ought to be. Is it women themselves, their lives and traditions, or is it the relations between men and women, their interlocking lives and traditions? The argument is serious, for a scholar's response will determine her, or his, methods, questions, and conclusions. *Rewriting the Renaissance* has chosen the second, and more expansive, focus. Its

vii

essays explore, then, immense social and cultural patterns, or, as Gayle Rubin has named them, sex/gender arrangements. They feature a divisive stress on *differences*, between genders, but also between classes, or races, or nationalities. The writers in this volume are especially sensitive to discourse, to the sign systems that "encode" and "enforce" individual specificity.

Given its intelligent commitment to spacious perspectives, *Rewriting the Renaissance* seeks to map junctures between sex/gender systems and other structures and processes, particularly those that determine class. Doing so demands several intellectual tasks: incorporating aesthetic and material investigations; exploring the intersections of reproductive and productive life; watching the representation of "reality" become ideology; placing the literary and pictorial text within the social text.

In brief, *Rewriting the Renaissance* legitimately demands that we regard the Renaissance as roundly and as sharply as possible. No single vision, however, no single person, can meet this demand. Boldly and correctly, *Rewriting the Renaissance* brings together scholars whose primary commitment is to a feminist perspective and scholars whose primary commitment is elsewhere. It juxtaposes the insights of feminism with those of Marxism, psychoanalysis, and deconstruction. Fearful of limiting themselves to the inquires of one academic discipline, the editors ensure that literary critics, art critics, historians will speak together.

Jostling together, essays question and refine each other. Yet they do not collapse into anarchic atomism. They have their unities. The volume acknowledges the strength of discourse in shaping history. The languages of representation serve as the genetic material of culture and of a culture. In the past, their most boisterous and powerful tongues have been those of the patriarchs. Yet languages can, and should, change. The silent can, and should, speak.

Rewriting the Renaissance contributes to the emerging languages of and about women, gender, and sexual difference. A sophisticated and solid text, it has as well the exuberance and spark of a revisionary act. As it looks back at the Renaissance and various interpretations of that period, the book also, perhaps paradoxically, burnishes a belief that the Renaissance helped to construct for us: a confidence, sometimes hopeful, sometimes ironic, in the metamorphic, self-reflective capacities of human intelligence itself.

Acknowledgments

As anyone who has seen a book through the press knows too well, even a single-authored volume is an extensive collaborative process. The present volume, with its many authors, multiple editors, and the collective occasion of its original inception, owes more than most books to the good will, interest, and care of a large group of people. Although the present collection of essays is by no means a record of the proceedings of the conference "Renaissance Woman/Renaissance Man: Studies in the Creation of Culture and Society," held at Yale University in March 1982, it is true that all of the authors represented in this volume were present at the conference, either as speakers or as members of the audience. Because the conference was the germinal occasion of the book, we wish then to thank the people who helped to make it possible: A. Bartlett Giamatti, president of Yale University, for his initial interest and support; Linda Downey and George Ferris of the Yale University Office of Grant and Contract Administration for their aid in seeking financial support for the conference; Laura Bornholdt, vice-president for education of the Lilly Endowment for the grant that funded the conference; Sheila Brewer of the Yale Renaissance Studies Program for her help with the initial mailings; and Susan Adler and Mary Beth Radigan of the Yale University Conference Office for their patience as well as eagerness to try something new. We wish also to acknowledge here the invaluable participation of all those who spoke at the conference; their contribution to the conversation begun then did not end with the close of that symposium and their work continues to be a part of the intellectual effort informing the present volume.

Among those who have helped us to transform the insubstantial pageant faded of the occasion of the conference into a book between covers, we wish to thank Catharine R. Stimpson for her initial interest and solid advice over breakfast in Los Angeles; Leah Marcus and an anonymous reader for the University of Chicago Press for their considered commentary on the essays, with particular thanks to Leah Marcus for her generous engagement in the revisions of the introduction; Kathleen Perry and Jennifer Roberts for their help with the bibliography; the Faculty Research Committee of Dartmouth College for providing support essential for the final preparation of the manuscript; and, finally, J. M. Matthews for such expert copyediting and enthusiastic reading.

Margaret W. Ferguson
Maureen Quilligan
Nancy J. Vickers

Note on the Jacket Illustration

Taken from a line drawing of Sir Thomas More's family that Hans Holbein apparently sent as a personal gift to Erasmus, the picture shows the urgent figure of Margaret Giggs, More's adopted daughter and a Greek scholar, bent over More's elderly father as she points out something in a book. The figure of Giggs was dropped from subsequent oil-painted versions of the famous portrait. We seek to redress her original marginalization and historical absence by putting her in the center of our picture; she stands as a fitting emblem of our enterprise.

The Contributors

Judith C. Brown teaches history at Stanford University, where she is associate professor. Her research centers on the economic and social history of early modern Italy. Her publications include *In the Shadow of Florence: Provincial Society in Renaissance Pescia* (1982) and recently *Immodest Acts: The Life of a Lesbian Nun in Renaissance Italy* (1986).

Elizabeth Cropper is professor of the history of art at the Johns Hopkins University. Her book *The Ideal of Painting: Pietro Testa's Düsseldorf Notebook* was published in 1984, and she has written extensively on the history and criticism of sixteenth- and seventeenth-century Italian art. She is currently working on the question of artistic plagiarism in seventeenth-century Rome.

Margaret W. Ferguson, associate professor of English and comparative literature at Yale University, is now working on a book tentatively entitled *A Room Not Her Own: Women as Readers and Writers in Early Modern Europe*. Her publications include *Trials of Desire: Renaissance Defenses of Poetry* (1983) as well as articles on Saint Augustine, Du Bellay, Nashe, Spenser, Shakespeare, and Milton.

Sheila ffolliott is associate professor of art history and European studies at George Mason University. She is the author of *Civic Sculpture in the Renaissance: Montorsoli's Fountains at Messina* (1984) and is currently at work on a major study of Catherine de' Medeci.

Carla Freccero is assistant professor of French and Italian at Dartmouth College, where she specializes in Renaissance comparative literature, modern literary critical theory, and feminist criticism. She is currently completing a book on Rabelais and has previously published articles on the function of woman in his text.

Jonathan Goldberg is professor of English at Brown University. He is the author of *Endlesse Worke: Spenser and the Structures of Discourse* (1981); *James I and the Politics of Literature: Jonson, Shakespeare, Donne, and Their Contemporaries* (1983); and recently *Voice Terminal Echo:*

Postmodernism and English Renaissance Texts (1986). Currently, he is coediting Milton (with Stephen Orgel) and writing on Shakespeare.

John Guillory, associate professor of English at Yale University, is the author of *Poetic Authority: Spenser, Milton, and Literary History* (1983). His earlier work on canon formation and ideology is now evolving into an extended study of literary canon formation.

Richard Halpern is assistant professor of English at Yale University, where he works in critical theory and sixteenth- and seventeenth-century texts. He has previously published on Skelton and is now completing a book, *The Poetics of Primitive Accumulation: English Literature in the Transition to Capitalism.*

Clark Hulse is associate professor of English at the University of Illinois at Chicago. He has written on Shakespeare and Spenser, on Renaissance historiography, and on the politics of Renaissance poetic language. His book, *Metamorphic Verse* (1981), is a generic study of the Elizabethan minor epic. Presently he is at work on a study of the relationship between poetry and painting in the Elizabethan Renaissance.

Ann Rosalind Jones is associate professor and chair of the Comparative Literature Program at Smith College. She has written on Renaissance poetry (Du Guillet, Labé, Scève, and Sidney) and fiction (Nashe) and is now completing a study of love poetry by sixteenth-century women. Her research includes work on contemporary literary theory—particularly Marxist and feminist debates—and twentieth-century narrative.

Constance Jordan's publications include articles on Montaigne, Deloney, Sir Thomas Elyot, and Pulci. Her first book, *Pulci's 'Morgante': Poetry and History in Fifteenth-Century Florence*, is forthcoming, and her second will focus on Renaissance defenses of women and the origins of modern feminism. She is assistant professor of English and comparative literature at Columbia University.

Coppélia Kahn, professor of English at Wesleyan University, is the author of *Man's Estate: Masculine Identity in Shakespeare* (1981). She has also coedited three anthologies: *Representing Shakespeare: New Psychoanalytic Essays* (1980); *Shakespeare's 'Rough Magic': Renaissance Essays in Honor of C. L. Barber* (1985); and *Making a Difference: Feminist Literary*

Criticism (1985). She is now working on the semiotics of gender in English Renaissance drama.

Louis A. Montrose is professor of English literature at the University of California at San Diego. He has published widely on Elizabethan drama and poetry, pastoral forms, and courtly performances. His work proposes to situate canonical Elizabethan literary texts within a larger field of Elizabethan social practices. He has recently completed *In Mirrors More than One: Elizabeth I and the Figurations of Power.*

Stephen Orgel teaches at Stanford. He is the author of *The Illusion of Power* (1975), *The Jonsonian Masque* (1981), and, in collaboration with Sir Roy Strong, *Inigo Jones* (1973). He has edited the court masques of Ben Jonson and Cristopher Marlowe's poems and translations, and has written extensively on Renaissance literature and culture. His edition of *The Tempest* is forthcoming in the Oxford Shakespeare.

Maureen Quilligan, associate professor of English at the University of Pennsylvania, is the author of *The Language of Allegory: Defining the Genre* (1979) and *Milton's Spenser: The Politics of Reading* (1983). She is currently at work on a book about female sovereignty in the sixteenth century.

François Rigolot is Meredith Howland Pyne Professor of French at Princeton, where he chairs the Department of Romance Languages and Literatures. He has published extensively on rhetoric, poetics, and textual problems in Renaissance literature. His books include *Les Langages de Rabelais* (1972), *Poétique et onomastique* (1977), and *Le Texte de la Renaissance* (1983). This year Flammarion will publish his edition of Louise Labé's complete works.

Lauren Silberman is assistant professor of English at Baruch College, City University of New York. She has published in the field of Spenser studies, and her current work is on Spenser's Hermaphrodite and the discourses of sexual difference in the 1590 *Faerie Queene*.

Peter Stallybrass is lecturer in the School of Cultural and Community Studies and covenor of the Graduate Program in Critical Theory at the University of Sussex. His research includes work on nationalism, popular culture, and the politics of gender in early modern England. He has published on popular ballads and festivals, on Shakespeare and

Sidney, and has coauthored (with Allon White) a forthcoming book, *The Politics and Poetics of Transgression.*

Nancy J. Vickers is associate professor and chair of French and Italian at Dartmouth College. She has published principally on Dante and Petrarch, although her most recent work has focused on description in Shakespeare, Petrarchan imitation in Ronsard, and artists and models in Cellini. Currently she is completing a book on the female body in the poetry and painting of the court of Francis I.

Marguerite Waller teaches Renaissance literature, literary theory, and film at Amherst College, where she is associate professor of English. She has written a book, *Petrarch's Poetics and Literary History* (1980), as well as articles on Wyatt and Surrey, Dante, Fellini, and George Lucas. Her current research draws upon poststructuralist and feminist theory to perform ideological analyses of early modern texts and their late modern readings.

Merry E. Wiesner is assistant professor at the University of Wisconsin-Milwaukee, where she teaches European history and women's history. She has recently completed a bibliography, *Women in the Sixteenth Century: A Bibliography* (1983), and a book, *Working Women in Renaissance Germany* (1986). Her current research focuses on women's defense of their public role in Renaissance Europe.

Introduction

Margaret W. Ferguson, with Maureen Quilligan
and Nancy J. Vickers

In his famous study *The Civilization of the Renaissance in Italy* (1860), Jacob Burckhardt wrote that "to understand the higher forms of social intercourse in this period, we must keep before our minds the fact that women stood on a footing of perfect equality with men."[1] This remarkable assertion is belied by its appearance in an eight-page chapter, "The Position of Women," in Burckhardt's massive book; and the argument of this chapter would doubtless have astonished Renaissance women whatever their social class. Even those privileged enough to participate in those "higher forms of social intercourse" that Burckhardt's book celebrates would have been less likely to agree with him than with the Venetian nun Arcangela Tarabotti, whose treatise *La Semplicitá Ingannata o la Tirannia Paterna* (*Simplicity Deceived or Paternal Tyranny*, 1654) describes the enormous obstacles women encountered whenever they attempted to engage in the quintessential humanist task of giving ideas public expression through writing. "I who know may freely testify," Tarabotti writes—with considerable irony, as what she is describing is precisely women's lack of freedom to testify—that when "women are seen with pen in hand, they are met immediately with shrieks commanding a return to that life of pain which their writing had interrupted, a life devoted to the women's work of needle and distaff."[2]

To oppose the virtually unknown voice of Tarabotti to Burckhardt's famous one is to highlight the simple but important fact that our views of the Renaissance have, until quite recently, been largely shaped by educated middle-class men writing for, and frequently about, other educated men. Burckhardt's account of the Renaissance as an era of splendid achievements in art and science—achievements made possible by the early humanists' rediscovery of the "freedom and dignity of man"—illustrates the ideologically significant skewing of perspective that occurs when cultural historians focus their attention chiefly on the beliefs and productions of a small elite group. The humanists constituted such a group, and although they did indeed advocate a certain equality of education for daughters and sons of wealthy burghers and patricians, they most certainly did not place women on a footing of "perfect equality" with men in Italy or elsewhere. On the contrary, as Margaret King has shown, humanist texts often dramatize profound social inequalities between men and women, both in the rhetoric of praise they use for learned ladies and in the actual programs of study they recommend for girls.[3] A pedagogic imperative like Leonardo Bruni's—that young women should study the liberal arts just as young men did but should on no account be introduced to rhetoric, which "lies absolutely outside the province of women"—went unnoticed by Burckhardt because he shared the common, although not universal, humanist assumption that women's province was the private rather than the public sphere.[4] The very distinction between these spheres, however, is a complex historical phenomenon that needs to be analyzed with reference to social and economic changes that occurred in the Renaissance.[5] Historians who want to understand women's relegation to a "private" realm cannot afford to view the period, as Burckhardt did, chiefly through the lens provided by the humanists themselves.[6] Too much is left out, and too much is at stake.

What is left out is not only the critical view of women's place in Renaissance society provided by witnesses like Tarabotti and by earlier Italian women like the scholar Isotta Nogarola, who lamented that she had ever been born female "to be scorned by men in words and deeds."[7] Also missing from Burckhardt's perspective, which has by no means ceased to inform more recent scholarship, particularly in the humanities, is a sense that history is more than the story of the political, artistic, and scientific achievements of great individuals. Only when we incorporate into our studies of Renaissance art and literature the findings of social historians who have begun to analyze new data about the lives of members of the lower as well as the upper strata of Renaissance society will we see how important the period is for students of modern society in general and for feminists in particular. What is at stake in a revaluation of the Renaissance is the possibility of a fuller, more historically grounded understanding of the socioeconomic system under which we now live, as well as a better appreciation of differences: not only those that distinguish late twentieth century western societies from those of Renaissance Europe but also those of class and gender that existed within the societies commonly designated by the term *Renaissance*.

According to another nineteenth-century German scholar whose view of history was at once darker and more comprehensive than Burckhardt's, the epochal significance of the years roughly between 1450 and 1700 in Western Europe lay in the gradual replacement during this era of a feudal mode of production by a capitalist one.[8] The experience of women and men in everyday life therefore underwent a change as profound as that which marked the transition from the socioeconomic system of late antiquity to the feudal one of the Middle Ages. From a Marxist perspective, European humanists were right to perceive a significant cultural rift between their era and the one that preceded it. The name given by the humanists to their era, however, was somewhat misleading, for if the period did see the "rebirth" (albeit in altered form) of certain aspects of ancient civilization in the realms of art, literature, law, historiography, and political theory, it also saw the emergence of social structures previously unknown on the stage of world history. The changes that occurred in the Renaissance, indeed, link that period more closely to our own than to the Middle Ages or to the classical era that the early humanists themselves thought they were in some sense privileged to see reborn, as historians in the last thirty years have suggested by referring to the Renaissance as the "early modern period."[9] The new name, which poses its own set of problems for theories of periodization, generally does not replace the old one but supplements it, calling attention to features of the period that Renaissance writers could not see as clearly as we can. Chief among those features important for the study of women during the period is the development of capitalism. Although debate continues among social and economic historians about the origins of capitalism and even about the meaning of the term, historians of various political perspectives have increasingly emphasized the idea that capitalism is a distinctive economic and social phenomenon, characteristic of a distinctive period of history. It entailed, among other things, a new type of relationship between workers and their work, on the one hand, and between workers and employers, on the other.[10] As production was organized on a larger scale, workplace and home were increasingly separated and an individual wage replaced the family earnings of domestic production; such changes had profound effects on women's lives and on their relations to men.[11]

In Western Europe and England, the gradual and uneven transition from feudal to capitalist societies was accompanied by at least two other developments that are important for an understanding of the social relations between the sexes in the early modern period. One is the emergence of those centrally administered nation states to which we owe the existence of powerful female queens within the royal dynasties of Spain, France, and England; the other is the significant set of changes that occurred in the structure of the family and therefore in women's roles during this era. Describing these latter changes in "The Rise of the Nuclear Family in Early Modern England," Lawrence Stone, for example, posits three major and interrelated developments. First, "the importance of the nuclear core increased, and the influence of the surrounding kin declined"; second, "the importance of affective bonds tying the conjugal group together increased, and the economic functions of the family as a distributive mechanism for goods and services declined"; and third, "the pre-existing patriarchal aspects of internal power relationships within the family" were strengthened.[12] Elaborating on this last point, Stone argues in *The Family, Sex and Marriage* that during the period between 1450 and 1630, "both Church and state provided powerful new theoretical and practical support" for a "reinforcement of the despotic authority of the husband and father— that is to say, of patriarchy." He adds that "a new interest in children, coupled with the Calvinist premise of Original Sin, gave fathers an added incentive to ensure the internalized submissiveness of their children."[13]

Although Stone focuses mainly on the upper and middle ranks of English society, Roberta Hamilton (among others) has shown that for lower class families too the Renaissance brought significant changes. The major one was that the family gradually lost its feudal function as a unit of production and became, as it still generally is today, a unit of consumption, dependent "either on the wage labor of individual family members or on capital."[14] Hamilton—like Stone, Philippe Ariès, and others who have studied the history of the early modern family—offers an important corrective to Marx's own view (shared by many modern feminists) that it was the Industrial Revolution that ushered in the most significant changes in the structure of the family and in women's roles within that unit and in society at large.[15] Hamilton argues persuasively that to understand the origins both of women's typical social roles and of the crucial differences among women of different classes in modern Western societies, we must look not to the period of industrialization in the eighteenth and nineteenth centuries but rather to the period of "early capitalization" in the late sixteenth and early seventeeth centuries.[16] For it was then that "women's work" was significantly redefined, as the opposition arose between the "idle" bourgeois wife and the proletarian woman. The role of the former is defined by her status as psychological helpmeet to her husband and mother to her children; her work in the household is not considered real because it does not directly contribute to capitalist production. The lower-class woman's work also becomes increasingly invisible during this period; whether she labors outside the home or within it (as a spinner, for instance), and whether she lives in the country or, as increasingly occurred in England, in the capital city whose population swelled with peasants uprooted from their farms by the practice of enclosure, her wages tend to be substantially lower than those of male workers—when she receives them at all, that is.[17] For as urbanization, rising prices, a rising population, and the dissolution of the monasteries in sixteenth century England contributed to the existence of pauperism "on a larger scale than ever before" in the country's history,[18] a growing number of lower class women found themselves unsupported by men and unable to earn a living for themselves and their children. Although some of them received welfare aid from their parishes, many suffered. Christopher Hill notes that pauperism in England "began to increase seriously just after the traditional means of coping with it [monastic alms-giving and the tradition of manorial hospitality] had been destroyed."[19]

Hamilton's argument is important because it addresses a question that most historians have neglected even to ask: how did the economic changes that occurred in the early modern period affect women as a group?[20] A similar question needs to be posed with respect to the political changes that occurred in Renaissance societies, both in the city states of Italy, where, Joan Kelly-Gadol has argued, "the exercise of political power by women was far more rare than under feudalism," and in those large monarchies that arose out of feudal societies elsewhere in Europe.[21] Perry Anderson's brilliant study of such monarchies—*The Lineages of the Absolutist State*—contains no separate index entry for women; moreover, Anderson explores the growth of monarchical government in France and England without ever considering the implications of the fact that the latter country was ruled for nearly fifty years by a queen. Rightly emphasizing that marriage was a crucial diplomatic as well as economic instrument of dynastic forms of government, Anderson nonetheless errs in attributing the growth of royal authority during Elizabeth's reign simply to her personal "popularity."[22] Had Anderson been more alert to the political significance of Elizabeth's gender, he would have needed to give a more complex account of her popularity, which derived not only from an accident of personality but also from her skillful manipulation of the social institution of marriage. She used that institution to reward the bureaucrats who helped her consolidate her power and to weaken aristocratic families that posed threats to the crown; she also used it symbolically to woo her people and literally to attract various suitors, foreign and domestic, to a royal hand she never finally gave.[23]

Because England was ruled so long and successfully by a female prince during a period when the relations between men and women at all levels of society were undergoing significant changes—many of which affected women adversely—that country offers a particularly rich field of inquiry for feminist scholars. Elizabeth's own strategies of self-presentation, especially when analyzed in relation to literary texts that figure and obliquely criticize her, dramatize certain contradictions in patriarchal ideology that impinged on the lives not only of court women but of their lower born sisters. As Ruth Kelso demonstrates in *Doctrine for the Lady of the Renaissance*, "the theory of the favored class" did not serve "to distinguish the lady from the inferior sort of womankind," because hierarchical social theories proclaimed "as the first law of woman . . . submission and obedience. Theory does not divide women into two groups, the rulers and the ruled, and prescribe to each a different set of laws . . . Practice did just that, but not theory. Theory said that all women must be ruled."[24] Kelso argues persuasively that, despite the significant and growing class differences among women in the Renaissance, they nonetheless constituted a distinct group within the discourse of patriarchal theory.

The Stuart kings who succeeded Elizabeth and who presided over the decline of the absolutist state created under the Tudors also provide fascinating material for students of patriarchal ideology. Partly in reaction against Elizabeth, the Stuarts aggressively promoted the image of the monarch as a father and husband of his country; and as several essays in this volume show, the royal self-presentations of the Stuart kings were refracted in the cultural productions of the period, including Shakespeare's later plays and the propagandistic painting centered on court personalities. If the present volume contains what seems a disproportionate number of essays about English court culture, this may be a sign of the crucial twist given to the ideology of gender in both the Elizabethan and the Jacobean eras by Elizabeth's problematic presence on the throne. For this reason, and also because England underwent a uniquely swift transition from abolutist state to the limited monarchy ushered in by the bourgeois revolution of the mid-seventeenth century, the moment of England's initial imperial expansion is of special interest to scholars who are beginning to look at Renaissance culture from an interdisciplinary, feminist perspective. Such a perspective gives rise to the large questions that underlie the essays collected here: how did relations between the sexes influence, and how were they influenced by, the new economic, social, and political arrangements of the early modern period?

To ask such questions is not only to interrogate the history of sexual difference and division of labor in our own culture; it is also to focus attention on social institutions and artistic productions that cannot be considered mere "reflections" of changes in a society's basic socioeconomic structure.[25] For example, an institution like the nuclear family was shaped by Counter-Reformation and Protestant ideologies as well as by changes in demographic patterns and labor relations. The family therefore needs to be studied in relation to what we shall call a society's "discourses of sexual difference." By that phrase we refer to the complex and heterogeneous sign systems that encode—and enforce—differences between the sexes. These differences are not natural; on the contrary, they constitute part of what Gayle Rubin has termed the "sex-gender system," that is, "a socio-historical construction of sexual identity, difference and relationship; an appropriation of human anatomical and physiological features by an ideological discourse."[26] The concept of the sex-gender system highlights the observation that while significant differences exist among women of various social classes, equally significant differences exist between men and women at all levels of society. Anatomy is not destiny, but biological differences between the sexes have, throughout human history, been translated by social institutions into codes of behavior and law that privilege men over women irrespective of class. And such codes profoundly affect the ways in which both men and women experience their sexuality.

By focusing attention on aspects of the sex-gender system of early modern Europe, the essays in the present volume contribute to the small but growing field pioneered by Alice Clark in her study of working women in seventeenth-century England and explored more recently by scholars like Joan Kelly-Gadol and Natalie Zemon Davis.[27] Such scholars view the Renaissance through a lens that may properly be called feminist because it places in the foreground phenomena that traditionally have been completely overlooked or relegated to the margins of scholarly discourse. By discovering or recovering previously ignored cultural documents, frequently by women who are considered to be "minor" figures (women such as Christine de Pizan or Arcangela Tarabotti, for instance, whose writings have only recently begun to receive the degree of critical attention they deserve), feminists mount a challenge to the very notion of a canonical tradition; they further challenge that notion by reading canonical texts, generally by men, in heretical ways.[28] Feminists who attempt such heretical readings often join forces with recent theorists who practice what Paul Ricoeur calls a "hermeneutics of suspicion."[29] This camp includes Marxist, psychoanalytic, and deconstructive interpreters who seek, in various ways, to analyze that which is suppressed or consigned to the margin by the dominant ideological discourses of a particular society; this camp also includes the growing number of social historians who are working, often without glamorous theoretical banners, on recovering types of historical evidence overlooked by traditional intellectual historians. Because the figures of women have been marginalized, if not rendered virtually invisible, in many cultural productions, and because the tradition of male scholarship has tended, with some notable exceptions, to reinforce this marginalization, feminist scholars necessarily engage in a certain polemical effort to decenter the map of knowledge that they inherit. In so doing, they illustrate Joan Kelly-Gadol's notion of a feminist "double vision": when we "look at ages or movements of great social change in terms of the liberation or repression of women's potential," she writes, "the period or set of events with which we deal takes on a wholly different character or meaning from the normally accepted one."[30]

The difference that Kelly-Gadol speaks of arises from a redefinition of the object of inquiry which in turn results from methodological changes in the approach to that object. *What* is seen depends on *how* it is seen. Moreover, as Renaissance artists themselves suggested in experiments with perspectival puzzles like anamorphosis, some objects (like the skull in Holbein's famous painting *The Ambassadors*) cannot be rightly perceived at all unless the viewer adopts an oblique rather than frontal perspective on the picture. Although the representations of Renaissance culture perceived and created in the present volume of essays are by no means complete or in perfect harmony with each other, they do represent a collective effort to see, and talk, across several sets of boundaries. These include the boundaries that inhibit communication between scholars of different generations, different academic disciplines, and different methodological schools within a single discipline. An equally significant boundary crossed in this volume is that between scholars whose work is explicitly motivated by feminist concerns and those whose work is not or is only beginning to respond, sometimes critically, to questions posed by the new scholarship on women. The conference "Renaissance Woman/Renaissance Man," which was held at New Haven in March, 1982, and from which most of these essays were drawn, provoked lively and sometimes sharp debate among its participants, both those who gave formal presentations and those who spoke from the audience. Some of the questions raised there about ideological presuppositions and interpretive methods are implicitly addressed, if not fully answered, in the revised versions of the essays printed here. The volume as a whole, therefore, represents a moment in a continuing conversation and invites further exchange between two intersecting interdisciplinary enterprises, Women's Studies and Renaissance Studies.

Feminists will find in this volume illustrations of the "comparative" or "relational" mode of inquiry advocated by scholars such as Joan Kelly-Gadol, Gerda Lerner, and Myra Jehlen, among others. "The activity, power, and cultural evaluation of women," Kelly-Gadol argues, "simply cannot be assessed except in relational terms: by comparison and contrast with the activity, power, and cultural evaluation of men, and in relation to the institutions and social developments that shape the sexual order."[31] By undertaking such comparative studies, these essays seek to define the world of women not as a separate enclave in the world of men but rather as what Myra Jehlen has called a "long border" or "no-man's land" that requires exploration—and mapping—with new conceptual tools.[32] The present volume, like the conference from which it derived, contributes to that project by addressing questions about the dynamics of women's social relations to men; it therefore pursues that path in feminist scholarship that leads from an initial emphasis on women in a room of their own toward an analysis of the sex-gender system itself as it at once shapes and is shaped by other cultural productions.

For scholars trained in traditional methods of literary criticism, art history, and history, the essays in this volume also provide models and pose challenges for future work. Literary critics here can be observed venturing beyond the boundaries of written texts to ask how and where such texts intersect with other kinds of cultural production, ranging from maps and paintings to royal progresses. Art historians explore a similar seam of connection between aesthetic objects and the discourses of political power. And the essays by historians, which analyze newly discovered data about women's work and social status, pose challenges both to traditional accounts of the Renaissance as a period of "human" progress and to Marxist accounts that emphasize economic changes and class conflict but rarely address specific questions about gender as a category of social thought.[33]

The essays in this volume are grouped in three sections. The first focuses on the pivotal structure of Renaissance patriarchy that served, both in theory and in practice, to organize power relations not only in the family but also in the state, according to the well-known analogy exploited by Robert Filmer in his *Patriarcha* (1634): "We find in the Decalogue that the law which enjoins obedience to Kings is delivered in the terms of: Honour thy Father."[34] The essays by Jonathan Goldberg, Coppélia Kahn, and Stephen Orgel that open this first section all examine facets of that "strengthening of patriarchy" which Lawrence Stone sees as characteristic of the transitional period in England between the "feudal or community organizations of medieval society, and the participatory limited monarchy . . . of the late seventeenth century onwards."[35] Goldberg shows how James I used the language of the family to legitimize his assumption of absolutist monarchical prerogatives. By presenting himself as a "loving-nourish father" to his country, as "head" to his subservient body politic, and as "husband" to his wife the realm, James domesticated or naturalized his claims to power. The patriarchal theory adumbrated in James's own writings and in other texts of the period also informs the genre of the family portrait. Goldberg examines a series of seventeenth-century paintings and engravings that "offer images of domestic life converted to state use." Such representations were structured to make "the natural event of procreation" seem an extension of male prerogative and power.

Kahn and Orgel are also concerned with cultural productions in which patriarchal ideology serves both to "naturalize" the political realm and to politicize the supposedly natural relations among family members. Arguing that the family functions as "a link between psychic and social structures, and as the crucible in which gender identity is formed," Kahn analyzes the ideologically skewed conception of the family that appears in *King Lear*, where the figure of the mother is suppressed—as it is in Filmer's version of the Fifth Commandment quoted above—and where the idea consequently arises that children "owe their existence to their fathers alone." Kahn uses psychoanalytic methods to interrogate this conception of the family; she seeks to excavate the hidden "maternal subtext" of the play, focusing in particular on Lear's characterization of his madness as hysteria, or "the mother." Studying another late play by Shakespeare in which the partial suppression of maternal figures acquires ideological significance, Stephen Orgel shows how the absence of Prospero's wife in *The Tempest* and the shadowy presence of Caliban's witch-mother Sycorax illuminate the complex relation between Shakespeare's play and Jacobean politics. By presenting Prospero as if he were the sole and sufficient parent of Miranda, Shakespeare appears to ratify the glorified image of patriarchal power that Jonathan Goldberg finds characteristic of Stuart ideology; but by showing Prospero's authority threatened by Caliban—whose own claims to power derive from his mother—Shakespeare may be commenting obliquely on the problematic derivation of the Stuarts' royal authority from two unruly "mothers," Queen Elizabeth I and Mary, Queen of Scots. Analyzing the "distinctly unstable" family paradigms figured in *The Tempest*, Orgel interprets Prospero's eventual surrender of Miranda and his relinquishing of his own art not simply as a conventional move toward reconciliation but also as a means of keeping patriarchal control over his usurping brother.

The question of patriarchal control—its strategies, its social and psychological causes—is also central in our next four essays. Louis Montrose views Shakespeare's *A Midsummer Night's Dream* as part of a general cultural obsession with Elizabeth, the Virgin Queen, an anomalous "unmastered" woman whose authority as female monarch generated peculiar tensions both for her subjects and for her royal successors. Montrose traces the ways in which Shakespeare's play attempts to neutralize the royal power to which it ostensibly pays homage; by staging the actions of all its female characters within the frame of Theseus's marriage to his conquered Amazon queen, the play symbolically places Elizabeth herself within a patriarchal frame that reaffirms the male right to "make women and make themselves through the medium of women."

Richard Halpern and John Guillory analyze another major poet's strategies for containing the complex threats symbolized by powerful women; focusing on the early and the late Milton respectively, Halpern and Guillory explore the ways in which his two dramas—*A Mask* and *Samson Agonistes*—recast, in mythological or "archaic" molds, contemporary ideological debates about relations both between the sexes and between members of different classes. The figures of Dionysus and the maenads that Milton's masque "half invokes in order to suppress," Halpern argues, embody twin threats to the bourgeois Puritan ideal of "married chastity"—an ideal that *A Mask* celebrates by depicting it as a "middle way" that avoids the posited "extremes" of savage virginity and promiscuity. The figure of the maenad, who lurks behind Milton's chaste Lady and reveals the latter's potential for deviating from the line that leads the virgin daughter to wifely obedience, points to the poet's desire to mark the limits of Christian liberty as it applied to women. For the maenad is a figure that "threatens not only the corporeal integrity of men, but also the integrity of the household as an arena for patriarchal control."

Examining the sexual division of labor as it is represented in *Samson Agonistes*, Guillory argues that Milton's characterization of Dalila, far from being a "version of a transhistorical misogyny," instead reflects specific tensions in seventeenth-century patriarchal ideology—and shows as well Milton's active "intervention" in contemporary social discourses. Milton intervenes "on behalf of a new social practice, *divorce*, which is not yet legitimated." His Dalila, unlike her biblical counterpart, is a *wife*, and this fact is central to Guillory's interpretation of the play as a "prototype of the bourgeois career drama" in which the man's work or vocation is threatened not by female sexuality per se but rather by the sphere of private domesticity that women came increasingly to symbolize within "the new discipline of the Protestant household."

Peter Stallybrass is also concerned with changing conceptions of the relations between the private and the public realms in the early modern period. His essay provides a broad overview of Renaissance definitions of woman as a male property category controlled or disciplined by codes that required of women a closed mouth (silence), a closed body (chastity), and an enclosed life in the home. Unlike medieval women—the peasant who engaged in productive agricultural labor in rough parity with her husband, or the noble lady who had the right both to inherit and on occasion to administer feudal property—Renaissance women of all classes were increasingly (although by no means universally) confined to a private sphere. Although humanist writers often defined this sphere with reference to the households of ancient Greece and Rome, it was in fact, as Stallybrass shows, a product of specific socioeconomic changes and those new canons of polite behavior brilliantly catalogued by Norbert Elias in *The Civilizing Process*.[36] Stallybrass concludes his examination of the Renaissance enclosure of the female body with a provocative reading of *Othello*: in this play, he argues, the woman's resistance to ideological containment—a resistance often signaled by depictions of female bodies as "grotesque" in their transgression of limits—is dramatized in the character of Emilia. At the tragedy's end, Stallybrass suggests, Emilia the "unruly woman" presides over the destruction of both literal and symbolic enclosures by questioning the very idea of the female body as the property of men.

Speaking almost as if occupying the position of the unruly woman described by Stallybrass, Carla Freccero opens the second section of this volume—"Modes of Marginalization"—with an essay that criticizes the tendency of many male critics to "impose hermeneutic closure" on Rabelais's corpus. Seeking to understand her own sense of exclusion, as a woman reader, from Rabelais's text, Freccero reinterprets Gargantua's emblem of the hermaphrodite, which most critics have taken to represent the union of male and female in marriage, as an image of erotic sameness that alludes to Plato's doubly male "circle being" in the *Symposium*. Far from symbolizing a union of sexual opposites, the emblem, in Freccero's view, figures the Renaissance ideal of male friendship in which man's love is "not for the Other, or Woman, but for that 'other' in himself, a [male] divinity."

Like Freccero, Marguerite Waller and Elizabeth Cropper are concerned with the strategies by which women are rendered marginal in works by male artists and critics. Waller notes that the tradition of commentary on Shakespeare's *Richard III*, and even the history of the play's performance, effectively reproduce the play's own silencing of those female characters who seek to articulate the "instability of identity which their losses have brought them to acknowledge." Using a deconstructive approach, Waller traces the play's revelation of the illusory nature both of Richard's construction of an autonomous and authoritative self and of Anne's participation in that construction. Waller's essay makes an important methodological point for feminist criticism by stressing the dangers of deploying a mode of discourse that revalues female characters without disrupting the conceptual dichotomies traditionally used to denigrate women.

In her study of Renaissance Italian portraiture, Cropper focuses on the problematic elision of female identity within the paintings themselves and the tradition of commentary upon them. She observes that while no unidentified male portrait is ever said to be a beautiful representation made for its own sake, "many portraits of unknown beautiful women are now characterized as representations of ideal beauty in which the question of the [sitter's] identity is immaterial." The rhetoric of Italian representations of women, like that of the Petrarchan lyrics to which the paintings often alluded, disregards the individual woman's identity: "the portrait of a beautiful woman belongs to a distant discourse from which the woman herself is necessarily absent."

History has not recorded the names of most of the women studied in the essays by Mary Wiesner and Judith Brown; but the importance of the work described in these essays (and of the original research that produced them) should not be underestimated. For if losses or gains for working women in the Renaissance are to be accurately assessed, there is no better place to begin to look for them than in the realm of cloth and clothing production. Until the late middle ages, as Wiesner observes, "all stages of [textile] production . . . were carried out in the home, usually by female members of the family or servants." In the Renaissance, this was no longer generally the case, and the complex changes that occurred in the textile industry had profound effects on women. If many of them continued to lead lives "devoted to . . . needle and distaff," as Arcangela Tarabotti complained, the meaning of their labor in the home was altered when *home* was defined with increasing frequency as a private place separate from the place where men worked. Wiesner's study of spinners and seamstresses in six-teenth-century Germany examines the economic and ideological factors that caused working women to suffer, despite some lively protest, a substantial loss both of earning power and of legal rights during this period. Wives, unmarried women, and widows all were increasingly excluded from the higher-paying stages of cloth produc-tion—a development that contrasts dramatically with the one Judith Brown finds in her study of women workers in sixteenth-century Tuscany. There, both in the cities and in the countryside, women became "increasingly active participants in the economy," Brown argues; and they did so "despite formidable barriers related to their lack of skills and capital, to prejudice about where women could work without losing honor, and to resentment on the part of male artisans." Although Brown speculates that the "success with which women gained access to paid employment and to productive labor" may be related—as an effect if not as a cause—to the "failure of the [Tuscan] economy to modernize" along capitalist lines, she also takes issue with feminist and marxist scholars who have, in her view, drawn prema-ture and perhaps erroneous generalizations about a causal relation between a decline in women's economic status and the development of capitalism. Her essay, like Wiesner's, continually tests explanatory models against the complex, heterogeneous, and always partial evi-dence uncovered, or recovered, as scholars have sought to understand the discrepancies and the congruencies between women's daily lives and the various documents, ranging from guild records to religious treatises, that described—and often prescribed—female behavior. To increase our understanding of women's lives, Brown cautions, "we need to look not only at the rules of society but at the ways in which men and women understood them, implemented them, and often circumvented them."

The essays in the final section elaborate that point by examining strategies employed by Renaissance artists and writers to transform margins into spaces of potential or actual strength. Each essay focuses on images or texts in which cultural presumptions of women's "naturally" subordinate status in the social hierarchy are carefully manipulated; each shows the construction of a female persona who, while participating in the rule of patriarchy, articulates her own power. The most striking examples of this phenomenon appear when high-born women assumed, or were in a position to assume, significant political roles. Sheila ffolliott and Constance Jordan, for instance, demonstrate how women who attempted to stand "upon the Slipper toppe / Of courts estate,"[37] as well as the men who advised or wrote about them, dealt with the conceptual and practical dilemmas presented by the very notion of a female prince. "The image . . . of a woman who is the political equal of man," writes Jordan, "is always an image of the culturally alien, a figure relegated to the borders of the culturally constituted community."

ffolliott's essay takes us quite directly to such borders as it studies a royal widow, Catherine de' Medici, who found herself not only isolated in a foreign land but also confronted with the possibility of governing it as regent. Catherine's position, ffolliott argues, was effectively reinforced by identification with a classical prototype, Artemisia, who figured an idea of "acceptable" female control—acceptable because it was cast as the legitimate concern of a dutiful widow and mother. Catherine-Artemisia, as depicted by French court artists, governs from a decentered position; standing at the margin of the space she controls—indeed at the borders of the tapestries that represent her—she is an apt emblem of the royal woman who would deviate from patriarchal rule. Jordan's interpretation of Thomas Elyot's *Defense of Good Women*—written, she persuasively argues, within the context of a conspiracy to depose Henry VIII and establish the regency of his rejected wife, Catherine of Aragon—also suggests that artful compromises were required in order to justify the idea of female rule. Elyot's polemical argument relies on the image of a pagan female "worthy," Queen Zenobia, who embodies, on the one hand, wifely obedience and maternal devotion but who represents, on the other, virile wisdom and strength. In the cases of both Catherines, classical allusion underscores the paradoxes of the royal woman's position.

The court of Elizabeth I, the royal woman who most adroitly manipulated the paradoxes inherent in her role as ruler, is the context for the works analyzed by Lauren Silberman and Clark Hulse. Figuring his most powerful reader in the very title of his epic—*The Faerie Queene*—Spenser, Silberman argues, was genuinely revisionary in his treatment of Petrarchan and Platonic traditions that marginalized women by objectifying them. Spenser deliberately sought to remedy some of the "injustices" to women perpetrated by previous poets and philosophers; in Silberman's view, Spenser's poem, and particularly his subtle characterization of the martial heroine Britomart, seriously address the question, "How does one write about a feminine reality for which men have made no room in their writs?"

Hulse, in his study of Sidney's *Astrophil and Stella*, seeks to show that the historical addressee of this sonnet sequence, Penelope Devereux Rich, is far more powerfully present in the poems than critics have acknowledged; the male speaker, Hulse argues, uses a double communicative code to address both his specific female reader (Penelope Rich or "Stella") and a male audience of courtiers. Stella, in Hulse's view, is not only presented as superior to the male audience but acquires a position of considerable authority, equal to the poet's.

Nevertheless, Stella's authority is granted—and controlled—by a male poet's text; Penelope Rich is an "absent presence" in Sidney's work as Queen Elizabeth is in Spenser's. The next essays turn to two Renaissance women who actively countered the paradoxical but powerful cultural notion that "women achieve the fame of eloquence," as Francesco Barbaro put it, "by silence."[38] François Rigolot's essay on Louise Labé and Ann Jones's on Labé and Veronica Franco focus on authors who were highly aware that their very act of writing was, in the eyes of male contemporaries, a transgression. Each of these poets seeks to define her place in a male-dominated discourse and to present herself as a public persona; both compose in a spirit of ambitious albeit anxious self-advancement. Rigolot shows how small grammatical anomalies in Labé's poems—variations of gender—are not accidental errors but rather sexually coded means of self-expression. A "devious yet indispensable gesture," this "gender scrambling" reaffirms Labé's identity as a woman and as a poet by subverting the "normal" order of language. Like the very existence of the Renaissance female prince, the work of this female poet challenges the ideological construct that defines the human as the male. Ann Jones expands Rigolot's interpretive frame of reference from text to social context by studying both Labé and Franco in their urban, middle-class settings. Both poets' rhetoric, she argues, is "shaped and contained" by the fact that men—who control entry into the social, cultural, and economic elites—are their "ultimate critics"; by refusing male injunctions to silence and modesty, however, both poets speak to and for women in ways that necessarily transform the sexual economy of traditional lyric.

This volume suggests that it is still too early for a definitive answer to Joan Kelly-Gadol's famous question, "Did women have a Renaissance?" We need to know much more about women's position relative to men of various social classes, in various countries, and at various moments of that period before we can speak confidently about what happened, during this geographically, politically, and temporally heterogeneous era, to women as a group. The conclusions drawn here, will, we hope, provoke discussion and may, in many cases, need to be revised as our knowledge of the period increases. Further work should take into account the growing body of information about aspects of women's "nature" and roles in early modern society that are mentioned only tangentially in these essays; definitions of women in medical theory and practice, for instance, and in legal systems that altered the rights of wives and widows during this era.[39] This volume shows scholars trained mainly in literary criticism, history, and art history working to broaden their perspective on a culture in which the boundaries among different fields of knowledge were much less rigidly drawn than they are today. By attempting, with varying degrees of boldness, to break down such barriers, these essays invite the reader to consider historical documents and aesthetic works no longer as isolated objects of specialized study but now as parts of a social text—a text constituted not only by economic forces and class ideologies but also by the complex ideologies of sexual difference.

Part One

The Politics of Patriarchy: Theory and Practice

I

Fatherly Authority:
The Politics of Stuart Family Images

Jonathan Goldberg

James I regularly described his relationship to his kingdom in familiar terms. His 1597 treatise on kingship, *The Trew Law of Free Monarchies,* is characterized by patriarchal arguments: "as the Father of his fatherly duty is bound to care for the nourishing, education, and vertuous government of his children," he wrote, "even so is the king bound to care for all his subjects" (*Political Works,* p. 55).[1] In the *Basilikon Doron,* written soon after and reissued in 1603, James claimed "fatherly authoritie" (p. 4). He did so on two counts: first, he addressed his son and heir; second, he instructed him as a natural father in his kingly duties. In large ways, James's statements are, of course, scarcely unprecedented. Cosimo de' Medici had been called *pater patriae* after his death, and his title points to Roman antecedents.[2] Yet, in England, no monarch since Henry VIII's time could have made James's assertions; Roman styles and patriarchal claims, in fact, found a new conjunction in his rhetoric; absolutist claims were domesticated. If James's subjects were his children, his kingdom was his wife. The connection between the two family images probably derives from an analogy found first in his 1597 treatise on kingship and repeated frequently thereafter, the comparison of king and country to head and body: "The head cares for the body, so doeth the King for his people" (pp. 64–65). Addressing his first parliament in England, the king declared: "I am the Husband, and all the whole Isle is my lawfull Wife; I am the Head, and it is my Body" (p. 272). "What God hath conjoyned . . . let no man separate," his sentence had begun, and coins of his reign proclaim the same text: "*Quae Deus Coniunxit Nemo Separet*" (fig. 1).

Late in the Caroline period, when Robert Filmer wrote a treatise on absolute rule, he adopted James's rhetoric and, replete with citations from *The Trew Law of Free Monarchies,* Filmer's *Patriarcha* was the result.[3] The title of Filmer's book immediately reveals its thesis, that

3

Fig. 1. Jacobean coin with motto, *"Quae Deus Coniunxit Nemo Separet."* Reproduced by courtesy of the Trustees of the British Museum.

the organization of the ideal state imitates the patriarchalism of the family. Filmer's argument, in fact, goes beyond merely making an analogy. For him, the king is quite literally the father of his country, for parents are, he says, "natural magistrates" and children, he asserts, "natural subjects" (p. 72); kings simply act within the "natural law of a Father" (p. 103) in making their absolute claims to obedience. Society is an extended family. Filmer's historical support for this belief takes him back to Adam as the first father. Not merely a model for kings and a model parent, Adam is, literally, the ancestor of kings. And the Adamic model of the "subordination of children is the fountain of all royal authority" (p. 57). Filmer's patriarchal theories justify absolutist rule: "the profound secrets of government" (p. 54) are corporealized, familiarized, and naturalized, supported by hierarchies of head and body, husband and wife, father and child. His theories seem to confirm an argument that has been made frequently about ideology, that ideology is never more apparent than when it is treated as a transparency and the political system is allowed to be an extension of natural laws and processes. As R. W. K. Hinton says in a stimulating study, "Husbands, Fathers, and Conquerors," Filmer's extreme patriarchal argument is powerful precisely as a "metaphor for the naturalness and inescapability of government."[4]

Head, husband, father. In these metaphors, James mystified and politicized the body. With the language of the family, James made powerful assertions. He rested his claims to the throne in his succession and based Divine Right politics there as well. Indeed, according to G. R. Elton, James's only real contribution to Divine Right theory lay in identifying his prerogative with the production of a legitimate male successor.[5] That is, unlike his Tudor predecessor, James located

Fig. 2. *Mary Queen of Scots and James VI.* From the collection of the Duke of Atholl in Blair Castle.

his power in a royal line that proceeded from him—hence his address to Prince Henry in the *Basilikon Doron,* with its claims to patriarchal and paternal prerogative. Hence, too, James's attempts to salvage his mother's reputation. James was haunted by the memory of Mary Queen of Scots, on her he rested his claims to the throne. Mother and son meet as alter egos in a double portrait dated 1583 (fig. 2). In fact, Mary and James were separated when he was ten months old and never saw each other again. But in this fantasized meeting sixteen years later, the two figures are parallel in stance and hands and eye glance. One face serves as a model for both. This picture says that children are the images of their parents. As a mirror of his mother, the king is located in a position of both dependence and obligation; but, also, an assertion of equality is being made. Rubrics name him as king of Scots, her as queen. The double portrait suggests that his power derives from re-production, literally and figuratively.

This family image functions as an ideological construct, as the family does in the writings of James and Filmer or in continental theorists of absolutism like Bodin. And not there alone. There is a pervasive politics of the family in the seventeenth century. Pointing to

Fig. 3. Holbein, *The Family of Sir Thomas More*. Offentliche Kunstsammlung, Kupferstichkabinett Basel.

what he calls the "restricted Patriarchal Nuclear Family" as one flourishing family system in the Jacobean period, Lawrence Stone has argued that "the growth of patriarchy was deliberately encouraged by the new Renaissance State on the traditional grounds that the subordination of the family to its head is analogous to, and also a direct contributory cause of, subordination of subjects to the sovereign."[6] Judging by representations of families in the sixteenth century, the "restricted Patriarchal Nuclear Family" emerged in England as a dominant Jacobean type. Before, as Holbein's depiction of the family of Sir Thomas More (fig. 3) or Hans Eworth's of William Brooke, Earl of Cobham and his family (fig. 4) suggest, the favored representation was more diffuse, a visual version of the commonwealth as Sir Thomas Smith had imagined it. Readings of the family in such political matrices are possible thanks to an ongoing revaluation of the idea of the family that owes its impetus to the pioneering work of Philippe Ariès, whose *Centuries of Childhood* first studied the family not as a natural unit but as a social institution with a history. In the past twenty-odd years, the history of the family has developed as a field of inquiry, and although many matters remain in dispute, one basic premise seems indisputable, that the institution of the family is an historical and cultural phenomenon. Stone's work represents a

Fig. 4. Hans Eworth (?), *William Brooke and His Family*. By permission of the Marquess of Bath, Longleat House.

recent trend, to recognize that a number of family structures exist at any time; discontinuities, disagreements and multiplicity are the norm. The sixteenth-century Elizabethan paintings, for instance, are closely related to Flemish family groups of the sixteenth and seventeenth centuries. Nonetheless, certain features of family life remain circumscribed in any historical period, and it is within these limits that the ideological function served by the domestic unit emerges, whatever its actual composition from locale to locale or from class to class may have been.

The ideology of the Renaissance family is opposed to modern, liberal views. The family in the Renaissance is inevitably a public unit. Marriages occurred between families; diplomacy was carried on through marriage; kings more and more stressed their legitimacy by pointing to their lineage and invented ancestries to further the sense that genealogy was destiny. Privacy was neither a value for itself, nor did it describe family life—the poor lived in one room, the rich in public rooms. The modern belief in the family as a retreat, as the place of comfort in an uncomfortable world, would scarcely have been recognized in the Renaissance, at least officially. Rather, the individual

7

derived a sense of self largely from external matrices among which the family and its place in society was paramount. The family was understood as part of the larger world, both as the smallest social unit from which the larger world was composed and as the essential link between persons. This idea goes back at least as far as the eighth book of Aristotle's *Ethics* and to the opening chapters of the *Politics*; there, too, ideological claims about the naturalness of political economy encompass household and domestic relations. It would be too large a subject to attempt here a history of this idea, for the fact that the family has an ideological function that can be traced back to antiquity does not mean that its relationship to the apparatuses of power has remained unchanged.

Nor could one write a history of the ideology of the family as if it were simply a reflection of social realities. The ideology of the family does not mirror the actuality of family life. Reproduction as trope is not reproduction in fact. These images function as part of the apparatus and discourse of power, and they embody such power. Hence, although we know that erotic relations were officially subordinated to larger social concerns, we know, too, that love matches were made. John Donne's is a famous case; and the disastrous social consequences that followed his marriage to Ann More suggest how strong the sanctions against it were. Even Donne's rebellion, however, subscribes to a cultural image; *Romeo and Juliet* might serve as a precedent for his behavior. A great frequenter of plays, Donne may have tried to live out a role he found there; some of the elegies, or "The Canonization," for instance, seem to have been written with texts like *Romeo and Juliet* in mind. The point may be, as Bacon said, that "the stage is more beholding to love than the life of man" (Essay 10), and that cultural images that contained rebellion left little room in real life to act outside them. Of course, Donne's life did not end with his marriage, and it proved possible to find ways of acting in his society. The system of patronage was not locked into family ideology. Still, his ten years of discontent suggest how closely the family and society functioned in the period, how powerful the ideology was. Such power, as Alan Sinfield writes, is always piecemeal and discontinuous, attempting to regularize the material contradictions that exceed its grasp, operating within the interstices of a culture to provide the illusion of overmastering structures.[7]

The family functioned in the Renaissance to reproduce society. This is not so simple as it sounds. On the one hand, family structures mirror the largest structures of society. But, on the other hand, procreation is not merely reproductive in a biological sense. Biology is transformed, and the family serves to reproduce society. The body is inscribed in a social system. The family/state analogy was embedded in the Renaissance habit of mind to think analogically and to explain events by understanding their origins; indeed, the analogy serves as an image of that ideational process. There is a family structure in thought, and to seek out the causes of things is to find their genealogical principles. In his *Fowre Hymnes,* Spenser, drawing upon Plato (and especially upon neoplatonic readings of Plato) makes the creation of the world the manifestation of eros. The Christian mystery declared the word made flesh. The pun with which *King Lear* opens—"*Kent.* I cannot conceive you. / *Gloucester.* Sir, this young fellow's mother could" (1:1, lines 12–13)[8]—can serve as an emblem of this habit of thinking, the connection between the generation of issues and issue.

Deprived his throne, Richard II has this fantasy: "My brain I'll prove the female to my soul, / My soul the father, and these two beget / A generation of still-breeding thoughts; / And these same thoughts people this little world" (5:5, lines 6–9). This family of ideas has a political function. We can observe it in Jonson's *Masque of Queens* (1609), in the scene of transformation—the routing of the witches and the arrival of Queen Anne as BelAnna—an event accomplished by Perseus, the embodiment of Heroic Virtue.[9] His virtue (or power) is described specifically as the power of giving birth. Heroic Virtue banishes terror to bring forth fame: "When Virtue cut off Terror, he gat Fame" (line 351); conception answers castration. "When Fame was gotten Terror died" (line 352), Perseus reiterates, concluding, "I was her parent, and I am her strength" (line 356). Parenting, Perseus acts as a kind of male mother here, a Zeus-like part King James had claimed for himself, calling himself a "loving nourish-father" (*BD*, p. 24) to his kingdom. Jonson extends Perseus's conceptual power to the king, for when BelAnna is brought forth, she is presented to him as to her source; the poet appropriates these powers for himself as well and, at the same moment, Perseus points to the House of Fame, newly arisen, "whose columns be / Men-making poets" (lines 361–62); what BelAnna's arrival has newly "brought forth" (line 303) is the poet's conception, and the queen submits to the sovereign light "all her worth / To him that gave it" (lines 402–3). At the masque's close, the penultimate song celebrates "this famous birth" (line 500) and the last couples virtue and power: "Who, Virtue, can thy power forget" (line 516). The masque delivers the poet's text and the queen's activities as the king's doing, embodying his power.

The masque links the generative powers of virtue, ideas, poetry,

Fig. 5. Willem van de Passe, *The Family of James I,* first state. Reproduced by courtesy of the Trustees of the British Museum.

and monarchy. Perseus, the poet, and James mirror each other, appropriating powers that might seem biological. In the masque, the body is consumed for the sake of ideology.

If we look now at some typical instances of family representation in the period, it is not difficult to make out their sexual politics or to see their connections to James's rhetoric or Jonson's masque. To uncover the politics of the family in the early seventeenth century, there is perhaps no better source than the paintings and engravings of the period. Family portraits developed as an important genre. These group portraits, posed, planned, and inescapably conceptualized, are cultural artifacts, official statements about family functions and relationships. Inevitably they offer images of domestic life converted to state use; inevitably they draw upon the metaphors of state power to express the bonds of kinship.

A most dramatic instance of the ideological functions of the family may be seen in two pieces of official portraiture, engravings by Willem van de Passe. The first (fig. 5) dates from the last years of James's reign (1622–24), the second (fig. 6) from the early years of Charles's (1625–30). In both engravings, James sits on the throne he proclaimed his in his divine lieutenancy. The scene, labeled the triumph of James as King of Peace, joins the imperial formula of

Fig. 6. Willem van de Passe, *The Family of James I,* second state. Reproduced by courtesy of the Trustees of the British Museum.

Augustan triumph to its Christian counterpart. The representational model for the king enthroned and serenaded by minstrel angels (a transformation of James's dead daughters) is familiar from countless Flemish paintings as well as Masaccio's Pisa polyptych. It is founded on representations of the Virgin, a familiar source, too, for portraits of Queen Elizabeth. Here, the model of the Holy Family undergoes a transformation. Before, as in *sacra conversazione* by Bellini, cherubs had serenaded mother and child, and the motif had been adopted to male saints, as in Vivarini's enthroned St. Mark or St. Ambrose in the Frari. Van de Passe undoubtedly belongs in this Venetian line, and his borrowing not only familiarizes sacred models for a Divine Right king, it also borrows the imagery of republican Venice to clothe absolutist claims, a striking instance of the rewriting involved in the transmission of images in Renaissance culture. The van de Passe engravings formally embody a visual version of the mixed state so favored by Renaissance political theorists. These implications coincide with other state ideals in this family group. Thus, one might argue that this undeniably hierarchical image of the royal family borrows from the Elizabethan family representations of the diffuse and extended family, perhaps (as George Starr has suggested to me) as a way to extend this absolutist image to the general audience intended by the engraver. Similarly, the coin of the realm proclaiming the king's marriage to his kingdom (fig. 1) had not made any hierarchical claims in its equal depiction of Scotland, Wales, and England.

Van de Passe locates James and his family in the court of heaven. The dead and the living are mingled, and not only in the angelic daughters. In both plates, the deceased Prince Henry and Queen Anne stand beside the throne; in the second state, James holds a skull. Although the representation has not changed, his status has; he, too, is dead. Replaced as monarch, he has not been deposed; he remains as a memorial image, dead and yet eternally alive. As Kantorowicz might say, the king has two bodies. The dead father remains as the father of his family and of the kingdom; he plays the role of a spiritual father. It was a part James had assumed before: in the preface to the *Basilikon Doron* he wrote as if from the grave, declaring that his book was his last will and testament; his claim to "fatherly authoritie" (p. 4) rested in his divinity. His disembodied words carried spiritual weight; they were meant to impress his son, to make him an imitation of his word. The principle governed the 1583 portrait of James and Mary Queen of Scots (fig. 2), and it can be seen, too, in an anonymous portrait of another father and son, Sir Walter Ralegh and his son, Walter (fig. 7). It is not only their names that echo. In stance and expression, and despite differences in costume (mere variations upon a theme), this picture also proclaims that children are the images of their parents.

Only a few years separate the two van de Passe engravings, and one could easily assume that the differences between them are simply accommodations to some natural events—that James died and Charles became king, married, and that his sister Elizabeth added to her enormous progeny. Yet the changes have their political point and affect, as we have seen, even constant elements like the enthroned *paterfamilias*. Charles's relationship to his father is refigured. In the first engraving, he stands with his hands placed on the Bible; the king's *Workes,* dignified with their Latin title, *Opera Regis,* lies beside it. Charles is being shown as the heir to James and in the first state of the engraving this means that he is the inheritor of the royal word. The literal and spiritual heir is balanced iconographically by the teeming family of Elizabeth and Frederick, the Elector Palatine, on the right side of the picture. The background of the picture reinforces the deployment of its figures. Behind Charles a deer park can be seen; behind Elizabeth there are church spires. The pleasures of the body and the demands of the spirit complement each other, books and deer, children and churches. Elizabeth's womb serves Protestant propa-

Fig. 7. *Sir Walter Ralegh and His Son.* By permission of the National Portrait Gallery, London.

ganda, Charles's study does not keep him from being cast fully in his father's image (the king was an avid sportsman). The background to the first state of the engraving offers a *paysage moralisé,* pleasure and virtue flanking the throne of the king of peace. Like the masque by Ben Jonson, this picture reconciles pleasure to virtue, and for the same reason, to suggest how all-pervasive the king's rule is and to extend the body politic into the body itself.

The most fundamental differences between the two engravings heighten the ideological function of the image of the family. First, Elizabeth's brood has increased and is more emphatic, although the labels naming the children are simply reassigned; these are not, in other words, representations of individuals. Second, although a spiritual father presides over the second engraving, other spiritual signs have been removed—the divine word and the books are gone as are the backgrounds with their emblematic meanings. The additional continental progeny and Charles's wife, Henrietta Maria, have obscured them. They are, perhaps, a subtext, hidden from view. In short, the spirit of James, the royal word, has, quite insistently, become flesh. The legitimacy of his rule has been translated into the bodies that fill the engraving. James's contribution to Divine Right theory has been fulfilled.

The transformation of state is equally notable in an engraving (fig. 8) of James I and his family by Gerrit Mountin (c. 1634) that is clearly based on the van de Passe plates. John Webster's verses, printed below it, provide an interpretive guide. The inexpressibility of James is Webster's rubric for the dead monarch: "Could Art his quistes of mind express as well, / no Picture in the World should this excell." That silent expression is imaged, however, in the "happy Coniunction" that Webster reads in the marriage of Charles and Henrietta Maria; they shed heavenly influence. As Roy Strong cogently remarks, not only does the neoplatonic love that Henrietta Maria fostered as a court style have a political meaning, "the blissful royal marriage and her ever fruitful womb are exalted almost to the level of a state philosophy. Charles and Henrietta are the first English royal couple to be glorified as husband and wife in the domestic sense."[10] Not surprisingly, the two masques written by Jonson for Charles I celebrate the love that united the royal couple. In *Love's Triumph through Callipolis* (1631), Charles, impersonating Heroic Love, leads the masquers to the queen in state; in *Chloridia* (1631), the action is reversed. Love is a "special deity in court" (line 18), the note prefacing *Love's Triumph* declares, and the masque concludes by

Fig. 8. Gerrit Mountin, *James I and His Family*. Reproduced by courtesy of the Trustees of the British Museum.

celebrating the imperial meanings in "Beauty and Love, whose story is mysterial" (line 184).

Strong's "domestic sense," the private sphere, is mystified, politicized, made into an ideological construct. This is intimated in the betrothal picture of the royal pair (fig. 9). Nothing less than an angel sanctifies their marriage. A similar meaning hovers in the background of a van de Passe engraving of Frederick and Elizabeth (fig. 10); God's name and a biblical text fill the sky, while directly beneath are the children produced by the unfortunate and ever more prolific winter monarchs. The conjunction of heaven and earth is, however, the familiar theme in representations of Charles and his bride and they normally domesticated the mythological energies of Mars and Venus by exchanging their attributes of laurel and olive, as they do in a Van Dyck portrait (fig. 11). This is a piece of royal mythology endlessly elaborated in Caroline masques. The politicization of their marriage and their private pleasures is beautifully captured in painting by Daniel Mytens (fig. 12). The couple appear ready to go hunting; however, only the dogs strain toward the countryside and the royal pair stands firm, hands clasped, an angelic putto showering them with roses. The Mytens painting poses the king before his palace, the queen before the landscape, and then unites them in their pleasure and virtue. A portrait by Henrick Pot of the couple with the first of their children (fig. 13)

Fig. 9. Francis Delaram, *Engagement of Charles I and Henrietta Maria*. Reproduced by courtesy of the Trustees of the British Museum.

conveys further the politics of family life. The king stands haloed and independently erect on the extreme right of the painting. On the left, Henrietta Maria sits and supports her seated and slightly tottering child. The long table is strewn with symbols, among them the olive and laurels. Charles's domestic hat rests beside him. Yet, at the center of the table, and at the center of the picture as well, is the crown, and the curtains, so dramatically drawn on this family group and the vast space between its members, open upon the symbol of power that is imaged as well in domestic relations.

And not only in the royal family. Patriarchalism is a regular feature of family life in which the natural event of procreation becomes an extension of male prerogative and male power. The family of Sir

Fig. 10. Willem van de Passe, *Frederick and Elizabeth of Bohemia.* By permission of the Rijksmuseum-Stichting, Amsterdam.

Fig. 11. Van Dyck, *Charles I and Henrietta Maria.* Archbishop's Palace, Kroměříž.

Fig. 12. Daniel Mytens, *Charles I and Henrietta Maria*. By permission of Her Majesty Queen Elizabeth II.

Richard Saltonstall as painted by David des Granges (c. 1637) nicely illustrates this (fig. 14). The husband draws the curtain to reveal the mother of his eldest son, who stands beside him, holding his hand. Sir Richard's wife, Elizabeth, is in the background, depicted in a way that was appropriate iconographically for the representation of a woman who died in childbirth, as comparison with a painting by John Souch reveals (fig. 15). This, in fact, is also apparently the case in the Saltonstall family; the woman seated on the right is Sir Richard's second wife, and she holds their first child. The composite picture serves, like the van de Passe engravings of the family of James I, as a kind of genealogical chart, and it suggests the place of natural production in the patriarchal family. The family line is symbolized by the joined hands that describe a line rising to the top hat of the *paterfamilias*; the ascending line is answered by Sir Richard's gaze toward his second wife and by his extended arm. The connection of hands is broken, however; the space between the extended hand of Elizabeth Saltonstall and Sir Richard is like the space in Pot's painting of the royal family (fig. 13). It is the gap between nature and power that patriarchal rhetoric transforms. It is the space in which patriarchal rhetoric is constructed, the space of the mystification of power. As in the *Masque of Queens,* the patriarch absorbs female creativity; James,

Fig. 13. Henrick Pot, *Charles I and His Family*. By Permission of Her Majesty Queen Elizabeth II.

we recall, had claimed such powers for himself when, in the *Basilikon Doron,* he said he was a "loving nourish-father" to his kingdom.

This transformative gap is worth further articulation because it draws attention to the juncture that ideological apparatuses attempt to close and foreclose. Yet, the breach remains as the visible scar in hegemonic processes. Although the gap in the portrait of the Saltonstall family is capable of eliciting patriarchal apparatuses of power, it reveals as well the fissure upon which it builds, a fissure also capable of toppling such impositions. For in that space, much can be read. Sir Richard's gesture might, for instance, be seen in relation to that of figures in *sacra conversazione,* pointing to, but not allowed to touch the center of numinous power; about his wife, there might be as strongly felt the corrupting and polluting powers of the dead.[11] To construct the painting as a piece of social discourse that affirms patriarchal power, the disjunctures represented by the gap must be suppressed. To exert pressure on the gap, however, would open the painting (or Jonson's *Masque of Queens,* for that matter) to the discontinuities and differences upon which the prevailing discourse rests, and could produce a reading that erodes the discourse by

Fig. 14. David des Granges, *The Family of Sir Richard Saltonstall*. By permission of the Tate Gallery, London.

throwing into question those differences. Male and female, parent and child, are constructed, constituted, produced as subjects and objects through the restructuring represented by the social discourse. As Louis Althusser says, "it is not their real conditions of existence, their real world, that 'men' 'represent to themselves' in ideology, but above all it is their relation to those conditions of existence which is represented to them there."[12] "Represent to themselves" is a problematic phrase for Althusser precisely because representation is always already in ideology; "men" is equally in question, since it is ideology that constitutes the subject. In the paintings we have been considering, as in Jonson's *Masque of Queens,* the emergence of the patriarchy depends upon the erection of controlling differences, male/female, parent/child, husband/wife. The sleight of hand that ideology performs is to render these categories obvious and natural, to deny, thereby, their production (or more exactly, their re-production of reproduction). The gap, for the moment, de-naturalizes and exposes the apparatuses of power. It is not so much representation as the abyss upon which representation rests. It is, perhaps, very close to what Foucault means by history as a discursive formation.

Fig. 15. John Souch, *Sir Thomas Aston at the Deathbed of His Wife*. By permission of the City of Manchester Art Galleries.

We can see the powerful presence of patriarchal discourse as a structuring apparatus (as a virtual formula of representation) if we turn to a few more examples. The powerful thematizing force of ideology does not quite still the ambivalences upon which it rests.

The living and the dead are strikingly and disturbingly present in William Dobson's picture of the Streatfeild family (fig. 16); mortality again divides the sexes. The mother, on the right, points to her dead child; behind her, a column topped with skulls testifies to the mortality of infants and the connection to the mother's as the body of death. Although the father gazes in the direction of the dead, he is tied to the earth. His hand rests on his son and heir's head, and the son embraces a younger child, a daughter who presents her father with a cherry. A curtain behind these tensely living children answers the funeral monument behind the more relaxed, smiling and dead, angelic

Fig. 16. William Dobson, *The Streatfeild Family*. Yale Center for British Art, Paul Mellon Collection.

child. This disturbing picture makes no final balance in the claims of the living and the dead; both the dead child and the heir engage the viewer's eyes, as does the gaze of the mother. The father looks away, and yet is attached to his children; but the circle of hands does not extend to his wife; hers encompass the dead child.[13]

Patriarchal formulas are fully in place in the portrait by Cornelius Johnson (c. 1639) of the royalist family of Arthur, Lord Capel (fig. 17). The picture again divides men and women (the younger sons are dressed in girls' clothing as was typical for boys in their early years). Males face forward, females look left. The youngest daughter pays homage to her latest brother. The flower is fittingly presented as a sign of natural obeisance to the patriarch—she is, Filmer would say, a "natural subject." The daughters, indeed, connect with the landscape behind them. Nature has already been ordered in the elaborate garden

Fig. 17. Cornelius Johnson, *The Family of Arthur, Lord Capel*. By permission of the National Portrait Gallery, London.

seen in the vista. Here, it is further subordinated to the civilized architecture that frames the family group of husband, wife, and sons. The old principle of echo is still there, too. Eldest son and father share the same tilt of the head, and Lord Capel's hat is above his son's head. The boy displays his own similar piece of headgear. Nature and its genealogical order are subordinated to the patriarchal line. In this picture, the facts of life serve the powers of state. There is no doubt who is the head, who the body.

Numerous family pictures develop these formulas. Van Dyck is especially interested in them. The equation of female and nature, male and culture, appears quite straightforwardly in the painting of Jan Wildens and his wife (fig. 18). In an early family group, we can see him working with similar elements. In this painting (fig. 19), the father's hand rests on a chair adorned with the family coat; lineage is declared by that gesture. The mother's hand is on the child, who holds a vase, perhaps a sign that the child is a female vessel, perhaps a token of infant mortality. Cross gazes and the placement of the curtain behind the mother (for once), nature behind the father, bind nature and art, depicting reproduction in both senses of the word; the child is the center of these meetings.

Finally, we can turn to a portrait of James's favorite, George Villiers, Duke of Buckingham, and his family, after Gerard Honthorst

Fig. 18. Van Dyck, *Jan Wildens and His Wife*. The Detroit Institute of Arts. Gift of James E. Scripps.

(fig. 20), for similar meanings, although in a somewhat disquieting context. In the painting, nature begins only with Kate, the duke's loving wife. His ties to culture are conveyed by the man-made wall behind him and the bit of writing in his hand. Mall, the couple's eldest daughter, presents the bounty of nature to her young brother, the duke's heir. (As is usual, the males all face one way, the females another.) Here, the horizontal lines of hands convey the patriarchal lineage. This was a family that James had doted over, and their domestic life was his royal concern; he advised Kate on weaning procedures and counseled her during pregnancies. On them he showered gifts, and from them he expected bounteous returns—foremost, of course, of the duke's love; this, too, was familiarly expressed—the duke was his "sweet child and wife," he wrote; the king had hopes of the fruit of the duke's conjugal lovemaking, too, imagining that he might "have sweete bed chamber boyes to play me with," or, as he ended a poem, he prayed that God would send them—and him—"a smilinge boy within a while."[14] Honthorst's painting celebrates the survival of Buckingham's male heir and

Fig. 19. Van Dyck, *Family Group*. Hermitage, Leningrad.

registers that event within the same language of patriarchal power
with which James embraced his favorite and declared his Divine
Right. However disturbing the conflicting claims evoked by this
picture, like other ideological constructs, it glosses over the
differences.

In examining the ideological connection between representation and
politics exemplified by early seventeenth-century English paintings of
family groups, the discussion thus far, has privileged the terms of
patriarchal discourse; we have been observing attempts at a
hegemonic transformation of private life into the public domain. This

Fig. 20. After Gerard Honthorst, *George Villiers and His Family*. By permission of the National Portrait Gallery, London.

is but one relationship between representation and authority, the one favored by the reigning monarch, jealous of his prerogative and anxious to extend his power to all corners of the realm; in this view, there is no sphere of privacy, and the body is mystified to serve the state. It should be noted that these images admit of further complexity in their ideological relations; for example, privacy could seize the public mode as a means to make counterassertions. This may, as Svetlana Alpers has suggested to me, provide further resonance to a Rubens family group to which I turn now, and it almost certainly helps to account for the ambiguous assertion that Van Dyck makes in casting himself as Icarus in the last painting that I will examine. Thus, although my main concern in these pages has been to illustrate how society shapes the representation of the family, it is important to add that its discursive practices define a society and give it shape; the full complexity of that countermotion is beyond the scope of this paper, but some gestures in that direction can be made in the examples below.

I have been arguing that the facts of life are what art re-presents, that the conditions of production have their place in the representation of reproduction. As one consequence of these conditions of representation, in family portraits in which self-portraiture is involved, the matrix of family images can serve as an image of artistic authority, too. This can be seen in a late painting of Rubens and his second wife, Hélène Fourment (fig. 21). This painting grows out of a Flemish tradition of domestic representation, and it is situated at some distance from some examples in the English tradition that we have been observing. In it, Rubens seems to adopt the absolutist model to enshrine family values and to proclaim his powers. There is, potentially, a subversive element here, or perhaps we could say that the absolutist frame contains its own subversion. In the painting, although Hélène's figure is a dominating one, and although landscape also predominates, familiar divisions obtain—flowers behind the woman, stone and statuary behind the man. The movement of eyeglances from husband to wife and child seems more intimate, less patriarchal than in other family groups. Nonetheless, the eyes move hierarchically.[15] The family seems self-involved, and the viewer's eye is engaged directly only by the statue behind the artist's head. Yet, that fixed gaze introduces an element into the painting that enforces meanings that drive away from apparent intimacy. The gaze signifies the relationship of artistic production to natural reproduction.

The statue—a female herm, a fixed gaze, a limit, a garden god without hands, an object made—that wholly artificial female virtually circumscribes the figure of the artist, save for his gloved right hand, which extends beyond its boundary. Elsewhere, the presence of deities or ghosts spiritualize the family; here, in the statue, we see what an artist might make, a phantom wife to replace the flesh and blood one engaged by his eye. (Similarly, the fountain behind Hélène seems to image her fecundity in a non-natural object; even a bird's feather has been turned into an object at the same time as it enforces a sexual theme.) And just as the stone female, a limit transcended by the artist's hand that makes it, points to male powers of making, so too that extended hand is raised almost in benediction over the couple's child. (The glove masks natural deformity.) Exactly which child from Rubens' second marriage this is is somewhat problematic; it is almost certainly not one of the first two children, Clara Joanna and Frans, whom Rubens had portrayed together with their mother in a painting now in the Louvre. The infant here is also represented in a sketch, and it has been identified usually as the third child of the marriage, Isabella Hélène. Possibly, however, the child is their fourth, named Peter Paul after his father. This identification has been maintained recently—on stylistic and iconographical grounds.[16] For the

Fig. 21. Rubens, *Rubens, His Wife Hélène Fourment, and Their Son, Peter Paul.*
Metropolitan Museum of Art. Gift of Mr. and Mrs. Charles Wrightman, 1981.

argument I am presenting, it is a most attractive hypothesis, since the position of the child in the painting—included in the group that is made up of the artist and his sculpted wife—would seem to invite the presence of a male child to complete its patriarchal theme. As I have suggested, however, the painting has a subversive strain in its self-proclamation and perhaps it extends, too, to the inclusion of a female child in the place that a male would occupy normally. In any case, the child is not Rubens' heir; there were two sons from his first marriage. The assertions made here, in other words, have translated claims about family lineage to another sphere. The canvas is divided and, on the left side, Rubens, the sculpted wife, and blessed child form a family group that are united as things made, products of the hand, works of art. Nature and art virtually split this picture, and art joins creation and procreation. And however subversive this painting may be in its celebration of the family, it is worth noting that a few weeks before his death, Rubens referred in a letter to his family as consisting of Hélène Fourment and "both my sons."[17] The daughters go unmentioned.

Such assertive and patriarchal meanings are supported by the event that appears to have occasioned the painting, the child learning to walk, especially through a bit of realistic rendering, the lead, a device commonly used in the period. Here, it defines a transitional moment, the child moving into humanity by standing up and walking. The rope connects the child to the family, tied to the mother. The lead extends from the hands and, although the artist's right hand hovers in benediction over the child's head, his other hand supports his wife's; she in turn holds the rope. The intimate pressure of his touch is undeniable; it echoes in his gaze and suggests the affection between the pair. Yet the hands also tell another story, of subordination, support, hierarchy, and ultimate separation. The child of woman is handed over to the man, let loose from its mother. The umbilical cord becomes a rope, nature replaced by art once again. The child, coming into its own, is coming into the father's sphere. Of the mother's sphere, the painting makes one further emblematic point. Flourishing amidst the flowers behind Hélène is a parrot, that imitative creature, mocker in nature of human speech. The parrot's head and the wife's face in parallel directions, as do the father's and child's. And the parrot's eye gazes out like the herm's. All that nature can do is imitate art and submit to its ideological imperatives. Much as one may wish to insist on the intimate joys of Rubens' domesticity, such sentimental responses need to be balanced by a recognition of the discourse of family relations in the period. And perhaps it is not entirely amiss to note that in a letter written less than a month after his marriage to Hélène Fourment, Rubens found no difficulty in mentioning his marital state in the same breath as political events. Thanking his correspondant for congratulating him on his recent marriage and on his successful diplomatic maneuvering, Rubens wrote, "I find myself most content in the conjugal state, as well as in the general happiness over the peace with England."[18] As in Jonson's *Hymenaei,* one language serves for both kinds of union.

We can find a similar range of meanings in a quite different painting, painted during Van Dyck's first visit to England in 1620 or shortly thereafter (fig. 22). It may serve to summarize much that we have been seeing about representations of the family and the relationship of art to society. The painting shows Daedalus and Icarus, father and son. Icarus, however, is a self-portrait done in the Venetian manner that Van Dyck came to master in part by viewing the paintings in the collections of the Earl of Arundel and the Duke of Buckingham. Van Dyck was taught—or quickly learned—a style that reflects the values of his patrons, and his self-portrait as a nude boy is clothed in a recognizable style; he masks *all'antica.* No actual masquer would be so undressed; but as in masques, disguise serves as self-revelation. This is a court style on more than one count, antique, Venetian; artistic self-assertion meets subservience to the prevailing winds of taste and style. The artist as Icarus may seem a strange choice, heavily loaded with tragic implication. But it has a wonderful ambiguity. As Carlo Ginzburg has shown, Icarus was undergoing a transformation in the early seventeenth century, turning into an emblem of intellectual daring.[19] Icarus, undaunted by the limits of knowledge, stood for the opening up of the intellectual community, the daring in natural science that ultimately was to challenge the hierarchies of power. The artist here takes that emblem for himself. His father, Daedalus, the mazemaker, gives instructions to the boy to keep him aloft, and his upward pointing finger is answered by the child's declining and horizontal gesture, keeping him on earth. Perhaps these gestures of father and son can be seen as a variant of a famous family group, Leonardo's *magna mater* and the Christ child in the St. Anne cartoon. If so, this antique family group has a Christian precedent, and behind patriarchal and filial assertions loom vast maternal powers. Whether the figure of Daedalus is also a portrait is unclear—it might be Van Dyck's father or his spiritual father, Rubens, although there is no reason to make either of those specific identifications. Rather, Daedalus is the transcendent father, a master artist. With his hermetic art, he stands for the sovereign power that would keep the boy

Fig. 22. Van Dyck, *Daedalus and Icarus*. Art Gallery of Ontario, Toronto. Gift of Mr. and Mrs. Frank P. Wood, 1940.

airborne. Placing himself in this family matrix, the artist alludes to his dependency on his forebears and qualifies his self-assertion with subscription to a higher authority. His extended hand links him with the powers that be. Daring as his self-assertion is, it is clothed in the understanding that the artist is produced and produces for those who stand behind him, and who survive his end. Fatherly authority reigns supreme.

2

The Absent Mother in *King Lear*

Coppélia Kahn

Fleeing Goneril's "sharp-tooth'd unkindness," Lear arrives at Gloucester's house in search of Regan, still hoping that she will be "kind and comfortable," although she was inexplicably not at home when he called before. He finds his messenger in the stocks, a humiliation that he rightly takes as directed at him personally. At first he simply denies what Kent tells him, that Regan and her husband did indeed commit this outrage. Then he seeks to understand how, or why. Kent recounts the studied rudeness, the successive insults, the final shaming, that he has endured.

For a moment, Lear can no longer deny or rationalize; he can only feel—feel a tumult of wounded pride, shame, anger, and loss, which he expresses in a striking image:

> O! how this mother swells upward toward my heart!
> *Hysterica passio!* down, thou climbing sorrow!
> Thy element's below.
>
> (2.4.56–58)[1]

By calling his sorrow hysterical, Lear decisively characterizes it as feminine, in accordance with a tradition stretching back to 1900 B.C. when an Egyptian papyrus first described the malady. Fifteen hundred years later in the writings of Hippocrates, it was named, and its name succinctly conveyed its etiology. It was the disease of the *hyster*, the womb. From ancient times through the nineteenth century, women suffering variously from choking, feelings of suffocation, partial paralysis, convulsions similar to those of epilepsy, aphasia, numbness, and lethargy were said to be ill of hysteria, caused by a wandering womb. What sent the womb on its errant path through the female body, people thought, was either lack of sexual intercourse or retention of menstrual blood. In both cases, the same prescription obtained: the patient should get married. A husband would keep that wandering womb where it belonged. If the afflicted already had a husband, concoctions either noxious or pleasant were applied to force or entice the recalcitrant womb to its proper location.[2]

In Shakespeare's time, hysteria was also called, appropriately, "the mother." Although Shakespeare may well have consulted a treatise by Edward Jordan called *A Brief Discourse of a Disease Called the Suffocation of the Mother*, published in 1603, like anyone in his culture he would have understood "the mother" in the context of notions about women. For hysteria is a vivid metaphor of woman in general, as she was regarded then and later, a creature destined for the strenuous bodily labors of childbearing and childrearing but nonetheless physically weaker than man. Moreover, she was, like Eve, temperamentally and morally infirm:—skittish, prone to err in all senses. Woman's womb, her justification and her glory, was also the sign and source of her weakness as a creature of the flesh rather than the mind or spirit. The very diversity of symptoms clustering under the name of hysteria bespeaks the capricious nature of woman. And the remedy—a husband and regular sexual intercourse—declares the necessity for male control of this volatile female element.[3]

Psychoanalysis was born, one might say, from the wandering womb of hysteria. Anna O., the star of *Studies in Hysteria*, published by Freud and Joseph Breuer in 1895, was its midwife. It was she who named psychoanalysis "the talking cure" and in a sense even discovered it. Afflicted with a veritable museum of hysterical symptoms, when Breuer visited her she spontaneously sank into a rapt, semiconscious state in which she insisted on talking about what bothered her, thus showing the way to free association as the distinctly psychoanalytic technique of treating mental disorders. For psychoanalysis and hysteria both, the discovery that its strangely disparate physical symptoms were in fact symbolic representations of unconscious mental conflict constituted a crucial breakthrough. Relocating the cause of hysteria in the head instead of in the womb, Breuer and Freud were able to make sense of it, treat it, and, to an extent, cure it. Yet, in the Viennese women they treated, we can see that hysteria does indeed come from the womb—if we understand the womb as a metaphor for feelings and needs associated with women. As Dianne Hunter suggests, what Anna O. talked out was her specifically *female* subjectivity.[4] She expressed through the body language of her paralyzed arm, her squint, and her speech disorders the effects on her as a woman of life in a father-dominated family and a male-dominated world that suppressed the female voice. The matrix of her disease was both sexual and social: the patriarchal family.

Because the family is both the first scene of individual development and the primary agent of socialization, it functions as a link between psychic and social structures and as the crucible in which gender identity is formed. From being mothered and fathered, we learn to be ourselves as men and women. The anthropologist Gayle Rubin describes psychoanalysis as "a theory of sexuality in human society . . . a description of the mechanisms by which the sexes are divided and deformed, or how bisexual androgynous infants are transformed into boys and girls . . . a feminist theory manqué."[5] A great Shakespearean critic, C. L. Barber, calls psychoanalysis "a sociology of love and worship within the family."[6] Freud, of course, viewed this family drama from the standpoint of a son; he conceived the development of gender as governed primarily by relationship with the father. Because Freud grounds sexual differentiation in the cultural primacy of the phallus, within the context of a family structure that mirrors the psychological organization of patriarchal society, he enables us to deconstruct the modes of feeling, the institutions, and the social codes in which much if not most of English literature is embedded.

But to use one of Freud's favorite metaphors, to excavate patriarchal sensibility in literature, we must sift through more than one layer. In the history of psychoanalysis, the discovery of the Oedipus complex precedes the discovery of pre-oedipal experience, reversing the sequence of development in the individual. Similarly, patriarchal structures loom obviously on the surface of many texts, structures of authority, control, force, logic, linearity, misogyny, male superiority. But beneath them, as in a palimpsest, we can find what I call "the maternal subtext," the imprint of mothering on the male psyche, the psychological presence of the mother whether or not mothers are literally represented as characters.[7] In this reading of *King Lear*, I try, like an archaeologist, to uncover the hidden mother in the hero's inner world.

Now, it is interesting that there is no literal mother in *King Lear*. The earlier anonymous play that is one of Shakespeare's main sources opens with a speech by the hero lamenting the death of his "dearest Queen."[8] But Shakespeare, who follows the play closely in many respects, refers only once in passing to this queen. In the crucial cataclysmic first scene of his play, from which all its later action evolves, we are shown only fathers and their godlike capacity to make or mar their children. Through this conspicuous omission the play articulates a patriarchal conception of the family in which children owe their existence to their fathers alone; the mother's role in procreation is eclipsed by the father's, which is used to affirm male prerogative and male power.[9] The aristocratic patriarchal families headed by Gloucester and Lear have, actually and effectively, no mothers. The only source of love, power, and authority is the father—an awesome, demanding presence.

But what the play depicts, of course, is the failure of that presence: the failure of a father's power to command love in a patriarchal world and the emotional penalty he pays for wielding power.[10] Lear's very insistence on paternal power, in fact, belies its shakiness; similarly, the absence of the mother points to her hidden presence, as the lines with which I began might indicate. When Lear begins to feel the loss of Cordelia, to be wounded by her sisters, and to recognize his own vulnerability, he calls his state of mind *hysteria*, "the mother," which I interpret as his repressed identification with the mother. Women and the needs and traits associated with them are supposed to stay in their element, as Lear says, "below"—denigrated, silenced, denied. In this patriarchal world, masculine identity depends on repressing the vulnerability, dependency, and capacity for feeling which are called "feminine."

Recent historical studies of the Elizabethan family, its social structure and emotional dynamics, when considered in the light of psychoanalytic theory, provide a backdrop against which Lear's family drama takes on new meaning as a tragedy of masculinity.[11] Recently, several authors have analyzed mothering—the traditional division of roles within the family that makes the woman primarily responsible for rearing as well as bearing the children—as a social institution sustained by patriarchy, which in turn reinforces it.[12] Notably, Nancy Chodorow offers an incisive critique of the psychoanalytic conception of how the early mother-child relationship shapes the child's sense of maleness or femaleness. She argues that the basic masculine sense of self is formed through a denial of the male's initial connection with femininity, a denial that taints the male's attitudes toward women and impairs his capacity for affiliation in general. My interpretation of *Lear* comes out of the feminist re-examination of the mothering role now being carried on in many fields, but it is particularly indebted to Nancy Chodorow's analysis.

According to her account, women as mothers produce daughters with mothering capacities and the desire to mother, which itself grows out of the mother-daughter relationship. They also produce sons whose nurturant capacities and needs are curtailed in order to prepare them to be fathers. A focus on the primacy of the mother's role in ego-formation is not in itself new. It follows upon the attempts of theorists such as Melanie Klein, Michael and Alice Balint, John Bowlby, and Margaret Mahler to cast light on that dim psychic region which Freud likened to the Minoan civilization preceding the Greek, "grey with age, and shadowy and almost impossible to revivify."[13] Chodorow's account of the mother-child relationship, however, challenges the mainstream of psychoanalytic assumptions concerning the role of gender and family in the formation of the child's ego and sexual identity.

Because I find family relationships and gender identity central to Shakespeare's imagination, the most valuable aspect of Chodorow's work for me is its comparative perspective on the development of gender in the sexes. For both, the mother's rather than the father's role is the important one, as crucial to the child's individuation (development of a sense of self) as to the child's sense of gender. It is only for the purpose of analysis, however, that the two facets of identity can be separated. Both sexes begin to develop a sense of self in relation to a mother-woman. But a girl's sense of femaleness arises *through* her infantile union with the mother and later identification with her, while a boy's sense of maleness arises *in opposition* to those primitive forms of oneness. According to Robert Stoller, whose work supports Chodorow's argument, "Developing indissoluble links with mother's femaleness and femininity in the normal mother-infant symbiosis can only augment a girl's identity," while for a boy, "the whole process of becoming masculine . . . is endangered by the primary, profound, primal oneness with mother."[14] A girl's gender identity is reinforced but a boy's is threatened by union and identification with the same powerful female being. Thus, as Chodorow argues, the masculine personality tends to be formed through denial of connection with femininity; certain activities must be defined as masculine and superior to the maternal world of childhood, and women's activities must, correspondingly, be denigrated. The process of differentiation is inscribed in patriarchal ideology, which polarizes male and female social roles and behavior.[15]

The imprint of mothering on the male psyche, the psychological presence of the mother in men whether or not mothers are represented in the texts they write or in which they appear as characters, can be found throughout the literary canon. But it is Shakespeare who renders the dilemmas of manhood most compellingly and with the greatest insight, partly because he wrote at a certain historical moment. As part of a wide-ranging argument for the role of the nuclear family in shaping what he calls "affective individualism," Lawrence Stone holds that the family of Shakespeare's day saw a striking increase in the father's power over his wife and children. Stone's ambitious thesis has been strenuously criticized, but his description of the Elizabethan family itself, if not his notion of its place in the development of affective individualism, holds true.[16]

Stone sums up the mode of the father's dominance thus:

> This sixteenth-century aristocratic family was patrilinear, primogenitural, and patriarchal: patrilinear in that it was the male line whose ancestry was traced so diligently by the genealogists and heralds, and in almost all cases via the male line that titles were inherited; primogenitural in that most of the property went to the eldest son, the younger brothers being dispatched into the world with little more than a modest annuity or life interest in a small estate to keep them afloat; and patriarchal in that the husband and father lorded it over his wife and children with the quasi-absolute authority of a despot.[17]

Patriarchy, articulated through the family, was considered the natural order of things.[18] But like other kinds of "natural order," it was subject to historical change. According to Stone, between 1580 and 1640 two forces, one political and one religious, converged to heighten paternal power in the family. As the Tudor-Stuart state consolidated, it tried to undercut ancient baronial loyalty to the family line in order to replace it with loyalty to the crown. As part of the same campaign, the state also encouraged obedience to the *paterfamilias* in the home, according to the traditional analogy between state and family, king and father. James I stated, "Kings are compared to fathers in families: for a king is truly *parens patriae*, the politic father of his people."[19] The state thus had a direct interest in reinforcing patriarchy in the home.

Concurrently, Puritan fundamentalism—the literal interpretation of Mosaic law in its original patriarchal context—reinforced patriarchal elements in Christian doctrine and practice as well. As the head of the household, the father took over many of the priest's functions, leading his extended family of dependents in daily prayers, questioning them as to the state of their souls, giving or withholding his blessing on their undertakings. Although Protestant divines argued for the spiritual equality of women, deplored the double standard, and exalted the married state for both sexes, at the same time they zealously advocated the subjection of wives to their husbands on the scriptural grounds that the husband "beareth the image of God." Heaven and home were both patriarchal. The Homily on the State of Matrimony, one of the sermons issued by the crown to be read in church weekly, quotes and explicates the Pauline admonition, "Let women be subject to their husbands, as to the Lord; for the husband is the head of the woman, as Christ is the head of the church."[20] In effect, a woman's subjection to her husband's will was the measure of his patriarchal authority and thus of his manliness.

The division of parental roles in childrearing made children similarly subject to the father's will. In his study of Puritan attitudes toward authority and feeling, David Leverenz finds an emphasis on the mother's role as tender nurturer of young children, as against the father's role as disciplinarian and spiritual guide for older children. Mothers are encouraged to love their children openly in their early years but enjoined to withdraw their affections "at just about the time the father's instructional role becomes primary." Thus the breaking of the will is accomplished by the father, rather than by both parents equally. This division of duties, Leverenz holds, fostered a pervasive polarity, involving "associations of feared aspects of oneself with weakness and women, emphasis on male restraint and the male mind's governance of female emotions, the separation of 'head' from 'body,' . . . a language of male anxiety, rather than of female deficiency."[21]

A close look at the first scene in *King Lear* reveals much about lordliness and the male anxiety accompanying it. The court is gathered to watch Lear divide his kingdom and divest himself of its rule, but those purposes are actually only accessory to another that touches him more nearly: giving away his youngest daughter in marriage. While France and Burgundy wait in the wings, Cordelia, for whose hand they compete, also competes for the dowry without which she cannot marry. As Lynda Boose shows, this opening scene is a variant of the wedding ceremony, which dramatizes the bond between father and daughter even as it marks the severance of that bond. There is no part in the ritual for the bride's mother; rather, the bride's father hands her directly to her husband. Thus the ritual articulates the father's dominance both as procreator and as authority figure, to the eclipse of the mother in either capacity. At the same time, the father symbolically certifies the daughter's virginity. Thus the ceremony alludes to the incest taboo and raises a question about Lear's "darker purpose" in giving Cordelia away.[22]

In view of the ways that Lear tries to manipulate this ritual so as to keep his hold on Cordelia at the same time that he is ostensibly giving her away, we might suppose that the emotional crisis precipitating the tragic action is Lear's frustrated incestuous desire for his daughter. For in the course of winning her dowry, Cordelia is supposed to show that she loves her father not only more than her sisters do but, as she rightly sees, more than she loves her future husband; similarly, when Lear disowns and disinherits Cordelia, he thinks he has rendered her, dowered only with his curse, unfit to marry—and thus unable to leave paternal protection. In contrast, however, I want to argue that the socially-ordained, developmentally appropriate surrender of Cordelia as daughter-wife—the renunciation of her as incestuous object—awakens a deeper emotional need in Lear: the need for Cordelia as daughter-mother.

The play's beginning, as I have said, is marked by the omnipotent presence of the father and the absence of the mother. Yet in Lear's scheme for parceling out his kingdom, we can discern a child's image of being mothered. He wants two mutually exclusive things at once: to have absolute control over those closest to him and to be absolutely dependent on them. We can recognize in this stance the outlines of a child's pre-oedipal experience of himself and his mother as an undifferentiated dual unity, in which the child perceives his mother not as a separate person but as an agency of himself, who provides for his needs. She and her breast are a part of him, at his command.[23] In Freud's unforgettable phrase, he is "his majesty, the baby."[24]

As man, father, and ruler, Lear has habitually suppressed any needs for love, which in his patriarchal world would normally be satisfied by a mother or mothering woman. With age and loss of vigor, and as Freud suggests in "The Theme of the Three Caskets," with the prospect of return to mother earth, Lear feels those needs again and hints at them in his desire to "crawl" like a baby "toward death."[25] Significantly, he confesses them in these phrases the moment after he curses Cordelia for her silence, the moment in which he denies them most strongly. He says, "I lov'd her most, and thought to set my rest / On her kind nursery" (1.1.123–24).

When his other two daughters prove to be bad mothers and don't satisfy his needs for "nursery," Lear is seized by "the mother"—a searing sense of loss at the deprivation of the mother's presence. It assaults him in various ways—in the desire to weep, to mourn the enormous loss, and the equally strong desire to hold back the tears and, instead, accuse, arraign, convict, punish, and humiliate those who have made him realize his vulnerability and dependency. Thus the mother, revealed in Lear's response to his daughters' brutality toward him, makes her re-entry into the patriarchal world from which she had seemingly been excluded. The repressed mother returns specifically in Lear's wrathful projections onto the world about him of a symbiotic relationship with his daughters that recapitulates his pre-oedipal relationship with the mother. In a striking series of images in which parent-child, father-daughter, and husband-wife relationships are reversed and confounded, Lear re-enacts a childlike rage against the absent or rejecting mother as figured in his daughters.

Here I want to interject a speculation inspired by Stone's discussion of the custom of farming children out to wet nurses from birth until they were twelve to eighteen months old; at that time they were restored to the arms of their natural mother, who was by then a stranger to them.[26] Many if not most people in the gentry or aristocracy of Shakespeare's day must have suffered the severe trauma of maternal deprivation brought on by the departure of the wet nurse. We know the effects of such a trauma from the writings of John Bowlby: a tendency to make excessive demands on others, anxiety and anger when these demands are not met, and a blocked capacity for intimacy.[27] Lear responds to the loss of Cordelia, the "nurse" he rejects after she seems to reject him, by demanding hospitality for his hundred knights, by raging at Goneril and Regan when they refuse him courtesy and sympathy, and by rejecting human society when he stalks off to the heath. After the division of the kingdom, he re-enters the play in the fourth scene with this revealing peremptory demand: "Let me not stay a jot for dinner; go, get it ready" (1.4.9–10): he wants food, from a maternal woman. I believe that Lear's madness is essentially his rage at being deprived of the maternal presence. It is tantalizing, although I can imagine no way of proving it, to view this rage as part of the social pathology of wet-nursing in the ruling classes.

The play is full of oral rage: it abounds in fantasies of biting and devouring, and more specifically, fantasies of parents eating children and children eating parents. The idea is first brought up by Lear when he denies his "propinquity and property of blood" with Cordelia; that is, he denies that he begot her, that he is her father, as he also denies paternity of Regan and Goneril later. He assures her,

> The barbarous Scythian,
> Or he that makes his generation messes
> To gorge his appetite, shall to my bosom
> Be as well neighbour'd, pitied, and reliev'd,
> As thou my sometime daughter.
>
> (1.1.116–20)

The savagery of the image is shocking; it indicates Lear's first step toward the primitive, infantile modes of thinking to which he surrenders in his madness. When Cordelia doesn't feed him with love, he thinks angrily of eating *her*. Lear again voices this complex conjunction of ideas about maternal nurture, maternal aggression, and aggression against the mother when he looks at Edgar's mutilated body, bleeding from its many wounds, and remarks,

> Is it the fashion, that discarded fathers
> Should have thus little mercy on their flesh?
> Judicious punishment! 'twas this flesh begot
> Those pelican daughters.

> (3.4.72–75)

Lear seems to think that Edgar first transgressed against his father by "discarding" him as Regan and Goneril discarded Lear, and that Edgar's father then got back at his child, his "flesh," *in* the flesh, as Lear would like to do. But this fantasy of revenge calls forth an answering fantasy of punishment against his own flesh—a punishment he deserves for begetting children in the first place. The image of the pelican may have been suggested to Shakespeare by this passage in a contemporary text, which I will quote because it elucidates both the reciprocating spiral of aggression and revenge and the close identification between parent and child, which possesses Lear's mind:

> The Pellican loueth too much her children. For when the children be haught, and begin to waxe hoare, they smite the father and mother in the face, wherefore the mother smiteth them againe and slaieth them. And the thirde daye the mother smiteth her selfe in her side that the bloud runneth out, and sheddeth that hot bloud upon the bodies of her children. And by virtue of the bloud the birdes that were before dead, quicken againe.[28]

The children strike their parents, the mother retaliates, then wounds herself that the children may nurse on her blood. "Is't not," Lear asks, "as this mouth should tear this hand / For lifting food to 't?" (3.4.15–16) referring to "filial ingratitude." His daughters are the mouths he fed, which now tear their father's generous hand; but at the same time, he is the needy mouth that would turn against those daughters for refusing to feed him on demand. Lear's rage at not being fed by the daughters whom, pelican-like, he has nurtured, fills the play. It is mirrored in Albany's vision of all humanity preying upon itself, like monsters of the deep (4.2.46–49), a vision inspired by the reality of Goneril turning her father out in the storm and shortly confirmed by the more gruesome reality of Regan and Cornwall tearing out another father's eyes.

Bound up with this mixture of love and hate, nurture and aggression, is Lear's deep sense of identification with his daughters as born of his flesh. When Goneril bids him return to Regan's house rather than disrupt her own, his first thought is absolute separation from her, like his banishment of Cordelia: "We'll no more meet, no more see one another." But immediately he remembers the filial bond, for him a carnal as much as a moral bond:

> But yet thou art my flesh, my blood, my daughter;
> Or rather a disease that's in my flesh,
> Which I must needs call mine: thou art a boil,
> A plague-sore, or embossed carbuncle,
> In my corrupted blood.
>
> (2.4.223–27)

Gloucester echoes the same thought when he says wryly to Lear on the heath, "Our flesh and blood, my lord, is grown so vile, / That it doth hate what gets it" (3.4.149–50).

Children are products of an act that, in Elizabethan lore, was regarded as the mingling of bloods. In the metaphor of Genesis, repeated in the Anglican wedding service, man and wife become "one flesh." With regard to mother and child, however, the fleshly bond is not metaphorical but literal. Lear (like Gloucester) ignores the mother-child fleshly bond and insists that his children are, simply, *his* "flesh and blood." In the pelican image, he assimilates maternal functions to himself, as though Goneril and Regan hadn't been born of woman. Like Prospero, he alludes only once to his wife, and then in the context of adultery. When Regan says she is glad to see her father, he replies

> if thou shouldst not be glad
> I would divorce me from thy mother's tomb,
> Sepulchring an adultress.
>
> (2.4.131–33)

These lines imply, first, that Lear alone as progenitor endowed Regan with her moral nature, and second, that if that nature isn't good, she had some other father. In either case, her mother's only contribution was in the choice of a sexual partner. Thus Lear makes use of patriarchal ideology to serve his defensive needs: he denies his debt to a mother by denying that his daughters have any debt to her, either.

Lear's agonizing consciousness that he did indeed produce such monstrous children, however, persists despite this denial and leads him to project his loathing toward the procreative act onto his daughters, in a searing indictment of women's sexuality:

> The fitchew nor the soiled horse goes to 't
> With a more riotous appetite.
> Down from the waist they are centaurs,
> Though women all above:
> But to the girdle do the Gods inherit
> Beneath is all the fiend's: there's hell, there's darkness,
> There is the sulphurous pit—burning, scalding,
> Stench, consumption; fie, fie, fie! pah, pah!
>
> (4.6.124–31)

Even if he did beget these daughters, Lear implies, he's not answerable for their unkindness, because they are, after all, women—and women are tainted, rather than empowered as men are, by their sexual capacities. Thus he presses into service another aspect of patriarchal ideology, its misogyny, to separate himself from any feminine presence.

To return for a moment to the social dimensions of Lear's inner turmoil, it is important here that generational conflicts entwine with and intensify gender conflicts. Lear and his daughters, Gloucester and his sons are pitted against one another because the younger generation perceives the authority of the elder as "the oppression of aged tyranny" (1.2.47–52). Stephen Greenblatt remarks that this period has "a deep gerontological bias," revealed in numerous claims that "by the will of God and the natural order of things, authority belonged to the old." At the same time, however, sermons, moral writings, and folk tales of the kind on which *King Lear* is based voice the fear that if parents hand over their wealth or their authority to their children, those children will turn against them.[29] The common legal practice of drawing up maintenance agreements testifies that this fear had some basis in actual experience. In such contracts, children to whom parents deeded farm or workshop were legally bound to supply food, clothing, and shelter to their parents, even to the precise number of bushels of grain or yards of cloth. Thus the law put teeth into what was supposed to be natural kindness. Lear's contest of love in the first scene functions as a maintenance agreement in that he tries to bind his daughters, by giving them their inheritance while he is still alive, into caring for him. This generational bargain is then complicated by the demands proper to gender as well—the father's emotional demand that his daughters be his mothers and perform the tasks of nurture proper to females.

Regan and Goneril betray and disappoint Lear by not being mothers to him, but in a deeper, broader sense, they shame him by bringing out the woman in him. In the following speech, Shakespeare takes us close to the nerve and bone of Lear's shame at being reduced to an impotence he considers womanish:

> You see me here, you Gods, a poor old man,
> As full of grief as age; wretched in both!
> If it be you that stirs these daughters' hearts
> Against their father, fool me not so much
> To bear it tamely; touch me with noble anger,
> And let not women's weapons, water-drops,
> Stain my man's cheeks! No, you unnatural hags,
> I will have such revenges on you both
> That all the world shall—I will do such things,
> What they are, yet I know not, but they shall be
> The terrors of the earth. You think I'll weep;
> No, I'll not weep;
> I have full cause of weeping, but this heart
> Shall break into a hundred thousand flaws
> Or ere I'll weep.
>
> (2.4.274–88)

He calls his tears "women's weapons" not only as a way of deprecating women for using emotion to manipulate men but also because he feels deeply threatened by his own feelings. Marianne Novy has argued that Lawrence Stone, in calling attention to the "distance, manipulation, and deference" that characterized the Elizabethan family, identified "a cultural ideal of Elizabethan society . . . a personality type that on the one hand kept feelings of attachment and grief under strict control, but on the other was more ready to express feelings of anger." "The model," she comments, "was primarily a masculine ideal."[30] In agreeing, I would suggest that this masculine ideal was produced by the extreme sexual division of labor within the patriarchal family, which made women at once the source and the focus of a child's earliest and most unmanageable feelings.

Despite a lifetime of strenuous defense against admitting feeling and the power of feminine presence into his world, defense fostered at every turn by prevailing social arrangements, Lear manages to let

45

them in. He learns to weep and, though his tears scald and burn like molten lead, they are no longer "women's weapons" against which he must defend himself. I will conclude this reading of the play by tracing, briefly, Lear's progress toward acceptance of the woman in himself, a progress punctuated by his hysterical projections of rage at being deprived of maternal nurture. In the passage that I just quoted, as he turns toward the heath, Lear prays that anger may keep him from crying, from becoming like a woman. He also, in effect, tells us one way to read the storm—as a metaphor for his internal emotional process: "I have full cause of weeping, but this heart / Shall break into a hundred thousand flaws / Or ere I'll weep" (2.4.286–88). Shakespeare portrays the storm as the breaking open of something enclosed, a break that lets out a flood of rain; it thus resembles Lear's heart cracking, letting out the hungry, mother-identified part of him in a flood of tears. Lear exhorts the winds to crack their cheeks and the thunder to crack Nature's moulds and spill their seeds; he envisions "close pent-up guilts" riven from "their concealing continents" (3.2.1–9, 49–59). He wants the whole world struck flat and cleft open, so that the bowels of sympathy may flow. What spills out of Lear at first is a flood of persecutory fantasies. He sees everyone in his own image, as either subjects or agents of persecution. Only daughters like his, he thinks, could have reduced Poor Tom to naked misery; Poor Tom and the Fool are, like him, stern judges bringing his daughters to trial. Gloucester is "Goneril, with a white beard," and then, someone who might weep along with Lear although he has only the case of eyes.

Before Shakespeare allows Lear to feel the weeping woman in himself or to face his need for Cordelia and his guilt for the wrong he did her, he evokes and excoriates a world full of viperish women. Interwoven with Lear's indictments of women during acts 3 and 4 are the imaginary lustful mistresses of Poor Tom's sophisticated past, the wearers of plackets and rustling silks, as well as the real Regan tearing out Gloucester's eyes, and the real Goneril, stealthy and lustful, seducing Edmund and sloughing off Albany. It is as though Shakespeare as well as his hero must dredge up everything horrible that might be imagined of women and denounce it before he can confront the good woman, the one and only good woman, Cordelia.

Cordelia's goodness is as absolute and inexplicable as her sisters' reprovable badness, as much an archetype of infantile fantasy as they are. When she re-enters the play, she is described as crying with pity for her father's sufferings, yet in her tears she is still "queen over her passion." Whereas Lear thought weeping an ignoble surrender of his masculine authority, Cordelia conceives her tears as a source of power:

> All blest secrets,
> All you unpublished virtues of the earth,
> Spring with my tears; be aidant and remediate
> In the good man's distress!
>
> (4.4.15–18)

In these scenes Cordelia becomes, now in a benign sense, that daughter-mother Lear wanted her to be. Like the Virgin Mary, she intercedes magically, her empathy and pity coaxing mercy from nature. Yet finally, as the Doctor's words imply, she can only be "the foster-nurse" of Lear's repose.[31]

Lear runs from the attendants Cordelia sends to rescue him, who appear just after he poignantly evokes the crying infant as a common denominator of humanity:

> Thou must be patient; we came crying hither.
> Thou know'st, the first time that we smell the air
> We wawl and cry . . .
> When we are born, we cry that we are come
> To this great stage of fools.
>
> (4.6.178–80, 182–83)

Here he comes closest to admitting his vulnerability, but he must immediately defend against it and see the proffered help as a threat. Stanley Cavell has argued that the reluctance to be recognized by those whom they love most, which characterizes Lear, Kent, Edgar and Gloucester, lies at the heart of this play; he holds that they are reluctant because they feel that their love bespeaks a demeaning dependency.[32] I agree—and I regard that embarrassed shrinking from recognition as part of a masculine identity crisis in a culture that dichotomized power as masculine and feeling as feminine.

And so Lear exits running in this scene, asserting his kingship ("Come, come, I am a king") but behaving like a mischievous child who makes his mother run after him ("Come, and you get it, you shall get it by running," 4.6.199, 201–202). When he reappears, he is as helpless as a child, sleeping and carried in by servants. He awakes in the belief that he has died and been reborn into an afterlife, and he talks about tears to Cordelia:

Thou art a soul in bliss, but I am bound
Upon a wheel of fire, that mine own tears
Do scald like molten lead.

(4.7.45–47)

These are the tears of ashamed self-knowledge, manly tears caused by
a realization of what his original childish demands on his daughters
had led to. In this scene, which I want to compare with the next scene
with Cordelia, Lear comes closer than he ever does later to a mature
acceptance of his human dependency. He asserts his manhood, and
admits Cordelia's separateness from him at the same time that he
confesses his need for her: he can say "I am a very fond foolish old
man" and yet also declare, "For (as I am a man) I think this lady / To
be my child Cordelia" (4.7.59, 69). I want to pause at those three
words "man," "lady," and "child." Lear acknowledges his manhood
and his daughter's womanhood in the same line and the same breath.
He can stop imagining her as the maternal woman that he yearned for
and accept his separateness from her. Yet he also calls her his child,
acknowledging the bond of paternity that he denied in the first act. He
need not be threatened by her autonomy as a person nor obsessed by
the fleshly tie between them as parent and child.

Lear's struggle to discover or create a new mode of being based on
his love for Cordelia continues to his last breath. Imagining their life
together in prison, he transcends the rigid structure of command and
obedience that once framed his world:

> Come, let's away to prison:
> We two alone will sing like birds i' th' cage;
> When thou dost ask me blessing, I'll kneel down
> And ask of thee forgiveness. So we'll live,
> And pray, and sing, and tell old tales, and laugh at gilded
> butterflies . . .

(5.3.8–11)

Parent and child are equal, the gestures of deference that ordinarily
denote patriarchal authority now transformed into signs of reciprocal
love. Moreover, Lear now views all power from a quasi-divine
perspective that charmingly deflates pretension or ambition as mere
toys, while nevertheless carrying a certain grandeur of its own. On the
other hand, Lear's characteristically fierce defensiveness continues to
shape his fantasy, which is provoked by Cordelia's request that they
confront their enemies: "Shall we not see these daughters and these

sisters?" The prospect of facing his bad mothers as well as his good mother impels Lear to conceive of Cordelia and himself as forming an impregnable dyad bound together by a complete harmony of thought and feeling more than by the circumstances of captivity. If he did agree to meet Regan and Goneril, he would have to abandon the fantasy that one good woman like Cordelia can triumph over or negate her evil counterparts, as well as the fantasy that a prison can be a nursery in which Cordelia has no independent being and exists solely for her father as part of his defensive strategy against coming to terms with women who are as human, or as inhuman, as men.

Cordelia's death prevents Lear from trying to live out his fantasy, and perhaps discover once again that a daughter cannot be a mother.[33] When he enters bearing Cordelia in his arms, he is struggling to accept the total and irrevocable loss of the only loving woman in his world, the one person who could possibly fulfill needs that he has, in such anguish, finally come to admit. No wonder that he cannot contemplate such utter, devastating separateness, and in the final scene tries so hard to deny that she is dead. At the end of King Lear, only men are left. It remains for Shakespeare to re-imagine a world in his last plays in which masculine authority can find mothers in its daughters, in Marina, Perdita, and Miranda—the world of pastoral tragicomedy and romance, the genres of wish-fulfillment, rather than the tragic world of King Lear.

3

Prospero's Wife

Stephen Orgel

This essay is not a reading of *The Tempest*. It is a consideration of five related moments and issues. I have called it *Prospero's Wife* because some of it centers on her, but as a figure conspicuous by her absence from the play, I take her as a figure of my larger subject: the absent, the unspoken, that seems to me the most powerful and problematic presence in *The Tempest*. In its outlines, the play seems a story of privatives: withdrawal, usurpation, banishment, becoming lost, shipwreck. As an antithesis, a principle of control, preservation, recreation, the play offers only magic, embodied in a single figure, the extraordinary power of Prospero.

1. Family History

Prospero's wife is alluded to only once in the play, in Prospero's reply to Miranda's question, "Sir, are you not my father?"

> Thy mother was a piece of virtue, and
> She said thou wast my daughter; and thy father
> Was Duke of Milan; and his only heir
> And princess: no worse issued.
>
> (1.2.55–59)[1]

Prospero's wife is identified as Miranda's mother, in a context implying that although she was virtuous, women as a class are not, and that were it not for her word, Miranda's legitimacy would be in doubt. The legitimacy of Prospero's heir, that is, derives from her mother's word. But that word is all that is required of her in the play; once he is assured of it, Prospero turns his attention to himself and his succession, and he characterizes Miranda in a clause that grows increasingly ambivalent: "his only heir / And princess: no worse issued."

Except for this moment, Prospero's wife is absent from his mem-

50

ory. She is wholly absent from her daughter's memory: Miranda can recall several women who attended her in childhood, but no mother. The attitudes implied toward wives and mothers here are confirmed shortly afterward when Prospero, recounting his brother Antonio's crimes, demands that Miranda "tell me / If this might be a brother," and Miranda takes the question to be a charge of adultery against Prospero's mother:

> I should sin
> To think but nobly of my grandmother:
> Good wombs have borne bad sons.
>
> (1.2.118–20)

She immediately translates Prospero's attack on his brother into an attack on his mother (and the best she can produce in her grandmother's defence is a "not proved"); and whether or not she has correctly divined her father's intentions, Prospero makes no objection.

The absent presence of the wife and mother in the play constitutes a space that is filled by Prospero's creation of surrogates and a ghostly family: the witch Sycorax and her monster child Caliban (himself, as becomes apparent, a surrogate for the other wicked child, the usurping younger brother), the good child/wife Miranda, the obedient Ariel, the violently libidinized adolescent Ferdinand. The space is filled, too, by a whole structure of wifely allusion and reference: widow Dido, model at once of heroic fidelity to a murdered husband and the destructive potential of erotic passion; the witch Medea, murderess and filicide; three exemplary goddesses, the bereft Ceres, nurturing Juno, and licentious Venus; and Alonso's daughter Claribel, unwillingly married off to the ruler of the modern Carthage and thereby lost to her father forever.

Described in this way, the play has an obvious psychoanalytic shape. I have learned a great deal from Freudian treatments of it, most recently from essays by David Sundelson, Coppélia Kahn, and Joel Fineman in the volume called *Representing Shakespeare*.[2] It is almost irresistible to look at the play as a case history—*whose* case history is a rather more problematic question and one that criticism has not, on the whole, dealt with satisfactorily: not, obviously, that of the characters. I want to pause first over what it means to consider the play as a case history.

In older psychoanalytic paradigms (say Ernest Jones's), the critic is the analyst, Shakespeare the patient, the plays his fantasies. The trouble with this paradigm is that it misrepresents the analytic situation in a fundamental way. The interpretation of analytic material is done in conjunction with, and in large measure by, the patient, not the analyst; what the analyst does is to *enable* the patient, to free the patient to interpret. An analysis done without the patient, like Freud's of Leonardo, will be revealing only about the analyst. A more recent paradigm, in which the audience's response is the principal analytic material, seems to me based on even more fundamental misconceptions, first because it treats an audience as an entity, a unit, and moreover a constant one; and more problematically, because it conceives of the play as an objective event, so that the critical question becomes, "This is what happened: how do we respond to it?"

To take the psychoanalytic paradigm seriously, however, and treat the plays as case histories, is surely to treat them *not* as objective events but as collaborative fantasies and to acknowledge thereby that we, as analysts, are implicated in the fantasy. It is not only the patients who create the shape of their histories, and when Bruno Bettelheim observes that Freud's case histories "read as well as the best novels," he is probably telling more of the truth than he intends.[3] Moreover, the crucial recent advances in our understanding of Freud and psychoanalysis have been precisely critical acts of close and inventive reading—there are, in this respect, no limits to the collaboration. But if we accept this as our paradigm and think of ourselves as Freud's or Shakespeare's collaborators, we must also acknowledge that our reading of the case will be revealing, again, chiefly about ourselves. This is why every generation, and perhaps every reading, produces a different analysis of its Shakespearean texts. In the same way, recent psychoanalytic theory has replaced Freud's central Oedipal myth with a drama in which the loss of the seducing mother is the crucial infant trauma. As men, we used to want assurance that we could successfully compete with or replace or supersede our fathers; now we want to know that our lost mothers will return. Both of these no doubt involve real perceptions, but they also undeniably serve particular cultural needs.

Shakespeare plays, like case histories, derive from the observation of human behavior, and both plays and case histories are imaginative constructs. Whether or not either is taken to be an objective report of behavior has more to do with the reader than the reporter, but it has to be said that Shakespearean critics have more often than not treated the plays as objective accounts. Without such an assumption, a book with the title *The Girlhood of Shakespeare's Heroines* would be incomprehensible. We feel very far from this famous and popular Victorian work now, but we still worry about consistency and motivation in

Shakespearean texts, and much of the commentary in an edition like the Arden Shakespeare is designed to explain why the characters say what they say—that is, to reconcile what they say with what, on the basis of their previous behavior, we feel they ought to be saying. The critic who worries about this kind of consistency in a Shakespeare text is thinking of it as an objective report.

But all readings of Shakespeare, from the earliest seventeenth-century adaptations through eighteenth-century attempts to produce "authentic" or "accurate" texts to the liberal fantasy of the old Variorum Shakespeare, have been aware of deep ambiguities and ambivalences in the texts. The eighteenth century described these as Shakespeare's errors and generally revised them through plausible emendation or outright rewriting. The argument was that Shakespeare wrote in haste and would have written more perfect plays had he taken time to revise; the corollary to this was, of course, that what we want are the perfect plays Shakespeare did not write rather than the imperfect ones that he did. A little later the errors became not Shakespeare's but those of the printing house, the scribe, the memory of the reporter or the defective hearing of the transcriber; but the assumption has always been that it is possible to produce a "perfect" text: that beyond or behind the ambiguous, puzzling, inconsistent text is a clear and consistent one.

Plays, moreover, are not only—and one might argue, not primarily—texts. They are performances, too, originally designed to be read only in order to be acted out, and the gap between the text and its performance has always been, and remains, a radical one. There always has been an imagination intervening between the texts and their audiences, initially the imagination of producer, director, or actor (roles that Shakespeare played himself), and since that time the imagination of editors and commentators as well. These are texts that have always had to be realized. Initially unstable, they have remained so despite all attempts to fix them. All attempts to produce an authentic, correct, that is, stable text have resulted only in an extraordinary variety of versions. Their differences can be described as minor only if one believes that the real play is a Platonic idea, never realized but only approached and approximately represented by its text.

This is our myth: the myth of a stable, accurate, authentic, legitimate text, a text that we can think of as Shakespeare's legitimate heir. It is, in its way, a family myth, and it operates with peculiar force in our readings of *The Tempest,* a play that has been, for the last hundred and fifty years, taken as a representation of Shakespeare himself bidding farewell to his art, as Shakespeare's legacy.

2. The Missing Wife

She is missing as a character, but Prospero, several times explicitly, presents himself as incorporating the wife, acting as both father and mother to Miranda, and, in one extraordinary passage, describes the voyage to the island as a birth fantasy:

> When I have decked the sea with drops full salt,
> Under my burden groaned, which raised in me
> An undergoing stomach, to bear up
> Against what should ensue.
>
> (1.2.155–58)

To come to the island is to start life over again—both his own and Miranda's—with himself as sole parent, but also with himself as favorite child: he has been banished by his wicked, usurping, possibly illegitimate younger brother Antonio. This too has the shape of a Freudian fantasy: the younger child is indeed the usurper in the family, and the kingdom he usurps is the mother. On the island, Prospero undoes the usurpation, recreating kingdom and family with himself in sole command.

But not quite, because the island is not his alone—or if it is, then he has repeopled it with all parts of his fantasy, the distressing as well as the gratifying. When he arrives he finds Caliban, child of the witch Sycorax, herself a victim of banishment. The island provided a new life for her too, as it did literally for her son, with whom she was pregnant when she arrived. Sycorax died some time before Prospero came to the island; Prospero never saw her, and everything he knows about her he has learned from Ariel. Nevertheless, she is insistently present in his memory—far more present than his own wife—and she embodies to an extreme degree all the negative assumptions about women that he and Miranda have exchanged.

It is important, therefore, that Caliban derives his claim to the island from his mother: "This island's mine, by Sycorax my mother" (1.2.333). This has interesting implications to which I shall return, but here I want to point out that he need not make the claim this way. He could derive it from mere prior possession: he was there first. This, after all, would have been the sole basis of Sycorax's claim to the island, but it is an argument that Caliban never makes. And in deriving his authority from his mother, he delivers himself into Prospero's hands: Prospero declares him a bastard, "got by the devil himself / Upon thy wicked dam" (1.2.321–22), thereby both disallowing any claim from inheritance and justifying his loathing for Caliban.

But is it true that Caliban is Sycorax's bastard by Satan? How does Prospero know this? Not from Sycorax: Prospero never saw her. Not from Caliban: Sycorax died before she could even teach her son to speak. Everything Prospero knows about the witch he knows from Ariel—her appearance, the story of her banishment, the fact that her pregnancy saved her from execution. Did Sycorax also tell Ariel that her baby was the illegitimate son of the devil? Or is this Prospero's contribution to the story, an especially creative piece of invective and an extreme instance of his characteristic assumptions about women? Nothing in the text will answer this question for us; and it is worth pausing to observe first that Caliban's claim seems to have been designed so that Prospero can disallow it, and second that we have no way of distinguishing the facts about Caliban and Sycorax from Prospero's invective about them.

Can Prospero imagine no good mothers, then? The play, after all, moves toward a wedding, and the most palpable example we see of the magician's powers is a betrothal masque. The masque is presided over by two exemplary mothers, Ceres and Juno; and the libidinous Venus with her destructive son Cupid has been banished from the scene. But the performance is also preceded by the most awful warnings against sexuality, male sexuality this time: all the libido is presumed to be Ferdinand's while Miranda remains Prospero's innocent child. Ferdinand's reassuring reply, as David Sundelson persuasively argues,[4] includes submerged fantasies of rape and more than a hint that when the lust of the wedding night cools, so will his marital devotion:

> . . . the murkiest den,
> The most opportune place, the strong'st suggestion
> Our worser genius can, shall never melt
> Mine honor into lust, to take away
> The edge of that day's celebration . . .
>
> (4.1.25–29)

This is the other side of the assumption that all women at heart are whores: all men at heart are rapists—Caliban, Ferdinand, and of course that means Prospero too.

3. The Marriage Contract

The play moves toward marriage, certainly, and yet the relations it postulates between men and women are ignorant at best, characteristically tense, and potentially tragic. There is a familiar Shakespearean paradigm here: relationships between men and women interest Shakespeare intensely, but not, on the whole, as husbands and wives. The wooing process tends to be what it is here: not so much a prelude to marriage and a family as a process of self-definition—an increasingly unsatisfactory process, if we look at the progression of plays from *As You Like It, Much Ado about Nothing, Twelfth Night* through *All's Well that Ends Well, Measure for Measure, Troilus and Cressida* to *Antony and Cleopatra* and *Cymbeline.* If we want to argue that marriage is actually the point of the comic wooing process for Shakespeare, then we surely ought to be looking at how he depicts marriages; and here Petruchio and Kate, Capulet and Lady Capulet, Claudius and Gertrude, Othello and Desdemona, Macbeth and Lady Macbeth, Cymbeline and his queen, Leontes and Hermione will not persuade us that comedies ending in marriages have ended happily—or if they have, it is only because they have ended there, stopped at the wedding day.

What happens after marriage? Families in Shakespeare tend not to consist of husbands and wives and their offspring but of a parent and a child, usually in a chiastic relationship—father and daughter, mother and son. When there are two children, they tend to be presented as alternatives or rivals: the twins of *The Comedy of Errors,* Sebastian and Viola, infinitely substitutable for each other; or the good son–bad son complex of Orlando and Oliver, Edgar and Edmund. We know that Shakespeare himself had a son and two daughters, but that family configuration never appears in the plays. Lear's three daughters are quite exceptional in Shakespeare, and even they are dichotomized into bad and good. We may also recall Titus Andronicus's four sons and a daughter and Tamora's three sons, hardly instances to demonstrate Shakespeare's convictions about the comforts of family life.

The family paradigm that emerges from Shakespeare's imagination is a distinctly unstable one. Here is what we know of Shakespeare's own family: he had three brothers and three sisters who survived beyond infancy, and his parents lived into old age. At eighteen he married a woman of twenty-four by whom he had a daughter within six months, and a twin son and daughter a year and a half later. Within six more years he had moved permanently to London, and for the next twenty years—all but the last three years of his life—he lived apart from his wife and family. Nor should we stop here: we do not in the least know that Susanna, Hamnet, and Judith were his only children. He lived in a society without contraceptives, and unless we want to believe that he was either exclusively homosexual or celibate, we must assume a high degree of probability that there were other children. That they are not mentioned in his will may mean that they did not survive, but it also might mean that he made separate, nontestamentary provision for them. Certainly the plays reveal a strong interest in the subject of illegitimacy.

Until quite late in his career, he seems to have expressed his strongest familial feelings not toward children or wives but toward parents and siblings. His father dies in 1601, the year of *Hamlet,* his mother in 1608, the year of *Coriolanus.* And if we are thinking about usurping bastard younger brothers, it cannot be coincidental that the younger brother who followed him into the acting profession was named Edmund. There are no dramatic correlatives comparable to these for the death of his son Hamnet in 1596. If we take the plays to express what Shakespeare thought about himself (an assumption that strikes me as by no means axiomatic) then we will say that he was apparently free to think of himself as a father—to his two surviving daughters—only after the death of both his parents: 1608 is the date of *Pericles* as well as *Coriolanus.*

One final biographical observation: Shakespearean heroines marry very young, in their teens. Miranda is fifteen. We are always told that Juliet's marriage at fourteen is not unusual in the period, but in fact it is unusual in all but upper-class families. In Shakespeare's own family, his wife married at twenty-four and his daughters at twenty-four and thirty-one. It was Shakespeare himself who married at eighteen. The women of Shakespeare's plays, of course, are adolescent boys. Perhaps we should see as much of Shakespeare in Miranda and Ariel as in Prospero.

4. Power and Authority

The psychoanalytic and biographical questions raised by *The Tempest* are irresistible, but they can supply at best partial clues to its nature. I have described the plays as collaborative fantasies, and it is not only critics and readers who are involved in the collaboration. It is performers and audiences, too, and I take these terms in their largest senses, to apply not merely to stage productions but also to the theatrical dimension of the society that contains and is mirrored by the theater. Cultural concerns, political and social issues, speak through

The Tempest—sometimes explicitly, as in the open-ended discussion of political economy between Gonzalo, Antonio, and Sebastian in act 2. But in a broader sense, family structures and sexual relations become political structures in the play, and these are relevant to the political structures of Jacobean England.

What is the nature of Prospero's authority and the source of his power? Why is he Duke of Milan and the legitimate ruler of the island? Power, as Prospero presents it in the play, is not inherited but self-created: it is magic, or "art," an extension of mental power and self-knowledge, and the authority that legitimizes it derives from heaven—*Fortune* and *Destiny* are the terms used in the play. It is Caliban who derives his claim to the island from inheritance, from his mother.

In the England of 1610, both these positions represent available, and indeed normative, ways of conceiving of royal authority. James I's authority derived, he said, both from his mother and from God. But deriving one's legitimacy from Mary Queen of Scots was ambiguous at best, and James always felt exceedingly insecure about it. Elizabeth had had similar problems with the sources of her authority, and they centered precisely on the question of her legitimacy. To those who believed that her father's divorce from Katherine of Aragon was invalid (that is, to Roman Catholics), Elizabeth had no hereditary claim; and she had, moreover, been declared legally illegitimate after the execution of her mother for adultery and incest. Henry VIII maintained Elizabeth's bastardy to the end; her claim to the throne derived exclusively from her designation in the line of succession, next after Edward and Mary, in her father's will. This ambiguous legacy was the sole source of her authority. Prospero at last acknowledging the bastard Caliban as his own is also expressing the double edge of kingship throughout Shakespeare's lifetime (the ambivalence will not surprise us if we consider the way kings are represented in the history plays). Historically speaking, Caliban's claim to the island is a good one.

Royal power, the play seems to say, is good when it is self-created, bad when it is usurped or inherited from an evil mother. But of course the least problematic case of royal descent is one that is not represented in these paradigms at all; it is one that derives not from the mother but in the male line from the father: the case of Ferdinand and Alonso, in which the wife and mother is totally absent. If we are thinking about the *derivation* of royal authority, then, the absence of a father from Prospero's memory is a great deal more significant than the disappearance of a wife. Some have dealt with this in a psychoanalytic framework, whereby Antonio becomes a stand-in for the father, the real usurper of the mother's kingdom.[5] Here again, however, the realities of contemporary kingship seem more enlightening, if not inescapable. James in fact had a double claim to the English throne, and the one through his father, the Earl of Darnley, was in the strictly lineal respects somewhat stronger than that of his mother. Both Darnley and Mary were direct descendents of Henry VII, but under Henry VIII's will, which established the line of succession, descendents who were not English-born were specifically excluded. Darnley was born in England, Mary was not. Indeed, Darnley's mother went from Scotland to have her baby in England precisely in order to preserve the claim to the throne.

King James rarely mentioned this side of his heritage, for perfectly understandable reasons. His father was even more disreputable than his mother; and given what was at least the public perception of both their characters, it was all too easy to speculate about whether Darnley was even in fact his father.[6] For James, as for Elizabeth, the derivation of authority through paternity was extremely problematic. Practically, James's claim to the English throne depended on Elizabeth's naming him her heir (we recall Miranda's legitimacy depending on her mother's word), and James correctly saw this as a continuation of the protracted negotiations between Elizabeth and his mother. His legitimacy, in both senses, thus derived from two mothers, the chaste Elizabeth and the sensual Mary, whom popular imagery represented respectively as a virgin goddess ("a piece of virtue") and a lustful and diabolical witch. James's sense of his own place in the kingdom is that of Prospero, rigidly paternalistic but incorporating the maternal as well: the king describes himself in *Basilicon Doron* as "a loving nourish father" providing the commonwealth with "their own nourish-milk."[7] The very etymology of the word *authority* confirms the metaphor: *augeo,* increase, nourish, cause to grow. At moments in his public utterances, James sounds like a gloss on Prospero: "I am the husband, and the whole island is my lawful wife; I am the head, and it is my body."[8] Here the incorporation of the wife has become literal and explicit. James conceives himself as the head of a single-parent family. In the world of *The Tempest,* there are no two-parent families. All the dangers of promiscuity and bastardy are resolved in such a conception—unless, of course, the parent is a woman.

My point here is not that Shakespeare is representing King James as Prospero or Caliban or both, but that these figures embody the predominant modes of conceiving of royal authority in the period. They are Elizabeth's and James's modes, too.

5. The Renunciation of Magic

Prospero's magic power is exemplified, on the whole, as power over children: his daughter Miranda, the bad child Caliban, the obedient but impatient Ariel, the adolescent Ferdinand, the wicked younger brother Antonio, and indeed, the shipwreck victims as a whole, who are treated like a group of bad children. Many critics talk about Prospero as a Renaissance scientist and see alchemical metaphors in the grand design of the play. No doubt there is something in this; but what the play's action presents is not experiments and empiric studies but a fantasy about controlling other people's minds. Does the magic work? We are given a good deal of evidence of it: the masque, the banquet, the harpies, the tempest itself. But the great scheme is not to produce illusions and good weather: it is to bring about reconciliation, and here we would have to say that it works only indifferently well. "They being penitent," says Prospero to Ariel, "The sole drift of my purpose doth extend / Not a frown further" (5.1.28–30). The assertion opens with a conditional clause whose conditions are not met: Alonso is penitent, but the chief villain, the usurping younger brother Antonio, remains obdurate. Nothing, not all Prospero's magic, can redeem Antonio from his essential badness. Since Shakespeare was free to have Antonio repent if that is what he had in mind—half a line would have done for critics craving a reconciliation—we ought to take seriously the possibility that repentence is not what he had in mind. Perhaps, too, penitence is not what Prospero's magic is designed to elicit from his brother.

Why is Prospero's power conceived as magic? Why, in returning to Milan, does he renounce it? Most commentators say that he gives up his magic when he no longer needs it. This is an obvious answer, but it strikes me as too easy, a comfortable assumption cognate with the view that the play concludes with reconciliation, repentence, and restored harmony. To say that Prospero no longer needs his magic is to beg all the most important questions. What does it mean to say that he needs it? Did he ever need it, and if so, why? And does he in fact give it up?

Did he ever need magic? Prospero's devotion to his secret studies is what caused all the trouble in the first place—this is not an interpretation of mine; it is how Prospero presents the matter. If he has now learned to be a good ruler through the exercise of his art, that is also what taught him to be a bad one. So the question of his need for magic goes to the heart of how we interpret and judge his character: is the magic a strength or a weakness? To say that he no longer needs it is to say that his character changes in some way for the better; that by renouncing his special powers he becomes fully human. This is an important claim. Let us test it by looking at Prospero's renunciation.

What does it mean for Prospero to give up his power? Letting Miranda marry and leaving the island are the obvious answers, but they can hardly be right. Miranda's marriage is *brought about* by the magic; it is part of Prospero's plan. It pleases Miranda, certainly, but it is designed by Prospero as a way of satisfying himself. Claribel's marriage to the King of Tunis looks less sinister in this light: daughters' marriages, in royal families at least, are designed primarily to please their fathers. And leaving the island, reassuming the dukedom, is part of the plan, too. Both of these are presented as acts of renunciation, but they are in fact what the exercise of Prospero's magic is intended to effect, and they represent his triumph.

Prospero renounces his art in the great monologue at the beginning of act 5, "Ye elves of hills, brooks, standing lakes and groves," and for all its valedictory quality, it is the most powerful assertion of his magic that the play gives us. It is also a powerful literary allusion, a close translation of a speech of Medea in Ovid,[9] and it makes at least one claim for Prospero that is made nowhere else in the play, that he can raise the dead. For Shakespeare to present this as a *renunciation* speech is upping Prospero's ante, to say the least.

In giving up his magic, Prospero speaks as Medea. He has incorporated Ovid's witch, prototype of the wicked mother Sycorax, in the most literal way—verbatim, so to speak—and his "most potent art" is now revealed as translation and impersonation. In this context, the distinction between black magic and white magic, Sycorax and Prospero, has disappeared. Two hundred lines later, Caliban too is revealed as an aspect of Prospero: "This thing of darkness I acknowledge mine."

But Caliban is an aspect of Antonio, the evil child, the usurping brother. Where is the *real* villain in relation to Prospero now? Initially Antonio had been characterized, like Caliban and Sycorax, as embodying everything that is antithetical to Prospero; but in recounting his history to Miranda, Prospero also presents himself as deeply implicated in the usurpation, with Antonio even seeming at times to be acting as Prospero's agent: "The government I cast upon my brother"; "[I] to him put the manage of my state"; "my trust . . . did beget of him / A falsehood," and so forth. If Prospero is accepting the blame for what happened, there is a degree to which he is also taking the credit. Antonio's is another of the play's identities that Prospero has incorporated into his own; and in that case, what is there to forgive?

Let us look, then, at Prospero forgiving his brother in act 5. The pardon is enunciated—"You, brother mine, that entertain ambition . . . I do forgive thee" (75–78)[10]—and qualified at once ("unnatural though thou art"), reconsidered as more crimes are remembered, some to be held in reserve ("at this time I will tell no tales" [128–29]), all but withdrawn ("most wicked sir, whom to call brother / Would even infect my mouth" [130–31]), and only then confirmed through forcing Antonio to relinquish the dukedom, an act that is presented as something he does unwillingly. The point is not only that Antonio does not repent here but also that he is not allowed to repent. Even his renunciation of the crown is Prospero's act: "I do . . . require / My dukedom of thee, which perforce, I know, / Thou must restore" (131–34). In Prospero's drama, there is no room for Antonio to act of his own free will.

The crime that Prospero holds in reserve for later use against his brother is the attempted assassination of Alonso. Here is what happened: Prospero sends Ariel to put all the shipwreck victims to sleep except Antonio and Sebastian. Antonio then persuades Sebastian to murder Alonso—his brother—and thereby become king of Naples. Sebastian agrees, on the condition that Antonio kill Gonzalo. At the moment of the murders, Ariel reappears and wakes Gonzalo:

> My master through his art foresees the danger
> That you his friend are in; and sends me forth—
> For else his project dies—to keep them living.
>
> (2.1.293–95)

This situation has been created by Prospero, and the conspiracy is certainly part of his project—this is why Sebastian and Antonio are not put to sleep. If Antonio is not forced by Prospero to propose the murder, he is certainly acting as Prospero expects him to do and as Ariel says Prospero "through his art foresees" that he will. What is clearly taking place is Prospero restaging his usurpation and maintaining his control over it this time. Gonzalo is waked rather than Alonso so that the old courtier can replay his role in aborting the assassination.

So at the play's end, Prospero still has usurpation and attempted murder to hold against his brother, things that still disqualify Antonio from his place in the family. Obviously there is more to Prospero's plans than reconciliation and harmony—even, I would think, in the forthcoming happy marriage of Ferdinand and Miranda. If we look at that marriage as a political act (the participants are, after all, the children of monarchs) we will observe that in order to prevent the succession of his brother, Prospero is marrying his daughter to the son of his enemy. This has the effect of excluding Antonio from any future claim on the ducal throne, but it also effectively disposes of the realm as a political entity: if Miranda is the heir to the dukedom, Milan through the marriage becomes part of the kingdom of Naples, not the other way round. Prospero recoups his throne from his brother only to deliver it over, upon his death, to the King of Naples once again. The usurping Antonio stands condemned, but the effects of the usurpation, the link with Alonso and the reduction of Milan to a Neapolitan fiefdom are, through Miranda's wedding, confirmed and legitimized. Prospero has not regained his lost dukedom; he has usurped his brother's. In this context, Prospero's puzzling assertion that "every third thought shall be my grave" can be seen as a final assertion of authority and control: he has now arranged matters so that his death will remove Antonio's last link with the ducal power. His grave is the ultimate triumph over his brother. If we look at the marriage in this way, giving away Miranda is a means of preserving his authority, not of relinquishing it.

A Bibliographical Coda

The significant absence of crucial wives from the play is curiously emphasized by a famous textual crux. In act 4 Ferdinand, overwhelmed by the beauty of the masque being presented by Prospero, interrupts the performance to say,

Let me live here ever.
So rare a wondered father and a wise
Makes this place Paradise.

(122–24)

Critics since the eighteenth century have expressed a nagging worry about Ferdinand's celebrating his betrothal by including Prospero but not Miranda in his paradise. In fact, what Ferdinand said, as Jeanne Addison Roberts demonstrated only in 1978, reads in the earliest copies of the folio, "So rare a wondered father and a *wife*," but the crossbar of the *f* broke early in the print run, turning it to a long *s* and thereby eliminating Miranda from Ferdinand's thoughts of wonder.[11] The odd thing about this is that Rowe and Malone in their eighteenth-century editions emended *wise* to *wife* on logical grounds, the

Cambridge Shakespeare of 1863 lists *wife* as a variant reading of the folio, and Furnivall's 1895 photographic facsimile was made from a copy that reads *wife,* and the reading is preserved in Furnivall's parallel text. Nevertheless, after 1895 the wife became invisible: bibliographers lost the variant, and textual critics consistently denied its existence until Roberts pointed it out. Even Charlton Hinman with his collating machines claimed that there were no variants whatever in this entire forme of the folio. And yet when Jeanne Roberts examined the Folger Library's copies of the book, including those that Hinman had collated, she found that two of them have the reading *wife*, and two more clearly show the crossbar of the *f* in the process of breaking. We find only what we are looking for or are willing to see. Obviously *wife* is a reading whose time has come.

4

A *Midsummer Night's Dream* and the Shaping Fantasies of Elizabethan Culture: Gender, Power, Form

Louis Adrian Montrose

1

I would like to recount an Elizabethan dream—not Shakespeare's *Midsummer Night's Dream,* but one dreamt by Simon Forman on 23 January 1597. Forman—a professional astrologer and physician, amateur alchemist, and avid playgoer—recorded in his diary the following account:

> I dreamt that I was with the Queen, and that she was a little elderly woman in a coarse white petticoat all unready; and she and I walked up and down through lanes and closes, talking and reasoning of many matters. At last we came over a great close where were many people, and there were two men at hard words. One of them was a weaver, a tall man with a reddish beard, distract of his wits. She talked to him and he spoke very merrily unto her, and at last did take her and kiss her. So I took her by the arm and put her away; and told her the fellow was frantic. And so we went from him and I led her by the arm still, and then we went through a dirty lane. She had a long, white smock, very clean and fair, and it trailed in the dirt and her coat behind. I took her coat and did carry it up a good way, and then it hung too low before. I told her she should do me a favour to let me wait on her, and she said I should. Then said I, "I mean to wait *upon* you and not under you, that I might make this belly a little bigger to carry up this smock and coats out of the dirt." And so we talked merrily and then she began to lean upon me, when we were past the dirt and to be very familiar with me, and methought she began to love me. And when we were alone, out of sight, methought she would have kissed me.[1]

It was then that Forman awoke.

Within the dreamer's unconscious, the "little elderly woman" who was his political mother may have been identified with the mother who had borne him. In an autobiographical fragment, Forman repeatedly characterizes himself as unloved and rejected by his mother during his childhood and youth; at the date of his dream, she was still alive, a very old woman.[2] When he has taken the old woman of his dream away from the "tall man with a reddish beard" who has kissed her, the dreamer begins to make his own erotic advances to her, anticipating that when they are alone, she will kiss *him*. The Oedipal triangle latent in this scenario is at once a psychological and social phenomenon: mother, mistress, and monarch merge in the dream figure of "the Queen." C. L. Barber has suggested that "the very central and problematical role of women in Shakespeare—and in Elizabethan drama generally—reflects the fact that Protestantism did away with the cult of the Virgin Mary. It meant the loss of ritual resource for dealing with the internal residues in all of us of the once all-powerful and all-inclusive mother."[3] What Barber fails to note is that a woman also had "a very central and problematical role" in the Elizabethan state and that a concerted effort was made to appropriate the symbolism and affective power of the suppressed Marian cult in order to foster an Elizabethan cult. Both the internal residues and the religious rituals were potential resources for dealing with the political problems of the Elizabethan regime. Perhaps, at the same time, the royal cult may also have provided Forman and other Elizabethans with a resource for dealing with the internal residues of their relationships to the primary maternal figures of infancy. My concern is not to psychoanalyze Forman but rather to emphasize the historical specificity of psychological processes, the politics of the unconscious. Whatever the place of this dream in the dreamer's interior life, the text in which he represents it to himself allows us to glimpse the cultural contours of a psyche that is both distinctively male and distinctively Elizabethan.

The virginal sex-object of Forman's dream, the "little elderly woman" scantily clad in white, corresponds with startling accuracy to descriptions of Elizabeth's actual appearance in 1597. In the year that Forman dreamt his dream, the ambassador extraordinary of the French king Henri IV described the English queen in his journal. At his first audience, "She was strangely attired in a dress of silver cloth, white and crimson . . . She kept the front of her dress open, and one could see the whole of her bosom, and passing low, and often she would open the front of this robe with her hands as if she was too hot . . . Her bosom is somewhat wrinkled . . . but lower down her flesh

66

is exceeding white and delicate, so far as one could see."[4] At the ambassador's second audience, the queen "was clad in a dress of black taffeta, bound with gold lace . . . She had a petticoat of white damask, girdled, and open in front, as was also her chemise, in such a manner that she often opened this dress and one could see all her belly, and even to her navel . . . When she raises her head, she has a trick of putting both hands on her gown and opening it insomuch that all her belly can be seen" (pp. 36–37). In the following year, another foreign visitor who saw the queen noted that "her bosom was uncovered, as all the English ladies have it till they marry."[5] Elizabeth's display of her bosom signified her status as a maiden. But, like the popular emblem of the life-rendering pelican (which Elizabeth wore as a pendant upon her bosom in one of her portraits), her breasts were also those of a selfless and bountiful mother. The image of the queen as a wet nurse seems to have had some currency. Of the earl of Essex's insatiable thirst for royal offices and honors, Naunton wrote that "my Lord . . . drew in too fast, like a childe sucking on an over-uberous Nurse."[6] The queen was the source of her subjects' social sustenance, the fount of all preferments; she was represented as a virgin-mother— part Madonna, part Ephesian Diana. Like her bosom, Elizabeth's belly must have figured her political motherhood. But, as the French ambassador insinuates, these conspicuous self-displays were also a kind of erotic provocation. The official portraits and courtly blazons that represent the splendor of the queen's immutable body politic are nicely complemented by the ambassador's sketches of the queen's sixty-five year old body natural. His perceptions of the vanity and melancholy of this personage in no way negate his numerous observations of her grace, vitality, and political cunning. Indeed, in the very process of describing the queen's preoccupation with the impact of her appearance upon her beholders, the ambassador demonstrates its impact upon him.

So, too, the aged queen's body exerts a power upon the mind of Dr. Forman; and, in his dream, he exerts a reciprocal power upon the body of the queen. The virginal, erotic, and maternal aspects of the Elizabethan feminine that the royal cult appropriates from the domestic domain are themselves appropriated by one of the queen's subjects and made the material for his dreamwork. At the core of Forman's dream is his joke with the queen: "I told her she should do me a favour to let me wait on her, and she said I should. Then said I, 'I mean to wait *upon* you and not under you, that I might make this belly a little bigger to carry up this smock and coats out of the dirt.' " The joke— and, in a sense, the whole dream—is generated from Forman's verbal quibble: to *wait* upon / to *weight* upon. Within this subversive pun is concentrated the reciprocal relationship between dependency and domination. With one vital exception, all forms of public and domestic authority in Elizabethan England were vested in men: in fathers, husbands, masters, teachers, preachers, magistrates, lords. It was inevitable that the rule of a woman who was unmastered by any man would generate peculiar tensions within such a "patriarchal" society.[7] Sir John Harington, a courtier and godson of the queen, recalled in a letter that when the earl of Essex returned to court from Ireland in defiance of his royal commission, Elizabeth "chaffed muche, walkede fastly to and fro, looked with discomposure in her visage; and, I remember, she catched my girdle when I kneelede to hir, and swore, 'By God's Son I am no Queen; that *man* is above me; —Who gave him commande to come here so soon? I did sende hym on other busynesse."[8] Likewise, Forman's dream epitomizes the indissolubly political and sexual character of the cultural forms in which such tensions might be represented and addressed. In Forman's wordplay, the subject's desire for employment (to *wait* upon) co-exists with his desire for mastery (to *weight* upon); and the pun is manifested physically in his desire to inseminate his sovereign, which is at once to serve her and to possess her. And because the figures in the dream are not only subject and prince but also man and woman, what the *subject* desires to perform, the *man* has the capacity to perform: for Forman to raise the queen's belly is to make her female body to bear the sign of his own potency. In the context of the cross-cutting relationships between subject and prince, man and woman, the dreamer insinuates into a gesture of homage, a will to power.

I find it a strange and admirable coincidence that the dreamer's rival for the queen should be a weaver—as if Nick Bottom had wandered out of Shakespeare's *Dream* and into Forman's. Forman's dream does indeed have affinities with the "most rare vision" (4.1.203) that Shakespeare grants to Bottom.[9] Bottom's dream, like Forman's, is an experience of fleeting intimacy with a powerful female who is at once lover, mother, and queen. The liaison between the fairy queen and the assified artisan is an outrageous theatrical realization of a personal fantasy that was obviously not Forman's alone. Titania treats Bottom as if he were both her child and her lover. And she herself is ambivalently nurturing and threatening, imperious and enthralled. She dotes upon Bottom and indulges in him all those desires to be fed, scratched, and coddled that make Bottom's dream into a parodic fantasy of infantile narcissism and dependency. The sinister side of

Titania's possessiveness is manifested in her binding up of Bottom's tongue and in her intimidating command, "Out of this wood do not desire to go: / Thou shalt remain here, whether thou wilt or no" (3.1.145–46). But if Titania manipulates Bottom, the amateur actor, she herself is manipulated by Oberon, the play's internal dramatist. A fantasy of male dependency upon woman is expressed and contained within a fantasy of male control over woman; the social reality of the player's dependency upon a queen is inscribed within the imaginative reality of the dramatist's control over a queen. Both Forman's private dream-text and Shakespeare's public play-text embody a culture-specific dialectic between personal and public images of gender and power; both are characteristically *Elizabethan* cultural forms.

It has long been recognized that *A Midsummer Night's Dream* has affinities with Elizabethan courtly entertainments. In his recent edition of the play, Harold Brooks cautiously endorses the familiar notion that it was "designed to grace a wedding in a noble household." He adds that "it seems likely that Queen Elizabeth was present when the *Dream* was first acted . . . She delighted in homage paid to her as the Virgin Queen, and receives it in the myth-making about the Imperial votaress" (*Arden* ed., pp. liii, lv). Although attractive and plausible, such topical connections must remain wholly conjectural. The perspective of my own analysis of the play's court connection is dialectical rather than causal, ideological rather than occasional. For, whether or not Queen Elizabeth was physically present at the first performance of *A Midsummer Night's Dream,* her pervasive *cultural presence* was a condition of the play's imaginative possibility. This is not to imply that *A Midsummer Night's Dream* is merely an inert product of Elizabethan culture. The play is rather a new *production* of Elizabethan culture, enlarging the dimensions of the cultural field and altering the lines of force within it. Thus, in the sense that the royal presence was itself represented within the play, it may be said that the play henceforth conditioned the imaginative possibility of the queen.

When Shakespeare's Duke Theseus proclaims that "The lunatic, the lover, and the poet / Are of imagination all compact," that "Lovers and madmen have such seething brains, / Such shaping fantasies, that apprehend / More than cool reason ever comprehends," he fails to apprehend that he himself and the fictional society over which he rules have been shaped by the imagination of a poet. My intertextual study of Shakespeare's *Midsummer Night's Dream* and symbolic forms shaped by other Elizabethan lunatics, lovers, and poets construes the play as calling attention to itself, not only as an end but also as a source of cultural production. Thus, in writing of "shaping fantasies," I mean to suggest the dialectical character of cultural representations: the fantasies by which the text of *A Midsummer Night's Dream* has been shaped are also those to which it gives shape. I explore this dialectic within a specifically *Elizabethan* context of cultural production: the interplay between representations of gender and power in a stratified society in which authority is everywhere invested in men—everywhere, that is, except at the top.

2

Harold Brooks summarizes the concensus of modern criticism when he writes that "love and marriage is the [play's] central theme: love aspiring to and consummated in marriage, or to a harmonious partnership within it" (*Arden* ed., p. cxxx). As Paul Olson suggested some years ago, the harmonious marital unions of *A Midsummer Night's Dream* are also in harmony with doctrines of Tudor apologists for the patriarchal family: marital union implies a domestic hierarchy; marital harmony is predicated upon the wife's obedience to her husband.[10] The opposed emphases of Brooks and Olson—the former, romantic; the latter, authoritarian—abstract and idealize what are in fact complementary features of the dramatic process whereby *A Midsummer Night's Dream* figures the social relationship of the sexes in courtship, marriage, and parenthood. The play imaginatively embodies what Gayle Rubin has called a "sex/gender system": a sociohistorical construction of sexual identity, difference, and relationship; an appropriation of human anatomical and physiological features by an ideological discourse; a culture-specific fantasia upon Nature's universal theme.[11] My concern is with how *A Midsummer Night's Dream* and other Elizabethan texts figure the Elizabethan sex/gender system and the queen's place within it.

The beginning of *A Midsummer Night's Dream* coincides with the end of a struggle in which Theseus has been victorious over the Amazon warrior:

> Hippolyta, I woo'd thee with my sword,
> And won thy love doing thee injuries;
> But I will wed thee in another key,
> With pomp, with triumph, and with revelling.
>
> (1.1.16–19)

Representations of the Amazons are ubiquitous in Elizabethan texts. All of the essential features are present in popular form in William

Painter's "Novel of the Amazones," which opens the second book of *The Palace of Pleasure*. Here we read that the Amazons "were most excellent warriors"; that "they murdred certaine of their husbands" at the beginning of their gynecocracy; that, "if they brought forth daughters, they norished and trayned them up in armes, and other manlik exercises . . . If they were delivered of males, they sent them to their fathers, and if by chaunce they kept any backe, they murdred them, or else brake their armes and legs in sutch wise as they had no power to beare weapons, and served for nothynge but to spin, twist, and doe other feminine labour."[12] The Amazons' penchant for male infanticide is complemented by their obvious delight in subjecting powerful heroes to their will. In Spenser's *Faerie Queene*, for example, Arthegall, hero of the Legend of Justice, becomes enslaved to Radigund, "A Princesse of great powre, and greater pride, / And Queene of Amazons, in armes well tride" (*FQ*, 5.4.33).[13] Defeated by Radigund in personal combat, Arthegall must undergo degradation and effeminization of the kind endured by Hercules and by the Amazons' maimed sons.

Sixteenth-century travel narratives often recreate the ancient Amazons of Scythia in South America or in Africa. Invariably, the Amazons are relocated just within the receding boundary of *terra incognita*. Thus, in Sierra Leone in 1582, the chaplain of an English expedition to the Spice Islands recorded the report of a Portuguese trader that "near the mountains of the moon there is a queen, empress of all these Amazons, a witch and a cannibal who daily feeds on the flesh of boys. She ever remains unmarried, but she has intercourse with a great number of men by whom she begets offspring. The kingdom, however, remains hereditary to the daughters, not to the sons."[14] This cultural fantasy assimilates Amazonian myth, witchcraft, and cannibalism into an anti-culture that precisely inverts European norms of political authority, sexual license, marriage practices, and inheritance rules. The attitude toward the Amazons expressed in such Renaissance texts is a mixture of fascination and horror. Amazonian mythology seems symbolically to embody and to control a collective anxiety about the power of the female not only to dominate or reject the male but to create and destroy him. It is an ironic acknowledgment by an androcentric culture of the degree to which men are in fact dependent upon women: upon mothers and nurses, for their birth and nurture; upon mistresses and wives, for the validation of their manhood.

Shakespeare engages his wedding play in a dialectic with this mythological formation. The Amazons have been defeated before the play begins; and nuptial rites are to be celebrated when it ends. *A Midsummer Night's Dream* focuses upon different crucial transitions in the male and female life cycles: the fairy plot, upon taking "a little changeling boy" from childhood into youth, from the world of the mother into the world of the father; the Athenian plot, upon taking a maiden from youth into maturity, from the world of the father into the world of the husband. The pairing of the four Athenian lovers is made possible by the magical powers of Oberon and made lawful by the political authority of Theseus. Each of these rulers is preoccupied with the fulfillment of his own desires in the possession or repossession of a wife. Only after Hippolyta has been mastered by Theseus may marriage seal them "in everlasting bond of fellowship" (1.1.85). And only after "proud Titania" has been degraded by "jealous Oberon" (2.1.60, 61), has "in mild terms begg'd" (4.1.57) his patience, and has readily yielded the changeling boy to him, may they be "new in amity" (4.1.86).

The diachronic structure of *A Midsummer Night's Dream* eventually restores the inverted Amazonian system of gender and nurture to a patriarchal norm. But the initial plans for Theseus's triumph are immediately interrupted by news of yet another unruly female. Egeus wishes to confront his daughter Hermia with two alternatives: absolute obedience to the paternal will or death. Theseus intervenes with a third alternative: if she refuses to marry whom her father chooses, Hermia must submit "Either to die the death or to abjure / Forever the society of men" (1.1.65–66). If Theseus finally overbears Egeus' will (4.1.178), it is because the father's obstinate claim to "the ancient privilege of Athens" (1.1.41) threatens to obstruct the very process by which Athenian privilege and Athens itself are reproduced. Hermia and Helena are granted their desires—but those desires have themselves been shaped and directed by a social imperative. Thus, neither for Oberon nor for Theseus is there any contradiction between mastering the desires of a wife and patronizing the desires of a maiden.

Theseus has characteristically Protestant notions about the virtue of virginity: maidenhood is a phase in the life cycle of a woman who is destined for married chastity and motherhood. As a permanent state, "single blessedness" (1.1.78) is mere sterility. Theseus expands Hermia's options only in order to clarify her constraints. In the process of tempering the father's domestic tyranny, the duke affirms his own interests and authority. He represents the life of a vestal as a *punishment,* and it is one that fits the nature of Hermia's crime. Each of the men who surround the maid—father, lovers, lord—claims a kind of property in her. Yet Hermia dares to suggest that she has a claim to property in herself: she refuses to "yield [her] virgin patent up / Unto his lordship whose unwished yoke / [Her] soul consents not to give sovereignty" (1.1.80–82). She wishes the limited privilege of giving herself. Theseus appropriates the source of Hermia's fragile power: her ability to deny men access to her body. He usurps the power of virginity by imposing upon Hermia his own power to deny her the use of her body. If she will not submit to its use by her father and by Demetrius, she must "live a barren sister all [her] life" (1.1.72). The female body is a supreme form of property and a locus for the contestation of authority. The self-possession of single blessedness is a form of power against which are opposed the marriage doctrines of Shakespeare's culture and the very form of his comedy.[15]

In the opening scene, Egeus claims that he may do with Hermia as he chooses because she is his property: "As she is mine, I may dispose of her" (1.1.142). This claim is based upon a stunningly simple thesis: she is his because he has *made* her. Theseus explains to Hermia the ontogenetic principle underlying her father's vehemence:

> To you your father should be as a god:
> One that compos'd your beauties, yea, and one
> To whom you are but as a form in wax
> By him imprinted, and within his power
> To leave the figure or disfigure it.
>
> (1.1.47–51)

Theseus represents paternity as a cultural act, an art: the father is a demiurge or *homo faber,* who composes, in-forms, imprints himself upon, what is merely inchoate matter. Conspicuously excluded from Theseus' account and from the whole play is the relationship between mother and daughter—the kinship bond through which Amazonian society reproduces itself. The central female characters of Shakespeare's comedies are not mothers but mother-to-be, maidens who are passing from fathers to husbands in a world made and governed by men. Hermia and Helena have no mothers; they have only fathers. And Theseus's lecture on the shaping of a *daughter* is, in effect, a fantasy of male parthenogenesis.

Titania's votaress is the only biological mother in *A Midsummer Night's Dream.* But she is an absent presence who must be evoked from Titania's memory because she has died in giving birth to a *son.* Assuming that they do not maim their sons, the Amazons are only too glad to give them away to their fathers. In Shakespeare's play, however, Oberon's paternal power must be directed against Titania's maternal possessiveness:

> For Oberon is passing fell and wrath,
> Because that she as her attendant hath
> A lovely boy, stol'n from an Indian king—
> She never had so sweet a changeling;
> And jealous Oberon would have the child
> Knight of his train to trace the forest wild;
> But she perforce withholds the loved boy,
> Crowns him with flowers, and makes him all her joy.
>
> (2.1.20–27)

A boy's transition from the female-centered world of his early childhood to the male-centered world of his youth is given a kind of phylogenetic sanction by myths recounting a cultural transition from matriarchy to patriarchy.[16] Such a myth is represented at the very threshhold of *A Midsummer Night's Dream*: Theseus's defeat of the Amazonian matriarchate sanctions Oberon's attempt to take the boy from an infantilizing mother and to make a man of him. Yet "jealous" Oberon is not only Titania's rival for the child but also the child's rival for Titania: making the boy "all her joy," "proud" Titania withholds herself from her husband; she has "forsworn his bed and company" (2.1.62–63). Oberon's preoccupation is to gain possession not only of the boy but of the woman's desire and obedience; he must master his own dependency upon his wife.

Titania has her own explanation for her fixation upon the changeling:

> His mother was a votress of my order
> And in the spiced Indian air, by night,
> Full often hath she gossip'd by my side;
> And sat with me on Neptune's yellow sands,
> Marking th'embarked traders on the flood:
> When we have laugh'd to see the sails conceive
> And grow big-bellied with the wanton wind;
> Which she, with pretty and with swimming gait
> Following (her womb then rich with my young squire),
> Would imitate, and sail upon the land
> To fetch me trifles, and return again
> As from a voyage rich with merchandise.
> But she, being mortal, of that boy did die;
> And for her sake do I rear up her boy;
> And for her sake I will not part with him.
>
> (2.1.123–37)

Titania's attachment to the changeling boy embodies her attachment to the memory of his mother. What Oberon accomplishes by substituting Bottom for the boy is to break Titania's solemn vow. As in the case of the Amazons, or that of Hermia and Helena, the play again enacts a male disruption of an intimate bond between women: first by the boy, and then by the man. It is as if, in order to be freed and enfranchised from the prison of the womb, the male child must *kill* his mother: "She, being mortal, of that boy did die." One can read the line as suggesting that mother and son are potentially mortal to each other: the matricidal infant complements the infanticidal Amazon. As later with Bottom, Titania both dotes upon and dominates the child, prolonging his imprisonment to the womb: "And for her sake I will not part with him." Thus, within the changeling plot are embedded transformations of the male fantasies of motherhood that are figured in Amazonian myth.

Titania represents her bond to her votaress as one that is rooted in an experience of female fecundity, an experience for which men must seek merely mercantile compensations. The women "have laugh'd to see the sails conceive / And grow big-bellied with the wanton wind"; and the votaress has parodied such false pregnancies by sailing to fetch trifles while she herself bears riches within her womb. The notion of maternity implied in Titania's speech counterpoints the notion of paternity formulated by Theseus in the opening scene. In Theseus's description, neither biological nor social mother—neither *genetrix* nor *mater*—plays a role in the making of a daughter; in Titania's description, neither *genitor* nor *pater* plays a role in the making of a son. The father's daughter is shaped from without; the mother's son comes from within her body: Titania dwells upon the physical bond between mother and child, as manifested in pregnancy and parturition. Like an infant of the Elizabethan upper classes, however, the changeling is nurtured not by his natural mother but by a surrogate. By emphasizing her own role as a foster mother to her gossip's offspring, Titania links the biological and social aspects of parenthood together within a wholly maternal world, a world in which the relationship between women has displaced the relationship between wife and husband. Nevertheless, despite the exclusion of a paternal role from Titania's speech, Shakespeare's embryological notions here remain distinctly Aristotelian, distinctly phallocentric: the mother is represented as a *vessel,* as a container for her son; she is not his *maker.* In contrast, the implication of Theseus's description of paternity is that the male is the only begetter; a daughter is merely a token of her father's potency. Thus these two speeches may be said to formulate, in poetic discourse, a proposition about the genesis of gender and power: men make

75

women, and they make themselves through the medium of women. Such a proposition reverses the Amazonian practice, in which women use men merely for their own reproduction. But much more importantly, it seems an overcompensation for the *natural* fact that men do indeed come from women; an overcompensation for the *cultural* facts that consanguineal and affinal ties between men are established through mothers, wives, and daughters.

We may recall here that what we tend to think of as the facts of life have been established as *facts* relatively recently in human history, with the development of microbiology that began in Europe in the later seventeenth century.[17] That seminal and menstrual fluids are in some way related to generation and that people have both a father and a mother are, of course, hardly novel notions. My point is that, in Shakespeare's age, they still remained *merely* notions. Although biological maternity was readily apparent, biological paternity was a cultural construct for which ocular proof was unattainable. More specifically, the evidence for *unique* biological paternity, for the generative link between a particular man and child, has always been exiguous. As Launcelot Gobbo puts it, "It is a wise father that knows his own child" (*The Merchant of Venice*, 2.2.76–77). In Shakespearean drama, this uncertainty is frequently the focus of anxious concern, whether that concern is to validate paternity or to call it into question. Thus, Lear tells Regan that if she were *not* glad to see him, "I would divorce me from thy mother's tomb, / Sepulchring an adult'ress" (*King Lear*, 2.4.131–32). And Leontes exclaims, upon first meeting Florizel, "Your mother was most true to wedlock, Prince / For she did print your royal father off, / Conceiving you" (*The Winter's Tale*, 5.1.124–26). In the former speech, a vulnerable father invokes his previously unacknowledged wife precisely when he wishes to repudiate his daughter; in the latter, a vulnerable husband celebrates female virtue as the instrument of male self-reproduction. A thematic complex that pervades the Shakespearean canon is dramatized in *A Midsummer Night's Dream*: a set of claims for a spiritual kinship among men that is unmediated by women, for the procreative powers of men, and for the autogeny of men.

The festive conclusion of *A Midsummer Night's Dream*, its celebration of romantic and generative heterosexual union, depends upon the success of a process whereby the female pride and power manifested in misanthropic warriors, possessive mothers, unruly wives, and willful daughters are brought under the control of husbands and lords. But while the dramatic structure articulates a patriarchal ideology, it also intermittently undermines its own comic propositions. The naturalization of the social doctrine of domestic hierarchy in the marriage of "jealous" Oberon and "proud" Titania calls attention to itself as an equivocal strategy of legitimation, one that authorizes not only the authority of husbands but also the unruliness of wives. The all-too-human struggle between the fairy king and queen—the play's already married couple—provides an ironic prognosis for the new marriages. The play ends upon the threshold of another generational cycle, in which the procreation of new children will also produce new mothers and new fathers. Within this ending is a potential for renewing the forms of strife exhibited at the opening of the play. Regardless of authorial intention, Oberon's blessing of the marriage bed of Theseus and Hippolyta evokes precisely what it seeks to suppress: the cycle of sexual and familial violence, fear, and betrayal begins again at the very engendering of Hippolytus. Shakespeare's romantic comedy is in fact contaminated throughout by a kind of intertextual irony. As Harold Brooks's edition has conclusively demonstrated, the text of Shakespeare's play is permeated by echoes not only of Plutarch's "Life of Theseus" but also of Seneca's *Hippolitus* and his *Medea*—by an archaeological record of the texts that shaped the poet's fantasy as he was shaping his play.[18] Thus, sedimented within the verbal texture of *A Midsummer Night's Dream* are traces of those recurrent acts of bestiality and incest, of parricide, uxoricide, filicide, and suicide, that the ethos of romantic comedy would evade. Shakespeare's sources weave the chronicle of Theseus's rapes and disastrous marriages, his habitual victimization of women, into the lurid history of female depravity that includes Pasiphae, Medea, and Phaedra. And Shakespeare's text discloses—perhaps, in a sense, despite itself—that patriarchal norms are compensatory for the vulnerability of men to the powers of women.

3

Such textual disclosures also illuminate the interplay between sexual politics in the Elizabethan family and sexual politics in the Elizabethan monarchy, for the woman to whom *all* Elizabethan men were vulnerable was Queen Elizabeth herself. Within legal and fiscal limits, she held the power of life and death over every Englishman, the power to advance or frustrate the worldly desires of all her subjects. Her personality and personal symbolism helped to mold English culture and the consciousness of Englishmen for several generations.

Although the Amazonian metaphor might seem suited to strategies for praising a woman ruler, it was never popular among Elizabethan encomiasts.[19] Its associations must have been too sinister to suit the personal tastes and political interests of the queen. However, Sir Walter Ralegh did boldly compare Elizabeth to the Amazons in his *Discovery of Guiana*.[20] In his digression on the Amazons, who are reported to dwell "not far from Guiana," Ralegh repeats the familiar details of their sexual and parental practices and notes that they "are said to be very cruel and bloodthirsty, especially to such as offer to invade their territories" (p. 28). At the end of his narrative, Ralegh exhorts Elizabeth to undertake a conquest of Guiana: "Her Majesty heereby shall confirme and strengthen the opinions of al nations, as touching her great and princely actions. And where the south border of *Guiana* reacheth to the Dominion and Empire of the *Amazones,* those women shall heereby heare the name of a virgin, which is not onely able to defend her owne territories and her neighbors, but also to invade and conquere so great Empyres and so farre removed" (p. 120). Ralegh's strategy for persuading the queen to advance his colonial enterprise is to insinuate that she is both like and unlike an Amazon, that Elizabethan imperialism threatens not only the empire of Guiana but the empire of the Amazons, and that Elizabeth can definitively cleanse herself from contamination by the Amazons if she sanctions their subjugation. The Amazonomachy that Ralegh projects into the imaginative space of the New World is analogous to that narrated by Spenser within the imaginative space of Faeryland. Radigund, the Amazon queen, can be defeated only by Britomart, the martial maiden who is Artegall's betrothed and the fictional ancestress of Elizabeth. Radigund is Britomart's double, split off from her as an allegorical personification of everything in Artegall's beloved that threatens him. Having destroyed Radigund and liberated Artegall from his effeminate "thraldome," Britomart reforms what is left of Amazon society: she

> The liberty of women did repeale,
> Which they had long usurpt; and them restoring
> To mens subjection, did true Justice deale:
> That all they as a Goddesse her adoring,
> Her wisedome did admire, and hearkned to her loring.
>
> (*FQ,* 5.7.42)

Unlike some of the popular sixteenth-century forms of misrule well discussed by Natalie Davis, this instance of sexual inversion would seem to be intended as an exemplum "of order and stability in a hierarchical society," which "can clarify the structure by the process of reversing it."[21] For Ralegh's Elizabeth, as for Spenser's Britomart, the woman who has the prerogative of a goddess, who is authorized to be out of place, can best justify her authority by putting other women in their places.

A few paragraphs before Ralegh exhorts Elizabeth to undertake an Amazonomachy, he exhorts his gentlemen-readers to commit a cultural rape: "Guiana is a Countrey that hath yet her Maydenhead, never sackt, turned, nor wrought, the face of the earth hath not beene torne, nor the vertue and salt of the soyle spent by manurance, the graves have not beene opened for gold, the mines not broken with sledges, nor their Images puld down out of their temples. It hath never been entred by any armie of strength and never conquered and possessed by any Christian Prince" (p. 115). Ralegh's enthusiasm is, at one and the same time, for the unspoiled quality of this world and for the prospect of despoiling it. Guiana, like the Amazons, is fit to be wooed with the sword and won with injuries. Such metaphors have a peculiar resonance in the context of an address to Elizabeth. Certainly, it is difficult to imagine Ralegh using them to represent the plantation of Virginia, which had been named by and for the Virgin Queen. When, in the proem to the second book of *The Faerie Queene*, Spenser conjoins "the Amazons huge river" and "fruitfullest Virginia" (*FQ*, 2.Proem.2), he is invoking not only two regions of the New World but two archetypes of Elizabethan culture: the engulfing Amazon and the nurturing Virgin. Later in the same book, they are conjoined again in Belphoebe, the virgin huntress who figures Queen Elizabeth in her body natural. Belphoebe is introduced into the poem with an extended blazon that concludes in an ominous epic simile comparing her both with the goddess Diana and with Penthesilea, "that famous Queene / Of *Amazons*, whom *Pyrrhus* did destroy" (*FQ*, 2.3.31). The female body—and, in particular, the symbolic body of the queen—provides a cognitive map for Elizabethan culture, a matrix for the Elizabethan forms of desire, and a field upon which the relations of Elizabethan power are played out.[22]

The queen herself was too politic, and too ladylike, to wish to pursue the Amazonian image very far. Instead, she transformed it to suit her purposes, representing herself as an androgynous martial maiden, like Spenser's Britomart. Such was her appearance at Tilbury in 1588, where she had come to review the troops mustered in preparation for a Spanish invasion. On that momentous occasion, she rode a white horse and dressed in white velvet; she wore a silver cuirass on her breast and carried a silver truncheon in her hand. The theme of her speech was by then already very familiar to her listeners: she dwelt upon the womanly frailty of her body natural and the masculine strength of her body politic—a strength deriving from the love of her people, the virtue of her lineage, and the will of her God: "I have always so behaved myself that, under God, I have placed my chiefest strength and safeguard in the loyal hearts and good will of my subjects . . . I know I have the body of a weak and feeble woman, but I have the heart and stomach of a king, and of a king of England too."[23] As the female ruler of what was, at least in theory, a patriarchal society, Elizabeth incarnated a contradiction at the very center of the Elizabethan sex/gender system. After the death of their royal mistress, Cecil wrote to Harington that she had been "more than a man, and, in troth, sometime less than a woman."[24] Queen Elizabeth was a cultural anomaly; and this anomalousness made her powerful and dangerous. By the skillful deployment of images that were at once awesome and familiar, this perplexing creature tried to mollify her male subjects while enhancing her authority over them.

At the beginning of her reign, Elizabeth formulated the strategy by which she turned the political liability of her gender to advantage for the next half century. She told her first parliaments that she was content to have as her epitaph "that a Queen, having reigned such a time, lived and died a virgin"; that her coronation ring betokened her marriage to her subjects; and that, although after her death her people might have many stepdames, yet they should never have "a more natural mother than [she] meant to be unto [them] all."[25] When she told the earl of Leicester, "I will have here but one Mistress, and no Master" (Naunton, *Fragmenta Regalia,* p. 17), she epitomized her policy on gender and power. As Bacon observed in his memorial of Elizabeth, "the reigns of women are commonly obscured by marriage; their praises and actions passing to the credit of their husbands; whereas those that continue unmarried have their glory entire and proper to themselves . . . And even those whom she herself raised to honour she so kept in hand and mingled one with the other, that while she infused into each the greatest solicitude to please her, she was herself ever her own mistress."[26] Elizabeth's self-mastery and mastery of others were enhanced by the promotion of her maidenhood into a cult of virginity; the displacement of her wifely duties from a household to a nation; and the modulation of her temporal and ecclesiastical supremacy into a nurturing maternity. She appropriated not only the suppressed cult of the Blessed Virgin but also the Tudor notion of the Ages of Woman. By fashioning herself into a singular combination of Maiden, Matron, and Mother, the queen transformed the normal domestic life cycle of an Elizabethan female into what was at once a social paradox and a religious mystery. Her emblem was the phoenix; her motto, *semper eadem, semper una.*[27] Because she was always uniquely herself, Elizabeth's rule was not intended to undermine the male hegemony of her culture. Indeed, the emphasis upon her *difference* from all other women may have helped to reinforce it. As she herself wrote in response to Parliament in 1563, "though I can think [marriage] best for a private woman, yet I do strive with myself to think it not meet for a prince" (Neale, *Elizabeth I and Her Parliaments 1559–1581*, p. 127). The royal exception could prove the patriarchal rule in society at large.

Nevertheless, from the very beginning of her reign, Elizabeth's parliaments and counselors urged her to marry and produce an heir. There was a deeply felt and loudly voiced need to insure a legitimate succession, upon which the welfare of the whole people depended. But there seems to have been another, more obscure motivation behind these requests: the political nation, which was wholly a nation of men, could sometimes find it frustrating or degrading to serve a prince who was, after all, merely a woman. Late in Elizabeth's reign, the French ambassador observed that "her government is fairly pleasing to the people, who show that they love her, but it is little pleasing to the great men and nobles; and if by chance she should die, it is certain that the English would never again submit to the rule of a woman" (De Maisse, *Journal*, pp. 11–12). In the 1560s and 1570s, Elizabeth witnessed allegorical entertainments boldly criticizing her attachment to a life of "single blessedness." For example, in the famous Kenilworth entertainments sponsored by the earl of Leicester in 1575, Diana praised the state of fancy-free maiden meditation and condemned the "wedded state, which is to thraldome bent." But Juno had the last word in the pageant: "O Queene, o worthy queene, / Yet never wight felt perfect blis / But such as wedded beene."[28] By the 1580s, the queen was past childbearing; Diana and her virginal nymph, Eliza, now carried the day in such courtly entertainments as Peele's *Araygnment of Paris.* Although "as fayre and lovely as the queene of Love," Peele's Elizabeth was also "as chast as Dian in her chast desires."[29] By the early 1590s, the cult of the unaging royal virgin had entered its last and most extravagant phase. In the 1590 Accession Day pageant, there appeared "a Pavilion . . . like unto the sacred Temple of the Virgins Vestal."[30] Upon the altar there were presents for the queen—offerings from her votaries. At Elvetham, during the royal progress of 1591, none other than "the Fairy Queene" gave to Elizabeth a chaplet that she herself had received from "Auberon, the Fairy King" (Nichols, *Progresses and Public Processions,* 3:118–19). From early in the reign, Elizabeth had been directly engaged by such entertainments: debates were referred to her arbitration; the magic of her presence civilized savage men, restored the blind to sight, released errant knights from enchantment, and rescued virgins from defilement. These social dramas of celebration and coercion played out the delicately balanced relationship between the monarch and her greatest subjects. And because texts and descriptions of most of them were in print within a year of their performance, these occasional and ephemeral productions could achieve a considerable cultural impact.

A Midsummer Night's Dream is permeated by images and devices that suggest these characteristic forms of Elizabethan court culture. Whether or not its provenance was in an aristocratic wedding entertainment, however, Shakespeare's play is neither focused upon the queen nor structurally dependent upon her presence or her intervention in the action. On the contrary, it might be said to depend upon her absence, her exclusion. In the third scene of the play, after Titania has remembered her Indian votaress, Oberon remembers his "imperial votaress." He has once beheld,

> Flying between the cold moon and the earth,
> Cupid all arm'd; a certain aim he took
> At a fair vestal, throned by the West,
> And loos'd his love-shaft smartly from his bow
> As it should pierce a hundred thousand hearts.
> But I might see young Cupid's fiery shaft
> Quench'd in the chaste beams of the watery moon;
> And the imperial votress passed on,
> In maiden meditation, fancy-free.
> Yet mark'd I where the bolt of Cupid fell:
> It fell upon a little western flower,
> Before milk-white, now purple with love's wound:
> And maidens call it 'love-in-idleness'.
>
> (2.1.156–68)

The resonant monologues of Titania and Oberon are carefully matched and contrasted: the fairy queen speaks of a mortal mother from the east; the fairy king speaks of an invulnerable virgin from the west. Their memories express two myths of origin: Titania's provides a genealogy for the changeling and an explanation of why she will not part with him; Oberon's provides an aetiology of the metamorphosed flower that he will use to make her part with him. The floral symbolism of female sexuality begun in this passage is completed when Oberon names "Dian's bud" (4.1.72) as the antidote to "love-in-idleness." With Cupid's flower, Oberon can make the fairy queen "full of hateful fantasies" (2.1.258); and with Dian's bud, he can win her back to his will. The vestal's invulnerability to fancy is instrumental to Oberon in his reaffirmation of romantic, marital, and parental norms that have been inverted during the course of the play. Thus, Shakespeare's royal compliment re-mythologizes the cult of the Virgin Queen in such a way as to sanction a relationship of gender and power that is personally and politically inimical to Elizabeth.

Shakespeare's comic heroines are in transition between the statuses of maiden and wife, daughter and mother. These transitions are mediated by the wedding rite and the act of defloration, which are brought together at the end of *A Midsummer Night's Dream*. When the newlyweds have retired, Oberon and Titania enter the court in order to bless the "bride-bed" where the marriages are about to be consummated. By the act of defloration, the husband takes physical and symbolic possession of his bride. The sexual act in which the man draws blood from the woman is evoked at the beginning of the play, in Theseus's vaunt: "Hippolyta, I woo'd thee with my sword, / And won thy love doing thee injuries." And it is immanent in the image that Oberon uses to describe the very origin of desire: "the bolt of Cupid fell / . . . Upon a little western flower, / Before milk-white, now purple with love's wound." Cupid's shaft violates the flower when it has been deflected from the vestal: Oberon's purple passion flower is procreated in a displaced and literalized defloration.[31]

Unlike the female *dramatis personae*, Oberon's vestal virgin is *not* subject to Cupid's shaft, to the frailties of the flesh and the fancy. Nor is she subject to the mastery of men. And it is precisely her bodily and mental impermeability that make possible Oberon's pharmacopoeia. Thus, ironically, the vestal's very freedom from fancy guarantees the subjection of others. She is necessarily excluded from the erotic world of which her own chastity is the efficient cause. Within *A Midsummer Night's Dream*, the public and domestic domains of Elizabethan culture intersect in the figure of the imperial votaress. When a female ruler is ostensibly the virgin mother of her subjects, then the themes of male procreative power, autogeny, and mastery of women acquire a seditious resonance. In royal pageantry, the queen is always the cynosure; her virginity is the source of magical potency. In *A Midsummer Night's Dream*, however, such magical powers are invested in the king. Perhaps three or four years before the first production of *A Midsummer Night's Dream*, in a pastoral entertainment enacted at Sudeley during the royal progress of 1591, the queen's presence was sufficient to undo the metamorphosis of Daphne, to release her from her arboreal imprisonment, and to protect her from the lustful advances of Apollo.[32] According to Shakespeare's Oberon, Helena's pursuit of Demetrius necessitates a metamorphosis of Ovid's text: "The story shall be chang'd: / Apollo flies, and Daphne holds the chase" (2.1.230–31). The response of the fairy king is neither to extinguish desire nor to make it mutual but rather to restore the normal pattern of pursuit: "Fare thee well, nymph; ere he do leave this grove / Thou shalt fly him and he shall seek thy love" (2.1.245–46). Unlike Elizabeth, Oberon uses his mastery over Nature to subdue others to their passions. Spenser and other courtly writers often fragment the royal image, reflecting aspects of the queen "in mirrours more then one" (*FQ,* 3.Proem.5). Similarly, Shakespeare splits the triune Elizabethan cult image between the fair vestal, an unattainable *virgin*; and the fairy queen, an intractable *wife* and a dominating *mother*. Oberon uses one against the other in order to reassert male prerogatives. Thus, in the logic of its structure, Shakespeare's comedy symbolically neutralizes the royal power to which it ostensibly pays homage.

Shortly before her death, Sir John Harington wrote of Elizabeth as "oure deare Queene, my royale godmother, and this state's natural mother." Shortly after her death, he reflected slyly on how she had manipulated the filial feelings of her subjects: "Few knew how to aim their shaft against her cunninge. We did all love hir, for she saide she loved us, and muche wysdome she shewed in thys matter" (*Letters and Epigrams,* pp. 96, 123–25). In Harington's image of the court, a metaphor from archery resonates as a metaphor of masculine genital aggression. But, like Oberon's Cupid, these children/courtiers are frustrated in their desire to master the sovereign mother/mistress with whom they are engaged in a subtle but ceaseless contest of wills. Bacon provides what is perhaps the most astute contemporary analysis of the queen's erotic strategies:

> As for those lighter points of character,—as that she allowed herself to be wooed and courted, and even to have love made to her; and liked it; and continued it beyond the natural age for such vanities;—if any of the sadder sort of persons be disposed to make a great matter of this, it may be observed that there is something to admire in these very things, which ever way you take them. For if viewed indulgently, they are much like the accounts we find in romances, of the Queen in the blessed islands, and her court and institutions, who allows of amorous admiration but prohibits desire. But if you take

them seriously, they challenge admiration of another kind
and of a very high order; for certain it is that these dalliances
detracted but little from her fame and nothing from her
majesty, and neither weakened her power nor sensibly hin-
dered her business. (*In Felicem Memoriam*, p. 460)

As Bacon suggests, the queen's personal vanity and political craft are
mutually reinforcing. He appreciates the generic affinities of the royal
cult, its appropriation and enactment of the conventions of romance.
And he also appreciates that, like contemporaneous romantic fictions,
the queen's romance could function as a political allegory. However,
symbolic forms may do more than *represent* power: they may actually
help to *generate* the power that they represent. Thus—although Bacon
does not quite manage to say so—the queen's dalliances did not
weaken her power but strengthened it, did not hinder her business but
furthered it.

By the same token, the queen's subjects might put the discourse of
royal power to their own uses. Consider the extravagant royal
entertainment of 1581, in which Philip Sidney and Fulke Greville
performed as "Foster Children of Desire."[33] "Nourished up with [the]
infective milke" (p. 313) of Desire—"though full oft that dry nurse
Dispaier indevered to wainne them from it" (p. 314)—the Foster
Children boldly claimed and sought to possess The Fortress of Perfect
Beauty, an allegorical structure simultaneously identified with the
queen's body and with her state. Elizabeth beheld the "desirous
assault" (p. 317) against her, in which "two canons were shot off, the
one with sweet powder, and the other with sweet water," and
"floures and such fansies" were thrown "against the wals" (p. 319).
During two days of florid speeches, spectacular self-displays, and
mock combats, these young, ambitious, and thwarted courtiers acted
out a fantasy of political demand, rebellion, and submission in
metaphors of resentment and aggression that were alternately filial
and erotic. They seized upon the forms in which their culture had
articulated the relationship between sovereign and subjects: they
demanded sustenance from their royal mother, favors from their royal
mistress. The Foster Children were finally forced to acknowledge the
paradox of Desire: "No sooner hath Desire what he desireth, but that
he dieth presentlie: so that when Beautie yeeldeth once to Desire, then
can she never want to be desired againe. Wherefore of force this
principle must stand, it is convenient for Desire ever to wish, and
necessarie that he alwaies want" (p. 325). The nobility, gentlemen,
and hangers-on of the court generated a variety of pressures that

constantly threatened the fragile stability of the Elizabethan regime. At home, personal rivalries and political dissent might be sublimated into the agonistic play forms of courtly culture; abroad, they might be expressed in warfare and colonial enterprise—displaced into the conquest of lands that had yet their maidenheads.

The queen dallied, not only with the hearts of courtiers but also with the hearts of commoners. For example, in 1600, a deranged sailor named Abraham Edwardes sent "a passionate . . . letter unto her Majesty," who was then sixty-eight years old. Edwardes was later committed to prison "for drawing his dagger in the [royal] presence chamber." The clerk of the privy council wrote to Cecil that "the fellow is greatly distracted, and seems rather to be transported with a humour of love, than any purpose to attempt anything against her Majesty." He recommended that this poor lunatic and lover "be removed to Bedlam."[34] By her own practice of sexual politics, the queen may very well have encouraged the sailor's passion—in the same sense that her cult helped to fashion the courtly performances and colonial enterprises of courtiers like Sidney or Ralegh, the dream-life of Doctor Forman, the dream-play of Master Shakespeare. This being said, it must be added that the queen was as much the creature of her image as she was its creator—the creature of images fashioned by Sidney and Ralegh, Forman and Shakespeare—and that her power to shape her own strategies was itself shaped by her society and constrained within the horizon of its cultural assumptions.[35] It would be an oversimplification to imply that the spiritual, maternal, and erotic transformations of Elizabethan power were merely instances of Machiavellian policy—were intentional mystifications and nothing more. Relationships of dependency and autonomy, desire and fear, characterize both the public and domestic domains of Elizabethan experience. If sexual and family experience were invariably politicized, economic and political experience were invariably eroticized. The social and psychological force of Elizabethan symbolic forms depended upon a play between the distinction and conflation of these domains.

The much-noted "metadrama" of *A Midsummer Night's Dream*—its calling of attention to its own artifice, its own artistry—analogizes the powers of parents, princes, and playwrights, the fashioning of children, subjects, and plays. Shakespeare's text is not only a cultural production but a representation of cultural production; a representation of fantasies about the shaping of the family, the polity, and the theatre. When Oberon blesses the bride-beds of "the couples three" (5.1.393), he metaphorizes the engendering of their offspring as an act of *writing*: "And the blots of Nature's hand / Shall not in their issue stand" (5.1.395–96). And when Theseus wryly describes the poet's "fine frenzy" (5.1.12), the text of *A Midsummer Night's Dream* obliquely represents the parthenogenetic process of its *own* creation:

> And as imagination bodies forth
> The forms of things unknown, the poet's pen
> Turns them to shapes, and gives to airy nothing
> A local habitation and a name.
>
> (5.1.14–17)

In its preoccupation with the transformation of the personal into the public, the metamorphosis of dream and fantasy into poetic drama, *A Midsummer Night's Dream* does more than *analogize* the powers of prince and playwright: It dramatizes—or, rather, *meta*-dramatizes—the relations of power *between* prince and playwright. The play bodies forth the theatre poet's contest, not only with the generativity of Elizabethan mothers but with the generativity of the royal virgin; it contests the princely claim to cultural authorship and social authority. To the extent that the cult of Elizabeth informs the play, it is itself transformed within the play. *A Midsummer Night's Dream* is, then, in a double sense, a *creation* of Elizabethan culture: for it also creates the culture by which it is created, shapes the fantasies by which it is shaped, begets that by which it is begotten.

5

Puritanism and Maenadism in
A Mask

Richard Halpern

Christianity gave Eros poison to drink; he did not die of it but
he degenerated into vice.

Nietzsche, Beyond Good and Evil

Despite the suggestions of union that inhere in the very word *wedding,*
it was no secret by Milton's time that the nuptial passage was rather
fraught. The vast apparatus of ceremonial and mythical harmony that
Renaissance humanists applied to it only threw its tensions, both
sexual and political, into greater relief.[1] It was John Milton's privilege
to live through these tensions with such disastrous intensity that his
art could illuminate them in a particularly telling way. Milton
composed *A Mask* in 1634, eight years before his first marriage. Yet
Milton seems particularly interested in the hymeneal associations of
the masque form, even though this takes the paradoxical shape of a
masque in praise of chastity.

Milton's ideological project in *A Mask,* I will argue, is to trace the
line that leads from virginity to married chastity. In one sense, of
course, this is only to retrace a line drawn by Spenser. Milton not only
invokes the Britomartian machinery at times but superimposes the
line of marriage onto that of romance, so that the hero's quest
represents the (incomplete) movement from virgin to bride. What
makes it possible for Spenser to formulate this identity, however, and
what therefore keeps Milton's project from becoming perfunctory,
was the increasing tendency of the marital line to wander. The formal
structure of romance—which throve on the tension between the
straight and teleological line of the quest, on the one hand, and the
curved and anarchic line of error, on the other—perfectly suited a
situation in which new historical circumstances threatened the efficacy
of marriage as an institution for containing women.

Along with his ideological theme, Milton inherits a field of literary instruments: specifically, a mythopoesis that tends to congeal into Neoplatonic and Christian allegory. The syncretic mythology of *A Mask,* and the ponderous symbolism of its action, draw on techniques common to both the Spenserian epic and the Jonsonian masque. Yet Milton's allegory lacks the coherence of its literary forebearers. *A Mask* seems to want to wed the Christian and classical virtues in a way that is appropriate to its hymeneal form. But the mythical vehicle keeps exceeding the allegory that it is supposed to express and thus subverts its coherence. The ambivalence of myth produces a surplus or residue of meaning that cannot be contained by allegory; hence Milton's masque begins to wander from its official ideological stance.

The surplus meaning of myth, which subverts the linearity of Milton's allegorical narrative, provides a privileged intersection of form and ideology in *A Mask,* where mythical contradictions are substituted for ideological ones. Nowhere is this more evident than in the Dionysian mythology that the masque half-invokes in order to suppress. The supremely ambivalent figure of Dionysus bursts the containment of his allegorical role, thereby revealing significant contradictions in Milton's sexual ideology.

1

Dionysus makes his only explicit appearance in Comus's geneal-ogy, the significance of which is easily read within the masque's dominant, allegorical code.

> Bacchus that first from out the purple grape,
> Crushed the sweet poison of misused wine
> After the Tuscan mariners transformed
> Coasting the Tyrrhene shore, as the winds listed,
> On Circe's island fell (Who knows not Circe
> The daughter of the Sun? whose charmed cup
> Whoever tasted, lost his upright shape,
> And downward fell into a groveling swine)
> This nymph that gazed upon his clustering locks,
> With ivy berries wreathed, and his blithe youth,
> Had by him, ere he parted thence, a son
> Much like his father, but his mother more,
> Whom therefore she brought up and Comus named.
> $(46-58)^2$

Both Circe and Bacchus are magical, both are associated with beasts and bestiality, intemperence, intoxication, promiscuous sexuality. Comus's lineage sets him in stark contrast to Milton's virginal, temperate Lady and indicates the grotesque animalism that awaits her if she falls prey to his wiles.

The threat to the Lady is clear; and yet something seems awry, for Circe's sexual magic is directed only against men. Bacchus may make a more sensible adversary, if we recall the lustful, vinous father of Mirth in *L'Allegro,* the language of which Comus echoes in his first dance. And yet, in *Lycidas* and later, Milton seems more interested in the very different legend of Orpheus's dismemberment by the maenads, or female followers of Dionysus. Because the maenad—a figure who, as we shall see, plays a role in *A Mask* as well—never attacks women but only beasts or men, a curious situation arises. Both of Comus's parents represent dangers that cannot overtake the Lady; rather, they would make her the bearer of a threat to men.

The thematic oppositions of *A Mask* are therefore questioned from its inception. That Dionysus should help begin this process is only appropriate, as in Hellenic culture he was the god of contradictions, embodying not so much a specific mythic or ritual content as a set of operations: Dionysus is a liminal god who either mediates or collapses or overthrows the structural oppositions on which Attic culture was based, oppositions that include male and female, citizen and slave, culture and nature, Greek and barbarian.[3] As even this partial list suggests, however, these are structures of domination as well as opposition. In *The Bacchae* and elsewhere, Dionysus overturns the oppressive structures that establish a dominant culture of Greek male citizens on the one hand, and, on the other, a world of slaves, women, barbarians and nature, which, through domination or exclusion, constitute the collective otherness of Greek culture.[4] Dionysus embodies the breaking in or revolt of this cultural otherness.

Maenadic worship directed its inverting energies against both the Attic state and the household. Practiced solely by women, the central ritual practice of maenadism was *omophagia,* or the eating of raw meat, which rejected cooking both as the basis of the state religion[5] and as the duty of a wife. Omophagia exemplified the thoroughgoing primitivism of maenadism, which, by reverting from culture to nature, temporarily evaded the patriarchal structures of both *polis* and *oikos.* Hence the wearing of animal skins, for example, abjured the traditional wifely tasks of weaving and spinning, and ecstatic dancing through the wood temporarily released women from the isolation and imprisonment of the Greek household.

In its animalism and its ecstatic dancing, maenadism presages Comus's orgiastic revels. Yet, as depicted by Euripides and others, maenadism was also chaste; bacchants did not drink wine or engage in sexual activity.[6] The amorous and cup-bearing Comus derives from a comic Bacchism that must be distinguished from the austere practices of maenadism, although it is precisely a function of Dionysian ambivalence that the god can encompass both chastity and promiscuity, asceticism and intoxication. Both strains emerge in Comus's seduction speech:

> It is for homely features to keep home,
> They had their name thence: coarse complexions
> And cheeks of sorry grain will serve to ply
> The sampler, and to tease the housewife's wool.
> What need a vermeil-tinctured lip for that
> Love-darting eyes, or tresses like the morn?
>
> (747–52)

The insinuating and aristocratic rhetoric of the cavalier poet, which expresses the promiscuity of comic Bacchism, also uncovers a maenadic theme: Dionysus will free the housewife from her spinning. By collapsing liberation into yet another seduction, Milton signals the dominance of the comic over the tragic Dionysus. Yet the ghost of maenadism still haunts the masque. When the heavenly spirit, disguised as the shepherd Thyrsis, fables his recent encounter with Comus's band, he patterns his tale after Orpheus's encounter with the maenads:

> I sat me down to watch upon a bank
> With ivy canopied, and interwove
> With flaunting honeysuckle, and began
> Wrapt in a pleasing fit of melancholy
> To meditate my rural minstrelsy,
> Till fancy had her fill, but ere a close
> The wonted roar was up amidst the woods,
> And filled the air with barbarous dissonance.
>
> (543–50)

The phrase "barbarous dissonance" reappears in the invocation to book 7 of *Paradise Lost,* whose explicit subject is Orpheus's dismemberment. Milton thus specifies the implied subtext of this earlier scene, which offers a menace to the male poet and not to the female protagonist.

Bacchus is introduced to reinforce the distinction between the Lady and Comus, which in turn expresses oppositions between temperance and intemperance, chastity and promiscuity. The logical as well as the practical substance of Milton's ethic rests on the discreteness of categories, to which the Lady gives dramatic expression by refusing Comus's advances. The univocal signification of allegory also reinforces this discreteness. But by embracing both sexual abstinence and excess, the Dionysian mode threatens to collapse the ruling antithesis of Milton's masque. For if aggressive virginity characterizes maenadism, then the Lady is already somehow Bacchic. A subterranean connivance between Comus and the Lady tends to undercut their ostensible opposition.

The formal disruption of *A Mask* both expresses and substitutes for a conceptual *aporeia*: virginity and promiscuity turn out to be doubles, not antitheses. The basis of this specular or imaginary reversal is, however, neither psychological nor semiological but ideological and political. More specifically, it derives from the contradictory place of women within Puritan sexual ideology, particularly with respect to the concepts of virginity and chastity. Roberta Hamilton has observed that the cultural prestige of women rose in England in the transition from Catholicism to Protestantism, even as their material condition declined in the virtually simultaneous transition from feudalism to capitalism.[7] One sign of this increased cultural prestige was the replacement of the Catholic ideal of female virginity with the Protestant ideal of chastity, that is, of a monogamous marital relationship. For the Puritans, woman was no longer a vessel of sin, a whore of Babylon whose sexuality was fearful and deadly, but a "helpmeet" for men, secondary in authority and yet primary as an embodiment of domestic purity. The reasons for this change are several: one was the Puritans' rather uncanny understanding of the importance of family life as a sphere for political and religious indoctrination; another was the Puritan doctrine of the priesthood of all true believers, which by its very logic demanded a rough equality for women.

This new cultural prestige helped Milton to choose a woman as the hero of his masque, a choice he was not again inclined to make after his marriage to Mary Powell. Yet the tension between the logic of feminine equality and the desire to impose a patriarchal family structure was one of the primary contradictions within Puritanism, expressing itself in the conflict between patriarchal Presbyterianism and radical sectarianism, the latter of which often supported both female and sexual liberation.

The sectarians attacked the Puritan family most directly by holding that a wife who was a true believer could divorce a heretical or atheistical husband. In *Tetrachordon,* Milton himself writes that "the wife also, as her subjection is terminated in the Lord, herself being the redeemed of Christ, is not still bound to be the vassal of him who is the bondslave of Satan."[8] Milton's language recalls the conflict between the Lady and Comus in his masque. Yet Milton was palpably uncomfortable with this position and more generally held that the husband could unilaterally divorce the wife.

Katherine Chidley gave a more spirited defense of woman's independence in 1641: "I pray you tell me," she says, "what authority [the] unbelieving husband hath over the conscience of his believing wife; it is true he hath authority over her in bodily and civil respects, but not to be a lord over her conscience."[9] In the same key, Milton's Lady warns Comus,

> Thou canst not touch the freedom of my mind
> With all thy charms, although this corporal rind
> Thou hast immanacled, while heaven sees good.
>
> (662–64)

The Lady, of course, is not yet a wife, although the masque intends that she eventually become one.[10] Yet in her speeches and those of her brothers, the words *virginity* and *chastity* are interchangeable, reflecting the Puritan belief that they are related and sequential virtues: the virginal girl becomes the chaste wife.[11] But the reasoning of the radical sectarians may also obtrude itself here.[12] If Christian liberty allows the virginal girl to refuse her seducer, might it not also allow the married woman to refuse her husband?

The dispute between Presbyterians and radical sectarians realized certain tensions that were always inherent in Puritan sexual ideology. In particular, the relation between virginity and chastity was more difficult than it might initially seem. In a purely empirical sense, of course, both stand opposed to sexual promiscuity by imposing a partial or total limitation on sexual activity. And the practice of patrimonial inheritance required both virginity and chastity, in sequence, to insure the legitimacy of the male line. Here it is a question of who controls, owns, or deploys female sexuality. The virginity of the pubescent or unmarried girl, held as untainted goods for the future husband or owner, comprises a passive virginity that suits a system of patriarchal control. Not only did the Puritan husband own his wife's sexuality in marriage, he owned it in advance.

Sectarian doctrine on divorce, however, suggested that a woman could, under certain circumstances, recoup her own person and sexuality. This repudiation of the husband's ownership I will call active virginity, a mode of sexual revolt at least as old as Lysistrata. If matrimonial monogamy, or chastity, is the dominant form of sexual control, then both promiscuity and active virginity violate it, although in different ways. Hence the uncanny doubling of apparent opposites in *A Mask*. The virtuous resistance of the Lady may become revolt if it is not relinquished at the proper moment. In excess, both virginity and sexuality overturn domestic rule.

Of course, the maenad was not the only figure for the fierce virgin available to Renaissance poetry. Amazons and the nymphs of Diana also withold their sexuality in ways that make them independent, strange, and frightening to men. All of these figures mark the point at which virginity ceases to denote submission and begins to denote revolt, at which purification becomes danger. In all of these cases, moreover, active virginity is marked by wandering, which contrasts with the stasis of domestic life. Here spatial containment figures political containment, and the freedom of the wilderness illuminates the structures of domestic space. Renaissance gynecological theory reproduced this figure by holding that the female uterus was an independent animal prone to wander from its proper place if not stabilized by regular insertion of the husbandly penis.[13] The virgin's wandering uterus is not unlike Diana, or the maenad, wandering through the hills, while the chaste or housewifely uterus, by contrast, is pinned in its place. It is one of the ironies of Milton's masque, then, that Comus captures and binds the wandering Lady. If, in one sense, this serves as a prelude to Bacchic perversion, in another it tames maenadic eccentricity. Comus seems to betray his father's epithet *Lyaeus,* "the looser" or "the releaser."

A question may arise: if *A Mask* works to reject or suppress the figure of the maenad, why does it extol the other fierce virgins? When the Second Brother asks what power can protect his supposedly helpless sister, his Elder Brother replies, in language that recalls Spenser's Britomart,

> 'Tis chastity, my brother, chastity:
> She that has that, is clad in complete steel,
> And like a quivered nymph with arrows keen
> May trace huge forests, and unharboured heaths,
> Infamous hills, and sandy perilous wilds,
> Where through the sacred rays of chastity,
> No savage fierce, bandit, or mountaineer
> Will dare to soil her virgin purity.
>
> (419–26)

He then invokes the goddess Diana, who, he says,

> set at nought
> The frivolous bolt of Cupid, gods and men
> Feared her stern frown, and she was queen o' the woods.
>
> (444–46)

The mythological panoply of the virgin queen, as it had been applied to Elizabeth, accompanies the usual explicit threat to men and the almost obligatory hints of castration or male sexual impotence. Since Acteon fared no better than Pentheus, one might ask why a masque that can celebrate Diana balks at the Greek Dionysus.

While Diana and the maenad both evade the household regime, their differing modes of doing so make the one tolerable and the other not. Diana's nymphs are virgins from birth; they simply abjure the domestic sphere while leaving it intact. Diana may be the patroness of virginity, but she also doubles as the patroness of childbirth. As consecrated figures, her nymphs are set off from the mass of women; the mythology surrounding Elizabeth, for example, regularly emphasized her singularity or uniqueness. By contrast, maenadism does not ignore the household; it ruptures it from within, as its votaries are wives and household slaves. For Puritanism, virginity before marriage is fine; virginity instead of marriage is less fine; but virginity within marriage, conceived as an explosive release from the domestic sphere, posed a grave threat at a time when the household was crucial as an arena for control but when sectarians were beginning to formulate dangerous ideas about a woman's right to release herself from wedlock. For Milton, then, the maenad mythologically embodies the logic of Christian liberty as it applied to women. The poet's anxiety takes the form of a figure who threatens not only the corporeal integrity of men but also the integrity of the household as an arena for patriarchal control.

"Licence they mean when they cry liberty," writes Milton in his twelfth sonnet, attacking those who misunderstood his divorce tracts. Bacchus, also known as Liber, marks the point at which, from Milton's perspective, Liber-ty exceeds its proper limits and becomes license. From another perspective, we may say that he marks the point at which liberty fulfills itself beyond the bounds set by Puritanism. Nathaniel Henry argued thirty years ago that Milton's twelfth sonnet is directed not against conservative Presbyterians offended by Milton's radicalism but against those radical sectarians who practiced what Milton preached.[14] Henry quotes Thomas Edwards's *Gangraena,* an attack on sectarianism published in 1644, where Edwards records that a Mrs. Attaway, "the mistress of all the she-preachers on Coleman

Street," came to consider leaving her husband after reading Milton on divorce. Mrs. Attaway, a kind of seventeenth-century maenad, embodied the feminine "licence" that Milton attacks in the sonnet's opening quatrain:

> I did but prompt the age to quit their clogs
> By the known rules of ancient liberty,
> When straight a barbarous noise environs me
> Of owls and cuckoos, asses, apes, and dogs.

By recalling Comus's band of revelers, this barbarous menagerie further clarifies the issues at stake in that earlier work.

In Milton's masque, the antidote to maenadism is offered by Sabrina, the nymph of the lake, who again represents both virginity and chastity. Sabrina's martyrdom—she drowns herself to avoid her "enraged stepdame"—has strong Christian overtones. But she also resolves a problem that blocks the way to the masque's implicitly hymeneal ending. Sabrina plays the part of the scapegoat, a structural necessity within the comic form. The evil that she bears off is nothing other than female aggressiveness—that of her almost maenadic stepdame—which, in imitation of Christian martyrdom, she wonderfully learns to turn against her own person. Where can maenadic violence safely be redirected? Why, at woman herself, who can become chaste only after she has sacrificed the power over her own sexuality. The Lady in Milton's masque is thus saved from imprisonment by Comus only in order that she may learn self-imprisonment at the hands of Christ. Thence the Lady is returned safe to her father's house (safe for whom, one wonders), and Thyrsis treats us to a heavenly vision at whose summit,

> Celestial Cupid . . . advanced,
> Holds his dear Psyche sweet entranced
> After her wandering labours long,
> Till free consent the gods among
> Make her his eternal bride.

> (1003–7)

Psyche, rescued from wandering, is *held* "sweet entranced," while Cupid has finally found a place to stick his "frivolous bolt." "Free consent," the liberty that, the Spirit tells us, only virtue can bestow, has somehow been transferred to the gods, for Psyche finds *herself* bestowed upon Cupid. Celestial visions, especially Milton's, have a peculiar way of reproducing, in sublimated form, the worst aspects of life on earth, rather in the way that hitting your thumb with a hammer can cause you to see stars. In *A Mask*, heavenly bliss seems to be only a trope for wedded bliss, with the result that no space remains for woman's liberty, even beyond the "sphery chime."

2

The sexual drama of *A Mask* arises from an historically specific struggle over the mode of reproduction, a struggle that is complexly interrelated with the struggle over the mode of production. The dynamic of the bourgeois marriage was founded by Protestantism at the same time that the bourgeois class was undertaking its two great historical tasks: wresting political power from the feudal aristocracy and seizing the means of production from the working class. Bourgeois strategies of sexual domination and of class exploitation mutually inform each other.

The Dionysian mythology of Milton's masque illustrates this intersection between class and gender struggles, for Dionysus (as well as his offspring, Comus) plays the same ambiguous role in class conflict that he does in gender conflict. The burlesque transvestitism that ends Pentheus's sexual mastery in *The Bacchae* also ends his tyranny over Thebes. Dionysis seems to emerge as a god of the people,[15] yet he becomes demagogic when he attempts to assert his divine birthright and extort worship from the Thebans.

The class ambiguities of Dionysian worship are reborn in Comus's festivities, which are both popular and courtly. While the tumult of his antimasque partakes of the popular mumming and misrule on which the masque form traditionally builds, Comus's castle and specious feast clearly represent the decadence of aristocratic entertainments. The speech in which the lady denounces Comus's apparently spontaneous copia as the product of a maldistribution of wealth (756–79) may be taken as the poet's critique of courtly festivity, including the masque, which mimics the more "natural" entertainments of a peasantry that it simultaneously exploits. When Comus disguises himself as a shepherd, he belatedly reassumes the tired dress of Spenser, Sidney, and his other courtly predecessors.

Yet if *A Mask* exposes courtly masquing as a decadent imitation, it holds that the original of this imitation is no less decadent. Puritansim made no secret of its desire to eradicate rural festivity, particularly Maypole dancing. Country sports represented everything about the "old Adam" that had to be eradicated or reformed by Christian discipline: these sports were sensual where the Puritans were ascetic, abandoned where they were restrained, pagan where they were Protestant. Maypole dancing defamed the Sabbath, and its adherents were dangerously prone to superstition and popery. It was spontaneous, anarchic, and leisurely when the times called for rigor and industry.[16]

The attempt to suppress country sports was a simple expression of the inability of Puritanism, as an urban bourgeois ideology, to assimilate the culture of the rural working class. Rural festivity was the vestigial form of a petty producing culture, now inherited only by the proletarianized stratum of that class. Maypole dancers were soon enough to fill the ranks of Digger radicalism and to threaten Puritanism with a revolution within the revolution. A Puritan minister complained in 1660 that May games made "the servant contemn his master, the people their pastor, the subject his sovereign, the child his father," and taught "young people impudence and rebellion."[17] For their part, rural laborers were not particularly eager to be reformed along Puritan lines. "The phallic maypole was for the rural lower class almost a symbol of independence of their betters: . . . In Stratford-on-Avon in 1619 popular libels were distributed, attacking the Puritan ruling group and calling for maypoles. The Puritans were described as economic oppressors, twisters of the law."[18] In the grotesque merriment of Comus's band lies not only the sexual but also the class threat of Dionysus. It endangers Puritan patriarchy as a specifically bourgeois patriarchy, that is, as the patriarchy of what was soon to be the new ruling class.

This class contradiction also expresses itself as a rural-urban antagonism, particularly as Puritan disdain for pagan festivities in the "dark corners of the land," of which Wales, the setting for Milton's masque, was one of the most notorious.[19] The murky woods of *A Mask* represent the spiritual as well as the physical darkness of the Welsh landscape, where popular affinities for both May games and Catholicism were rampant. Comus may be taken as a *genius loci* of this "dark corner," and his followers as the local rambunctious peasantry. The Lady herself suggests this identification when she mistakes Comus's revels for country sports:

> This way the noise was, if mine ear be true,
> My best guide now, methought it was the sound
> Of riot, and ill-managed merriment,
> Such as the jocund flute, or gamesome pipe
> Stirs up among the loose unlettered hinds,

> When for their teeming flocks, and granges full,
> In wanton dance they praise the bounteous Pan,
> And thank the gods amiss. I should be loth
> To meet the rudeness, and swilled insolence
> Of such late wassailers.
>
> (169–78)

While the Lady seems implicitly to fear a sexual assault, her language dwells on region and social class—appropriately enough, since rural festivities were viewed as orgiastic by urban Puritans, whose mouthpiece she seems to be here.

If Puritanism objected to country sports, however, the monarchy was pleased to encourage them as a means of social control. Not only were they traditional royalist symbols, but they were deemed preferable to meetings in alehouses and coventicles where seditious ideas might be discussed. Further, encouraging the games enlisted the support of the rural masses against the Puritans.[20] On the other hand, the crown also recognized the connection between country sports and recusancy. *The Book of Sports,* first issued by James in 1617 and later reissued by both James and Charles, sought to promote country sports within limits, "the same to be had in due & convenient time, without impediment or neglect of Divine Service."[21]

Royal encouragement of country sports partly underlies that doubling whereby Comus appears as both a wanton country dancer and a dissolute aristocrat. In this he simply imitates his original in Jonson's *Pleasure Reconciled To Virtue,* a masque that celebrates James's *via media* in attempting to reform without destroying both country and courtly pleasures.[22] Jonson's masque depicts the Stuart court as an Hesperian realm, which refines the antimasque of Comus into a chaster footing, banishing the excesses of courtier and clown while avoiding the opposite extreme of Puritan prudishness.

Milton's satiric riposte to Jonson begins when Comus leads his riotous dances under the light of Hesperus, an acknowledgement that none of Jonson's moralizing was ever able to moralize the English court. When the Lady attacks Comus for his prodigality, she does so in language that would have been unthinkable, and indeed downright dangerous, in a royal masque:

> If every just man that now pines with want
> Had but a moderate and beseeming share
> Of that which lewdly-pampered Luxury
> Now heaps upon some few with vast excess,
> Nature's full blessings would be well-dispensed

In unsuperfluous even proportion,
And she no whit encumbered with her store,
And then the giver would be better thanked,
His praise due paid, for swinish gluttony
Ne'er looks to heaven amidst his gorgeous feast,
But with besotted base ingratitude
Crams, and blasphemes his feeder.

(767–78)

The Lady's reasoning begins to move beyond the ethical to the structural; she attacks the morals of the aristocracy less than she does their position as a ruling class (I fail to see how Alice Egerton and her family could avoid applying this speech to themselves). It is hard to imagine how personal temperance could solve the maldistribution of wealth described here; hence Jonsonian exhortations give way to an unspecified threat. At the same time, however, the masque seems to approve of the poor only when they are suffering, not celebrating.[23] The decline of the Hesperian indicates not only the debauchery of the Stuart court but a movement from the western realm of England to the even further western realm of Wales, where the rural poor were felt to be especially savage and superstitious. Milton's masque begins in an age too late for Jonsonian compromise and suggests that both ends of the social scale have gotten out of hand.

In what is both a political and rhetorical ploy, Milton resolves this problem by appropriating the Jacobean-Anglican *via media,* or middle way, for the Puritan middle class. When the Lady first hears Comus's band, which she mistakes for a group of country revelers, she sounds less like a country aristocrat than like a Puritan bourgeois. Only the middle class, Milton seems to say, can steer a chaste course between the debaucheries of the aristocracy and those of the rural laboring class, just as chastity itself, the bourgeois form of sexual control, avoids the extremes of savage virginity and promiscuity.

The offending practices of popular festivity, to which the coordinated class and gender controls of Puritanism respond, do not stop at unrestrained sexuality, however.[24] In addition, "popular festivals and customs . . . show much play with switches in sex roles and much attention to women on top."[25] Husband-beating, for instance, formed a frequent theme for festivals and at least once provided the basis for a courtly entertainment. John Lydgate wrote the speeches for "A Mumming at Herford," which was performed for King Henry VI around 1430. The manuscript describes it as "a disguysing of the rude vplandisshe people compleyning on hir wyves, with the boystous [*sic*] aunswere of hir wyves."[26] In this proto-masque, "certeyne sweynes" present themselves to the king in order to complain

> Vpon the trouble and the crueltee
> Which that they haue endured in theyre lyves
> By the felnesse of theyre fierce wyves.
>
> (11–13)

These wives, they say, stay out drinking all day, refuse to cook dinner, beat them with distaffs, scratch their faces with their nails, and pummel them until they bleed. When it comes their turn to speak, the wives defend rather than deny their ferocity:

> Touching the substance of this hyeghe discorde,
> We sixe wyves beon ful of oon acorde
> Yif wordes and chyding may vs not avaylle,
> We wol darrein it in chaumpcloos by bataile.
>
> (163–67)

This was about as near to maenadism as England was going to get.[27] Lydgate's disorderly wives not only represent class and gender revolt but, by acting as a group, they also provide a model for mass disobedience, something that exceptional figures like Britomart cannot do.[28] The incredible strength of the maenads is no doubt a physiological effect of religious ecstasy; but it may also figure forth the strength of the collective.

In Milton's masque, the threat of the rural masses is, by a familiar trope, portrayed as bestialism: Comus's cup "transforms [the face] of him that drinks, / And the inglorious likeness of a beast / Fixes instead" (527–29). The ferocity of country wives thus assumes a theriomorphic form, "like stabled wolves, or tigers at their prey" (533). Peasants are explicitly transformed into animals in the twelfth sonnet, where the "barbarous noise" of Milton's detractors reminds him of "when those hinds that were transformed to frogs / Railed at Latona's twin-born progeny." Here the class allegory is relatively unproblematic: the poor who have the nerve to rise against their betters—Milton, in this case—are turned into animals (apparently, the next lowest step on the cosmological scale), thereby enacting the already-present equation between Ovid's *rustica turba* and Milton's "owls and cuckoos, asses, apes, and dogs." Nathaniel Henry notes that "Mrs. Attaway . . . was apparently uneducated and belonged to a social and economic level considerably different from that of Milton,"[29] as did most of the radical sectarians. Fear of maenadism is not only fear of women, then, but also fear of the working class mob, whose turbulence threatens the crystalline integrity of the bourgeois order.[30]

All of the inversions discussed above are conceived as somehow alien, imported by the foreigner Comus to plague the order of English Puritan culture. The Dionysian antinomy between Greek and barbarian thus asserts itself, here figured primarily as an opposition between England and Wales, although this national opposition in turn represents breaks within English culture. Ben Jonson had already played with the "barbarous" Welsh tongue in his masque, *For the Honor of Wales,* a piece that evidently influenced *A Mask.*[31] The "barbarous dissonance" of Comus's crew probably alludes in part to the unintelligible Celtic speech of the Welsh peasantry.[32] Yet as Jonson's masque suggests, the concept of the barbarous is not strictly limited to the tongues of a different national or ethnic group. For even when Jonson's peasants speak English—a comically grotesque exaggeration of the dialect in some of Spenser's eclogues—they are difficult to understand. The absolute incomprehensibility of the Welsh, a pure linguistic otherness, becomes a hyperbolic trope for class and regional differences within the same linguistic system. The discourse of the peasantry as a class is "barbarous" and unassimilable to the court and to the urban bourgeoisie.

Comus, who roved "the Celtic and Iberian fields" (60) before settling in Wales, represents the barbarian or foreign in general, just as Dionysus does in *The Bacchae.* Yet Dionysus, who comes from Asia Minor but claims his birthright in Thebes, confuses the distinction between native and barbarian. Milton introduces similar perplexities by locating his masque in Wales, so that a "native" or English culture breaks in on a foreign one and thus finds itself in the situation of an alien intruder. When Comus greets the Lady with the words "Hail foreign wonder," he introduces a dangerous cultural relativism (and further obscures the distinction between himself and the Lady). The structural opposition between native and barbarian can be stabilized only by the dominance of one culture over the other: in this case, of England's over Wales's. When the Lady defeats Comus, her victory is an imperial one that definitively inscribes Wales as the inferior or barbarian culture.[33]

But maenadism entails the concept of the barbarian or foreign not only because it comes from a strange land but also because the maenad becomes foreign or alien to men by forfeiting her domesticity. In *The Bacchae,* therefore, the Theban wives come to resemble the Lydian women, even surpassing them in ferocity, when they take up maenadic practices. The opposition of inner/outer, which defines the problem of barbarism, situates itself on the border of a space in which the *oikos* and the *polis* become one: in which, that is, the interior of the household represents civilization (for women, at least), and its exterior represents savagery or barbarism. To redomesticate the Theban wives would be to resanctify the cultural borders of the state as a whole, to close the wound that Dionysus has inflicted on its limit.[34]

While this project fails spectacularly in *The Bacchae*, patriarchy and imperialism do triumph together in *A Mask*. The site of their linguistic intersection is the word *home*, which signifies both the domestic sphere and the familiarity of English culture. Upon first hearing the Lady sing, Comus declares that

> such a sacred, and home-felt delight,
> Such sober certainty of waking bliss
> I never heard till now. (261–63)

The Lady's song temporarily "domesticates" the reveler and in so doing renders him conscious of his own foreignness. This moment presages her eventual return to her father's house and the triumph of its civilizing values. On the way, however, she must resist Comus's offer to separate her from those "homely features . . . [who] keep home" (747), for acceptance would transform her into a "foreign wonder" in relation to her own native English culture.

The coincidental problems of femininity and barbarism are, however, not only a structural or mythic base for Milton's masque; they are, I would argue, consciously taken up into its allegorical code. For the root haemony, which Thyrsis offers as protection against Comus's spells, represents married chastity as a vehicle for both patriarchal and imperial domination. When the Elder Brother suggest a martial assault on Comus in order to liberate his sister, Thyrsis replies,

> Alas good venturous youth,
> I love thy courage yet, and bold emprise,
> But here thy sword can do thee little stead,
> Far other arms, and other weapons must
> Be those that quell the might of hellish charms,
> He with his bare wand can unthread thy joints,
> And crumble all thy sinews.
>
> (608–14)

The sword and the wand invoke the two extreme forms of sexuality between which the masque tries to steer a middle course. The sword represents an anti-erotic aggressiveness that has already been associated with virginity through the figure of armed Diana. The wand, by contrast, represents the promiscuous phallic sexuality of Comus. Because these ostensible opposites are actually allied within Puritan ideology, the brothers' armed attack on Comus would be co-opted, just as the Lady's "armed" virginity was.

Thyris, however, finds a better way. A shepherd lad once taught him the secrets of herbs, he claims, and

> Amongst the rest a small unsightly root,
> But of divine effect, he culled me out;
> The leaf was darkish, and had prickles on it,
> But in another country, as he said,
> Bore a bright golden flower, but not in this soil:
> Unknown, and like esteemed, and the dull swain
> Treads on it daily with his clouted shoon,
> And yet more med'cinal is it than the Moly
> That Hermes once to wise Ulysses gave;
> He called it haemony, and gave it me,
> And bade me keep it as of sovran use
> 'Gainst all enchantments, mildew blast, or damp
> Or ghastly Furies' apparition.
>
> (628–40)

Such are the horizons of Milton's vision that yet a third phallus is found to "liberate" the Lady. The reference to moly suggests that female sexuality is the real culprit here, the primary object of resistance and control. Although both the wand and the sword only encourage its recalcitrance, the humbler haemony is able to master its magic. Most interpretations of haemony have placed it within a theological allegory, which indeed is clearly present. Yet whatever else it may be, as a cure for sexual magic, haemony seems to represent married chastity—boring, perhaps, and unsightly in appearance, but powerful in its effects. Such an interpretation seems at least not to violate the literary context. That the "dull swain / Treads on it [haemony] daily with his clouted shoon" may refer to the traditional lower-class rejection of church marriage, a practice that horrified Puritans and that was particularly prevalent in those rural "dark corners" where church and state had difficulty enforcing their jurisdiction. "Norden the surveyor," writes Christopher Hill,

> spoke of people bred amongst the woods, "dwelling far from
> any church or chapel," who "were as ignorant of God or of

any civil course of life as the very savages amongst the infidels." Contemporaries explained the whoredoms of the Welsh by the mountain air: the modern historian more wisely sees them as the natural product of a society which refused to accept English protestant marriage laws.[35]

One wonders whether, according to Hill's own argument, contemporaries weren't at least dimly aware of the true reasons for the "whoredoms of the Welsh." At least, they tended to treat Wales as a particularly noxious "dark corner."

In such a context, the opposition between "this soil" and "another country" takes on a more than merely theological resonance: it distinguishes between the soil of Wales, where the masque occurs and where the "whoredoms" of the inhabitants blind them to the virtues of Protestant marriage, and that other country, England, where married chastity bears its bright flower of sexual and social control. In this remarkable moment, then, the gender, class, and imperial codes of the masque seem temporarily to coalesce. Wales provides a barbarian setting (which in itself offers a hyperbolic nightmare image of the rural proletariat) where "savage" marital practices release the dangers of feminine sexuality. Woman can be rehoused but not on this soil and amongst this class; English bourgeois life provides the proper "home" for the home itself.

6

Dalila's House: *Samson Agonistes* and the Sexual Division of Labor

JOHN GUILLORY

1. Sexual Subjection and Division of Labor

Both the sexual division of labor and the sexual subjection of women are apparently universal constituents of culture and may therefore be said to lie within the historical horizon of any literary work. We scarcely need to observe that *Samson Agonistes* assumes the subjection of women, a practice to which Milton gives his unequivocal endorsement; but is there any sense in which that practice of subjection is modified by the contemporaneous form of the sexual division of labor? I would like to propose an answer to this question, an answer that should move criticism of Milton's work beyond the impasse of observing in such figures as Dalila merely an intensified version of a transhistorical misogyny.

Lévi-Strauss has reminded us that the sexual division of labor is quite arbitrary and need not imply the subjection of one sex to another.[1] This fact bears importantly on the historical specificity of relations between men and women, because it suggests that while neither the division of labor nor the subjection of women may be easy to identify as determined by conditions particular to a given period, there may well be at certain times unique *conjunctures* between them. Feminist historians have located such a conjuncture in the emergent bourgeois society of the sixteenth and seventeenth centuries, a period that saw, according to Roberta Hamilton, "the decline of the family as an economic unit of production" and the rise of several new, or newly gender-inflected distinctions: "The separation of production from consumption, work from home, housework from work, and public from private."[2] It has been demonstrated with reasonable assurance that this mutation brings into unprecedented alignment and mutual reinforcement the two transhistorical practices of sexual division of labor and the subjection of women.[3] The conjunction constitutes the historicity of seventeenth-century misogynistic discourse, which

would otherwise be recognized as only conventional. As the sociol-
ogist Annette Kuhn has written, the sexual division of labor is now
"overdetermined by the separation of work and home," and that
separation becomes the ground of those ideological subjections
loosely denominated as the system of partriarchy.[4] The disqualification of housework as work, or the appearance of the subsidized
woman in the middle-class household, removes labor to an exclusively masculine domain of representation, and produces a fresh
equation of the feminine and the domestic. I will assume in the
following argument that the conjuncture of sexual subjection and
division of labor forms a functionally indivisible complex, even when
only a part of that complex, like one face of a solid, presents itself to
view.

Identification of the historical horizon for a text such as *Samson
Agonistes* is complicated by Milton's habit of displacing his immediate
concerns onto biblical narratives. Such a displacement tends to qualify
at the outset any interpretation of the drama as merely reproducing the
discourse of its time. Rather, it should be said that Milton actively
intervenes in the very social circumstances that simultaneously determine the conditions of his intervention. As such an intervention,
Samson Agonistes can be characterized as an act of legitimation that
strategically employs the authority of a biblical narrative, in this case,
a narrative both tactfully distanced and resonating with current social,
political, and religious concerns. Milton intervenes on behalf of a
social practice, divorce, which is not yet legitimized; or better,
unsuccessfully legitimized by Milton's former prose productions, the
divorce tracts. In advancing this hypothesis, I do not mean to reduce
Samson to its polemical motives, much less to the single motive of
defending divorce. In fact the story in Judges serves Milton as a kind
of allegorical narrative for several crises of legitimation, political,
religious, and aesthetic. It is the ability of the Samson story to embody
these crises, or project images of their resolution, that attracts Milton.
Nevertheless, my concern here is largely with Dalila, specifically with
the figure of Dalila's house.

If Milton's rewriting of the Samson story puts into circulation a
newly effective, because recontextualized, biblical narrative, the process of recontextualizing requires a major revision of the narrative
itself. At the center of the new story, the "tragedy" of Samson, is an
extra-biblical encounter with Dalila, the burden of which is a rejection
of her offer to take Samson *home*—not to his father's house, to which
his body is eventually returned, but to *her* house. Dalila's house is not
the marginal fact that would seem to be indicated by its status as a

rejected offer; it represents, on the contrary, the central fact of what *must* be rejected if Samson is to accomplish his divinely ordained task. The narrative is restructured as an exclusive choice between the poem's two houses, the father's and Dalila's. The demands emanating from these houses result in the acting out of a social contradiction, whose remedy Milton had glimpsed in the 1640s in the practice of divorce.

The projection of divorce onto the biblical narrative can of course be undertaken only by first supposing a marriage between Samson and Dalila not hinted at in the original text. In the same way that Milton adjusts the biblical story to serve as a setting for the contemporary institution of marriage, Samson's struggle against the Philistines is modernized as a kind of election, in the densely ambiguous Puritan senses of that concept:

> such as thou has solemnly elected,
> With gifts and graces eminently adorn'd
> To some great work, thy glory . . .
>
> (677–80)[5]

The election or vocation of Samson ("the work to which I was divinely call'd") is further recontextualized as representative of masculine labor, because Samson's failure is construed both as an effeminization ("effeminately vanquished") and as a failure to serve his God. The moment of failure is represented by the complex figure of castration, by which Samson is unmanned as well as unfitted to complete his task. For Milton, the cutting off of Samson's hair, not simply by a woman but by his *wife,* is the precise point of impact on the narrative of its historical conditions. The very flexible misogynistic discourse condemning female sexuality can be said to recognize the specificity of these social relations by misrecognizing them.[6] What is recognized in the conflict between Samson and Dalila if not a conflict between vocation and marriage, between two *institutions*? If Samson and Dalila were Milton's contemporaries, would we not say that the labor of the male has confronted as its antagonist the sexuality of the female? But even this recognition is as yet only misrecognition, because what brings the vocation of the male into apparent conflict with the sexuality of the female is the sexual division of labor, the social and economic condition by which the wife can be seen to *oppose* rather than cooperate with the productive labor of the husband.[7] In *Samson Agonistes* the sexual division of labor is misrecognized as the conflict between sexuality and labor (the institutions of marriage and vocation). The transhistorical distinction in gender thus has the mysterious effect of sorting out, like magnetic poles, what belongs (but not necessarily) to the male—labor—and what belongs (but not necessarily) to the female—sexuality.

2. Public and Private

Milton has no need to refer the narrative in any conspicuous way to the contemporary division of labor, except at those moments when Samson faces idleness as an alternative, clearly not preferable, to his labor at the mill:

> To what can I be useful, wherein serve
> My Nation, and the work from Heav'n impos'd
> But to sit idle on the household hearth,
> A burdenous drone . . .
>
> (564–67)

The image of the drone acknowledges the sexual division of labor in the society of the bee colony, a natural matriarchy, but only very parenthetically. Nevertheless the image suggests an important thematic obsession in the play with the relation between Samson's vocation and his public role: his most terrible punishment would be confinement to the "household." The distinction between the active vocation and the idle household is more usually expressed as the classical distinction between public and private:

> I was no private but a person rais'd
> With strength sufficient and command from Heav'n
> To free my Country . . .
>
> (1211–13)

Samson's vocation and his public role are identified by reference to the same convention that associates the private domain with women. Here, classical credentials of the public-private distinction matter more than any suppositions about the actual organization of classical culture. The discourse of public and private is mobilized for its prestige; it functions as one layer in a complexly sedimented system of ideology, the layer signifying the authority of tradition. For classical culture, the public world makes the higher claim. Privacy, on the other hand, means deprivation, a certain incapacity to act; and action is defined against both leisure and labor—if labor is not just for slaves, it is something that belongs to the household, the *domus*.[8] In Milton's time, the domestic world is positively revalued in relation to the political; as many historians of the family have established, the household, relieved of its productive function and now the antithesis rather than the site of economic behavior, becomes the locus of new social values as well as the refuge from the public world.[9] The private is no longer the realm of deprivation. At the same time, the classical distinction between public and private is retained as the bad conscience of the domestic retreat, setting an ideological limit to the valuation of the private. The importance of this point must be grasped if we are to understand why the antagonist that confronts Samson throughout the drama is not finally another person but rather the offer to go home.

Just as Samson's failure can be expressed as the failure of his public life, Dalila's self-defense can be expressed as the complaint of the housewife, the complaint of the private world against the public. Here is the domestic voice that Milton's critics have been disposed not to hear, because Dalila has been dismissed as merely a liar. In fact, she speaks the conventional truth of the household:

> I knew that liberty
> Would draw thee forth to perilous enterprises.
> While I at home sat full of cares and fears
> Wailing thy absence in my widow'd bed . . .
>
> (804–6)

Dalila conceives of Samson's calling merely as a dangerous occupation with the additional unpleasant prospect of his meeting other sexual objects on the road ("partners in my love"). Interestingly, Milton is closer to the bourgeois career drama of Cecil B. DeMille, who projected that drama back onto the magnified figure of the biblical hero, than he is to his Hebraic source. I intend to show that *Samson Agonistes* is a prototype of the bourgeois career drama, which conventionally sets the vocation of the husband against the demands of the housewife. It does not matter to the structure of the narrative that Samson's vocation is not productive labor, that it takes the form of a violent struggle against the Philistines. That sort of vocation is no less vulnerable than a secular career to pressures from the household.

When Samson rejects as mendacious Dalila's expressed motive of keeping him "at home," Dalila responds by invoking the system of the classical *polis* in an obvious attempt to turn the ideological tables. She reinterprets her betrayal of the private marital contract as the subordination of private to public interests; in this act of subordination she becomes what Samson ought to have been, the deliverer of her people from the foreign enemy:

> at length that grounded maxim
> So rife and celebrated in the mouths
> Of wisest men, that to the public good
> Private respects must yield, with grave authority
> Took full possession of me and prevail'd . . .
>
> (865–69)

An archaic ideology reappears, like the ghost of Hamlet's father, to demand a response already obsolete. The invocation of "that grounded maxim" does not answer to the situation of either Samson or Dalila. Yet Dalila's strategy of adopting the hierarchical distinction of public and private has the serious consequence of inverting the gender assignments of the very discourse she is calling to her aid. The real question all along has been that of sexual distinction. In her simulacrum of the Samsonian life—Dalila as deliverer of her people— she crosses from the private to the public realm, passing Samson as he moves in the opposite direction. Hence, while Dalila continues to urge a domestic resolution, as though she really would prefer a happy marriage to her recent fame, it would seem to be her status as Samson's female double that is perceived as most threatening and that accounts for the detail with which her figure as deliverer is drawn. Most tellingly she describes her projected fame and memorial cere- monies (980–96) in language very much like Manoa's at the end of the drama (1732–42). Dalila's betrayal of Samson and of the household is implicitly an *imitation* of her husband. No doubt the resemblance of Dalila to Samson is an unintended effect of Milton's construction of the worst possible case against her. She is allowed an array of defenses so that she may be condemned out of her own mouth. Yet that design becomes overextended when Dalila voices and embodies a masculine dread specific to Milton's own time. The question of sexual domina- tion (or of its failure, "female usurpation") is not simply a matter of relation between the sexes but of the maintenance of the nonproduc- tive household as a refuge from, but not an obstruction to, whatever occupies the public life of the male. Dalila's failure as a wife might well have meant her public success; for Milton they are equally to be condemned.

3. Seduction

In addition to the narrative pressures of the biblical material, Samson's elected task confronts as its antagonist Dalila's sexuality. The antecedent of the tragic action, the apparent failure of the vocation, is for Milton therefore a scene of seduction: the sexual crisis becomes the political crisis. Samson rehearses the scene of his seduction several times in the course of the drama, and Dalila's reappearance is a repetition of that scene. Her entrance is made emblematic of female seductiveness, as the chorus attempts to focus its masculine gaze upon a constellation of gender signs:

> But who is this, what thing of Sea or Land?
> Female of sex it seems,
> That so bedeckt, ornate, and gay,
> Comes this way sailing
> Like a stately Ship
> Of Tarsus, bound for th'Isles
> Of *Javan* or *Gadire*
> With all her bravery on, and tackle trim,
> Sails fill'd, and streamers waving,
> Courted by all the winds that hold them play,
> An Amber scent of odorous perfume
> Her harbinger, a damsel train behind;
> Some rich Philistian Matron she may seem,
> And now at nearer view, no other certain
> Than *Dalila* thy wife.

(710-24)

The foregrounding of Dalila's clothing temporarily effaces her identity, an important point to which I will return later. At the moment I want to observe that the rhetorical amplification of Dalila's integuments of seduction is so atypical of the drama's style that we are led to suspect a particular source governing the momentary extravagance. Likening women to ships is quite conventional, but the specific combination of details here belongs unmistakably to one source, the set piece on Cleopatra's barge in *Antony and Cleopatra*. Milton follows Shakespeare in most details—ship, sails, amorous winds, scent, train—and adds a signature of derivation: The "ship of Tarsus" recalls not only the biblical emblem of pride ("Thou breakest the ships of Tarshish," Psalm 48) but also the same city on the river Cydnus where Cleopatra meets Antony.[10] When Milton's text hesitates at the threshold of allusion, that hesitation takes the form of a question: what thing of sea or land? In a slightly different form, the question is critical in Shakespeare's play, where it is Antony's decision to fight by sea that his lieutenants find so perverse (a choice belabored in Plutarch as well). At Actium, Cleopatra's fleeing galley completes the movement begun on her Silician barge. Milton's allusion might be said to read the battle at Actium as wholly a conflict between Antony and Cleopatra, although he might not otherwise find congenial the intense erotic wager. The pressure of the Shakespearean plot—there the political crisis becomes the sexual crisis—breaks through the surface of Milton's text at the entrance of Dalila, because the scene is of her *entrance,* like Cleopatra's, the epiphany of the female.

The allusion therefore holds out the possibility of a triumphant sexuality, of another defeat at Actium. Yet the meaning of such a defeat (or conversely, of victory) is very poorly explicated by conventional allegories: for example, of male reason and female passion. The question of sex will irrevocably disrupt the moral equilibrium of Milton's psychomachia, as we shall see, in some surprising ways. The allusion to Shakespeare's play locates the meeting of Samson and Dalila just at the intersection of two homologous chains of symbolic equations: the first sequence, femininity-clothing-ship-Dalila/Cleopatra, intersects crucially with a second, which can be extrapolated from passages such as the following:

> How could I once look up, or heave the head,
> Who like a foolish Pilot have shipwreckt
> My vessel trusted to me from above,
> Gloriously rigg'd . . .
>
> (197–200)

The "vessel" collects or implies the constituent elements of Samson's election: his strength, the secret of his hair (which he must contain), his ordained mission. The second chain is thus: masculinity-election-ship-Samson/Antony. Representing both Samson and Dalila as ships repeats at the level of the drama's figurations their narrative doubling. The figurative and intertextual chains intersect at the point at which Samson is seduced ("shipwrecked") or at which certain properties specific to Samson's identity can be transferred to Dalila. That point also marks the loss of an authority that Milton generally signifies by *posture*: "How could I once look up or heave the head." References to posture are distributed throughout the drama, from the "languished head unpropped," Samson's opening stance, to the "head erect" with which he addresses his final taunt to the Philistines. Indeed it is characteristic of Milton's major works to register the condition of the protagonist by the capacity to "stand." At this point, we may subsume all such figures under the master sign of the phallus, in Lacanian psychoanalytic theory the signifier by which the hierarchy of sexual difference structures and is structured by language itself.[11] As the master term in both the practice and the rhetoric of sexual difference, the phallus organizes the figurative complexes of Milton's drama. For example, Dalila is what Freud called the "phallic woman," by which he does not mean a "masculine" woman but the fantasy of a woman who possesses a phallus.[12] Dalila's appropriation of the phallic property is quite selective, but her "usurpation" has the effect of a horrifying revelation, an *unveiling*: "She's gone, a manifest Serpent by her Sting / Discovered in the end, till now concealed" (997–98). The chorus is reacting at this moment to Dalila's presentation of herself as deliverer of her people (975–95). Such a revelation exposes her femininity as only a mask, but is that not what femininity has already been determined to mean in the scene of Dalila's entrance, with its foregrounding of clothing? Dalila is always an image of *heightened* femininity.[13] The figure who emerges from her portrait, and who is empowered to double the masculine protagonist as the phallic woman, possesses no consistent identity but displays a shifting mask, the moral sign of deviousness or concealment.

On the other hand, it is Samson's fixity that constitutes his identity, his idée fixe. He must identify himself with his election, a concept virtually defined by singleness of purpose. The successful assertion of that identity is thus united to the completion of his ordained task: "Samson hath quit himself like Samson." The structural antithesis between Samson's election and Dalila's sexuality accords with the psychoanalytic hypothesis that identification is at base sexual identification.[14] The paradigm for the subversion of identity is thus the confusion of gender, as in the incident where masculine and feminine dress are exchanged in *Antony and Cleopatra* (2.5.20–23); clothing conceals and therefore contains the phallus. At one point Antony is compelled to assert, "I am Antony yet" (3.12.92), a virtual admission of the contrary. Later the admission is outright, this time imaged as the rupture of a container or as the state of dissolution ("here I am Antony, / Yet cannot hold this visible shape" 4.14.13). *Samson* enacts the same drama of masculine identification with the same complex figures. To say that Samson is no longer Samson, that he is no longer a man, that he is no longer God's chosen, is in every case to say that he is drowned in the sea upon which both Cleopatra and Dalila embark in their potent vessels.

It should be possible now to estimate the general as well as local effects of Milton's allusion to *Antony and Cleopatra*. The association of Antony with Samson, Cleopatra with Dalila, places Milton's redaction of the Judges story into the context of a seduction narrative that reflects a mythological archetype in the relationship of Mars and Venus (or of the martial and the venereal). When Milton recalls the archetype in his allusion to Shakespeare, the effect is to archaize a conflict that would otherwise establish itself in immediate relation to the contemporary Puritan institutions of vocation and marriage. The archetypal contest of the martial and venereal (a primitive "division of labor") can be invoked as the precedent for the conflict between Samson and Dalila, but it is not really possible for the conflict to be resolved in those anachronistic terms. The allusion is intended as an ideological buttress to the argument against "female usurpation"; the martial-venereal complement is superimposed upon the contradiction between work and home by means of allusion to Shakespeare's play. The pressure of that contradiction is exposed, as though the text had worn thin, in the transformation of Cleopatra's barge into a merchant vessel. The richness associated with Cleopatra's seductiveness, a wealth that seems inexhaustible, becomes in the figure of Dalila an uncertain return upon an investment. Shakespeare's story of seduction outside of marriage delights in its prodigality, its refusal of economic rationality. Cleopatra's person "beggar[s] all description." Milton tends to represent sexual relation rather as an investment of libido, if not money.[15] The difference between the Shakespearean pretext and Milton's merchant vessel is determined by the latter's subordination of sexuality to the most rational form of the libidinal economy— marriage.

Samson is in the very odd position of having been seduced by his own wife, but for Milton no other seduction could have been more powerful. Seduction within marriage removes the narrative from the domain of sexual ethics and places it within the newer Protestant practice of the discipline of everyday life. While traditional Christian morality demanded moderation of sexual appetite even within marriage, these demands became particularly urgent when sex was as rigorously confined to marriage as it was in the new discipline of the Protestant household.[16] As Foucault has demonstrated in his recent researches, such supposed inhibitions enhance the *value* of sexuality.[17] Samson falls into the trap of overvaluing the erotic object not because he has yielded to a sinful sexual relation (within marriage, how could he?) but rather because the sexual relation has come to signify the *whole* of domestic life. We are already well within the synecdoche of sexuality-for-the-domestic upon which psychoanalysis is founded.[18]

The containment of sexuality within marriage—and hence the need to control the body of the female, the repository of libidinal wealth or capital—produces a new discipline and a new historical form of discipline's failure. Seduction by the female means really what seduces the male away from the public vocation, means really seduction by the domestic realm itself. The language of asceticism and of traditional sexual morality are carried over into the Protestant disciplinary regime not as an accurate reflection of practice but as the condition for the misrecognition of the contradiction between work and home. Where the division of social life promises to deliver an area of relaxation from discipline (the private household), *there* is the crucial arena of struggle. This contradiction in the discourse and practice of privacy is the condition of Milton's analysis of marriage (including Samson's marriage) and the occasion for the remedy of divorce.[19]

4. Castration

In the sexualized language by which the narrative represents the contradiction of work and home, Samson's seduction by Dalila results in his castration or effeminization. If the disciplinary requirement of sexual restraint even (or especially) within marriage functions to attach phallic symbology to Samson—he is identified as both masculine and indivisible when his body represents the phallus to his constituents—then we are in a position to understand why the sexual union of Samson and Dalila will evoke castration. Of course, such a thesis is less than surprising, but I would like to propose that in fact there is no castration in the biblical story. There Samson's relation to Dalila is simply one of desire and gratification. She wears him down with pleading, not by any arts of sexual seduction.[20] That Milton diverges from his biblical pretext also is doubtless no surprise, yet there is an essential discrimination to be made here. Castration in *Samson* is consequent upon the failure of the disciplinary regime, which does not avoid temptation but seeks it out. This discipline means just the opposite of Origen's *reductio ad absurdum,* his extreme assertion of sexual abstinence. Hence, while in symbolic castration the allusion is always to the loss of the sexual organs, castration enters the story of Samson not to indicate this loss but to have this loss figure something else, namely the failure of the political aim, the liberation of the Israelites.

Some of Freud's disciples have argued that we should understand by castration any primal or traumatic "cutting off," a meaning certainly broad enough to include the "sense of Heav'n's desertion." I would rather maintain the strictly Freudian view and ask why this desertion must be represented as a phallic loss. What can be demonstrated now, in looking more closely at the scene of castration, is the peculiar victory of the private, the domestic, over the public, even the political. By this victory I do not mean only the victory of Dalila over Samson, which is of course temporary. I refer to the victory of privatization, by which the interior sexual drama comes to seem more real than the public life, by which the public life comes to seem only a version of the libidinal economy. Hence the scene of castration displays nothing so much as the original *subversion* of the public by the private:

> Fearless of danger, like a petty God
> I walk'd about admir'd of all and dreaded
> On hostile ground, none daring my affront.
> Then swoll'n with pride into the snare I fell
> Of fair fallacious looks, venereal trains,
> Soft'n'd with pleasure and voluptuous life;
> At length to lay my head and hallow'd pledge
> Of all my strength in the lascivious lap
> Of a deceitful Concubine who shore me
> Like a tame Wether . . .
>
> (529–38)

The passage narrates a fall from public fame into private pleasure, but at the same time it tells this story as if the phallus were the protagonist. The movement of the phallus through the passage blatantly imitates the trajectory of coition. Here the distinction between the phallus and the penis is of particular relevance, because what is "standing" for one is just the opposite for the other. Indulgence in sexual pleasures is already effeminization; to be "swoll'n" is already to be "soft'n'd." This is the paradox by which egregious exercises of restraint come to signify patriarchal standing.[21]

If Samson's failure is necessarily represented as sexual seduction, however, we need to remember that the phallic narrative is a translation of what actually occurs—the telling of the secret, the failure to contain certain words. Sexuality is only the context for this utterance, yet the scene of telling is so completely encased in its erotic shell that it disappears from view. In his recounting, Samson substitutes an erotic gratification for the telling of the secret. So far from having yielded with irritation or weariness to Dalila's importunity, this version makes the telling a pleasure, even a sexual pleasure. The moment of telling represents a contamination, which operates in both directions—not only the politicization of an erotic bond, but the sexualization of the public life. Samson confuses his secret with the private pleasure of his sexual relation: when he "publishes" the secret, he constructs a verbal bridge by which sexuality itself invades the realm of the public. The narrative of Samson's life is thus written upon what moves back and forth from the public to the private—his *body*. His hair, his eyes, his genitals signify in both domains. Or perhaps it would be more accurate to say that the public and the private already inhabit the body, precisely as the difference between Samson's hair as a public testimony of the Nazarite vow and as the secret repository of his strength, or as the difference between the phallus and the private parts.[22]

The failure of discipline acknowledged in the seduction, the "blab-bing" of his secret, discovers a metonymy by which the materiality of language is itself signified in the exchange of body parts, an exchange occasioned and regulated by a severe linguistic-sexual discipline. Samson's loss of control over his tongue, instrument of both seduc-tion and betrayal, is a kind of parapraxis. In order to prevent such a slip, not only the body must be controlled—language must be controlled. That control doubtless has a transhistorical element in the simple sense that the dominant have always embedded their domina-tion in the "nature" of language itself. But in the early modern period, that control is reorganized and intensified as a means of dealing with the ambivalence excited by the newly privatized domain of the bourgeois household, the site of enhanced discipline *and* pleasure. In Milton's drama, this ambivalence is signaled by Samson's desire to tell his secret, the secret that is none other than the secret of sexual subjection, the same secret psychoanalysis still elicits from its subjects by relaxing the discipline of speech. The narrative of seduction has the paradoxical effect of obscuring the fact of this desire for unregulated exchange (of speech, of bodies). When Dalila seeks to discover Samson's "capital secret," she is really asking for the knowledge that is also power. We might paraphrase her request as "What is the source of Samson's [masculine] strength?" The symbolic avatar of the phallus is revealed to Dalila in a reified form, accurately characterized by Samson as "slight," as truly an imposture. By cutting his hair, Dalila effects a double coup, obstructing Samson's public calling and over-turning the hierarchy of the *domus*—but again, only temporarily. It is important to emphasize that sexual subjection is not merely a matter of withholding knowledge from the female, but that it is perpetuated as an actually indivisible complex of knowledge and power, as the conjunction of phallocentrism with an enforced division of labor. Hence, while a desire to be relieved of phallic responsibility can be indulged in the fiction of being seduced, the invisible but still potent division of labor will reassert itself when necessary by *dissolving* the household.

5. Divorce

Telling his secret removes Samson from public life, interrupts his vocation, and places him in the power of the insubordinate female tongue (hence the complaint elsewhere in the drama about Dalila's "tongue batteries"). We can consider now a rhetorico-anatomical formula for Samson's castration: the subordination of the phallus to the tongue. Yet that subordination has also been secretly desired: it is a catastrophe and at the same time a relief from phallic discipline. If language and the body are indissolubly linked in the system of sexual subjection, we may say that the female tongue speaks for the otherwise silent female organ, the vagina.[23] Samson falls by the agency of the tongue but he falls into Dalila's "lap" (one meaning of which in the seventeenth century was "female pudenda"). Neither for Samson nor for Milton's contemporaries is this an unequivocally unfortunate fall. The vagina is the first home and the model of the *domus*; it is the bower that Milton associates frequently in *Paradise Lost* with the female body. It is also what Samson calls, in an exquisite image of ambivalence, a *snare* (230: "my accomplisht snare"; other examples at 409, 532, 931). In fact *Samson* provides a lexicon of specular images for the female genitalia: *trains, gins, toils,* and everything else that entangles man with woman. I propose now to consider what the disentangling of Samson from Dalila means, and to do this we need to look at what marital reconciliation might restore. Here is Dalila making her strongest offer:

>   though sight be lost
> Life yet hath many solaces, enjoy'd
> Where other senses want not their delights
> At home in leisure and domestic ease,
> Exempt from many a care and chance to which
> Eyesight exposes daily men abroad.
> I to the Lords will intercede, not doubting
> Thir favorable ear, that I may fetch thee
> From forth this loathsome prison-house to abide
> With me, where my redoubl'd love and care
> With nursing diligence, to me glad office,
> May ever tend about thee to old age

With all things grateful cheer'd, and so supplied,
That what by me thou has lost thou least shall miss.

(914–27)

The contradiction within the home between pleasure and discipline is seen to recapitulate the crisis of transition from pre-Oedipal to Oedipal sexuality. Dalila offers a restoration not simply of the marital bond but of the pre-Oedipal condition of maternal bonding. It is this choice that underlies the alternatives of returning to the father's house or to the wife's. Dalila will relieve Samson of his grief by reinstating the relation that preceded the anxiety of phallic loss; only the threat of that loss had the power once to dislodge the male child from his narcissistic attachment to the mother. What Dalila offers to Samson then is a return to a privacy much more intense than a marital reconciliation could ever establish. "At home" with her, Samson would be both husband and child ("in most things as a child"); infantilization is disclosed as the state beyond or (historically) before castration. The Oedipus complex precedes and heralds, in introducing the rule of the father, the divorce enacted by the husband in each gesture of sexual subjection, in each departure from the home. The finalization of Samson's divorce becomes inevitable when Dalila is made to take up a position not only against the duty of Samson's vocation but against the father. Dalila's house is one that no father will ever enter; and therefore Samson will never "miss" what by Dalila he has "lost."

It has been my assumption that *Samson Agonistes,* as the prototype of the bourgeois career drama, already reads that drama against the background of its Oedipal precursor. But this is by no means to say that relations between work and home are determined by eternal psychological verities. On the contrary, the historically specific constitution of the home is the condition for the way in which psychogenesis is recalled—Freud's "*Nachträglichkeit*"—or called to the aid of particular social practices of subjection. This is never more the case than with Freud's discovery in the female subject (wife and mother) of a natural hostility to civilization, by which he means the labor of the male:

> Women represent the interests of the family and of sexual life.
> The work of civilization has become increasingly the business
> of men, it confronts them with ever more difficult tasks and
> compels them to carry out institutional sublimations of which
> women are little capable. Since a man does not have unlimited

quantities of psychical energy at his disposal, he has to
accomplish his tasks by making an expedient distribution of
his libido. What he employs for cultural aims he to a great
extent withdraws from women and sexual life. His constant
association with men, and his dependence on his relations
with them, even estrange him from his duties as a husband
and father. Thus the woman finds herself forced into the
background by the claims of civilization and she adopts a
hostile attitude towards it.

(S. E. 21:103–4)

The hypothesis of a psychically determined female antipathy to
masculine labor is the transhistorical theory by which the sexual
division of labor is misrecognized as the conflict between sexuality and
labor. It is no longer possible to deny that the disqualification of
female labor as work, even the total subsidization of the wife in some
bourgeois households, is a historical form of the sexual division of
labor. Yet it must also be said that psychoanalysis provides a
paradoxically accurate account of the *operation* of misrecognition,
since Freud's conflation of infantile psychogenesis and human prehis-
tory is very much like Milton's transposition of contemporary social
formations to the context of an ethically paradigmatic biblical narrative. We need only advance the concept of *Nachträglichkeit* onto the
terrain of history to remember what Freud always misremembers,
that the "civilization" of which he writes is bounded by the bourgeois
revolutions of the early modern period, and to remember as well that
the marriage of Samson and Dalila is an example of a seventeenth-
century social practice.

The difficult historical question passed over by Freud's theory is
posed, without answer, by Norbert Elias in his major study, *The
Civilizing Process*: "Why the occupational work that became a general
way of life with the rise of the bourgeoisie should necessitate a
particularly strict disciplining of sexuality is a question in its own
right."[24] Indeed, it is the overwhelming question of Foucault's
researches into the history of discipline, and while we can do no more
here than acknowledge the magnitude of the question, we can be
relatively certain that the modern forms of sexual subjection derive
their programs from the conjuncture between the disciplining of
sexuality and the reorganization of social and economic life in the
sixteenth and seventeenth centuries.[25] Milton belongs to the history of
discipline most especially as the advocate of divorce, which is for him
not so much a relaxation of discipline as it is the remedy of the

contradiction between work and home.[26] Divorce sacrifices marriage itself (or the wife) to the higher calling of the male, when the household no longer functions efficiently as both the refuge from the discipline of masculine labor and as the locus for the disciplining of sexuality (what Freud recognizes in his phrase, "an expedient distribution of . . . libido"). The contradiction of work and home is the condition for the representation of Samson's ascetic vocation, as it is for the representation of Dalila's seduction of Samson within marriage. The central panel of *Samson Agonistes* is thus recognizably an example of that domestic drama with which we are now so familiar, not the comedy of courtship but the "tragic" social practice Milton called the discipline of divorce, a programmatic attempt to control the bodies of men and women—as a last resort—by disentangling them.

7

Patriarchal Territories:
The Body Enclosed

Peter Stallybrass

In his essay "Techniques of the Body," Marcel Mauss uses the term *habitus* to define the acquired abilities—the motions, postures, and gestures—of the body:

> These "habits" do not just vary with individuals and their imitations, they vary especially between societies, educations, proprieties and fashions, prestiges. In them, we should see the techniques and work of collective and individual practical reason rather than, in the ordinary way, merely the soul and its repetitive faculties. [1]

To analyze the habits of the body, then, is not only to trace the individual development of the subject but also to investigate what Pierre Bourdieu calls "the insignificant details of dress, bearing, physical and verbal manners" as the inscribed principles of "the arbitrary content of the culture." [2]

> The social formation of the body is the more effective because it extorts the essential while seeming to demand the insignificant: in obtaining the respect for form and forms of respect which constitute the most visible and at the same time the best hidden (because most "natural") manifestation of submission to the established order, the incorporation of the arbitrary abolishes what Raymond Ruyer calls "lateral possibilities," that is, all the eccentricities and deviations which are the small change of madness. [3]

To examine the body's formation is to trace the connections between politeness and politics. But because these connections are never simply given, the body can itself become a site of conflict.

In *Rabelais and His World*, [4] Bakhtin attempts to map out that site, although he concentrates on the body as *locus* of class conflict to the

123

exclusion of gender, a point to which I shall return. Bakhtin's interpretation of the differentiated "habits" of the Renaissance body works out from the rhetorical ploys of Rabelais's text to an opposition between the grotesque body and the classical body. The grotesque body is "unfinished, outgrows itself, transgresses its own limits" (p. 26); it is "not separated from the world by clearly defined boundaries" (p. 27). The classical body is, on the contrary, an image of "finished, completed" man; as it is formed within the canons of the absolutist state, "the opaque surface and the body's 'valleys' acquire an essential meaning as the border of a closed individuality that does not merge with other bodies and with the world" (p. 320). The grotesque emphasizes those parts of the body "that are open to the outside world," "the open mouth, the genital organs, the breasts, the phallus, the potbelly, the nose" (p. 26). If it privileges an area, it is the anus and it celebrates dung as the fertilizer of material life, whereas the classical emphasizes the head as the seat of reason, transcending the "merely" bodily. The grotesque body's favored space is the marketplace where it enjoys "a certain extraterritoriality in a world of official order and official ideology" (p. 154); in the "liberties" of the marketplace it can speak the language of festive obscenity and abuse. The language of the classical body, by contrast, is the "tongue of official literature or of the ruling classes," a language governed by the hierarchy and etiquette of "palaces, churches, institutions, and private homes" (p. 154). It is precisely these privileged places that the grotesque interrogates and subverts, since it rejects "all the forms of inhuman necessity that direct the prevailing concept of the world" (p. 49).

This opposition between the grotesque and the classical defines two canons "in their pure, one might say extreme form" (p. 30). But historically, as Bakhtin notes, they were not fixed and immutable. They were indeed diacritical, each in turn formed by the redrawing of the boundaries of the other. If we can imagine a precise shape for the grotesque body in the sixteenth and seventeenth centuries, it is only in opposition to the development of new canons that distinguished the "correct" techniques of the body even as they carefully distinguished between "familiar speech and 'correct' language" (p. 320). It is the formation of these "correct" techniques that Norbert Elias examines in *The History of Manners,* the first volume of *The Civilising Process.*[5] At first sight, this book looks like a curious collection of quotations (mainly from the sixteenth and seventeenth centuries) arranged into chapters "On Behaviour at Table," "On Blowing One's Nose," "On Spitting," "On Behaviour in the Bedroom," etc. But in the context of the second volume of *The Civilising Process, Power and Civility,* it is clear that Elias is actually mapping out the relation between state formation and the formation of new kinds of behavior "under the watchword of *civilité*."[6]

In particular, Elias traces the development of concepts of *civilité* following the publication of Erasmus' massively influential *De civilitate morum puerilium* (1530), a book concerned with "outward bodily propriety." Elias argues that during the sixteenth century "in conjunction with the new power relationships the social imperative not to offend others becomes more binding."[7] But the very notion of social "offence" depended upon transformed thresholds of embarrassment and shame that marked a simultaneous process of social and bodily differentiation:

> In the sixteenth century, Monteil tells us, in France as everywhere else, the common people blow their noses without a handkerchief, but among the bourgeoisie it is accepted practice to use the sleeve. As for the rich, they carry a handkerchief in their pockets; therefore, to say that a man has wealth, one says that he does not blow his nose on his sleeve.[8]

The adoption of handkerchiefs, forks, separate eating bowls in the sixteenth and seventeenth centuries was a means of establishing social purity through bodily purity. The enclosure of the body, the "cleansing" of the orifices, emphasized the borders of a closed individuality at the same time as it separated off the social elite from the "vulgar."

During the same period, sumptuary laws were extended and enforced. In England, the Act of 1533 closely defined the relation between social status and dress, and in Elizabeth's reign the Act was reinforced through nine royal proclamations on apparel. In 1559–60, watches were appointed in London to look for people wearing "great hose and other unlawful apparel," and in May 1562 a proclamation was specifically directed against the "monstrous abuse of apparel almost in all estates, but principally in the meaner sort."[9] The etymological connections between "decoration" and "decorum," "polite" and "police" were made into legal connections. If, as Bourdieu says, "the concessions of *politeness* always contain *political* concessions,"[10] polite society still needed policing to ensure those "concessions" in "the meaner sort."

But bodily definitions were as important in the mapping out of gender as of class, although Bakhtin and Elias are largely silent on this issue, assuming an "ungendered"—i.e., implicitly male—body. In this they repeat the early Elizabethan proclamations on apparel that legislate men's dress but are silent on women's. It was not until 1574

that a proclamation regulated the details of women's apparel.[11] This
tardiness in the statutes should be seen as a sign less of women's
liberties than of the implicit assumption that women's bodies were
already the object of policing by fathers and husbands. Thus Gouge,
for instance, demanded that the wife submit herself to her husband as
"a King to governe and aid her, a Priest to pray with her and for her,
a Prophet to teach and instruct her." Even "such tokens of familiarity
as are not withall tokens of subjection and reverence are unbeseeming
a wife."[12] And William Whately clearly defined the position of the
"ideal" wife in his wedding sermon, *A Bride-Bush*: "The whole duty
of the wife is referred to two heads. The first is, to acknowledge her
inferiority: the next to carry her selfe as inferior."[13] But Whately, like
many writers of Renaissance conduct books, detected a problem: how
could the "necessary" obedience be inscribed in what he considered
the most recalcitrant of animals, woman? Only, he suggested,
through a rigorous program of "education," reinforced by the implicit threat of violence. Woman is a horse to be broken in, only
properly trained when "shee submits herselfe with quietness, cheer-
fully, even as a well-broken horse turnes at the least check of the riders
bridle, readily going and standing as he wishes that sits upon his
backe."[14] And Snawsel listed the techniques to "tame" a wife
(including beating and deliberate changes of mood) and compared
them favorably to the methods used "to tame lions, bulls, and
elephants."[15]

Gouge, Whately, and Snawsel share with Erasmus the desire to
inculcate new techniques of the body. Where they differ from
Erasmus is in the assumption that woman's body, unlike the prince's,
is *naturally* "grotesque." It must be subjected to constant surveillance
precisely because, as Bakhtin says of the grotesque body, it is
"unfinished, outgrows itself, transgresses its own limits."[16] The
surveillance of women concentrated upon three specific areas: the
mouth, chastity, the threshold of the house. These three areas were
frequently collapsed into each other. The connection between speaking and wantonness was common to legal discourse and conduct
books. A man who was accused of slandering a woman by calling her
"whore" might defend himself by claiming that he meant "whore of
her tonge," not "whore of her body."[17] And Toste wrote in a
marginal gloss to his translation of Varchi's *The Blazon of Jealousie*:

> Maides must be seene, not heard, or selde or never,
> O may I such one wed, if I wed ever.
> A Maide that hath a lewd Tongue in her head,
> Worse than if she were found with a Man in bed.[18]

Similarly, Barbaro writes in his treatise *On Wifely Duties*: "It is proper . . . that not only arms but indeed also the speech of women never be made public; for the speech of a noble woman can be no less dangerous than the nakedness of her limbs."[19] Silence, the closed mouth, is made a sign of chastity. And silence and chastity are, in turn, homologous to woman's enclosure within the house. Thus Vives writes that "maides should be kept at home, and not goe abroad, except it be to heare divine service," and Samuel Rowlands in a poem denouncing "Salomons Harlot" claims that, in her "brutish filthynesse," she

> Is noted to be full of words,
> And doth the streets frequent,
> Not qualitied as Sara was,
> To keepe within the tent.[20]

The signs of the "harlot" are her linguistic "fullness" and her frequenting of public space. In contrast, the ideal wife is represented by Venus with her foot upon a tortoise, signifying in Alciati's *Emblematum liber* (1531) "that women should remain at home and be chary of speech."[21] We are not, of course, addressing here the local mechanisms of social control, differentiated by both class and region, to which women were subject, nor women's resistances to them both collectively and individually, but the production of a normative "Woman" within the discursive practices of the ruling elite. This "Woman," like Bakhtin's classical body, is rigidly "finished": her signs are the enclosed body, the closed mouth, the locked house.

In the process, "woman," unlike man, is produced as a *property* category. The conceptualization of woman as land or possession has, of course, a long history. The Commandments catalog wife, maid, ox, and ass side by side as a man's assets and in the Jewish code betrothal was classified as a form of masculine acquisition, related to the acquisition of slaves, cattle, and other belongings.[22] In early modern England, "woman" was articulated as property not only in legal discourse ("by marriage the very being or legal existence of a woman is suspended")[23] but also in economic and political discourse. Economically, she is the fenced-in enclosure of the landlord, her father, or husband. Thus Toste states:

> Property or Right is a kinde of Interest or Clayme, which one challengeth to any thing as his owne, and as peculiar and proper to himselfe, and wherein no other can (truely) demand

any share or part. Yea, so peremptory are some men in this point (especially if they know that they may lawfully challenge this high pris'd commoditie of love as their owne, and that they have payed for the same) as they have cast off their Wives, and Mistresses, onely upon a meere suspicion. . . .[24]

Though Toste does not approve such "castings off," he has no doubt that men can claim "this high-pris'd commoditie of love" as their property or right. But unlike most property, this property can bring dishonor to the landlord even as he possesses it. *"Covert,"* the wife becomes her husband's symbolic capital; "free," she is the opening through which that capital disappears. So, Toste argues, "when this our high-pric'd Commoditie chanceth to light into some other merchants hands, and that our private Inclosure proveth to be a Common for others, we care no more for it" (p. 20). By constructing the beloved entirely within the economic discourses of commodities and enclosures, Toste is able to maintain the distinction between woman as passive possession (even in adultery) and man as active agent, as merchant.

This clear-cut opposition comes under stress in Marlowe's *The Massacre at Paris*, where Guise's possession of his wife is threatened by his "tenant" Mugeron, to whom a soldier says:

> you put in that which displeaseth him, and so forestall his market, and set up your standing where you should not; and whereas he is your landlord, you will take upon you to be his, and till the ground which he himself should occupy which is his own free land; if it be not too free—there's the question. . . .[25]

The landlord (the Duke) possesses his "free land" (the Duchess) only on condition that it is safely fenced off against trespassers. But the concept of "free" property becomes radically unstable when applied to a person. The Duchess is both Guise's freehold, his commodity, and free in that, however hedged about, her will may be "liberal." She is in other words a version of the Renaissance *topos* that presents woman as that treasure which, however locked up, always escapes. She is the gaping mouth, the open window, the body that "transgresses its own limits" and negates all those boundaries without which property could not be constituted.

We find this same fear of instability when woman is mapped out within political discourse. Thus, Wye Saltonstall's "A Mayde" is inscribed both as enclosure for fear that she will become common land and as monarchy for fear that she will become a commonwealth:

> Let Maids then give to one their loves and selfe,
> To be a Monarchy no Commonwealth.[26]

But most contemporary political apologists were at pains to deny any opposition between monarchy and commonwealth. Saltonstall tries to negotiate this problem in the following lines:

> Though good be better'd by community,
> Yet since that love and Soveraighnty do know
> No partners, but consist in unity:
> Maids should not let their loves too common grow.[27]

This is scarcely a resolution. It is claimed both that good is "better'd by community" and that monarchy depends upon "unity," but this leaves the "maid" in the contradictory position mapped out in Saltonstall's preface to the poem, where she is commanded to be "modest, curteous, constant" and, at the same time, "not too coy."[28] "Too coy"/"too common": the maid is constituted as the inevitable object of criticism. She lacks either kindness or chastity.

When women were themselves the objects to be mapped out, virginity and marital "chastity" were pictured as fragile states to be maintained by the surveillance of wives and daughters. But paradoxically the normative "Woman" could become the emblem of the perfect and impermeable container, and hence a map of the integrity of the state. The state, like the virgin, was a *hortus conclusus*, an enclosed garden walled off from enemies. In the Ditchley portrait, Elizabeth I is portrayed standing upon a map of England.[29] As she ushers in the rule of a golden age, she is the imperial virgin, symbolizing, at the same time as she is symbolized by, the *hortus conclusus* of the state. In a Dutch engraving of 1598, Elizabeth's body encloses all Europe:[30] her breasts are France and the Low Countries, her left arm is England and Scotland, her right arm is Italy. Under her left arm, an island is enclosed by a fence against the Catholic navies. What the two pictures share is the conjuncture of imperial virgin and cartographic image, which together constitute the terrain of Elizabethan rule.

The meaning of that symbolic conjuncture should be located within specific developments of the state. The map on which Elizabeth stands in the Ditchley portrait is Saxton's map of 1583, and the major advances in English mapmaking during the 1570s and 1580s were determined by the administrative needs of central government. Those "needs" were shaped both by foreign policy and by internal colonialism: for the former, maps were required to chart the coast and to prepare defensive fortifications against invasion; for the latter, they were needed in the appropriation and "redistribution" of Irish land, in depicting the locations of justices of the peace, in "determining the best routes for the increasing volume of correspondence between the administrative centre and the periphery," and in the formation of "a more detailed knowledge of the internal topography and resources . . . of provincial society within England."[31] Mapping was, then, an instrument in the charting of ideological, as well as geographical, boundaries.

And as the nation-state was formed according to new canons of incorporation and exclusion, so was the female body refashioned. In this refashioning, Elizabeth functioned both as emblem of national "integrity" and as embarrassing contradiction. As emblem of "integrity," she was the privileged term in a system of antithetical thinking (what Le Roy called the "comparing of contraries")[32] that was central to absolutist political theory. Within one English version of this theory, Elizabeth was Una, the unity of church and state, the pure virgin who had abandoned "the cuppe of spirituall abhominations";[33] she was set in opposition to Duessa, the false church, a whore who, in *The Faerie Queene*, has at "her rompe" a fox's tail "with dong all fowly dight" (1.8.48). The enclosed body is valorized by contrast to the demonized grotesque. Duessa's dirt is, as Mary Douglas says of all dirt, "the by-product of a systematic ordering and classification of matter, in so far as ordering involves rejecting inappropriate elements."[34] Dirt is necessary to construct the concept of cleanliness, or as James I put it in his *Daemonologie*, "there can be no better way to know God, than by the contrarie."[35] It is as the contrary of "Bloody Mary" that the Virgin Queen could be constituted in Breton's "Elogy" as "*semper eadem*, alwaies one, zealous in one religion, believinge in one God, constant in one truth, absolute under God in her selfe, one Queene, and but one Queene," the transformer of her kingdom into "a paradice on earth" or, at least, "a gardein of no smale grace."[36] But not only was Elizabeth the maker of that "paradice" or "gardein"; her enclosed body *was* that paradise (a word derived from the Persian *pairidaeza*, meaning a royal enclosure).[37] Projected onto a religious plane, her body was the garden of the Song of Songs, which was interpreted both as the body of the Virgin and as the body of a church that John King portrayed as "a several, peculiar, enclosed peece of ground," a *hortus conclusus* that "lieth within a hedge or fense," separated off from "the *grape of Sodome* or *cluster of Gomorrhe*."[38]

We are dealing here with an ideological configuration that had real effects. The contraries or "inappropriate elements" were concepts applied to actual women, constituting them as sinners and criminals to be purified or exterminated. The godly mother is opposed to the witch who gives suck to a satanic familiar. The pelican who pecks her breast to feed her young on her own blood has as her demonized opposite the woman who kills her child. There were legal consequences to these "comparing of contraries": after 1560, "infanticide, rarely recorded in fourteenth- and fifteenth-century assize files, began to be regularly indicted, an English symptom of the 'infanticide craze' which affected much of western Europe, and which may have resulted in more executions than the famous witch craze."[39] The ideological formation of the family and the state was staked out across the physical bodies of "criminalized" women.

But how could a Virgin Queen be an appropriate emblem for an absolutist theory that founded state rule (*imperium*) in family rule (*dominium*)?[40] For Bodin, as for Filmer, the family is established by the enclosure of private property, and that property is under the absolute control of the father.[41] The patriarchalist connection between father and monarch is clearly stated in Filmer's *Observations . . . Touching Forms of Government*, where he writes:

1. That there is no form of government, but monarchy only.
2. That there is no monarchy, but paternal.
3. That there is no paternal monarchy, but absolute, or arbitrary.[42]

Filmer, of course, was writing in the seventeenth century under a male monarch, but the relation between Elizabeth and family rule had deeply troubled Elizabethan patriarchalists. In 1559, John Aylmer claimed that "a woman maye rule as a magistrate, yet obey as a wife."[43] And Edmund Tilney dedicted *A Brief and Pleasant Discourse of Duties in Mariage* (1568) to Elizabeth I but he had no doubts in his book that "the man both by reason, and law, hath the soveraigntie over his wyfe" and he thought that equal rights for women might be appropriate for barbarians but not for Christians.[44]

Spenser opened up the problematic terrain of the relation between *imperium* and *dominium* in his presentation of Britomart, an Amazonian maiden. Her overpowering of Guyon at the beginning of book 3 of

The Faerie Queene is the occasion for a digression on a golden age in which women were warriors:

> But by record of antique times I find,
> That women wont in warres to beare most sway,
> And to all great exploits them selves inclind:
> Of which they still the girlond bore away,
> Till envious Men fearing their rules decay,
> Gan coyne streight lawes to curb their liberty. . . .
>
> (3.2.2)

If Britomart is in part a compliment to Elizabeth I, she nonetheless threatens to subvert the basis of *dominium* even as she establishes *imperium*. But when Spenser returns to the problem of female rule in book 5, the book of justice, it is to reassert "mans well ruling hand." Radigund, a "Queene of Amazons" (5.4.33), overcomes Artegall, and makes him her vassal, clothing him "In womans weedes, that is to manhood shame" (5.5.20). Spenser does not leave the moral of the tale in any doubt:

> Such is the crueltie of womenkynd,
> When they have shaken off the shamefast band,
> With which wise Nature did them strongly bynd,
> T'obay the heasts of mans well ruling hand,
> That then all rule and reason they withstand,
> To purchase a licentious libertie.
> But vertuous women wisely understand,
> That they were borne to base humilitie,
> Unless the heavens them lift to lawfull soveraintie.
>
> (5.5.25)

Elizabeth, then, like Britomart, is the exception who proves the rule of women's "base humilitie"; the patriarchal basis of legitimate authority is restored. But female rule still looks precarious. Why was Elizabeth not subject to "the shamefast band" of "wise Nature"? Why did she not obey "mans well ruling hand"? These questions that troubled the "legitimate" discourses of patriarchalism could also be inscribed within popular sedition. Thus, John Feltwell, a laborer, argued that the queen was "but a woman and ruled by noblemen," and Thomas Wenden, a Colchester yeoman, claimed that the queen was "an arrant whore."[45]

The elaboration of the cult of Elizabeth was partly an attempt to neutralize these contradictions. On the one hand, she was the object of "amorous admiration," and hence the people's love was, as Harrington put it, "their choice, and not her compulsion."[46] As woman, then, she could be the idealized beloved, to whom was ascribed the devotion of amatory discourse. But, on the other hand, she belonged to an anomalous category, being both mother of her people and virgin. Thus, as Shirley Ardener argues, she could escape the category of "woman" and "take advantage of being the 'third sex,' and available for deification."[47]

Within the dominant discourses of early modern England, then, woman's body could be both symbolic map of the "civilized" and the dangerous terrain that had to be colonized. These conceptualizations can be related to the contradictory formation of woman within the categories of gender and of class. To emphasize gender is to construct women-as-the-same: women are constituted as a single category, set over against the category of men. To emphasize class is to differentiate *between* women, dividing them into distinct social groups. Insofar as women are differentiated, those in the dominant social classes are allocated privileges they can confer (status, wealth). In societies where heterosexuality and marriage are prescribed, those privileges can only be conferred back on *men,* so the differentiation of women simultaneously establishes or reinforces the differentiation of men. The deployment of women into different classes, then, is in the interests of the ruling elite, because it helps to perpetuate and to naturalize class structure.

Oppressed groups, on the other hand, by denying the class differentiation of women, may attack aristocratic privilege. But when the elimination of class boundaries is produced by the collapsing of women into a single undifferentiated group, that elimination is commonly articulated within misogynistic discourse. This may help us to understand the contradictory attitudes of the malcontent on the Elizabethan stage. While he sees the social order as an arbitrary and unjust system of court corruption, his political critique leads into a disquisition on the corruption of the court lady. In the first scene of *The Duchess of Malfi,* for instance, whereas Antonio praises the French court for "seeking to reduce both State, and People / To a fix'd Order" (1.1.6–7),[48] Bosola declares that "places in the Court, are but like beds in the hospitall, where this mans head lies at that mans foote, and so lower, and lower" (1.1.67–69). But in the next act, contempt for the court is displaced onto contempt for an old lady, whom Bosola abuses for the "deepe rutts" and "fowle sloughs" of her face, now concealed by her "scurvy face-physicke" (2.1.26, 24). The lady serves no function in the scene except as an emblem of corruption, but in reviling her, Bosola displaces his own abjection onto a person even more marginal and vulnerable. However much he may despise his own "outward forme of man," he has asserted his gender status over women with their "shop of witchcraft" (2.1.47, 37). Similarly, Flamineo's language in *The White Devil* is a mine of misogynistic commonplaces ("women are like curst dogges" [1.2.188–89]; "Trust a woman? never, never" [5.6.161]). It is notable how frequently the malcontent's analysis of power and corruption reverts to a withering contempt for the artifices of the powerless.

In the process, the malcontent's own situation is effaced, for he himself is the most notable practitioner of the artifices of the powerless. For like the women he despises, he is bought by the highest bidder; like them, his only role is service. On the face of it, it is true, he stands opposed to the "feminization" of a court culture in which, as Joan Kelly-Gadol has argued, the courtier adopted " 'woman's ways' in his relations to the prince."[49] Certainly, the malcontent does not have the "purified" language, the fashionable clothes, or the accomplished manners of the manipulative courtier. But the abrupt "independence" of his discourse obscures the structural dependency he shares with the court lady.

So far, I have posited only two class positions, the one attempting to maintain social closure and exclusion, the other subverting class but reinforcing gender hierarchy. But we may define a third position: that of the class aspirant. Like the members of the male elite, the class aspirant has an interest in preserving social closure, since without it there would be nothing to aspire *to*. But, as the same time, that closure must be sufficiently flexible to incorporate *him*. His conceptualization of woman will as a result be radically unstable: she will be perceived as oscillating between the enclosed body (the purity of the elite to which he aspires) and the open body (or else how could he attain her?), between being "too coy" and "too common."

This unstable conceptualization of the woman corresponds to the instability of the class aspirant's own position. A naked interest in the acquisition of status or wealth through marriage exposes him, like Malvolio, to the contempt of dominant and subordinated classes alike. But within literary discourse, class aspiration can be displaced onto the enchanted ground of romance, where considerations of status are transformed into considerations of sexual success. In the form of desire, this success is the always-deferred moment of final incorporation; in the form of attainment, it is, paradoxically, the imminent threat of loss inscribed within the unstable conceptualization of woman as simultaneously enclosed and open, the passive conferrer of status, and, in the act of union with the aspirant, the active transgressor of status boundaries.

This slippage between women-as-the-same (woman categorized by gender) and women-as-differentiated (woman categorized by class) is foregrounded in *Othello*. It is only if woman is differentiated by class (and race) that Othello's marriage to Desdemona is significant. The prescribed transgression of romance is the displaced condition of Othello's legitimation as Venetian. But that *pre*scription of transgression can only be defined in relation to the *pro*scription that it breaks. Because Desdemona is involved in that transgression, her status is necessarily made problematic. Othello interprets her first as emblem of what Coryat called "that most glorious, renowned and Virgin Citie of Venice"[50] and then as the type of female wantonness, precisely because of her marriage to him, the culturally demonized Other.

In what is still, I believe, the best account of *Othello*, Kenneth Burke wrote:

> Add the privacy of Desdemona's treasure, as vicariously owned by Othello in manly miserliness (Iago represents the threat implicit in such cherishing), and you have a tragic trinity of ownership in the profoundest sense of ownership, the property in human affections, as fetishistically localised in the object of possession, while the possessor is himself possessed by his very engrossment. . . . The single mine-own-ness is thus dramatically split into the three principles of possession, possessor and estrangement (threat of loss). Hence, trust and distrust, though *living in* each other, can be shown *wrestling with* each other. . . . Property fears theft because it is theft.[51]

But to analyze the "conspiracy" (to use Burke's term) that the play performs, we need to add that the "possessor" (Othello) does not have a cultural entitlement to his "possession" (Desdemona) and that, consequently, Desdemona is for Othello a particular form of acquisition. As Burke puts it, "we should encounter also in Othello as lover the theme of the newly rich, the marriage above one's station."[52] For Othello to "gain," though, there must be a mark against him that will be overcome by his marriage. That mark can be located in the construction of Othello as "black."

In an emblem entitled "Art cannot take away the vice of nature," Thynne wrote:

> The healthfull bathe which daielie wee doe see
> to cure the sores and fleshe of lothsome skinn,
> cann never make the Negro white to bee,
> or clense the harlot from her loathed sinne.[53]

In *Othello,* "Negro" and "harlot" are alike the objects of scrutiny: that is, the discourses of racism and misogyny are deployed and interrogated in the play. It is the mark of race (what an imperialist culture labeled "the vice of nature") that is seemingly overcome in the action of the first three scenes. Othello's "lothsome skinn" is transformed: his virtue makes him, in the Duke's words, "far more fair than black" (1.3.290).[54] But to demonstrate his virtue in dramatic terms, it is necessary to portray him not as alien transgressor but as a worthy object of affection. Accordingly, Desdemona is portrayed not as passive beloved but as "half the wooer" (1.3.176). Desdemona's active choice is the seal on Othello's incorporation as Venetian and on his repudiation of the "unhoused, free condition" (1.2.26). But if act 1 depicts the "civilizing" of the military Moor, it also depicts the "uncivilizing" of the city. Desdemona is drawn from "house affairs" (1.3.147) to tales of an undomesticated landscape "of antres vast and deserts idle, / Rough quarries, rocks and hills whose heads touch heaven" (1.3.140–41). And her withdrawal from house affairs and the government of her father marks her out as "untamed."

There is a corresponding transition in the play from the interrogation of Othello's "witchcraft" to the interrogation of "A maiden, never bold" (1.3.94) who transgressed "Against all rules of nature" (1.3.101). The play up until act 2, scene 1 has "a perfect comic structure in miniature," as Susan Snyder has pointed out.[55] Othello triumphs over all obstacles: the *senex iratus,* Brabantio; the accusation of racial inferiority; the storm that separates him from Desdemona; even his own passions, the "light-wing'd toys / Of feather'd Cupid" (1.3.268–69). As acquirer, he is totally successful. But as possessor, he lives with the imminent threat of loss. The very fact that Desdemona was "open" to him endangers her status as his spiritual enclosure, the impermeable container of his honor. So her body must be interrogated and deciphered. But the voyeuristic gaze encounters only the opaque surfaces of the body. If Othello does indeed "grossly gape" (3.3.395), it is not because of any bodily sexuality but because of a linguistic wantonness that ceaselessly elides the cultural opposition between the woman who married him and the category of "woman" constructed within misogynistic discourse, between woman as differentiated by class (the elite maiden) and woman as unified by gender (the daughters of Eve). Deciphering her hand he finds it "liberal" (3.4.46): that is, it is both a generous hand (it "gave away" [3.4.45] her heart to him) and a wanton one. The liberty of her marriage necessitates that she now has "A sequester from liberty" (3.4.40). The problematic within which Othello operates here is one he shares with Renaissance conduct books. Vives, for instance, objects to the maid giving any sign of affection to the man she is going to marry: "For if she love him afore she have him, what shall he think but that she will as lightly love another as she hath done him."[56] For Othello, though, even the signs of Desdemona's oppression become radically ambivalent. In act 4, scene 1 he strikes her and, as she leaves, calls her back again. But her submissive obedience to his command is seen as further evidence of her wantonness:

> Sir, she can turn, and turn; and yet go on
> And turn again. . . .

> (4.1.253–54)

Turning becomes a figure for her inconstancy: as she can turn to him, so she can lie to him or turn to the arms of another man. In other words, even those discourses that inscribe Desdemona as his (her "liberality," her obedience) simultaneously disqualify her.

The contradictions that are, in a culturally pathological manner, staked across the body of woman are generated in *Othello* with particular acuteness around the handkerchief. It is at once emblem of Othello's exotic genealogy and hence of his family honor, and emblem of Desdemona's honor. But honor is a gendered concept. Applied to Othello, the concept includes military prowess, virility, his "name" or reputation. Applied to Desdemona, the concept means, above all, chastity. As Ruth Kelso notes in *Doctrine for the Lady of the Renaissance,* "let a woman have chastity, she has all. Let her lack chastity and she has nothing."[57] But through marriage, the woman's honor, like her property, is incorporated into her husband's. It is no coincidence that the disputed readings of 3.3.386, "Her name . . . is now begrim'd," "My name . . . is now begrim'd," make equal sense. Desdemona's "name," like her handkerchief, is Othello's.

But the handkerchief is *detachable.* Its passage from Othello to Desdemona implies the possibility of further passages:

> *Iago:* But if I give my wife a handkerchief—
> *Othello:* What then?

Iago: Why then 'tis hers, my Lord, and being hers,
             She may, I think, bestow't on any man.
Othello: She is protectress of her honour, too;
             May she give that?

                                    (4.1.10–15)

" 'Tis hers," Iago says of the handkerchief, but only a few lines later Othello calls it "my handkerchief" (4.1.22). The handkerchief, like her honor, is both hers and his. But if the handkerchief is detachable, is not her honor, and therefore his, also detachable? Hence, the anguished "May she give that?" The handkerchief is, indeed, "ocular proof" (3.3.360) of the process of exchange that Othello himself initiated. It is and is not his, just as Desdemona is and is not his:

                      O curse of marriage!
      That we can call these delicate creatures ours,
      And not their appetites!

                           (3.3.268–70)

The handkerchief, indeed, has a peculiar relation to "appetites" in the geography of the body. In this context, we may note Othello's speech before his fit:

      It is not words that shakes me thus. Pish!
      Noses, ears and lips. Is't possible? Confess?
      Handkerchief? O devil!

                           (4.1.41–43)

If it is "not words," it is the body ("Noses, ears and lips") that shakes him. But as I have argued, there can be no simple opposition between language and body because the body maps out the cultural terrain and is in turn mapped out by it. The connection between the handkerchief and "Noses, ears and lips" is not only metonymic; it is also metaphoric, since those parts of the body are all related to the thresholds of the enclosed body, mediating, like the handkerchief, between inner and outer, public and private. Moreover, within the body geography of the Renaissance, the nose in particular mediates between above and below, since it is a part of the head, the seat of reason, and yet it is analogous to the phallus—hence the enormous noses of carnival and the grotesque celebrations such as Hans Sachs's *Nasen-Tanz*. So Othello, observing what he imagines to be "the fleers, the gibes, and notable scorns / That dwell in every region" (4.1.82–83) of Cassio's face, says "O, I see that nose of yours, but not that dog I shall throw't to" (4.1.142–43). And the ears and lips point to the connection between private betrayal and public degradation, since they are the organs both of whispered secrets and of the blabbing of which Cassio is accused (4.1.25–28). In Othello's mind, the handkerchief, metonymically associated with the operations of the body, is metaphorically substituted for the body's apertures, and its transference from hand to hand comes to imply both the secret passage of "an essence that's not seen" (4.1.16) and a ritual of public humiliation ("O thou public commoner" [4.2.73]).

The transformation of the handkerchief from *locus* of privileged meaning to commonplace is a paradigm of Iago's method. That transformation depends upon a simultaneous process of desublimation and reduction that we can observe in act 2, scene 1. The equivocal forms of words (e.g., "liberal") and of objects (e.g., the handkerchief) are presaged there in the equivocal status of gestures. The public gesture of homage ("let her have your knees" [2.1.84]) and the elaborate courtesy of Cassio constitute Desdemona as "divine," "our great captain's captain" (2.1.73, 74). But the fingers with which Cassio displays his "excellent courtesy" (2.1.175) will serve him no better than "clyster-pipes" (2.1.177) (medical syringes used for enemas), in Iago's apposite image of physical debasement. What Iago achieves is the reinterpretation of the gestures of a class elite (the gestures of patrician courtesy) as purely gendered signs, the gestures of sexual promiscuity.

This reinterpretation is possible not because Iago is superhumanly ingenious but, to the contrary, because his is the voice of "common sense," the ceaseless repetition of the always-already "known," the culturally "given." This helps us, I believe, to account for 2.1.100–166 where, in a passage that has consistently troubled editors, Iago reworks familiar misogynistic *topoi*: beauty disguises folly; the "fair" and the "foul" practice the same "foul pranks"; the "fair" are either unchaste or only fit "To suckle fools and chronicle small beer." But what are here presented as comic diversions (even Desdemona engages in the interchange) will later be revealed as the ideological "truisms" that destroy Desdemona. Thus, Othello comes to see "The fountain from the which [his] current runs" as "a cestern for foul toads / To knot and gender in" [4.2.59, 61–62]. The concept of engendering is knotted and twisted by the contradictory cultural constructions of gender.

Iago is the manipulator of these contradictions, working both upon woman-as-differentiated and woman-as-the-same, since both undermine Othello's assurance as possessor. To emphasize Desdemona's distinctiveness it is enough for Iago to remind Othello of her status.

Will not her "better judgement" (3.3.236), then, draw her back to the racial and social elite (the matches "Of her own clime, complexion, and degree" [3.3.230]) to which Othello can only vainly aspire? Equally, Iago can work on the fear that women are, as a category, impure. Hence, Othello is either the "knee-crooking knave" (1.1.45), forever despised by his lady, or the master of an insubordinate servant, who has made him an object of contempt. In both cases, Othello's place in the social order is subverted.

But dramatically, that subversion is localized and demonized in the figure of Iago. Thus the play allows those who laughed at the misogynistic jokes of act 2, scene 1 to misrecognize in Desdemona's dead body the workings of "a devil" (5.2.287), just as Othello's final speech permits an imaginary resolution in which the "Virgin Citie of Venice" is reenclosed, as the island of Cyprus had been earlier in the play, against the demonized Other, the "turban'd Turk" (5.2.353). Thereby, the discursive contradictions that generate the text are displaced from the center to the periphery. For Iago is the projection of a social hierarchy's unease in the hypostatized form of envy. And the complicities of the dominant culture in a Desdemona "Still as the grave" (5.2.94) are reinterpreted as the marginal operations of an individual.

This is not to deny that the ideological configuration demonized in Iago may have a social location outside the discourses of the literate. The transformation of Iago's implacable negation of "the duteous and knee-crooking knave" into misogyny can be paralleled, for instance, in the winter carnival of 1580 in Romans. There, according to the magistrate Guérin, the plebeian "kingdom" of the Capons was stirred to action by the patrician carnival queen "who was so sumptuously dressed that she was all aglitter."[58] Guérin claimed that the subsequent slaughter of the peasants was retaliation for the intended rape of the patrician women. In his reports, he declared that the plebeians had planned "to begin on Mardi Gras to kill the nobility . . . and afterwards even kill their own women, and marry the wives of the said notables whom they had killed and whose property they had seized and divided up".[59] We need not accept Guérin's account at face value, since it was he who organized the attack on the peasants, but nor can we simply dismiss it, for we know that groups of apprentices practiced gang rape in the region during the same period.[60] Indeed, insofar as the "sumptuously dressed" woman was deliberately paraded as the symbol of aristocratic prestige, it is plausible that she became the focus of displaced class conflict. In Romans, as in Othello, woman's body could be imagined as the passive terrain on which the inequalities of masculine power were fought out.

In reality, of course, that "passive terrain" had a voice, however much the historical records have effaced it. In *Othello,* though, the female voices are constituted *fictionally,* by a male author. It is not sufficient, then, to "recover" Desdemona's silenced voice; we must also ask how it is *constructed.* I have suggested that Othello is a function of a particular form of class aspiration through romance. And Iago can be seen as a function of the projected fears of class hierarchy and sexual possession. But Desdemona, I suggest, fulfills two different functions. The Desdemona of the first half of the play is an active agent, however much she may be conceived of as the "spiritualization" of Othello's legitimation. She is accordingly given the freedom we tend to associate generically with the comic heroine. In fact, in the first two acts it is Othello who is the primary object of scrutiny, and who is correspondingly portrayed as controlling his "appetite" (1.3.262). It is only when Desdemona becomes the object of surveillance that she is reformed within the problematic of the enclosed body. Hence, in the second half of the play, the worse Iago's insinuations, the more she is "purified." In other words, the play constructs two different Desdemonas: the first, a woman capable of "downright violence" (1.3.249); the second, "A maiden, never bold" (1.3.94). Desdemona's subservience, enforced by her death, has already been enforced by the play's structure.

If the cost of rescuing Desdemona's "honor" is her transformation into aristocratic enclosure, is it not surprising that the value of that enclosure is called in question at the end of the play? Adultery, says Emilia, is "a small vice" (4.3.69). Kenneth Burke explains Emilia's function as an embodiment of the audience's resistance to the "*excessive* engrossment*" of a tragic plot. But

> though in her role she represents a motivation strong with the audience, she is "low" while tragedy is "high." Hence in effect she is suggesting that any resistance to the assumptions of the tragedy are "low," and that "noble" people will choose the difficult way of Desdemona.[61]

If, then, Emilia "purifies" Desdemona (who, in opposition to Emilia, would not commit this "small vice" for "the whole world" [4.3.79]), she also demonstrates the connection between class and the enclosed body. But is Burke right in arguing that Emilia simply siphons off an audience's "low" thoughts, thus reinforcing the tragic engrossment?

Would it not be equally plausible to say that Emilia exposes "the universe of what is taken for granted"[62] in the play? And this exposure is both thematic ("They are all but stomachs, and we all but food" [3.4.104]) and structural. For as the agent who unravels the plot, that is, as the agent of "truth," Emilia must open the closed mouth, the locked house. As wife, she is subject to the husband's command ("charm your tongue"; "hold your peace"; "get you home" [5.2.183, 219, 194]), but at the same time she is "bound to speak" and will "ne'er go home" [5.2.184, 197]. Emilia, then, serves contradictory functions: even as she elevates the "high" purity of her "sweet mistress" [5.2.121] she subverts the enclosed body.

I have analyzed the enclosed body mainly as a function of the antithetical thinking of the developing Renaissance state and as a target of the displaced resentment of the subordinated classes. But the subversive intervention of Emilia suggests a third possibility: the rejection of enclosure and the validation of the female grotesque. If woman was constituted as rampant sexual animal within medical discourse[63] and as innate heretic within religious discourse (in *Malleus Maleficarum*, *Femina* is derived from *Fe* and *Minus*, "lacking faith"),[64] her "recalcitrant" nature could become the symbol not only for "temporary release from traditional and stable hierarchy" but also "part and parcel of conflict over efforts to change the basic distribution of power within the society."[65] The "unruly woman" presided over the destruction of literal and symbolic enclosures alike. In 1605, women accused of "hiding behind their sex" tore down enclosures; in 1629, Captain Alice Clark "headed a crowd of women and male weavers dressed as women in a grain riot near Malden in Essex"; in 1626–28, and again in 1631, enclosure riots in Wiltshire and Gloucestershire were led by a man dressed as "Lady Skimmington"; in 1637 Scottish resistance to Charles I's imposition of the English prayer book was led by "rascally serving women," who stoned the doors and windows of Saint Giles' from which they had been evicted.[66] The female grotesque could, indeed, interrogate class and gender hierarchies alike, subverting the enclosed body in the name of a body that is "unfinished, outgrows itself, transgresses its own limits."[67]

Part Two

The Rhetorics of Marginalization: Consequences of Patriarchy

8

The Other and the Same: The Image of the Hermaphrodite in Rabelais

CARLA FRECCERO

One of the problems in Rabelais studies over the years has been critics' desire to impose hermeneutic closure on the four or five books that are attributed to his name. Despite admonitions against a reductive reading of this multileveled discourse, many still attempt to find a key that will open the work as a philosophically and poetically harmonious whole. It would seem that the effort to control or dominate meaning in discourse is only encouraged when the text opposes this strategy in its every rhetorical move.

Rather than seek to reduce chaos, I propose to allow it to seep through the cohesive surface of Rabelais's discourse. I want to examine the conflict of rhetorical strategies in this text that, because it is figurative and figured, can never speak a literal truth. I do this not simply as an exercise in perversity (although it is also that) but because I wish to see the text's declared ambiguity at work, both in the discourse itself and in the subtexts and intertexts that inform it. My reading is perverse in that it addresses those strategies on the fringes of the master discourse and that speak my exclusion, as feminine subject, from the economy of the work. My desire for inclusion, ultimately, motivates this exercise and gives a perspective that is radically "other" from the text.

The passage in question, then, is the following, from *Gargantua*, chapter 7:

> Pour son image avoit, en une platine d'or pesant soixante et huyt marcs, une figure d'esmail compétent, en laquelle estoit pourtraict un corps humain ayant deux testes, l'une virée vers l'aultre, quatre bras, quatre piedz et deux culz, telz que dict Platon *in Symposio* avoir esté l'humaine nature à son commencement mystic, et autour estoit escript en lettres Ioniques: ΑΓΑΠΗ ΟΥ ΖΗΤΕΙ ΤΑ ΕΑΥΤΗΣ.[1]

As his hat medallion, he had a fine piece of enamelled work set in gold plate weighing a hundred and thirty-six ounces, on which was displayed a human body with two heads turned toward one another, four feet and two rumps—the form, according to Plato in his *Symposium,* of man's nature in its mystical beginnings; and around it was written in Ionian script: Charity seeketh not her own (p. 56).

Gargantua's image is a device or *impresa,* a picture with an accompanying motto, a polyvalent symbol expressing an individual's personal philosophy. Ambiguity, it seems, is the rule. As Erasmus points out concerning his own device, "Concedo nulli," in a letter to Alfonso Valdes in 1528: "in devices of this kind one actually aims at a certain degree of obscurity in order to exercise the guessing powers of those who look at them."[2] Once again, then, this most coy of texts has inscribed its own enigma, determining a history of debates much like those mocked in the prologue to *Gargantua.*

The debate addresses the physical peculiarities of the "figure" and the relationship between image and motto in the passage. Most regard it as an exemplary case of Renaissance syncretism, with pagan imagery assimilated by Christian doctrine, the reconciliation of eros (in the pagan representation of Rabelais's expression, "faire la beste à deux dos") and agape (as described by the quotation from St. Paul), opposed notions synthesized into a harmonious, if humorous, symbol of the spirit of Evangelical Humanism.[3] To cite just one example:

> The grotesque androgyne of Plato's Aristophanes is explicated by the Greek of Saint Paul: "Charity seeketh not her own." This medallion not only gives shape to the deepest of Rabelais's values; it also bears witness to the unity of wisdom which, for the Christian humanist, lies at the heart of ancient thought and scriptural revelation alike.[4]

The figure referred to as "androgyne" derives, writes Rabelais, from a passage in the *Symposium,* where Aristophanes describes mankind's sexual origin(s):

> First of all I must explain the real nature of man, and the change which it has undergone—for in the beginning we were nothing like we are now. For one thing, the race was divided into three; that is to say, besides the two sexes, male and female, which we have at present, there was a third which partook of the nature of both, and for which we still have a name, though the creature itself is forgotten. For though

"hermaphrodite" is only used nowadays as a term of contempt, there really was a man-woman in those days, a being which was half male and half female . . . each of these beings was globular in shape, with rounded back and sides, four arms and four legs, and two faces, both the same, on a cylindrical neck, and one head, with one face one side and one the other, and four ears, and two lots of privates, and all the other parts to match.[5]

According to the syncretist interpretation, Rabelais is referring to the Aristophanic description of the "man-woman." Rabelais who, as far as we know, was the first to employ this image in sixteenth-century France, alliteratively inscribes a difference in his version of the creature. The two heads, "l'une virée vers l'aultre," face each other. Jerome Schwartz, in his article "Scatology and Eschatology in Gargantua's Androgyne Device," seeks to reconcile this element not only with the serious, Neoplatonic Christian interpretation of Aristophanes' fable but also with the comic aspect of the myth.[6] Marsilio Ficino, translator and interpreter of Plato for the sixteenth century, provides a Christianizing exegesis for the passage, likening it to the Fall:

> Summa vero nostre interpretationis erit huiusmodi. *Homines,* id est, hominum anime. *Quondam,* id est, quando a deo creantur. *Integre sunt,* duobus sunt exornate luminibus, ingenito et infuso. Ut ingenito equalia et inferiora, infuso superiora conspicerent. *Deo equare se voluerunt.* Ad unicum lumen ingenitum se reflexerunt. *Hinc divise sunt.* Splendorem infusum amiserunt, quando ad solum ingenitum sunt converse statimque in corpora cecidere. *Superbiores facte iterum dividentur,* id est, si naturali/nimium restitit quodammodo extinguetur.[7]

> The gist of our interpretation will be this. "Men" (that is, the souls of men) "originally" (that is, when they were created by God), "were whole" and equipped with two lights, one natural, and the other supernatural; by the natural light they beheld inferior and co-equal things; and by the supernatural light, superior things. "They aspire to equal God"; they reverted to the natural light alone. Hereupon "they were divided," and lost their supernatural light, were reduced to natural light alone, and fell immediately into bodies.

Humankind's nostalgia, later described by Aristophanes, which draws each half together again, represents the soul's longing for reintegration

with the divine light. Schwartz notes that Ficino interprets this myth
through the words of St. Paul, "For now we see through a glass
darkly, but then face-to-face" (1 Corinthians 13:12), thus possibly
providing a subtext for the creature's position as well as for a
Neoplatonic synthesis of two concepts of love, eros becoming the
mediator for agape.[8]

Ficino's reading, however, cannot account for the humor in both
the Platonic text and in Rabelais's passage. He fails to take into
account the peculiar complexity of the dialogue, whereby
Aristophanes, rather than Socrates, recounts the myth. The story is
Babelian: it narrates the division of sexuality (its "origin") as resulting
from the (circle-) man's desire to displace the gods. Love, then, comes
to be defined as the half-creature's longing for its original, material
wholeness. The myth may be, among other things (including the
metaphorical embodiment of poetic discourse in its opposition to
philosophy), Aristophanes' proleptic critique of the Socratic theory of
love expounded further on in the dialogue. To Socrates's idealistic and
mystifying definition of human eros as a mediating force in man's
pursuit of transcendence (what we think of as Neoplatonic love),
Aristophanes, the comic poet, opposes a wholly material explanation
of human desire. He concludes: "And so all this to-do is a relic of that
original state of ours, when we were whole, and now, when we are
longing for and following after that primeval wholeness, we say we
are in love."[9] The passage in Rabelais seems to emphasize, in the
specificity of its description (recalling Aristophanes' own humorous
and minutely detailed portrait) the physicality of the hermaphrodite
rather than its (Ficinian) allegorical function.

Furthermore, the Aristophanic fable emphasizes the self-sufficiency
of the circle-men and their arrogance in attempting to overthrow the
gods. Rabelais seems to emblematize the circle-men's implied narcissism by turning his creature's heads inward so that the figure
contemplates itself. This inward turning posture seems, in turn, to
contradict the Pauline motto, which stresses an essentially God-
oriented notion of love. Schwartz considers this aspect of the figure:

> There is the . . . theme of self-love or philautia implied by the
> relationship between image and motto. Charity does not seek
> the things of itself while one half of the Androgyne seeks its
> other half. As a device, Gargantua's medal may be seen as a
> means of representing a fusion between elements that may
> appear at first as irreconcilable if not mutually exclusive.[10]

The problem of the ironic twist in the creature's heads can be resolved, in Schwartz's view, by examining Renaissance interpretations of the androgyne provided by Eusebius and Leone Ebreo.[11] The turning of the heads to face each other might, then, represent the post-lapsarian androgyne who struggles, through coition and marriage, to regain primeval wholeness. In this case Rabelais would be both exercising his comic skills in the reference to coitus and making the theological point that Christian marriage attempts to reestablish a harmonious union lost to humanity.

These interpretations undoubtedly inhere in any late Christian reading of Gargantua's medallion. However, it seems to me that critics, in their effort to read syncretism into Renaissance textual endeavors, have made too many assumptions about the figure described in *Gargantua* 7. By clinging to the notion of a harmonious transfer of the Platonic passage into the vocabulary of Christian Humanism, they have often overlooked elements of the discourse that militate against its integration into such a scheme (much as the Aristophanic fable subverts the Socratic theory of love) and have blinded themselves to the description in order to force it to conform to the requirements of the concept "Christian Humanism."

One text standing between Plato and Rabelais that might influence our reading of the "hermaphrodite" is Ovid's *Metamorphoses*. It is perhaps because of this text that today we make a slight distinction between the terms *androgyne* and *hermaphrodite,* the former being a spirtualized union of male and female aspects, the latter connoting a monstrous hybrid, characterized not only by a merging of the two sexes, but by the deformation of each required to effect the union.[12]

Hermaphroditus, according to Alcithoe's story in book 4, is a boy, and the story of his transformation provides a basis for the evil reputation of the fountain Salmacis.[13] A water-nymph, whose name the fountain bears, sees Hermaphroditus and desires him. He rejects her, whereupon she waits, hidden, until he has stripped and is bathing in the pool, at which point she dives in, praying to the gods that they might never be separated:

> velut, si quis conducat cortice ramos,
> crescendo iungi pariterque adolescere cernit,
> sic ubi conplexu coierunt membra tenaci,
> nec duo sunt et forma duplex, nec femina dici
> nec puer ut possit, neutrumque et utrumque videntur.[14]

> as when a twig is grafted
> On parent stock, both knit, mature together,
> So these two joined in close embrace, no longer

Two beings, and no longer man and woman,
But neither, and yet both.

At this point, although the two are ostensibly joined, Salmacis seems
to disappear and it is Hermaphroditus whose consciousness governs
the new creature:

Ergo ubi se liquidas, quo vir descenderat, undas
seminarem fecisse videt mollitaque in illis
membra, manus tendens, sed iam non voce virili
Hermaphroditus ait: "nato date munera vestro,
et pater et genetrix, amborum nomen habenti:
quisquis in hos fontes vir venerit, exeat inde
semivir et tactis subito mollescat in undis!"[15]

    Hermaphroditus
Saw that the water had made him half a man,
With limbs all softness. He held out his arms,
lifted a voice whose tone was almost treble,
Pleading: "O father and mother, grant me this!
May every one hereafter, who comes diving
Into this pool, emerge half man, made weaker
By the touch of this evil water!"

Thus, in Ovid's account, hermaphroditism becomes a curse, the
reduction of an essentially masculine nature. The myth has interesting
parallels with the account in book 3 of Narcissus and Echo in that
both youths are strikingly beautiful, virginal, and desired by water-
nymphs who lose their identities (Echo cannot speak, she can only
repeat, and loses her body entirely, while Salmacis's body echoes
femininity only as a modification of the masculine, and she cannot
speak at all), leaving them trapped in an enamored or horrified
self-contemplation.

    The suggestive connections between these myths, as well as the loss
of feminine identity incurred by the merging of masculine and
feminine, may well have implications for Rabelais. Certainly, Ovid's
myth of Hermaphroditus casts a more than skeptical shadow across
attempts to view this merging as a positive symbol of union. For the
Middle Ages, at least, that shadow was important. Versions of the
"moralized Ovid" tend to interpret the hermaphrodite as a symbol of
lust and concupiscence,[16] as does Dante when, in canto 24 of the
Purgatorio, Guido Guinizelli declares:

Nostro peccato fu ermafrodito;
ma perchè non servammo umana legge,
seguendo come bestie l'appetito . . .[17]

Our sin was hermaphrodite;
but because we observed not human law,
following appetite like beasts . . .

It would seem, then, that the hermaphrodite carries with it a great
deal of *in malo* interpretive potential for the Renaissance. As Marie
Delcourt and Mircea Eliade both indicate, a great distance lies between
the spiritualized concept androgyne and its physical realization (or
description) as the monstrous hermaphrodite.[18]

It remains to be seen whether Rabelais's description might be taken
in any way as a figure of a man and a woman copulating. One could
assert that as an eternal archetype the androgyne (or the hermaphrodite) necessarily represents both male and female components. While
such a solution may seem the obvious one and apparently resolves the
enigma of the device, there is nothing in the language of the passage
to support such an interpretation. Rather, the play of presence and
absence between the Platonic subtext and its Rabelaisian representation suggests that the latter strains against the very syncretic coherence
it seems, at the same time, to imply. In the very place where the
hermeneutic leap to a resolution of the enigma might be made, the
text lacks those terms of comparison that would remove such an
interpretation from the realm of speculation.

It may be important, first of all, to emphasize that the text describes
one figure, not two. If difference is being asserted, it is within a
context of sameness, further emphasized by the lack of features
distinguishing one body from the other. The description proceeds by
doubling or, inversely, halving a single entity.

In a later Renaissance text, the language of doubling and halving a
single entity becomes explicitly linked to the bond between men,
which suggests that Rabelais's figure may indeed be symptomatic of a
more widespread Renaissance thematics. Montaigne describes the
relationship between himself and Etienne de la Boétie:

Le secret qu j'ay juré de ne deceller à nul autre, je le puis, sans
parjure, communiquer à celuy qui n'est pas autre: c'est moy.
C'est un assez grand miracle de se doubler; et n'en cognois-
sent pas la hauteur, ceux qui parlent de se tripler (p.
239). . . . et les plaisirs mesmes qui s'offrent à moy, au lieu de
me consoler, me redoublent le regret de sa perte. Nous

estions à moitié de tout; il me semble que je luy desrobe sa
part . . . J'estois desjà si fait et accoustumé à estre deuxiesme
par tout, qu'il me semble n'estre plus qu'à demy (p. 241).[19]

> The secret I have sworn to reveal to no other man, I can impart
> without perjury to the one who is not another man: he is
> myself. It is a great enough miracle to be doubled, and those
> who talk of tripling themselves do not realize the loftiness of
> the thing (p. 142). . . . And the very pleasures that come my
> way, instead of consoling me, redouble my grief for his loss.
> We went halves in everything; it seems to me that I am robbing
> him of his share . . . I was already so formed and accustomed
> to being a second self everywhere that only half of me seems
> to be alive now ("De l'Amitié," p. 143).

Rather than an androgynous reconciliation of erotic differences, the
figure portrayed on Gargantua's medallion, like Montaigne's description, presents a doubly powerful image of erotic sameness.

It is precisely that image of sameness—one man doubled or one man
halved—that Rabelais could have found in Aristophanes, whose text is
not confined to the portrayal of hermaphroditism but also describes
the appearance of all three "original" genders:

> Men who are slices of the male are followers of the male, and
> show their masculinity throughout their boyhood by the way
> they make friends with men, and the delight they take in
> lying beside them and being taken in their arms. And these
> are the most hopeful of the nation's youth, for theirs is the
> most virile constitution.[20]

All of the sexes, male, female, and hermaphrodite, were circle-people
or double beings, and they were all divided in half. This explains the
genesis of homosexuality and in turn gives rise to the possibility that
Rabelais's comment on the double-headed being, "telz que dict
Platon, *in Symposio,* avoir esté l'humaine nature à son commencement
mystic," refers to the doubly masculine being. The omission of the
sexual organs included in Aristophanes' portrayal ("two lots of
privates") in the otherwise physically detailed description (itself
miming Aristophanes' painstaking catalogue of parts) marks the
ambiguity of Rabelais's suggestive image. The submergence of this
detail points to sexuality as the locus of tension within this representation of erotic and "agapic" love.

On the linguistic level, the passage displays some resistances to the syncretic interpretation assumed by many of its readers. The words employed in the text seem to emphasize the androcentricity of the image rather than the merging of two opposite-sexed beings: for example, sexual allusion and punning may be contained in the words *testes (testis)* and *culz* (as a reference to sodomitic sexuality). The couple *virée vers,* alliteratively overdetermined as a reference to the distortion of the Platonic subtext, excludes, in its morphemic masculinity, the entry of the feminine into the duality of the turned heads, *virée* containing *vir,* the Latin word for man. Ida Nelson, in her book *La sottie sans souci: essai d'interprétation homosexuelle,* has attempted to create a typology for what she calls the "registre homosexuel," a linguistic code present in the wordplays, paradoxes, and puns of farcical poems and plays called *sotties,* performed or recited during Carnival in medieval and Renaissance France. While some of the patterns she discerns are suggestive and plausible, at least in the case of Rabelais, she herself acknowledges the risk involved in assigning homosexual connotations to a vocabulary "qui n'était jamais enregistré directement comme possédant ce sens."[21] Nelson isolates four major semantic fields that carry homosexual connotations. One such category is "l'idée de tourner comme virer."[22] The use of the word *virer* for turning is relatively rare, and its radical *vire* also carries the meanings of "leg," "arrow," and "stick."[23] I choose the example of this word because of its importance in the context of the description, but it would be possible to go farther, as does Nelson, cataloguing similar connotations in the passage, particularly as the text easily lends itself to enigmatic wordplay and distortions as well as to erotic references.[24] She suggests that, just as on the thematic level Bakhtin has shown how Carnival procedes by "le morcellement, le démembrement, la décomposition des choses dans un but de renouvellement, de recréation, de renaissance," so on the linguistic level, one can show writers of carnivalesque texts proceeding in a similar fashion: "Ils ont disloqué, écrasé, morcelé, décomposé les mots pour les recréer dans un autre registre sémique."[25] Although caution is necessary in deducing the nature of Rabelaisian wordplay, readers of this playful and playfully disguised text should not be surprised that such possibilities exist within the economy of a discourse so exclusively masculine in its thematic horizons.

Other passages in Rabelais corroborate an androcentric reading of the hermaphrodite. The episode of the "haulte dame de Paris," for instance, provides an occasion for the courtly (and the feminine) to be excluded as an important element of the "hero's" life. Panurge verbally degrades and physically befouls a haughty Parisian noblewoman. In doing so he mocks the Petrarchan hierarchy and exonerates Pantagruel from possible charges of discourtesy for having abandoned his own lady in favor of male companions and the epic quest. The chapter that follows involves a destruction of the lady's missive (in the effort to decode it) and frees Pantagruel, through a comparison with Aeneas, to leave his lady definitively behind.[26] The *Gargantua*'s "Abbaye de Thélème," a glaringly exceptional place in Rabelais's *corpus*, includes women, but only as part of a rigid reversal of values, which it seeks to enforce in as legal and restrictive a manner as the religious institutions that constitute its opposite.[27] The arguments in favor of a Rabelaisian "feminism" often focus on the inclusion of women in this utopistic society. But the text deconstructs the very notion of utopia: an ominous "enigme" underlies the foundation of the institution and causes it (so to speak) to crumble. Thélème cannot be considered a point of resolution in Rabelais's text, either thematically or narratively, for the artificiality of the closure it imposes is defeated by the recapitulative structure of the *Pantagruel*, which reopens and continues the narrative. Thélème cannot be the exception that disproves the rule of silencing the feminine in the text of Rabelais, for it serves to demonstrate, through its failure as an institution, the untenability of simply reversing social (and linguistic) value-systems.[28] Furthermore, upon leaving Thélème, a man is not absolutely free to choose what he will do, while a woman seems to have little choice at all:

> Par ceste raison, quand le temps venu estoit que aulcun d'icelle abbaye, ou à la requeste de ses parens, ou pour altres causes, voulust issir hors, avecques soy il emmenoyt une des dames, celle laquelle l'auroit prins pour son devot, et estoient ensemble mariez; et, si bien avoient vescu à Theleme en devotion et amitiyé, encores mieulx la continuoient ilz en mariage, et autant se entreaymoient ilz à la fin de leurs jours comme le premier de leurs nopces.[29]

> For that reason, when the time came that anyone in that abbey, whether at his parents' request or for any other reason, wished to leave it, he took with him one of the ladies, the one who had accepted him as her admirer, and they were married to one another; and if at Thélème they had lived in devotion and friendship, they lived in still greater devotion and friendship when they were married. Indeed, they loved one another to the end of their days as much as they had done on their wedding day (pp. 159–60).

This tacit command may constitute part of the campaign to promote marriage, which M. A. Screech considers one of the animating principles of the *Tiers Livre*.[30] The *Tiers Livre*, however, although concerned with marriage, effectively defers its realization beyond the bounds of the book, while defining *woman* by the hysteria (displayed, comically enough, by Panurge in the course of his adventures) emanating from her womb.[31] Here, once again, Montaigne's summary of the situation may prove illuminating:

> Quant aux mariages, outre ce que c'est un marché qui n'a que l'entrée libre (sa durée estante contrainte et forcée, dependant d'ailleurs que de nostre vouloir), et marché qui ordinairement se fait à autres fins, il y survient mille fusées estrangieres à desmeler parmy, suffisantes à rompre le fil et troubler le cours d'une vive affection; là où, en l'amitié, il n'y a affaire ny commerce que d'elle mesme. Joint qu'à dire vray, la suffisance ordinaire des femmes n'est pas pour respondre à cette conference et communication, nourrisse de cette saincte couture; ny leur ame ne semble assez ferme pour soustenir l'estreinte d'un noeud si pressé et si durable.[32]

> As for marriage, for one thing it is a bargain to which only the entrance is free—its continuance being constrained and forced, depending otherwise than on our will—and a bargain ordinarily made for other ends. For another, there supervene a thousand foreign tangles to unravel, enough to break the thread and trouble the course of a lively affection; whereas in friendship there are no dealings or business except with itself. Besides, to tell the truth, the ordinary capacity of women is inadequate for that communion and fellowship which is the nurse of this sacred bond; nor does their soul seem firm enough to endure the strain of so tight and durable a knot (pp. 137–38).

Montaigne's description of marriage might almost be a commentary on Panurge's vicissitudes throughout the *Tiers Livre,* while the theme of the essay, friendship, points to a vital yet relatively unexplored component of Rabelais's text. Montaigne's narrated "encounter" with Etienne de la Boétie in "De L'Amitié" provides an explicit clarification for Pantagruel's mysterious reaction to the "shadow" or trickster-figure of the book, Panurge:

> Si on me presse de dire pourquoy je l'aymois, je sens que cela

ne se peut exprimer, (c) qu'en respondant: "Par ce que c'estoit luy; par ce que c'estoit moy."

. . . Et à nostre premiere recontre, qui fut par hazard en une grande feste et compagnie de ville, nous nous trouvasmes si prins, si cognus, si obligez entre nous, que rien dès lors ne nous fut si proche que l'un à l'autre.[33]

If you press me to tell why I loved him, I feel that this cannot be expressed, (c) except by answering: Because it was he, because it was I. . . . And at our first meeting, which by chance came at a great feast and gathering in the city, we found ourselves so taken with each other, so well acquainted, so bound together, that from that time on nothing was so close to us as each other (p. 139).

Pantagruel, upon encountering Panurge in chapter 9 of the *Pantagruel*, testifies similarly to the great bond of love that is immediately established between them:

"Car, par ma foy, je vous ay jà prins en amour si grande, que, si vous condescendez à mon vouloir, vous ne bougerez jamais de ma compaignie, et vous et moy ferons ung nouveau per d'amytié, tell que fut entre Enée et Achates."[34]

"I've taken such a liking to it [*sic*], I swear, that if I have my way you'll never stir from my side. Indeed you and I will make such another pair of friends as Aeneas and Achates" (p. 201).

This relationship, and its juxtaposition in Montaigne's essay with a discussion of marriage, may shed light on the apparent effacement of the feminine from Rabelais's image of love in *Gargantua* 7.[35]

Both Rabelais and Montaigne cite the *Symposium* in their texts on love. While the Socratic discourse ultimately places spirit over body, thus enabling men metaphorically to appropriate the capacity of giving birth (in order to become philosophers or writers of texts), the *Symposium* ultimately remains a playful and solemn celebration of masculine eros and, as such, cannot be completely assimilated within the framework of orthodox Evangelical Humanism.[36] Montaigne dismisses the question of pagan eroticism by commenting, "Et cet'autre licence Grecque est justement abhorrée par nos moeurs."—p. 234. ("And that other, licentious Greek love is justly abhorred by our morality"—Frame, p. 138), while continuing to describe friendship in physical terms that liken it to Rabelais's hermaphrodite:

En l'amitié dequoy je parle, elles se meslent et confondent l'une en autre, d'un melange si universel, qu'elles effacent et ne retrouvent plus la couture qui les a jointes. . . . Nos ames ont charrié si uniement ensemble, elles se sont considerées d'une si ardente affection, et de pareille affection descouvertes jusques au fin fond des entrailles l'une à autre . . .[37]

In the friendship I speak of, our souls mingle and blend with each other so completely that they efface the seam that joined them, and cannot find it again (p. 139). . . . Our souls pulled together in such unison, they regarded each other with such ardent affection, and with a little affection revealed themselves to each other to the very depths of our hearts . . . (p. 140).

In Rabelais's text the erotic question is addressed through the juxtaposition of the *figure d'esmail* and the quotation from 1 Corinthians 13:5: "Charity . . . seeketh not her own." The motto ironically underscores the specularity of the figure that, in looking at an other-image, contemplates itself. This hermaphroditic self is an other, its other a self. The Pauline statement mitigates the heterodox eroticism of the figure's masculine self-absorption by introducing the notion of spiritual or "brotherly" love, man's love for that which is "other" in himself, or God.[38] St. Paul, in Corinthians, discusses both love and marriage. Here too, women are subordinated in the spiritual hierarchy to the love between man and God, a subordination achieved, in part, through marriage:

But I would have you know, that the head of every man is Christ; and the head of the woman *is* the man; and the head of Christ *is* God . . . (5) But every woman that prayeth or prophesieth with *her* head uncovered dishonoureth her head: for that is even all one as if she were shaven . . . (7) For a man indeed ought not to cover *his* head, forasmuch as he is the image and glory of God: but the woman is the glory of the man. (8) For the man is not of the woman; but the woman of the man. (9) Neither was the man created for the woman; but the woman for the man.[39]

Like Salmacis joined to Hermaphroditus in the *Metamorphoses,* women are silenced within the body of the church:

Let your women keep silence in the churches: for it is not permitted upon them to speak; but *they are commanded* to be under obedience . . .[40]

Paul's "Charity . . . seeketh not her own" in the Rabelaisian passage repeats, in spiritual terms, the depiction of difference incorporated into sameness in the hermaphrodite. The relation of otherness defined by the text is one of man to God, or man to himself through (in) God. The other is the other of the same and not, in fact, Otherness, or woman.[41] Thus, the strategy whereby phallocentric ideology excludes the feminine from the possibility of identity or presence, and the consequences of this strategy, are literally figured here: the text deforms its subtext; the heads are twisted inward, locked into the distorting, imaginary gaze of Narcissus.[42] The result is a double-headed monster. Yet, the text has enlisted the blind complicity of its (masculine) interpreters, who find in the image of Rabelais's hermaphrodite a symbol of human totality.

9

Usurpation, Seduction, and the Problematics of the Proper: A "Deconstructive," "Feminist" Rereading of the Seductions of Richard and Anne in Shakespeare's *Richard III*

MARGUERITE WALLER

About that title. It strikes me as verbose, pretentious, overly Latinate, typographically busy, and quite probably off-putting. But I do not know how else to indicate to you or to myself what I am trying to do at this moment in a collaborative attempt to reread (or rewrite) the Renaissance from a number of recently conceived political and especially "feminist" positions. I have trouble naming either my topic or my approach, not least because it is a certain violence implicit in naming itself that I want to make available for closer examination. Jacques Derrida, the formulator of the non-name, non-concept "deconstruction," has argued that it is this violence, a violence of or in language, that underwrites the traditional discourses of reference and meaning in which, as he and several feminist theoreticians have gone on to demonstrate, "woman" always comes off badly.[1] It is this violence that continues to frustrate even the most thorough-going "deconstructive" attempts to open Western discourses of knowledge to the discourses of women.[2] I place "feminist" and "deconstructive" in quotation marks here and in my title, then, to call attention to this violence, the structure of which we will presently examine in greater detail.

I also want to suggest a second, related, problem. That is, the two terms are not necessarily compatible. They do not signal a harmonious, homogeneous, co-extensive set of concerns and practices. By reading deconstructively I may be able to de-literalize or re-figure the figure "man" so as to show how the speaking, writing, knowing subject of the discourse of knowledge does not itself escape its violent rhetorical origins, how its own status as a linguistic artifact precludes the possibility of its serving as the ground of meaning and being. I might go on, as Derrida has done in *Spurs: Nietzsche's Styles,* to demarcate "man" by means of gender.[3] The issue would then become how the category "man," when it is de-figured, interpreted as literal, comes to operate linguistically in ways that compel gender discrimination. I could point out that "man," seen as working beyond rhetorical determinations, compels the subordination of the category "woman." Woman appears as the dangerous, supplemental, figural term; man as the stable, literal one. She becomes a secondary deprivileged entity, an object to be investigated; man the primary term, the subject who performs the investigation. She can be seen only in her relation to men, while men are seen as transcending such networks of relations.

But such deconstructive reading appears unable to ask why it was that man became the unscrutinized term in the first place. And as Gayatri Spivak has recently asked, is the position of woman really being interrogated when the philosopher moves into what he has determined to be her position the better to ask what "man" is? Doesn't the deconstruction of the general sign of man still depend upon the figural determination of woman inherited from what is now seen to be a phallocentric system of thought, and isn't woman, therefore, not better spoken for or about, but doubly displaced, at the very moment when she appears to inaugurate the new regime of quotation marks?[4]

There seems to be a failure, then, of the questions posed by deconstruction and those posed by feminism to match up. Not that this failure necessarily takes the form of an opposition. The nonrelation of deconstruction and feminism to which Spivak points may allow the two to work together fruitfully as demarcations of each other's explanatory limits. The logic of deconstruction suspends the conditions under which it makes sense to ask direct, historical, and epistemological questions (such as, how, when, why did "man" become the subject and referent of our knowledge about, among other things, gender? What does it mean to be a woman? What has it meant and what might it come to mean?). But feminism reminds us that the position of woman in language, by its very difference from "man's," "means" that "man's" discourse, even in the form offered by Derrida, which strives toward ending the centrality of "man," has its own particular kind of boundary. Not that we can "know" something about "woman" that goes unproblematized by deconstruction's insights into discourse, but that between deconstructive and feminist logic there now emerges the event of their "missed encounter."[5] That is, the nonconfrontation between deconstruction and feminism can be seen as an event (although an event of a different order from that constituted by traditional epistemology) accessible as a historical reality. As Shoshana Felman suggests in a canny analysis (from which I have just been drawing) of J. L. Austin's speech act theory and its comparable discontinuities with continental linguistic thought, such misfires, instances of the impossibility of translating from one argument into another, give us a different kind of referent to consider—what she calls a "material knowledge of language."[6] Such knowledge, Felman stresses, "has to do with reality" because referential knowledge about language "is itself—at least in part—what this reality is made of." But this referent is conceived of as an act, that is a dynamic movement of modification of reality."[7] The quotation marks in my title are intended to evoke this kind of successful failure, one that performs an act modifying rather than reinforcing the reality suggested by either approach in the absence of the other. In the context of a reading of seduction scenes in Shakespeare's *Richard III*, I would like to think of this act as an anti-seduction. As I present my argument—that Shakespeare's characters Richard and Anne and many of the play's commentators are seduced by the dream of a common language in which the radical potential of this heteronomy is suppressed—my commitment is to the subversion of such suppression.

1

> Cette fissure n'est pas une fissure parmi d'autres. Elle est *la* fissure: la nécessité de l'intervalle, la dure loi de l'espacement.
> —Jacques Derrida, *De la grammatologie*

Academic commentators on *Richard III* have found much to admire in the character Richard. He has been called, among other things, "buoyantly vital," "fascinating," "creative," "self-knowing," "a great artist," "a great actor," "a wit," "an ironist," "a human representative, bolder than ourselves, resisting the oppression of history," "a ruthless, demonic comedian with . . . the seductive appeal of an irresistible gusto."[8] By contrast, the female characters within the play refer to him as a "wretch," a "villain slave," "the slave of nature," "a toad," "a bottled spider," "a dissembler," and "the troubler of the poor world's peace." In the slightly more politicized language of the deposed queen, Margaret, he is "that excellent grand tyrant of the earth / That reigns in galled eyes of weeping souls."[9] Were I to judge Richard, a critical gesture that I find of questionable political or epistemological usefulness either to the female figures in the play or to my project, the catalogue of epithets might read as follows: Richard is politically and intellectually stupid, cowardly, and boring. A sentimental writer and reader of himself and of others, he is a relatively common species of manipulative narcissist. My point, however, is not that my position or that of the play's internal critics of Richard is right and the positions of various twentieth-century male (as it happens) critics are wrong. I want to call attention instead to the enormous discrepancy concerning what judgment is to be made of, what value is to be seen in, the figure of Richard. Such discrepancies present us with a dramatic eruption of the kind of violence, an unavoidable violence, that underwrites the making of all moral and aesthetic judgments. It will prove a useful detour in an investigation of seduction—itself, etymologically a leading aside or detour—to turn our attention first to that fundamental violence implicated in this instance of critical disagreement.

Like other kinds of naming, such judgments participate in what Derrida, in an essay on Claude Lévi-Strauss, has called "the violence of the letter,"[10] Explicitly in that essay and implicitly throughout his work, Derrida has concerned himself with the structure and effects of the way in which language necessarily effaces or represses its indeterminate origins in the infinite play of phonemic difference. If, as structural linguists maintain, meaning is diacritical, the product of the free play of difference, then in order for words to seem "proper," to appear as stable, self-identical entities endowed with stable meanings, this play of difference must be effaced. The indeterminate origins of linguistic signification must be repressed. It is Derrida's breakdown into stages of this effacement or repression that I have found especially pertinent to the case at hand.

Derrida (or his text, which here performs a little exemplary violence on "proper" French) has termed the first stage the "violence originaire" of language.[11] The term, *originaire* or "originary," not to be found in either the French or the English lexicon, and not meaning "original" or "primary" but something prior to the possibility of such concepts, aptly enacts the way in which a word can never be "proper," literal, only and wholly itself. Derrida's gnarled explication of the term tries to confront and combat our commonsense feel for the order of things as it lays out a different, difficult to conceptualize schema:

> To name, to give names . . . such is the originary violence of
> language which consists in inscribing within a difference, in
> classifying, in suspending the vocative absolute. To think the
> unique *within* the system, to inscribe it there, such is the
> gesture of the arche-writing: arche-violence, loss of the
> proper, of absolute proximity, of self-presence, in truth the
> loss of what has never taken place, of a self-presence which
> has never been given but only dreamed of and always already
> split, repeated, incapable of appearing to itself except in its
> own disappearance.[12]

In other words, names are never simply what they are but are
identified by what they are not as well. The violence done to and
through difference by naming works by constituting a presence which
then seems to precede difference. This implies, among other things,
that the substantiality that a name "literally" suggests or seems to
promise is fundamentally illusory.[13] There occurs, however, a second,
"reparatory" violence, implied by and inseparable from the first,
whereby this "loss of the proper . . . of what has never been given but
only dreamed of" is concealed and compensated for. In a violent
rewriting of the originary violence, the "proper" becomes the proper.
Rather than a mere appearance made possible by, but doing violence
to, difference, "literal" meaning comes to appear as itself the ground
from which contraries and conflicts emerge. It is the emergence of
these contraries and conflicts in the form of a third violence, empirical
violence, that we tend to interpret in moral, legal, and other evaluative
ways. For Derrida, though, this last violence remains unrecuperated
and anything but neutralized by normative systems of law and value.
Instead, empirical violence refers back to the complex, abyssal structures of rhetorical violence that underwrite it. Thus, in a way,
empirical violence undoes the work of the first two stages. "In effect
it reveals the first nomination which was already an expropriation . . .
it denudes also that which since then functioned as the proper, the
so-called proper . . ."[14] Though not often, and not always advisably,
seen this way, war, murder, rape—and verbal disagreement—violently strip away "the reassuring seal of self-identity" of nations,
persons, and ideas.[15]

If, as I have been urging, the attempt to judge Richard's performance aesthetically or morally in no way escapes this problematics of
the proper, then it should come as no surprise that there are—and had
better be—disagreements among such readings. The mistake would
be not to expect such conflicts or to try to resolve or abolish them on

the assumption that this would make one's own critical position secure. Such a gesture would be structurally analogous to Richard's elimination of everyone who appears to threaten his claim to absolute authority and is magnificently undercut by the irony emplotted in Richard's homicidal progress toward the throne. As he systematically kills off those against whom he defines himself, he fails to understand that the dream of self-identity and self-determination (which he identifies with the throne) necessarily recedes from his grasp. His rhetorical situation just before the end of the play, on the morning of the battle of Bosworth, anticipates what is about to become his empirical situation—nonexistence. Richard says, "I myself / find in myself no pity to myself" (5.3.203–4), echoing the tortured attempt to name the self of Petrarch's famous line-"di me medesmo meco mi vergogno."[16] The play's evocation at this moment of Petrarch's *Canzoniere,* one of the foremost Renaissance investigations of the indeterminate, fragmenated situation of the self as it is "known" in and through language, signals just how far off-base Richard's "self-knowledge" has become.[17] His lack of self-knowledge shortly proves fatal. His collision with Richmond on the battlefield gives the lie to his sense of a stable, self-conscious, sovereign subjectivity, proving it no more than a fragile linguistic construct. Had he recognized the provisional nature of the self, he might have chosen to do things differently. As it is, we see him crash blindly against an "enemy" paradoxically generated out of his own ever-increasing need for antagonistic others.

There will be more to say about Richard's unselfconscious use of Petrarchan discourse later, but first, let me complete the analogy between Richard's usurptive position and a certain kind of position-taking by literary critics. This time my point of departure is the emphasis placed by two feminist critics, Madonne Miner and Irene Dash, on the extent to which male-authored performances of and commentaries on *Richard III* have almost completely overlooked, and invariably subordinated, the women in the play, even though only female characters undergo significant changes in outlook and feeling.[18] As the seemingly endless pattern of usurpations in the *Henry VI* and *Richard III* tetralogy systematically destroys their legal, emotional, and biological bonds to men, Elizabeth and Margaret give up the competitive back biting of the latter play's first act, and, in act 4, together with Richard's mother, they collaboratively redefine their positions in precisely the terms to which Richard's mode of self-definition blinds him—in terms, namely, of the instability of identity that their losses have brought them to acknowledge. Margaret, especially, can see not only the fact, but the positive advantages of such instability, preferring to become a Shakespearean prototype of the "new French feminist" than to stay in the English court.[19] To Elizabeth she announces:

> Now thy proud neck bears half my burdened yoke,
> From which even here I slip my wearied head
> And leave the burden of it all on thee.
> Farewell, York's wife, and queen of sad mischance!
> These English woes shall make me smile in France.
>
> (4.4.111–15)

This scene has been criticized for being "impersonal," "mainly ritual," and "rigidly formalized," and has often been cut from performances.[20] The passages of lamentation in which Richards and Edwards become indistinguishable as murderers and victims, usurpers and usurped, are found to be particularly objectionable. The recognition that these characters *are* fundamentally self-destructive and structurally indistinguishable, then, does not occur. Nor can the scene lend its support to Coppélia Kahn's theory that the means whereby the male characters know and define themselves is very much at issue in the play.[21] By subordinating this scene, or leaving it out of account, one misses the contrast, for example, between Margaret's farewell speech and Richard's hectic defense of his identity, his inability or unwillingness to slip its burden: "What do I fear? Myself? There's none else by. / Richard loves Richard: that is, I am I" (5.3.183–84). On a larger scale, one misses the relation between Richard's discourse in the first part of the play, his so-called "creative," "self-knowing," soliloquies and manipulations, and his subsequent disintegration and defeat. The turn of events then has to be accounted for with such critical constructs as "the Tudor myth of history," "a divine moral plan," or some other arbitrary check to what is perceived as Richard's power.[22] Clearly this is the feminist in me talking. My dislike of this particular critical reduction or misreading (and every reading, for by now obvious reasons, will be partial) has everything to do with my "being" a feminist woman. The deconstructionist in me, however, no less urgently, wants to call attention to the failure of this position to acknowledge the *illusoriness* (not the "wrongness") of its ground. It is in this sense that, intentionally or not, such a position participates in and perpetuates Richard's politics—sexual and other.

The feminist reader is, I hasten to elaborate, just as subject to the problematics of the proper as are the more traditional critics upon whose texts I have been commenting. If one assumes that the women in the play would be all right were it not for their dependence upon the power and privilege of their fathers, husbands, brothers, and sons, one may be poorly placed to investigate the levels of sheerly rhetorical violence to which this arrangement complexly refers.[23] Put another way, the dream of a female self that appears to itself as autonomous and authoritative as the male selves of Shakespeare's Lancastrian and Yorkist courts would sustain rather than undermine the kinds of position the male characters in the play are portrayed as occupying. It is precisely her susceptibility to this dream, in fact, that dooms Lady Anne. In order to analyze the part played in the extinction of *both* Richard and Anne, not only by male supremacy and misogyny but also by an essentializing discourse that may be employed by either sex, it becomes important not to take these characters' word either for themselves or for the social organization within which we see them embedded, but to examine closely the rhetorical structure of the characters' language about themselves. It then becomes possible to begin to describe how these selves, as they are rhetorically constituted, interlock with one another and how they are related to the usurpations and seductions that figure so largely in this play. Why is it, for example, that Richard can contemplate usurpations by others with irony, but, nevertheless, feel compelled unironically to perpetrate one of his own? Why, if Lady Anne is already at the mercy of her politically antagonistic suitor (repeating the pattern of the two queens, Margaret and Elizabeth, in the *Henry VI* plays), is Richard drawn to commit the apparently gratuitous violence of making her abandon her personal and emotional, as well as her political allegiances? My hope is not that we shall then be in a better position from which to indulge in such self-aggrandizing gestures as judging Richard and Anne or the social structures portrayed in the play but that this Renaissance text, among others, may become a more active site of the cultural self-critique with which both deconstruction and feminism, however asynchronously, are currently engaged.

2

It is not simply a question of literature's ability to say or not to say the truth of sexuality. For from the moment literature begins to try to set things straight on that score, literature itself becomes inextricable from the sexuality it seeks to comprehend.

—Barbara Johnson, *The Critical Difference*

The seduction of Anne, the occasion that has generated most of the positive commentary on Richard, is not, I would maintain, the first seduction in the play. In the opening soliloquy of act 1, Richard's own discourse enacts a kind of leading aside or away from one's own cause very similar to that which occurs to Anne in the second scene. It will be important, then, to attend closely to the means of self-definition— or as I would prefer to call it, self-seduction—in the opening scene, before trying to determine who does what to whom in scene 2. The soliloquy begins with a memorable but ironic catalogue of the antitheses presented by the "peacetime" court of Edward IV (Richard's brother) to the civil strife it replaces:

> Now is the winter of our discontent
> Made glorious summer by this sun of York
> And all the clouds that loured upon our house
> In the deep bosom of the ocean buried.
>
> (1.1.1–4)

As the antitheses pile up, Richard wittily compresses the oppositions into single lines:

> Now are our brows bound with victorious wreaths,
> Our bruised arms hung up for monuments,
> Our stern alarum changed to merry meetings,
> Our dreadful marches to delightful measures.
> Grim-visaged War hath smoothed his wrinkled front.
>
> (1.1.5–9)

and then formulates a longer, more involved contrast:

> And now, instead of mounting barbed steeds
> To fright the souls of fearful adversaries
> He capers nimbly in a lady's chamber
> To the lascivious pleasing of a lute.
>
> (1.1.10–13)

These antitheses are ironic in the sense that Richard hardly shares the pretensions of Edward's court, a court that we know, either from the *Henry VI* plays or, shortly, from Anne's lament over the corpse of Henry VI, does not represent a reconciliation of two warring factions but rather a temporary or apparent suppression of one faction by the other. This peacetime, then, and the sovereignty of the usurper Edward, can be thought of fundamentally not as the cessation of violence but as its institutionalization. In Richard's extended figure for the current situation, it is still "grim-visaged war," merely presenting a peaceful front, that has transferred its activities from the battlefield to the bedroom. To use the rhetorical terms introduced earlier, what Richard seems to appreciate is the nonproper or "improper" status of his brother's position. This position is congruent with the rhetorical violence of naming, being constituted by the structurally analogous compound violence first of civil war—in which each side sees the other as that which prevents itself from appearing proper, unique, and authoritative—then of peace—in which the dream of the proper made possible (and impossible) by war is rewritten by the "winning" side as the ground and governing principle of national, political, and social identities.

Abjuring that ground determined by Edward's usurpation (and the position dictated for him in Edward's court), Richard ought logically to extend his ironic insight to himself. A second antithesis—between the erotic activities in terms of which Edward's peace is defined and Richard's place within that schema—does make Richard's self-characterization doubly problematic:

> But I, that am not shaped for sportive tricks
> Nor made to court an amorous looking glass;
> I, that am rudely stamped, and want love's majesty
> To strut before a wanton ambling nymph . . .
>
> (1.1.14–17)

Not only does the antithetical construction itself display each term's dependence upon the other but the first term of the antithesis, amorous peace, has already been presented as highly unstable. At this point, however, the point where a subject, an "I," begins to be elaborated, Richard's discourse parts company with rigor. The self that first emerges as the antithesis to the second term of a previous antithesis comes to appear instead as itself the ground of these antitheses. In a long anacoluthon (the perfect grammatical correlative for seduction, being a sentence or expression in which there is a change of direction, an abandonment of one type of construction in favor of another) Richard translates his ironic, antithetically-constituted figure of the self into the unproblematic origin or source of his speech and actions, locking himself into the sense of autonomous selfhood that leads him to be such a poor legislator and poet in the end.

The passage whose first four lines I just quoted continues:

I, that am curtailed of this fair proportion
Cheated of feature by dissembling Nature,
Deformed, unfinished, sent before my time
Into this breathing world scarce half made up,
And that so lamely and unfashionable
That dogs bark at me as I halt by them;
Why, I, in this weak piping time of peace,
Have no delight to pass away the time,
Unless to spy my shadow in the sun
And descant on mine own deformity.

(1.1.18–27)

Suddenly, here, "peace" is peace and "I" am I; the constitutive negativity of Richard's self-image is skewed in the translation to become merely a negative (but otherwise stable, transparent) self-image. Like the narcissist that the reference to his shadow suggests that he is, Richard becomes attached to this *image* of what and where he is—an image first formulated, you recall, as an image of what and where he is not—at the expense of any apparent awareness or memory of the rhetorical operations that produced this illusory ground.[24] He confounds the power of his demystifying insight into Edward's authority with a power that would generate the freedom of an authority of his own (a confusion that seduces many resistance groups, including feminists). In spirit he has already become a usurper—someone who holds a position without right and by force—not least in the sense that he now claims to be self-determining, a position that can be maintained only by doing both rhetorical and empirical violence to the figures and factors that constitute his position. "And therefore, since I cannot prove a lover," Richard concludes with logical illogic, "To entertain these fair well-spoken days, / I am determined to prove a villain / And hate the idle pleasures of these days" (1.1.28–31).

Richard, then, continues to deceive himself when he says at the close of the second scene, the seduction of Anne, that he cannot see in himself, as Anne seems to, a "proper" man. The powerfully seductive appeal of the narcissistic or rhetorical reflection by which Richard translates his analyses of others' positions and constructs his plots for their expoitation or extinction is precisely that it allows him to conceive of himself as a substantial being, a knowing and knowable "proper" subject, capable of autonomy and self-sovereignty. Anne is then delegated the unenviable task of sustaining and extending the business that Richard has begun in his soliloquy. She, for instance, can allow him to see reflected in her a self that is not deformed but proper in the sense of physically complete and sexually eligible. Anne's role, that is, will not prove to be determined in some simple cause and effect way by the sovereign subject Richard takes himself to be; on the contrary, it will be greatly determined by the insatiable need of such a "sovereign" subject to set up for itself new challenges to surmount in an ever-intensifying evasion of its own unraveling.

But distracting attention from how scene 2 breaks down the notion that Richard and Anne are two independent subjects, controversy over their interaction has focused on the much safer question of whether or not their dialogue is credible.[25] Does it display Richard's brilliance and dramatic power that he can persuade Anne to marry him even though he has killed her husband and her father-in-law, even though he woos her over the corpse of her father-in-law, the murdered King Henry VI? Or is Anne a singularly weak woman? Or does the scene present an unplayable violation of dramatic and psychological probability, attributable, perhaps, to Shakespeare's immaturity as a playwright?[26] None of these approaches will yield readings that account for the etiology of the appetites of a self-seducer like Richard or the particular vulnerability of Anne and Richard to each other.[27] Those who argue that this scene is a brilliant display of Richard's talents simply reiterate Richard's own self-serving, long-winded, but unfounded assessment of his performance as a *tour-de-force* carried out in the face of every improbability:

> What! I that killed her husband and her father
> To take her in her heart's extremest hate,
> With curses in her mouth, tears in her eyes,
> The bleeding witness of my hatred by,
> Having God, her conscience, and these bars against me,
> And I no friends to back my suit at all
> But the plain devil and dissembling looks,
> And yet to win her, all the world to nothing!
>
> (1.2.230–37)

Conversely, but also similarly, those who find Anne weak or the scene improbable so thoroughly defend themselves against its shock effect that they see nothing to be investigated.

Thus commentators have generally not noted that it is Anne who first sets the terms for scene 2, nor have they said what those terms are. In her description of the dead Henry VI, we find her opposing signs of various kinds to more substantial realities that she takes to be transcendentally, genealogically, and even physiologically grounded:

Poor key-cold figure of a holy king,
Pale ashes of the house of Lancaster
Thou bloodless remnant of that royal blood.

(1.2.5–7)

The figures, that is, by which Anne has been defined, and continues to define herself when she identifies herself as "poor Anne, / Wife to thy Edward, to thy slaughtered son" (1.2.9–10), are posited, not as themselves figural or allegorical indicators of the rhetorical and empirical violence constitutive of political dominance (as Richard was able to see in instances other than his own) but as the literal embodiments of the authority they exercised. Though it might be seen that the Wars of the Roses would long since have radically disturbed, or displayed as disturbable, the status of names and titles associated with the houses of Lancaster and York, war can just as well, as I have mentioned, promise to each side the kind of stability of identity whose seductive appeal seems to govern the English court.

But Anne does not assume for herself quite the same kind of unproblematic position that she assumes for royal men. Implicit in her scheme of things is a kind of double focus or double-bind whereby a woman's position and identity are thought of as derivative, and therefore in some sense representative, of a male position, while a woman is also supposed to possess the kind of autonomous subjectivity (akin to the subjectivity that we have watched Richard elaborate) that could ground distinctions like the ones Anne makes here between the figural and the literal. The prophetic curse in Anne's opening speech, spoken, let it be noted, before Richard's entrance, displays the strange logic of her situation more obviously:

If ever he have wife, let her be made
More miserable by the life of him
Than I am made by my young lord and thee [Henry VI].

(1.2.26–28)

As much an anacoluthonist as Richard, she reasons that as her own unhappiness is an extension of the deaths of her husband and father-in-law, so the harm she wishes to Richard would be heightened and extended if his wife, should he ever have one, were to suffer on his account. This hypothetical wife (who will, of course, turn out to be Anne herself) would reflect her husband's condition, yet this reflection would also act somehow as a constituent of the condition it is supposed to reflect. Richard's role in the seduction of Anne is, thus, less self-initiated than it might at first appear. In a sense it is written for him, in Anne's discourse, before he ever approaches her. He need only respond to the double nature of her bereavement—her loss of her male points of reference and her role as a subjectivity that thinks of *itself* as authoritative. He can make her "amends," as he puts it at the end of scene 1, by repeatedly inviting her to see herself *reflected in him*, as immensely powerful. Whatever the fundamental incoherence and self-destructiveness of it, the position to which Anne is thus restored is consistent with (and might well seem even stronger than) the position out of which she has been cast.

It remains to be seen in greater detail how Anne's empirical seduction both evidences and screens from view Richard's and Anne's respective self-seductions, and, especially, how the image of male supremacy that Richard contrives to see reflected in Anne blinds him to the second major step on his course toward disaster. Two examples, one from the beginning of the dialogue and one from near the end, will have to suffice here to suggest in outline the remarkable transaction carried out in this complex, highly nuanced exchange. A moment after Richard has terrorized the pallbearers and been defied by Anne, he hails her as someone who has a more positive, powerful part to play than that of bereaved and beleaguered widow: "Sweet saint, for charity, be not so curst" (1.2.49), he intervenes unexpectedly. By doing so, he pays her the compliment of adopting her constellation of terms—she has just called him a devil and a "dreadful minister of hell" (1.2.46)—and names her in a way that lends the authority of virtue to her claims and curses—an authority that she evidently accepts in her lengthy, eloquently vituperative response to Richard's address. Her acceptance of his use of her terms, as well as his appropriation of her terms, however, sets up a paradoxical dependency. In order for Anne to remain the author, the creator, of the terms she is using and to retain her sense that hers is the definitive description of the situation—in order to be a speaker at all, really—she will have to remain in conversation with Richard, as in fact she does—their extensive *repartée* serving to consolidate this dependence. On the other hand, Richard's encouragement of Anne's sense of her own power over herself and Richard—which reaches its apotheosis when Richard offers her his sword and encourages her to kill him—encourages Richard, too, to think of himself as author and director of the situation, making him, in turn, paradoxically dependent upon Anne's continuing sense of authorship.

Anne, if the other female characters in the tetralogy are any indication, has no habitual or socially available alternative. These are the conditions, we can surmise, under which she would always have operated, and, on balance, Richard seems to offer her more rather than less self-determination. But how does Richard manage to have Anne serve as a testimonial to his manipulative talents and still recuperate her as a powerful, power-giving figure? His failure (and Anne's) to understand that both figures are shadowy projections of his own rhetorical blindness is enacted in their closing exchange where Anne reluctantly accepts Richard's ring. Anne, mistakenly, asserts, "To take is not to give" (1.2.203–4), to which Richard cynically, but with inadvertent accuracy, responds:

> Look how my ring encompasseth thy finger,
> Even so thy breast encloseth my poor heart.
> Wear both of them, for both of them are thine.
>
> (1.2.230–32)

Anne, that is, reflecting her insistence upon an illusory autonomy, tries to take the ring and run, to extricate herself from the conversation with her sense of her separateness from Richard intact. In the act of doing so, however, she gives, or seems to give, Richard exactly what he wants, namely that very separateness. It is *precisely* the moment at which Anne reasserts her autonomy that is seized upon by Richard in order to see reflected in her an objective, external indicator of his power. (Later, in an effort to repeat and eternalize this maneuver, he will arange to make the appearance of her autonomy permanent by having her murdered.) His unselfconscious use of a Petrarchan conceit to do so, however, labels him as at once a show-off and a dupe. Ironically a much better index of his situation than his supposed success with Anne, the discourse he employs as a sign of his literary and amorous sophistication, remains, in an important sense, unreadable to him. Because of his unironic assumption of mastery *over* his own (and Petrarch's) discourse, he remains utterly blind to what it has to say about the futility of his logic.

What Richard's words display, without necessarily expressing, might be put this way: If Anne's acceptance of his ring validates Richard's capacity to determine what will signify what to whom, then the "heart" or being of Richard, itself a product of signification, could be said to be "enclosed" within—in the sense of limited by—Anne's acceptance. It follows that Richard retains no autonomous self but could be described as a kind of ornament, set off to great advantage as presented or worn by Anne. Anne's own status is, of course, neither more nor less problematic than Richard's, as is suggested by the contorted image of her wearing the heart that her breast also encloses.

That Richard can offer and Anne can accept these words without either of them becoming alive to these implications then underscores one further aspect of their situation—namely, that because of their kindred, though asymmetrical, attachments to rhetorically impossible ideals of selfhood, both Richard and Anne cut themselves off from what discourse might have to tell them. The final irony is, of course, that the abstraction of the self from language that they seek is exactly that which, in a sense not consciously intended, they also find.

3

Some repercussions of my project of Richard's misappropriation of language are by now obvious. If either deconstruction or feminism were to triumph over the other, I would have to count it a loss for both. To criticize one discourse at the expense of the other would not prove that the first is better, nor must we try to make them consistent with each other in order to be rigorous. Indeed such projects can make sense only within the kind of totalizing discourse with which I have been taking issue. If I have not seen a way simply and directly to extricate Anne from her predicament, owing to my insistence upon analyzing her situation rhetorically rather than empirically, neither have I, I hope, encouraged a utopian feminism that would be compatible with other, non–woman-centered, utopian dreams—of which, after all, Richard's is one.

IO

The Beauty of Woman: Problems in the Rhetoric of Renaissance Portraiture

Elizabeth Cropper

The first painting, Alberti used to tell his friends, was a portrait, created by Narcissus as he embraced his own image on the surface of the pool. Portraits brought pleasure to those who recognised them and admiration for the artist who presented a convincing likeness. They made the absent present and gave life to the dead.[1] But portraiture, even in Alberti's day, is not so easily defined. The image reflected in the mirror is grasped only by the self, which the face both betrays and masks. The particular myth of origin chosen by Alberti suggests that the true likeness can be painted only by love through a process that threatens the existence of both subject and beholder-creator. Indeed, the same ancient rhetorical tradition that inspired Alberti's treatise *On Painting* had challenged the very validity of the painted portrait. In Lucian's *Essay in Portraiture* one orator describes an imaginary painted statue representing the physical beauty of Panthea, the Emperor Verus's mistress, whom he has seen only once.[2] The other portrays in words a whole series of pictures, each devoted to one of her virtues revealed to him over time and through conversations in their common tongue. In the end the two orators will combine their portrayals of her body and soul in a book. Although they frequently compare the beauty of Panthea to famous paintings and sculptures, the orators claim that their literary portrait will be more enduring and more pleasing to the sitter than any portrait by Apelles, Parrhassios, or Polygnotus. Theirs will be the most accurate portrait, for in a literary description extrinsic and intrinsic beauty, or the *effictio* and *notatio* of the rhetorical *descriptio personarum,* are combined.

Lucian, whose description of Apelles' *Calumny* is recommended by Alberti as the sort of text that prompts the painter's invention, opposes the power of images to the power of epideictic rhetoric to paint in words.[3] In the dialogue *Essays in Portraiture,* it is the portrayal of a beautiful woman that stands characteristically for the descriptive power of words. In the theory and practice of Italian Renaissance painting, both deeply indebted to Lucian's definition of the *paragone,* the portrayal of a beautiful woman also came to function as a synecdoche for the beauty of painting itself. In this context distinctions between the representation of beauty and the beauty represented are often elided, and, as a result, peculiar problems of identity and efficacy are attached to the interpretation of female portraiture.

The problem of identity may be illustrated by a few famous examples. In about 1534 Titian immortalized the beauty of Isabella d'Este (fig. 1).[4] And yet, if we did not know this to be Isabella, we would never recognise her. In 1534 she was sixty, and Titian's refashioning of an earlier portrait by Francia is a deceptive anachronism. A portrait by Parmigianino of an unidentified woman (fig. 2), painted at about the same time, presents the contemporary ideal of beauty that Titian made it possible for Isabella to rival.[5] Isabella's greater wealth is apparent, and she wears her favorite hairstyle, but the two women are similarly dressed in intricately embroidered dresses, with frilled cuffs emerging from the scalloped edges of the sleeves, and both are adorned with pearl earrings and marten furs. Beyond this, however, both portraits represent the same ideal of beauty as if it were nature, and the clear intensity of each woman's gaze is rendered ambiguous by a potential smile. We would not confuse the identity of the two women, even as we would not confuse Titian with Parmigianino, but the women's beauty is clearly synchronic, aspiring to the same idea: it establishes a similarity that outweighs difference, and only chance survival of the historical record points to Isabella as the subject of Titian's image.

Parmigianino's portrait poses the problem of identity in a different way, for the name of the sitter is not documented. In 1671 Barri identified her as Antea and as the artist's beloved. Antea in turn came to be identified with the famous, and unfortunate, courtesan of the same name.[6] Such an identification of an unknown beautiful woman as a representation of the painter's mistress and as a courtesan belongs to a long tradition, the underlying arguments of which continue to influence interpretation. Principally these are, that certain women were portrayed for their physical beauty alone, that individual artists had favorite models who conformed to their ideal of beauty and whose portrayal implies no specific identity, and that in painting female beauty the artist must first possess it.[7] Some of these arguments were also articulated by Renaissance critics and may be found to have been implicated in the creation of works of art. But the extent to

Fig. 1. Titian, *Portrait of Isabella d'Este*. Kunsthistorisches Museum, Vienna.

Fig. 2. Parmigianino, *Antea*. Gallerie Nazionali di Capodimonte, Naples.

which this is true has never been established, for modern criticism, accepting many of the same assumptions, has found them too useful to define. Many portraits of unknown beautiful women are now characterized as representations of ideal beauty in which the question of identity is immaterial. No unidentified male portrait, on the other hand, is ever said to be a beautiful representation made for its own sake.

Support for the theory that many images of women are not truly portraits, to be considered in relation to an individual sitter, but rather unproblematic objects made for simple delectation, has been found in the famous letter from Francesco Maria della Rovere, duke of Urbino,

concerning Titian's portrait known as *La Bella* (fig. 3).[8] The duke
wanted the picture for his collection and asked that Titian finish "that
portrait of that lady in the blue dress" so that it would be beautiful.
The duke's readiness to buy a beautiful picture of a woman whose
name he does not mention, and probably did not even know, has led
to revealing speculation about Titian's purpose in painting it, and, as
in the case of Parmigianino's *Antea,* his relationship to the sitter.
Pope-Hennessy (1966) attributes the sensuous beauty of the artist's
portrayals of women in general to "one of the chinks in Titian's
armour of detachment"—his suceptibility to charm.[9] Wethey (1977)
considers *La Bella* to be a portrait (as the duke of Urbino indeed called
it) but, finding the woman's look and attitude "impersonal," he
characterised the portrait as an ideal one. Seeing in the woman the
decorous reserve appropriate to a high-born lady, Wethey argues that
Titian approached her on bended knee.[10] However, in the so-called
Girl in the Fur Coat, Wethey identifies the same woman. Now she is
a model, a vision of youthful beauty, but no longer a person of
stature.[11] In neither case does he distinguish between the representation and the figure represented. In 1980, Charles Hope brought the
argument around full circle, in the most uncritical comment of all.
According to him the figure of *La Bella* is not even a decorous lady,
but "just a pretty girl." The portrait is "merely a particularly fine
example of a standard type of mildly erotic painting available in
Titian's studio."[12] In the *Venus of Urbino,* Hope recognises the same
model, now in "an elaborate erotic genre scene."[13] He admits that
such a realistic image would be unique in the sixteenth century and
sees the closest parallel in Manet's *Olympia,* thereby also destroying
Manet's gesture in painting it. If Hope is right, then all that distinguishes *La Bella* from *The Girl in the Fur Coat,* or from Paris
Bordone's many lightly draped women, is the degree of their undress.
Titian has effectively charmed his critics into believing that his
paintings mirror the truth and require no interpretation.

Critical interpretation of many of these images of women becomes
possible only when it is recognised that they belong to a special class
of paintings existing in relation to a particular set of expectations on
the part of the beholder and painter. A Renaissance portrait of a
beautiful woman is not, in other words, simply a portrait with a
female rather than a male subject, and if we look at Renaissance
criticism with this in mind it is possible to begin to define a series of
problems affecting the representation of female beauty, whatever the
particular circumstances of the commission and in relation to which
internal or external evidence about the social, historical, or economic

Fig. 3. Titian, *La Bella*. Palazzo Pitti, Florence. Photo: Alinari.

status of the person represented is secondary. In part these problems derive from those ancient rhetorical traditions of the *descriptio personarum* and the *paragone* of the literary and painted, or sculptured, portrait exemplified by Lucian's dialogue, in which the choice of a female subject sets the scene for a discussion of the particular difficulty of the representation of beauty. More immediately, they derive from the conventions of lyric poetry and courtly love, which provided the motive for nonnarrative images of women, even as epic poetry and history provided the motives for history painting. Broadly stated, these problems are the following: that the physical beauty of the beloved is necessarily beyond representation, that the representation of intrinsic beauty is specifically beyond the painter's reach, and finally, that the painting of a beautiful woman, like the lyric poem, may become its own object, the subject being necessarily absent.

All of these problems are raised by Castiglione's story in *The Book of the Courtier*.[14] On seeing a portrayal of Campaspe by Apelles, says the count, Alexander decided to give his mistress to the painter because the love inspired by beauty gives greater pleasure to the one who discerns it best. In other words, Apelles' painted image corresponded more perfectly to the ideal of beauty than the image of Campaspe that Alexander had formed in his own mind. In reply to Cesare Gonzaga's objection that he sees more beauty in the woman *he* loves than could Apelles, the count explains that it could only have been Campaspe's physical, or extrinsic, beauty that inflamed Apelles and Alexander, whereas Cesare's love relies on the knowledge that he is loved in return and upon his long acquaintance with his beloved's manners, intellect, and movement. His observation reflects not only upon the servile status of the beautiful Campaspe but also on the painter's inability, which Lucian also indicated, to represent those qualities of character disclosed only over time. Furthermore, in this story of the magnanimity of the noble Alexander, whose superior judgment recognised the discernment of the painter in making something more beautiful than nature, the woman is displaced by the work. In this transaction, the object of Campaspe's love is not, however, similarly displaced, for the count believes that she was sorely grieved to exchange a king for a painter. Apelles' art, in turn, does not make him more noble or more judicious than Alexander, but his ability to represent perfect beauty is prized more highly than the beauty of the woman he represents.

The issue raised by Cesare Gonzaga's objection and the count's reply to it constituted the most fertile paradox to painters seeking to portray beautiful women and, by extension, to paint beauty itself.

Even as the portrayal of woman provided a figure for the beauty of painting, the very possibility of representing beauty was denied. Implicated in this paradox is the poet's claim that intrinsic beauty of character, upon which a true and virtuous identity is founded, cannot be communicated in the single beautiful moment of painting. The inadequacy of the painter's representation of the beauty of the beloved woman places the possibility of any true representation in doubt.

In the Renaissance, the *locus classicus* for the claim that perfect beauty is beyond representation is, of course, Petrarch's two sonnets on Simone Martini's portrait of Laura.[15] In the first the poet denies, as would Cesare Gonzaga, that even Polyclitus could see the smallest part of the beauty that has conquered his heart, though the artist compete with every other famous artist for a thousand years. Simone's portrait could only have been painted in paradise, for on earth, where the body is a veil to the soul, his eyes would have been clouded by his senses. In the second sonnet Petrarch laments that the joy of Pygmalion is denied him: Simone has provided a figure that seems humble and kind, yet voice and intellect are forever lacking. Although Laura appears to listen benignly, she will never come alive and reply. This inability of the portrait to respond is fundamental to the story of Narcissus to which Alberti referred the origin of painting, and it epitomises Plato's objection to representation in general.[16] In the painting and criticism of the Italian Renaissance, it is the portrayal of beautiful women, however, that carries the burden of these doubts.

Pietro Bembo's two sonnets addressed to Giovanni Bellini's portrait of his beloved testify to the continuing vigor of the problem stated by Petrarch, for they imitate his sonnets directly.[17] The notion of the inexpressibility of the image in the poet's heart could not easily be circumvented, and Bembo presents the strengths and weaknesses of Bellini's painted representation of the face of the woman that is carved upon his own heart as another paradox. The resemblance of portrait to sitter lies in the fact that both are cold enamel in Bembo's gaze, even as he is enflamed by them. It is the very presence of the image before him that makes it unlike its absent subject—his beloved, who hides when he seeks her out. In the second sonnet Bembo compares the eyes, brow, and locks of the painted figure with those that have conquered him. In the brow of the face impressed upon his soul he sees Love enthroned. On one side fly his own hope, pleasure, fear, and pain. On the other his beloved's judgment, value, beauty, *leggiadria,* nature, and art, are scattered like stars. None of the qualities expressed in this *blason* can be encompassed in the silent docility of the painted representation of her face.

Both pairs of sonnets challenge the possibility of portraying the ideally beautiful woman and therefore the possibility of perfect representation itself. In the Petrarchan tradition, the object of desire is necessarily dismembered and physically absent; figurative and color-istic metaphor consciously deny specific mimetic reference. The operation of the painter who, like Zeuxis gathering together the beauties of the virgins of Croton, reunites scattered beauty, is the direct antithesis of the poet's fragmentation of presence in the *Rime sparse.*[18]

In an important article Giovanni Pozzi has examined how, faced with this challenge, several painters attempted to accommodate the metaphors of poetry in their representations of beautiful women.[19] An attempt at literal, and therefore unsuccessful, translation cited by Pozzi is Bartolomeo Veneto's painting of a woman, variously identi-fied as a marriage portrait, a portrait of Giulia Farnese, or of Lucretia Borgia, or as a Flora (fig. 4).[20] The metallic curls, the flowers she holds, and the white veil and shift would stand for the gold, ivory, roses, and snow of the lyric poem, here reduced almost to a still life. Pozzi believes that many so-called Floras may belong to this type, in which jewels and ivory skin tinged with pink serve to provoke a mental reconstruction, not of the woman herself but of the poetry in which they serve as figures. Such literal reference is avoided in two of the most successful attempts to rival poetic metaphor through the autonomous power of painting. In Titian's so-called *Vanità,* physical beauty confronts us directly (fig. 5).[21] Gold, pearls, and jewels are figured in the reflecting pool of the mirror, the fugitive quality of beauty being underlined by the presence of the Fate. In Giorgione's *Laura* (fig. 6), Pozzi's second example, again variously identified as Petrarch's Laura, a woman called Laura, a courtesan, or a marriage portrait, the laurel provides the single referent to the Petrarchan figure. This established, all others are denied, and the painter claims the power to represent the colors of natural beauty that are beyond the reach of poetic metaphor.[22]

To Pozzi's example should be added Leonardo's portrait of a woman now identified as Ginevra de' Benci (figs. 7 and 8).[23] Facing us is the image of the physical beauty of Ginevra that only the painter can represent. As in Giorgione's *Laura,* the bush behind her provides the single referent to her as the beloved. In this case the species, juniper, identifies her specifically as Ginevra, but the pun on her name operates only through the analogy with laurel. The emblematic image on the reverse (fig. 8), figuring her inexpressible qualities, confirms this. The emblems are not, like those in Titian's mirror, metaphors for her

Fig. 4. Bartolomeo Veneto, *Portrait of a Woman,* Städelsches Kunstinstitut, Frankfurt.

Fig. 5. Titian, *Allegory of Vanity*. Bayerische Staatsgemäldesammlungen, Alte Pinakothek, Munich.

Fig. 6. Giorgione, *Laura*. Kunsthistorisches Museum, Vienna.

Fig. 7. Leonardo da Vinci, *Ginevra de' Benci.* National Gallery of Art, Washington; Ailsa Mellon Bruce Fund.

beauty but figures of her character. Against a background of simulated porphyry, a curling ribbon encircles a sprig of juniper and embraces branches of laurel and palm. It is inscribed *VIRTUTEM FORMA DECORAT*—with her Beauty she adorns Virtue. Again the branches establish the reference to Petrarch, for they are the "ramoscel di palma / et un di Lauro" that the spirit of the dead Laura brings from the empyrean to comfort him in a vision.[24] "The palm is victory," she explains, "and I when still young conquered the world and myself; the laurel means triumph, of which I am worthy, thanks to that Lord who gave me strength."[25] Laura chides the poet for seeking her lost

Fig. 8. Leonardo da Vinci, reverse of *Ginevra de' Benci*. National Gallery of Art, Washington; Ailsa Mellon Bruce Fund.

corporeal beauty when he asks "is this the blond hair and the golden knot that still binds me, and those the beautiful eyes that were my sun?" But to help him in his travail, it is given to her to appear as she once was and to promise that she will be more beautiful than ever, more dear to him. Through this emblem and its associations, Leonardo circumvented the inability of painting to portray the beloved: Ginevra's beauty, like Laura's, adorns her virtue. The poet's denial of the validity of painted appearance is refuted through painting itself. At the same time, however, the withdrawn presence before us is not Ginevra but her redeeming appearance, more beautiful than ever, a memory image that fills the void of her absence.[26] The porphyry on the reverse stands for her nobility, the stony obduracy of her chastity than can yet strike a flame in the heart, and, through its association with the tomb, the metaphysical death suffered through absence. Leonardo has painted the silence of the portrait of the beloved that Petrarch could only describe. In a beautiful paradox he makes the problem of representation manifest rather than suppressing it.[27]

Leonardo accepted the challenge of the *paragone* more aggressively than his contemporaries, determining to express the beauty of the soul through the representation of the graceful movements of the body. He opposed the natural, universal language of painting to the conventions of poetry. "What poet," he asks of the lover, "can put before you the true effigy of your idea with such truth as the painter?"[28] In the portrait of *Mona Lisa,* he severed the reference to the emblems of poetry upon which the portrait of Ginevra relies. Responding to the poet's challenge, he represented the form and character of an individual woman as the effigy of the perfect idea in the lover's heart. He claimed the autonomous power of painting to set before the lover a living presence in a single moment, to which his eyes would be drawn by nature.[29] Mona Lisa herself is absent, but the portrait has the ability to make her seem present, or, in the words of Lorenzo de' Medici addressed to a portrait of a woman, "come se fussi viva e pura," at least some of the time.[30] The woman is not replaced by the work, but representation is no longer impossible.

Leonardo's sublimation of the objections raised in the *paragone* of painting and poetry against the validity of the painter's representation of ideal beauty through his portrayal of a perfect illusion of natural beauty provides a definition of High Renaissance art. His achievement, and that of Raphael and Michelangelo in emulation of it, was not long sustained. By the 1530s and 1540s the relative merits of poetry and painting in the representation of intrinsic and extrinsic beauty had again become favorite topics for debate.[31] The representation of a beautiful woman continued to provide the figure for this *paragone,* and the sonnets by Petrarch and Bembo were frequently introduced as evidence for arguments in which many of the productive distinctions we have observed were dissolved or transformed.[32] Ludovico Dolce, for example, argued that Ariosto's description of the beautiful Alcina—another favorite text in the *paragone* of painting and poetry in the Cinquecento—was the work of a painter: when the poet described her cheeks as a mixture of privet and roses, he was painting like Titian. Conversely, the painter could do no better than to paint what the poet had described.[33] Paralleling this rapprochement, as Mendelsohn has shown, sixteenth-century treatises on painting came to be modeled on contemporary treatises on love, and not only on the texts of ancient rhetoric.[34]

In the Renaissance *paragone* of painting and poetry, the portrayal of a beautiful woman is not merely an example. It is the test the poet sets the painter, and the primary figure for the truthfulness of the representation of beauty itself. Not all portraits of beautiful women were painted in direct response to the changing arguments of this debate, but, given the inextricability of the image of the beloved from the problem of the *paragone,* so firmly established by Petrarch, few paintings of women stand completely outside it. Sometimes the metaphors of poetry prevail, sometimes the natural colors of painting dominate, and, as we have seen in the case of Leonardo's two images, the issue of the *paragone* is correspondingly more or less apparent. But the portrait of a beautiful woman belongs to a distinct discourse from which the woman herself is necessarily absent. In portraying his mistress, it is the art of painting that the painter desires to possess, even as the poet embraces his own laurels.

II

Spinsters and Seamstresses: Women in Cloth and Clothing Production

MERRY E. WIESNER

Unlike other crafts, the production of cloth and clothing throughout most of western history has been a women's occupation. Until the late middle ages, all stages of production, from carding raw wool or cooking flax to making the final finishing touches on garments, were carried out in the home, usually by female members of the family or servants. As late as 1500, Jacob Wimpheling in *Germania* (dedicated to the city of Strasbourg) praised Margaret, daughter of Duke Louis of Bavaria and wife of Phillip, the elector Palatinate, his contemporary, with the comment: "She was active during her whole life with feminine occupations, consisting mainly of spinning and weaving of wool and silk, sewing and all sorts of embroidery, which she did together with her entire female retinue."[1] She was certainly not an exception, as letter exchanges between noble women often include references to spinning and requests for yarn, with clear indication that the ladies were doing this themselves.[2]

Beginning in the thirteenth century, however, particularly in urban areas, male artisans began to take over some stages of production from women, gradually forming guilds of weavers and cloth cutters. As with all guilds, systems of apprenticeship were set up, which usually did not allow for female participation. Only the initial stages, such as carding and spinning, or the production of cheaper cloth, especially that specifically made for women's clothing, such as veils, were left to unorganized women workers.

This gradual exclusion of women from the skilled trades has usually been examined in the context of more general economic changes going on during the early modern period—the growth and decline of the guilds in both political power and economic strength, the rise of rural cottage industry, the gradual economic decline of many towns, the growth of capitalism.[3] The model that has been the most useful in explaining the declining opportunities for women has been a Marxist one: with the growth of capitalism, production was organized on a larger and larger scale, workplace and home were separated, and an individual wage replaced the family wage of domestic production. Women rarely controlled enough financial resources to act as investors and so remained in the market economy as underpaid wage labor or disappeared from the market economy to the unpaid (and therefore devalued in a capitalist society) domestic realm.[4] The cloth industry has been seen as the prime example of this, in England with the growth of rural cottage industry and in Florence and Flanders with a similar, although urban, "putting-out" system.[5]

When one examines other areas of Europe, however, the Marxist model is less appropriate. In most of the German cities during this period, for example, cloth production remained under the control of small-scale master craftsmen, with most tasks still carried out in small domestic workshops. Nevertheless, women were increasingly excluded from the higher paying stages of production in the same way as in areas with a "modernizing" economy. Thus a solely economic model is not sufficient.

Recent feminist scholarship has provided other explanations and has linked this exclusion of women from the world of work to a number of other changes going on in contemporary European society. Natalie Davis and Joan Kelly see it as related to an increased emphasis on the patriarchal family as the basic social unit.[6] Cities increasingly forced women to live (and work) in male-headed households and restricted the right of women to make economic decisions of any type.[7] Other observers tie women's exclusion from nondomestic work to increasing misogyny, both scholarly and satirical, a misogyny that found its most devastating expression in the great witch craze.[8] Restrictions on women's work are also seen as an example of the increasing division between public and private, a split in which women were relegated to the private, domestic realm.[9] These analyses recognize the ideological content in the restrictions but are often impressionistic and based primarily on prescriptive sources—sermons, law codes, behavior manuals, political treatises, and literature.

Feminist social historians have begun to go beyond the prescriptive literature to explore why and how women's work changed during the early modern period, paying attention to both the economic and ideological context. The work of Olwen Hufton, Louise Tilly, and Joan Scott on the impact of industrialization in the eighteenth century offers sophisticated analysis of the relations between women's work, the family, and the larger economy.[10] For the pre-industrial period,

Natalie Davis has focused on the situation in Lyons, Lyndal Roper on Augsburg, Susan Karant-Nunn on Zwickau, Grethe Jacobsen on Malmö, Annette Winter on Trier, Heide Wunder on East Prussia, Judith Brown on Florence, and I, in my earlier work, on Nuremberg.[11] Marxist, feminist, and other models can best be tested by examining a fairly small geographic area in which economic, political, social, religious, and ideological factors can all be taken into account.

This study continues that line of research, looking at a single industry—cloth and clothing production—in a few cities in Germany. I explore cloth and clothing production precisely because it had been women's work, so that the exclusion of women was a significant change, and I concentrate on German cities because the mode of production did not change dramatically. Here "modernization" cannot be the sole explanation. I will first examine the process by which women's work was limited and then put forth some of the factors I see as operating in the process. The study is based, wherever possible, on actual cases, for, as we shall see, women protested against, circumvented, or ignored any rule or regulation by which a guild or city council attempted to restrict their activities, so a study of the laws alone can be misleading.

First, let us look briefly at the medieval period. As weavers and other guilds were gradually being formed in the late thirteenth and fourteenth centuries in Germany, women were involved in a huge variety of occupations. In Frankfurt, fourteenth-century tax records list twenty-four somewhat different occupations for women in cloth and clothing.[12]

The Munich tax records for the fifteenth century include weavers, seamstresses, dyers, veilmakers, silk embroiderers, glove knitters, bag makers, nappers, bag and glove embroiderers, and spinsters who are clearly working on their own and not simply as widows carrying on their husband's shop.[13] In Trier, Annette Winter finds women in many of the same crafts.[14]

The situation is much the same in other German cities. A partial list of weavers in 1434 in Strasbourg includes sixty-eight men and thirty-eight women, some labeled as widow or daughter but some as "single woman" (Jungfer) or with nothing but their name. About half of these women made a larger payment than normal with the note, "if they want to make cloth, they will do like the others," so apparently they were paying extra for the privilege of being in the guild without making cloth.[15] Some of these female weavers were quite successful, as their income and property made them responsible for supporting an armored knight and horse for the city's defense.

The number of weavers of all types in a city like Augsburg, Frankfurt, or Ulm—between two hundred and five hundred—necessitated a huge number of additional workers, most of whom do not appear in any records. Each weaver, with the help of one or two journeymen, often produced as much as sixty to a hundred bolts of cloth annually. Fifteenth- and sixteenth-century techniques of production necessitated at least twenty carders and spinners per weaver.[16] These pieceworkers, paid by the weaver, were generally women who carded and spun in their own homes or in the weaver's house, but who are almost never identified by occupation in tax lists because they paid no independent taxes on their work, as they were considered members of a male-headed household.

About thirty cities in Germany saw independent female tailors, some of them assuredly master's widows but some also women who seem to have joined the guild on their own.[17] Tailors often had female wage workers who did much of the actual sewing for them.[18] In addition to tailors, seamstresses were to be found in every city.

In Ulm, several women took part in the *Barchantschau,* the examination and approval of linen cloth, admittedly as folders and other sorts of manual laborers, but they were sworn to secrecy and to do their job quickly and efficiently just as was every other official at the *Schau,* and they were paid the same as male assistants.[19]

It is evident, then, that women were independently involved in a huge number of textile-related occupations well into the fifteenth century. The large majority of them were wageworkers involved in preparing thread, finishing clothing, or assisting weavers, but some were weavers or tailors themselves, either carrying on a shop as a widow or having somehow gained the right to run a shop on their own.

As early as the fifteenth century, however, one begins to see the restrictions, which intensify and sharpen in the sixteenth and seventeenth centuries. The barrage of restrictions falls roughly into four categories: (1) limitations on master's widows; (2) restrictions on the family background and conduct of the master's or journeyman's wife; (3) controls on or total prohibition of the use of female labor by masters; (4) direct restrictions on independent work by women, often with certain specific exceptions. Each of these categories is justified and enacted in certain distinct ways.

Limitations on the rights of widows are the most common and widespread of all restrictions. The earliest guild ordinances make no mention at all of widows, who seem to have had unrestricted rights to carry on the husband's shop after his death or at least as long as they remained unmarried.[20] The earliest restrictions limit the time a widow was allowed to continue operating the shop, at first, usually to one or two years and later to as little as two months. In other cases, she was limited to only finishing work already begun or was allowed to work at all only if there was a son who could possibly inherit the shop.[21] If she remarried fairly soon, she might be forbidden even to sell what her first husband had made if the second was not in the same guild.[22]

During the fifteenth and sixteenth centuries, guilds often required a widow to pick a journeyman to run the shop, or the guild picked one for her. The stereotypical scenario is that she then married the journeyman, for most guilds made it easier and cheaper to get in if one married a master's widow. By the seventeenth century in some guilds, however, widows were forbidden to use journeymen in an attempt to keep their shops as small as possible.[23]

Sometimes restrictions on widow's work came under the guise of technological improvement. For example, a new dying process was introduced in sixteenth-century Lübeck; in 1546 the city council there allowed the old *Tuchscherer* to continue working but not their widows. Only men who had been trained in the new techniques were to be allowed to dye cloth after the old *Tuchscherer* had all died out.[24]

Widows as a rule ran smaller workshops and had a smaller income, even when allowed to continue to work independently. Claus-Peter Clasen, in his new study of the Augsburg weavers around 1600, finds that 15 percent of the master weavers were women, but they employed only 5 percent of the journeymen and assistants.[25] Over two-thirds of the widows in the Munich tax lists paid the smallest amount of taxes, a statistic repeated in other cities as well, at a time when 20 to 25 percent of the households in most cities were headed by women, usually widows.[26]

One can easily understand why widows were allowed to carry on a business—the tools, equipment, and organization were already there, contracts had been made, the household still needed to be supported, the widow was usually skilled enough to carry on the work, and cities prized order and continuity in households, which of course were the tax units. Why then would widow's work be restricted at all? To answer this question, we need first to look at the justifications given by various guilds and then try to extrapolate the real reasons from these.

The longest list of justifications that I have found is in a case involving the Frankfurt stonemasons. In 1624, a stonemason's widow asked to be allowed to continue working, as she had a large amount of stone left that her husband had purchased just before his death and that no one was willing to buy. Several stonemasons answered her with the comment that it was now the practice in Frankfurt and elsewhere that widows were allowed to work only four weeks after their husband's death. They followed this with a long string of justifications for not giving her special consideration. First, other widows would want the same rights, as had happened once before. Second, her husband had been the most successful stonemason in town, and the others felt he had taken business away from them and were bitter about it. If his widow continued the shop, there would be many disputes between her and the other masters. Besides, her husband had been vigorously opposed to letting any widow work longer than normally allowed, so why should they go against his wishes in the case of his own wife? Third, she could not oversee the shop properly so that stone might be destroyed and work not done properly, "which would bring shame to her and to the whole guild." Fourth, she could not control the journeymen, who might marry and have children; but if they were accused of bad work, they might leave their wives and children, who would then need public support. Fifth, because she could not control the journeymen, they would want to work in her shop and not for the other masters. The city council in Frankfurt wrote first to Strasbourg asking about the practice there and, on finding that stonemason's widows there were also limited to four weeks work, refused to allow the widow her request, despite her pleas for Christian charity.[27]

Many of these justifications also appear in other cases in other crafts. In a 1604 complaint by the Munich linen weavers against a woman, they include disorder among the crafts, bad products, masters' widows and orphans left without support, poor masters who could no longer pay their taxes, and suspicious persons coming in to the city. Quite a list.[28]

In this complaint and the stonemasons' answer, we can see a number of things emerging: petty jealousy and envy of the most successful master, suspicion between masters and journeymen, feigned or real concern about the guild's quality standards and the city's security, flagrant attempts to win over the city council with the spectre of more public welfare charges. These kinds of reasons certainly figure in other decisions to limit widows' rights in many crafts, lending unintentional irony to the words of the Strasbourg city council that the action was taken "because of a number of especially important reasons, all too long to mention here but which are known to all."[29] Limitation of the rights of widows was one way in which the guilds tightened up in the sixteenth century and controlled the number and size of workshops operating.

This tightening up can also be seen in the second category, restrictions on the family background and conduct of wives. Beginning with the earliest guild laws, master's wives as well as masters had to be legitimate and have an "honorable" lifestyle. A woman was also responsible for the conduct of her parents; even if they were guild members, if one of them acted or had acted dishonorably in any way, she was suspect and would often not be married.[30]

Occasionally this concern was carried to what seem to be bizarre extremes. The shoemakers' guild in Bremen, for example, appears to have had the right to physically examine the wife of a shoemaker before the couple's first copulation to see whether or not she was a virgin. In the words of the ordinance, which are, admittedly, confusing, "the two youngest guild officials, with the hand they have sworn their oath with, touch or grab, as a sign of her undisturbed virginity." Following this, the young couple had to provide the two officials with a meal.[31] Some authors have interpreted this to mean that the officials actually touched the woman's sexual organs, which, given the fact that contemporary doctors did not go that far when making diagnoses, I think is highly unlikely. Whatever it was that they actually touched or grabbed, however, the guilds' close involvement and interest in the most intimate personal details comes out clearly.

The guilds were much more strict than city councils or even the Roman Catholic or Protestant churches in regulating conduct. A couple whose first child was born too soon after their marriage was often expelled, and appeals went all the way to the emperor, although the state and church, of course, accepted such children as fully legitimate. A man who had committed adultery was usually expelled immediately from the guild; if his wife was guilty and he decided to go on living with her, he was also thrown out. Such cases appeared often before city courts, which had to decide between keeping households and marriages together and keeping the guilds happy; they usually decided in favor of the household and ordered the guilds to take such masters back. Even when they grudgingly agreed to do so, the guild usually at least forbade the guilty woman to accompany her husband to any guild functions and often tried to deny her any widows' rights or deny her children entrance rights to the guild.[32] The guilds also objected when a city council occasionally allowed a woman to continue operating a shop after her husband had been banished for one reason or another. The council again was motivated by the desire to keep households together and keep them self-supporting, to prevent any avoidable drain on public finances, the guild by the desire to limit numbers and keep up its reputation.[33]

During the sixteenth and seventeenth centuries, journeymen became even more stringent than masters. Journeymen's ordinances, which were first written down separately in the late sixteenth century, forbade all contact with prostitutes, even standing next to them in a public place.[34] Journeymen often refused to work with another who had married a woman in some way "dishonorable" until guild masters or city councils stepped in and ordered them to do so. As one can easily imagine, the atmosphere in a workshop where this had happened was not pleasant.

This atmosphere of tension and a constant concern for what everyone else was doing, or had once done, can be seen as a result of feeling threatened, which guilds and especially journeymen came to feel with the economic decline of the late sixteenth century. Excluding someone on any possible grounds meant one less competitor for a position; if a whole family could be excluded through the actions of one member, so much the better. The third category of restrictions, those on the use of female labor by master craftsmen, also points to the jealousies, petty quarrels, and power plays that were so common in guild life. Women were used by cloth masters more often than by masters of other guilds as the women were adept at the kinds of skills needed and the work could be easily subdivided, with the master and his journeyman simply providing the finishing touches. The borders between domestic service and domestic industry were often very fluid; maids might actually spend most of their time spinning or carding or doing other production-related tasks.

Objections often came first from journeymen who felt they were losing work to women. In 1597, the journeymen cord makers (*Posamentierer*) in Frankfurt complained to the city council that although cordmaking had recently been made a guild, the masters were still hiring no one but young women or girls, although this was not tolerated by most guilds. The masters replied that their teaching girls as well as boys was a sign of their openness and generosity; if they were to be strict like other guilds, the journeymen themselves would suffer as they would all have to produce a proof of legitimate birth and a letter of apprenticeship. Nevertheless, ten years later, the journeymen's arguments were successful, and the masters were allowed to use only their own daughters and no other relatives or nonrelated maids. Even the number of daughters they could use was limited to two, and they were only allowed to work at "finishing small tasks".[35]

The work of maids was often restricted to assisting or packing or to some of the most unpleasant tasks, such as dying and bleaching.[36] Even in occupations that today seem traditionally feminine, such as stocking knitting, maids were restricted to carding and spinning the wool and were not to be taught to knit; this was the province of the master, journeymen, and apprentices.[37]

Not only the journeymen but also other guilds made objections to masters using women. In 1615, the Munich strap makers (*Riemern*) complained that the belt makers were using their wives and maids to do stitching with an awl, which was forbidden to everyone but the strap makers. The city council ordered the belt makers not to use female hands for tasks that they themselves were not allowed to do.[38] During the mid-seventeenth century, the Strasbourg wool weavers had come to such hard times that they were spinning wool for the linen weavers, for their production of linsey-woolsey. They forced through a regulation that allowed the linen weavers only one spinning maid instead of the large number they had had previously; they had to buy all the rest of their wool thread from the wool weavers.[39]

Occasionally these disputes ranged beyond city boundaries. In the 1530s, the journeymen bag and glove makers in Nuremberg objected to having to work next to a maid, but the city council continued to allow women to work. Shortly after, the bag and glove makers in Strasbourg complained about the cheap price of Nuremberg gloves and persuaded the city council there to write to Nuremberg. This complaint was effective, and the women were forbidden to work.[40] The same sort of pressure was put on the Fulda hat makers by those in Frankfurt. The latter refused to take on journeymen who had been trained in Fulda as long as the Fulda hat makers continued to use "all sorts of servants, maids and embroideresses," and once again women were excluded.[41]

We can point to several causes for this exclusion: inter-guild rivalries, journeymen's fears, worries about competition from guilds in other cities, conflicts between masters and journeymen. All of these and others come to play in the fourth category of limitations, direct restrictions on independent work by women.

In some cities, women were specifically limited to making narrow cloth (*Halb-tuch*) and veils, as in 1360 in Speyer and in 1375 in Hamburg; in 1458 even the number who could do that in Hamburg was limited to thirty.[42] In Strasbourg, the female *Halb-tuch* weavers could only have one bench, and the male weavers attempted to limit all women to veil weaving alone, 'because the majority of the male weavers have to earn their living making *Halb-tuch*."[43] In 1470 women were excluded totally from weaving in Leipzig, in 1403 in Göttingen, and in 1450 in Richlitz in Saxony; in the last case some women continued until the guild appealed to the duke of Saxony and got a ducal order demanding that they stop.[44] The Basel weavers complained repeatedly in the mid–fifteenth century that the women who were supposed to weave only headcloths were also weaving *Halb-tuch*; the city council required these women to pay the normal guild dues from then on but did not require them to quit weaving—indeed, 25 percent of the linen weavers in Basel in 1469 were women, but Basel is somewhat of an exception.[45]

The 1598 weaving ordinance for a number of small towns in the duchy of Württemburg recommends that no girls be taken on as apprentices, and if one was, she was to pay a higher entrance fee than a boy. If she became a master weaver, she could only weave *Halb-tuch* and could not use a maid or apprentice to do any weaving for her; if she married outside the craft, she could weave only veils. The Stuttgart ordinance from the same year is even more specifically antifemale, as it directly forbids taking on new female apprentices, with a huge four gulden fine and a fine of three gulden for any present *Meisterin* who took on an apprentice.[46] It does allow women to continue boiling flax, one of the most unpleasant tasks in cloth preparation, but only under the direct supervision of a master.

Augsburg also saw disputes about veil weaving. Up to 1560, this was a free art (*Freie Kunst*) open to anyone. At this point, the weavers and some of the veil makers demanded that anyone who made veils buy into the weavers' guild (*Webergerechtigkeit*), justifying this with the claim that the art of weaving veils had changed and become more complicated, so that only those learned in the craft should weave. The city council asked for a compromise, and in 1561 the veil weavers were given an ordinance requiring all to buy the *Webergerechtigkeit*, except for those "few women" who had been weaving already, who could now have only two looms. These women also had to register immediately with the council, to buy all their yarn in the city, and to be married or widowed with their own household. This last clause was objected to immediately by a number of single veil weavers who had learned veil weaving "because it is a fine and honorable female trade" and who were supporting elderly parents; only in a few cases, however, did the city council make exceptions and allow single women to work.[47]

This concern about single women working on their own also comes out in several other cases in Augsburg. In 1577, the weavers complained that they couldn't find enough maids to spin for them as all the women coming to the city were working independently, living with other families or renting a small room somewhere. Five years later the council forbade all noncitizen women to live and work independently, but to no avail. In 1597, the weavers were even more incensed, as women were saying openly that they were not so dumb as to work as spin maids for the weavers when they could earn three times as much spinning on their own. This was an intolerable situation, according to the weavers, as these women had complete freedom in when they worked and when not and freedom to walk around with young journeymen all during the week; they were a bad example for girls coming in from the countryside, and even for local girls, who decided to live on their own rather than becoming maids. The city council enacted a series of harsh ordinances, banishing women who made demands of their employers and forbidding all unmarried women, citizens or not, from having their own household, but these were probably just as ineffective as earlier laws.[48]

In most cases, the guilds were successful in their restrictions on women's work. City councils did make individual exceptions, but these usually allowed women, for example, to weave for customers but not for the free market, and only for customers who came to them;[49] to repair clothing and furs but make nothing new;[50] to make shirts and underclothing but no suits or expensive garments;[51] to bleach only those veils they had woven themselves;[52] or to knit stockings with needles but not on frames.[53] In short, to make or do things that were simple and not very expensive. Even these were forbidden if the city council did not feel that the woman was poor or worthy or needy enough, so that women's individual pleas are filled with statements stressing their age, poverty, number of dependent children (some of whom are usually sickly or still nursing), sick husbands, and war losses; the women threw themselves on the mercy of the council: "because as a poor old widow I have nothing but what I earn with trials and work in sour sweat . . . as I already have one foot in the grave and few days left to live . . . I would see (your permission) as such great generosity that I would constantly and fervently pray to God for your health and salvation."[54] Granted that sixteenth- and seventeenth-century language is flowery, but one certainly senses great desperation in mothers who ask that the piece of bread not be taken out of their child's mouth, that they be allowed to continue working.[55]

Despite these individual exceptions, by the mid-seventeenth century, we find very few references to female weavers and tailors, and there are restrictions on women's work even in stocking knitting, which became a guild in Germany only in the late sixteenth century. What then were women still doing? According to the Munich tax lists, a few single individuals were making lace, embroidering, weaving veils, making string, carding, or working satin.[56] A list of linen weavers in Munich includes 156 masters, and only 3 widows.[57] They were still seamstresses; the Memmingen city council occasionally provided the fees for girls to learn that trade and provided desperately poor seamstresses with food in the hospital.[58] There were still a few weavers, as Clasen finds in his study of the Augsburg weavers. On the 2,165 people who actually had a loom and weaver's bench, 115 were women; of these 115, 47 had no journeyman or servant. Therefore they either wove themselves or let the loom stand unused, which was very unlikely. Clasen simply doesn't know what to think on the matter, because there was no provision in guild ordinances for female apprentices and some of these women were not widows.[59] I don't find this terribly surprising, as with only one loom they were not major weavers; the tax records indicate they were very poor anyway. Their presence was most likely simply tolerated as it was easier and cheaper to let them weave a bit than provide them with poor relief.

Most of all, women were spinning. When households were liquidated for debt and everything was sold down to the last spoon, the widow was still allowed to keep her spinning wheel.[60] In even the most desperate cases, women were expected to continue spinning: a woman charged with stealing had merited a harsh punishment, according to the Memmingen city council, but because she had been forced to steal by her now deceased mother and was very sickly, she was to be chained in the paupers' room in the city hospital "in a way that she can still spin."[61] The Strasbourg city council was offered the prospect of a young woman "with no hands and only one foot, but who can still do all sorts of handwork, like spinning"; the man who had found her wanted to show her to the public, and the city council agreed, allowing him to charge a penny an onlooker.[62]

As Alice Clark says of the seventeenth century in England, "Spinning became the chief resource of the married women who were losing their hold on other industries, but its return in money value was too low to render them independent of other means of support."[63] Whether married or single, a spinner was always dependent on the weaver for her livelihood, and as more women turned to spinning, she could not demand a decent wage for her work.

Thus by the mid-seventeenth century, women were limited to the lowest paid and least pleasant tasks within the cloth industry, to work that they could do part time even if they needed to work full time to support themselves, or to work that was outside the guild structure, which men did as well as a side occupation. Their labor was essentially proletarianized, and their economic security was minimal. They generally worked in isolation in their own homes; thus, unlike male weavers and also unlike market women, who worked together or in competition with one another, they developed little work identity and did not organize as a group.

This process of removing women from the workplace took centuries, and involved, as I have pointed out, a variety of causes. Some of these were economic. With the decline of the late sixteenth century, guilds and journeymen attempted to limit the number of workers outside the guild system who could be hired in any shop. This worked against the labor of male piece workers as well as that of women and was one of the reasons that enterprising investors began to organize production in the rural areas away from guild restrictions. Interguild rivalries intensified, as guilds attempted to produce a broader range of products, thus infringing on the range of another guild. Competition between towns also increased, and guilds often charged their competitors, both local and distant, with breaking ordinances in order to produce a product more cheaply. The easiest way to produce a cheaper product was to hire cheaper labor, which all guilds recognized would often mean hiring women; this might be disguised by claiming that they were domestic servants or even adopted daughters.

Some of these causes were political. Women's work was a handy arena for battles between guilds and city councils over control of the economic life of the city—the guilds arguing that they should control it as part of their regulation of quality standards and production levels, the councils that they should as part of their oversight of public welfare. Thus each request by a woman to be allowed to make or do something to support herself and her family took on a symbolic importance far greater than the actual threat posed to the guild by her labor. This was also true for cases involving disputes between guilds and journeymen concerning who would control who was allowed to work in a shop and what tasks they were allowed to do.[64]

Some of these causes were personal. Individual widow's requests were often turned down if their husband had been disliked or their lifestyle was seen as questionable. Groups of women, like the Augsburg veil weavers, were opposed because their attitude and demeanor offended the guild concerned.

No matter what the underlying causes, the language used to justify and accomplish these moves became more and more antifemale. Crafts that traditionally had been free arts strove to become guilds, expressly to prevent "old women, charlatans and rogues" from carrying out their craft.[65] Restrictions on pieceworkers refer to "women and all sorts of people" or "women and other unskilled workers."[66] Gradually the two, "women" and "unskilled," came to be equated in the minds of those making the regulations. Language that had begun perhaps as rather common, offhand misogyny became an integral part of the restrictions.

We can see this in the answers to women's individual supplications. Increasingly the guilds expressed their objections, not by noting that the individual was untrained or not a guild member, but simply that she was a woman.[67] In their denial of women's requests, city councils also generalized and stated that the work involved was not "women's work."[68] This did not work the other way, however. Councils never made blanket statements about the rights of women *per se* to work in a given occupation. If a council agreed to an individual supplication, they often pacified the guild concerned by noting that this was an extraordinary case and normally such requests would be denied.[69]

As more and more women worked at tasks that were unskilled and low paying, any occupation in which a significant number of women were involved became devalued. This vicious circle has been traced in the twentieth century with librarians, secretaries, and telephone operators, but we can see it working here as well.[70] "Women's work" was by definition, low-status, unskilled, and badly paid.

For the cloth and clothing trades, this posed a particular problem. Because cloth and clothing production had traditionally been women's work, weavers and associated craftsmen had to make the distinction between what they did and this devalued "women's work" more sharply than did other trades. Certain stages of production, such as weaving and cloth-cutting, became increasingly defined as men's work, and certain stages, primarily spinning, as women's. This distinction was an economic one, as I have noted above, as the men's tasks were generally the higher-status and higher-paid, but it was also what might be called an ideological one. Women were not to do certain tasks because their doing them would devalue them and thus threaten the status and self-esteem, as well as the income, of the men who did them. The Augsburg weavers, for example, clearly felt that a few female weavers posed a threat that went beyond economics, judging by the violence of their reactions. In other cities, too, weavers often led the fight against women working independently in any allied trade.[71]

The situation was even more problematic for journeymen. As journeymen's work also became proletarianized—that is, as their chances of ever becoming masters dimmed and they could expect to remain wage laborers in a master's shop for their whole lifetime—journeymen attempted to save a shred of their old position and honor by sharply differentiating their work from that of women. They became the group most fervently opposed not only to independent work by women but also to any work by women in the shop.[72] As most production was still small scale and domestic, this meant creating a line between men's work and women's work within the walls of a household-workshop.

Women's tasks within the workshop were reduced to those that were essentially domestic-cleaning up, packing, preparing materials—which created within a shop an artificial division between the public realm of production and the private domestic realm. This worked to both the economic and ideological advantage of the journeymen, as they were assured a certain number of workplaces and their work was distinguished from women's work. It was also an important symbolic victory in their disputes with guild masters. The women who worked in the shop—the master's wife, daughters, and maids—were a symbol of the patriarchal system that everyone in the household, including journeymen and apprentices, worked under. By restricting the women's work, the journeymen showed that they had some power; although their own lives were increasingly controlled by the master, they at least had some control over his female dependents.

This flat prohibition of women's work occasionally worked against the journeymen's own economic interests, for they supported prohibitions of widows using journeymen, which meant they lost workplaces. Their own wives—for they had succeeded in their demands to be allowed to marry—could also not work at a trade for decent wages. What the journeymen did in the shop was to be a male province; what their wives, and all women, did was to be done at home, in spare moments, by the piece or by the day, badly paid, but often earning money desperately needed to keep the family going.

Thus women's work came to have an ideological content far beyond its economic significance. Not only does it become an epithet for the boring, mundane, domestic tasks beneath the dignity of a man—"that's women's work"—and women's occupations remain the lowest paid, but any work done by a woman, even if it is the same as (or "of comparable value" to) that done by a man, is *prima facie* worth less. Although virtually every society has had a sexual division of labor, with men's labor generally valued higher than women's, the Renaissance brought a much sharper division and a harsher devaluation of women's labor. The spinners and seamstresses of the seventeenth century, and the typists and teachers of the twentieth, have all felt the results of this in both pocketbook and pride.

12

A Woman's Place Was in the Home: Women's Work in Renaissance Tuscany

JUDITH C. BROWN

In her pioneering essay, "Did Women Have a Renaissance?" the late Joan Kelly suggested that the very developments that opened up new possibilities for Renaissance men, namely the consolidation of the state and the emergence of capitalism, affected women so adversely that for them there was no renaissance. Although she was aware that "the state, early capitalism, and the social relations formed by them impinged on the lives of Renaissance women in different ways according to their different positions in society," she argued that "women as a group, especially among the classes that dominated Italian urban life, experienced a contraction of social and personal options . . ."[1] This contraction could be measured in part by looking at changes in the economic and political roles of women, "the kind of work they performed as compared with men, and their access to property, political power, and the education or training necessary for work, property, and power."[2] The strengths of Kelly's thesis are her willingness to consider a radically different periodization for women's history and her clear outline of what we need to know to establish whether there was a "loss or gain with respect to the liberty of women." But the weakness of her essay lies in the demonstration of her thesis, which rests on a comparison of literary sources from medieval France, such as Andreas Capellanus's *The Art of Courtly Love* and Chretien de Troyes's *Lancelot,* with those of Renaissance Italy, especially Baldassare Castiglione's *The Courtier* and Leon Battista Alberti's *Book on the Family.*

The difficulties with this approach are many. Quite aside from the problem of comparing literary traditions and genres from different parts of Europe, the insurmountable problem from the perspective of the works of women is that such comparison is incapable of demonstrating the constraints faced by women in the world of work and economic power. For one, as Kelly herself admits, literary sources can be prescriptive rather than descriptive. They tell us much about the attitudes of the literate groups that produced them and about the public that read them, but they may not correspond to social realities. Secondly, because she confined the demonstration of her thesis to the social conventions constraining upper-class women, she could not readily penetrate the web of economic relations that affected most women in their daily lives. The one possible area that might have bridged this gap would have been the rules governing access to property, which presumably applied to women of all classes. Yet, surprisingly, Kelly's essay does not explore inheritance laws or the laws regarding the management of property. In short, while she sheds much light on male ideals about women's economic roles, she does not show that women, patrician or lower class, faced increasing economic constraints.

In this essay, I hope to analyze the issue of women's economic status from a different perspective. I will use a variety of sources—guild records, population surveys, and literary evidence—to explore the lives of working women in Renaissance Florence and their relation to paid employment. By looking at this one aspect of the lives of working women in one city, I hope to illuminate broader questions of women' economic power, although obviously the plight of working class women ought not to be equated with that of women of other classes, and the direction of change in one city does not preclude different developments in other areas of Europe. Furthermore, access to paid employment is not the only, or even the most important, determinant of economic power. As scholars continue to work on this subject, they will undoubtedly consider class, property rights, marriage relationships, and many other social and economic factors before they can arrive at any broad interpretations of the economic and social status of Renaissance women. Nonetheless, if we are to determine whether or not there was a renaissance for women in the economic realm, and by that, like Kelly, I mean an expansion of options available to them, then access to paid employment, the kinds of work women did, how and how much they were paid in comparison with men, all have to be given prominent consideration. Such an examination for Renaissance Florence may well reveal a different pattern from the one suggested by Kelly.

An exploration into the world of women's work will perforce make use of, but not limit itself to, economic theory. While economics is a necessary point of departure that can tell us a great deal about the economic implications and the effects of sexual discrimination, as the economist Kenneth Arrow has pointed out, it cannot explain its causes.[3] To understand the full range of rules and constraints faced by working women in the Renaissance, we must turn not only to economic factors but also, albeit briefly, to the realm of culture and social values that affected the world of work.

Urban Women

Recent writings about women's work in the cities of Renaissance Italy suggest that Joan Kelly's observations about "the declining power of women of rank and the enforced domestication of middle-class women" also hold for those of the working class.[4] Unlike the Northern European women described in recent years by Louise Tilly, Joan Scott, Natalie Davis, and Olwen Hufton, Italian city women allegedly had very limited economic functions.[5] Because of their low participation rates in the urban economy, women were of little economic value. Indeed, it has been argued that the meagerness of their contribution to the productivity of households helped to bring about the decline of once flourishing urban centers.[6]

This conception of women's work, based primarily on data from about 1350 to 1500, only partially describes the experience of urban working women. Florence, one of the most industrialized cities of Renaissance Italy, exhibited a more complex pattern. To begin with, as in all other premodern cities, women often worked as helpers to their husbands, fathers, and brothers in workshops located in their homes. Although their work was economically significant both to their households and to the economy as a whole, its value was reflected only indirectly in the income earned by the males they helped. Their contribution to the productivity of their households is impossible to measure because it left few traces in the historical record, but this is not to say that it had no value. As Natalie Davis has shown, in their wills and other bequests, husbands and fathers frequently alluded to the approximate cash value they placed on the unpaid work performed by the women of their households.[7]

Furthermore, in trying to estimate women's contribution to the urban economy, we must realize that the trend of women's participation in market related activities—that is, paid work—was neither unilinear over time nor was it monocausal. For different reasons Florentine women were engaged in paid work in varying numbers depending on the time period and the occupation examined. Employment data, to be sure, are not extensive until the late Renaissance, but scattered references in fiscal, legal, and literary records can help us reach plausible conclusions about changes in women's participation in the workplace and the reasons for them.

In contrast to the large numbers of working women mentioned in documents of the late thirteenth and the first half of the fourteenth centuries, the records of the next two centuries reveal very few. The principal Florentine industry, woolen cloth manufacturing, which until the last quarter of the fourteenth century relied primarily on female weavers, turned to males, many of them foreigners, in the subsequent period.[8] The nascent silk industry also relied primarily on male workers.[9] While women continued to exercise certain traditionally female occupations such as midwifery, wet nursing, and domestic service, the guild records, wills, property transfers, and other legal documents no longer mention the large variety of female occupations evident in the notarial records and literary sources of the pre-plague period. The absence of working women from the historical records of the early Renaissance may simply be an anomaly, but that is not very likely in view of the large numbers of documents for this period. An explanation for this shift in employment patterns is readily available in regard to the wool industry: female weavers were replaced by male weavers from Germany. The reasons for the absence of women in other occupations are more difficult to discern. One plausible argument, advanced by David Herlihy and Christiane Klapisch, is that lower demographic pressures after 1348 enabled women to avoid the labor market and to enter the marriage market instead.[10]

The long absence of women from the ranks of wage labor ended in the late sixteenth century, when once again women began to appear as part of the urban labor force. The account books of silk and wool manufacturers indicate that they made up a rising percentage of workers in the textile sector, which from mid-sixteenth century to mid-seventeenth century still employed between one-half and one-third of the labor force.[11] By 1604, 62 percent of the weavers and approximately 40 percent of all wool workers were women, not counting the spinners who resided mostly in the outskirts of the city and who had always been female. Surveys of both the silk and the wool industries completed in 1662–63 show that female employment remained high in the seventeenth century. Women made up 38 percent of wool workers and 84 percent of workers in the silk industry (see tables 1 and 2).[12]

The causes for the increased participation of women in the labor market are rooted in changes in the Florentine economy that will be explored briefly below. We must be careful, however, not to be misled into thinking that women were as well represented outside the

TABLE 1. Sex-Specific Distribution of Labor in the Wool Industry, 1663

Occupation	Male	Female	Total
Wool merchants & staff	113	—	113
Warehouse owners & staff	107	—	107
Weavers-Camaldoli	84 (35)[a]	157 (65)	247[b]
Weavers-San Barnaba	13 (4)	290 (96)	303
Beaters	217	—	217
Wool cleansers	48	—	48
Warpers	1 (4)	26 (96)	27
Cloth scourers	37	—	37
Tenterers	10	—	10
Dyers	96	—	96
Shearers & menders	37	—	37
Total	763 (61)	473 (38)	1,242

a. Numbers in parentheses are row percentages.
b. Includes six weavers of undetermined sex.

SOURCE: ASF, *Miscellanea Medicea*, 311, ins. 8. Reprinted from Judith Brown and Jordan Goodman, "Women and Industry in Florence," *Journal of Economic History* 40 (1980):73–80.

TABLE 2. Sex-Specific Distribution of Labor in the Silk Industry, 1663

Occupation	Male	Female	Total
Dyers			
Masters	20 (100)[a]	—	20
Apprentices	71 (100)	—	71
Children (under 15)	75 (48)	80 (52)	155
Weavers			
Masters	393 (22)	1,393 (78)	1,786
Apprentices	319 (41)	456 (59)	775
Children	1,078 (47)	1,238 (53)	2,316
Throwsters			
Masters	36 (35)	66 (65)	102
Apprentices	104 (22)	376 (78)	480
Children	156 (48)	169 (52)	325
Winders			
Masters	—	4,716 (100)	4,716
Children	—	3,288 (100)	3,288
Total	2,252 (16)	11,782 (84)	14,034

a. Numbers in parentheses are row percentages.

SOURCE: Jordan Goodman, "The Florentine Silk Industry," p. 72. Reprinted from Judith Brown and Jordan Goodman, "Women and Industry in Florence," *Journal of Economic History* 40 (1980):73–80.

textile sector. Although their numbers are difficult to determine, women did not make up such a large percentage of the paid labor force in most other activities. A very rough indication of their participation can be obtained from the 1631 census, a household survey of the Florentine population. In addition to recording the number and sex of all household residents, the document sometimes includes the occupation of the head of the household and some of his or her dependents. Of the 2,504 females whose occupations were listed, only 20 percent were employed in nontextile related activities such as seamstressing (5.9 percent), prostitution (4 percent), domestic service (3 percent), food production, and a small range of other activities. Because many occupations required no specialized equipment, the census undoubtedly underrepresents the number of women outside of the wool and silk industries. Probably the most underaccounted occupation was that of domestic servant. In the census of 1552, which was similar in most respects to that of 1631 but which identified the servants in each household, there were 8,890 servants, two-thirds of them women. From what we know about Florentine society in the seventeenth century, there is no reason to think that there would have been significant alterations in the intervening years.[13]

The inadequacies of the 1631 census as a survey of employment are of course many. In addition to systematically underrepresenting certain occupations, it does not help us to identify the actual employment of many of the women who are identified as working women. A food vendor, for instance, might also do spinning, a servant might help her master with weaving. Moreover, the census, and for that matter the surveys of the silk and wool industries, do not tell us the number of hours that women worked. Both types of documents probably conceal chronic underemployment. Yet, despite these problems, the census and the industry surveys help to confirm that, by the end of the Renaissance, women were employed in very large numbers. If in order to make a worst case situation, we assume that 80 percent of all working women were employed by the wool and silk industries, as the 1631 census suggests, that all females between the ages of six and seventy-nine were employable, and that approximately half of the population of mid-seventeenth century Florence was female, then we can calculate from the number of female workers included in the 1663 surveys of the wool and silk guilds that at least 63 percent of all working age females in the city in 1631 were active in the workplace.[14] This is surely a conservative estimate, because the 1631 census underreports the number of women in nontextile occupations and does not include either less visible activities performed by wives or female servants in city workshops or the activities of the large number of female religious who often worked preparing wool and silk for production inside the convent walls. Moreover, the wool guild's survey of 1663 does not mention the spinners who resided in the city. Finally, my own assumptions about the productive ages of women may be stretching the biological limits. A different set of assumptions could yield a female work force of 73 percent of the working age women of Florence.[15] The point, however, is clear, whatever set of assumptions one chooses. A large number of Florentine women were paid for their labor and their efforts added considerably to the urban economy.

The growth of paid employment for city women in late Renaissance Florence is related to structural changes that took place in the urban economy. In the last half of the sixteenth century the artisan sector flourished, as many of the old crafts expanded and a new set of luxury crafts developed in response to the growing demand by the European public for luxury products. Florentine workers eagerly set to accommodating the taste for ceramics, books, jewelry, furniture, coaches, and other objects with which the bourgeoisie and nobilities of Europe sought to enhance their prestige and their standards of material life.[16] The emergence of a more diversified world of goods in the late sixteenth century created new employment opportunities for the Florentine population. Although few women found openings in the artisan sector, as men shifted from the production of textiles to that of luxury crafts, the women began to perform many of the previously male tasks in the wool and silk industries. This, more than anything else, probably explains the larger participation of women in the labor force.[17]

Another reason may be the altered status of the guilds in the political economy of late Renaissance Florence. There is a small but growing body of evidence to indicate that throughout Europe there was an inverse relation between the ability of guilds to regulate economic activity and the extent of female participation in the labor force. Merry Weisner's work on women's occupations in Nuremberg suggests that as guilds consolidated their power in the sixteenth and seventeenth centuries, they passed regulations excluding women from traditional occupations and relegated them to the margins of the world of work. Similarly, evidence cited by Alice Clark for a variety of English towns suggests that starting in the sixteenth century guilds passed prohibitions against women weavers.[18] In Florence, however, the guilds received a major setback as regulators of economic and political activity with the creation of the Medici principate in 1532.

During the first twenty years of their rule, the Medici abolished the most vital political functions of the guilds and reorganized them as eleven universities whose officers and economic policies were controlled by government officials.[19] Since the early Medici dukes were particularly interested in promoting economic activity, they aimed in various ways to make the guilds less exclusive and more open to competition, whether from neighboring cities in the state or from within the ranks of Florentine labor.[20] It is not surprising therefore to see women enter certain sectors of the labor force at a time when the guilds were at their weakest. This is not to argue that the Medici were champions of the economic emancipation of women or that women after the mid-sixteenth century had equal status in the guilds. Even in mid-seventeenth century, when there were many women masters in the wool and silk industries, very few appear in guild matriculation records and none became guild consuls. Still, the greater tolerance toward female workers in some types of work is revealed in the different ways that two guilds, one in the fourteenth century and the other in the sixteenth, reacted to the presence of women competitors. In the late fourteenth century, the guild of used clothing dealers (*rigattieri*) for a time barred women as itinerant hawkers, claiming that they infiltrated people's houses and "persuaded the women to buy to the detriment of their men [that is, of the men of their household]."[21] Two centuries later, the linen guild, which now included the *rigattieri,* faced with large numbers of female tailors, did not seek to prohibit them from practicing their trade but argued instead that if they were going to work as tailors and maintain shops, they should pay the modest fee to matriculate in the guild.[22]

While such structural factors may account for the increased participation of women in the labor force of late Renaissance Florence, they do not explain why Florentine males worked in luxury crafts while women were employed in the textile industries and a smaller number of other occupations. What determined the sexual segregation of labor in Florentine society? For an understanding of such problems, economists have relied in part on the very useful theory of human capital. According to this theory, investment in human capital, that is, in the acquisition of skills either through education, on-the-job training, or general training, has generally paid individuals a substantial rate of return because it has enabled them to learn difficult skills or to engage in a wide variety of well-paid occupations. Women are generally found in poorly paid, low-skilled occupations because they accumulate less human capital through their work experience. Women's function in the household economy as childbearers, providers of childcare, and domestic labor results in their more limited and discontinuous presence in the job market, making it harder for them to acquire the training necessary for highly skilled work.[23] Barriers to skill acquisition, moreover, could be higher in premodern economies in which training often took place in the home. There was little incentive for parents to teach their daughters complex and hard to learn skills that they would hardly put to use before they married and left the paternal house. In Italy, where urban women married when they were still in their teens, this would have been a particularly important consideration. While some parents may have counted this training as part of their daughters' dowry, as was the case in some parts of Northern Europe, such an indirect return on their investment was far from certain as it might be difficult to find a husband whose trade could make use of the specialized skills previously acquired by his bride. Evidence from sixteenth-century Lyon and Venice suggests that very few women married men in the same occupations as their fathers.[24] If the same were true in Florence, and preliminary analysis of the 1631 census and of guild records suggests that it was, then it would be better for young girls to work on less skilled tasks where there were immediate returns and where the minimal skills acquired could be easily transferred to their new households. Once there, the young wives of Florentine artisans would be in no position to acquire sophisticated new training. The cares of childrearing and domestic work would ensure that they would simply maintain their previous skills or acquire only those new ones that were easily learned.

The distribution of labor in late Renaissance Florence in large measure accords with the pattern predicted by the human capital approach. Highly skilled artisans were men, and women were relegated to textile work where there were fewer skill requirements. In this regard, it is revealing that in the early Renaissance, when Florence produced a small quantity of simple woolen cloths alongside the more elaborate woolens and silks for which the city became famous, a small number of women appear in the account books of Florentine wool manufacturers as weavers of the plainer and coarser wools. None worked as weavers in the silk industry, which was entirely devoted to the production of luxury cloths requiring a high degree of skill. In the late Renaissance, however, when both wool and silk production shifted to cheaper, coarser, and simpler cloths, women formed the majority of weavers in the two industries. But, significantly, the silk manufacturers who continued to produce elaborate patterned silks generally turned to male weavers for those cloths while retaining women to work on the rest.[25]

The accumulation of human capital then is clearly one of the determinants in the distribution of labor in the Florentine economy. But how are we to explain the high concentration of women in certain relatively low-skill jobs and their absence in others? Why are most women wool workers engaged in weaving, warping, and spinning, but not in cleaning, combing, or carding wool? Consistent with the human capital approach is the notion that women have had first and foremost a reproductive responsibility in the home. This would limit employment outside. Textile manufacturing was organized according to a putting-out system in which the merchant consigned the raw silk or wool to workers who did much of the processing of the raw material into cloth in their own homes. Occupations such as weaving, which were carried out in the home, could fit around childrearing and household tasks. The compatibility of these different types of work is illustrated by the fact that in the early seventeenth century, roughly 800 of the 1,025 female weavers surveyed by the Florentine wool guild had children.[26] Other occupations in the textile sector, such as cleaning or carding, were done in central workshops and would have required women to give up their productive roles within the household. It is not surprising then to find that there were no women engaged in those types of jobs.[27]

Yet much more than the physical requirements of production were involved in the locational barriers to women's work. If an occupation such as itinerant vendor, for instance, placed a woman outside the home, even though the hours might be flexible and could be accommodated around household chores, it would include few women. The exclusion of women from publicly visible roles was so thorough that in 1610 Grangier de Liverdes commented, "in Florence women are more enclosed than in any other part of Italy; they see the world only from the small openings in their windows."[28]

Women had not always been so restricted. Their confinement to domestic spaces had started much earlier, growing gradually over the course of the thirteenth and the first half of the fourteenth centuries, until they were barred even from attending the funerals of their kinsmen.[29] Explanations for this shift are complex and partly rooted in changes in inheritance systems and family structures too involved to explore in a brief essay; but one contributing factor was that women were seen, not merely as the caretakers of the material welfare of their home, but also as the guardians of its religious and moral values. From the fourteenth through the sixteenth centuries, moralists like St. Bernardino of Siena and Lodovico Dolce advised women to become proficient in two areas: household management and religion.

The importance of the latter, is made clear in St. Bernardino's early fifteenth-century description of the religious function of women in the family:

> Just as the sun is the most beautiful work in the sky and the world, so a graceful, virtuous, and honest woman, who is fearful of God, is a sun; who like the sun gives life to all things, so does she give life to her husband and to all her family. And if her husband has no faith, she will comfort him and bring him into the faith and into good morals, honest words and honest ways and deeds. And so with her sons and daughters.[30]

Because these were the tasks of women, it was important that their lives and reputations be unblemished by any hint of scandal. "Shun every sort of dishonor," Giannozzo Alberti admonished his wife in Leon Battista Alberti's treatise on the family. "Use every means to appear to all people as a highly respectable woman. To seem less so would be to offend God, me, our children, and yourself."[31] Men thought that the best way to avoid such scandal was to limit women's exposure to the public world, because for all their moral responsibility women were considered mentally weak and easily led into immoral behavior. In Castiglione's *The Courtier,* Gasparo Pallavicino articulates the views of most sixteenth-century men when he states that "women . . . due to the frailty of their sex, give in to their appetites much more than men . . . Therefore men have instilled in women the fear of infamy as a bridle to bind them as by force to this virtue . . ."[32] Indeed, their very faith and credulity, which made them the repositories of religious instruction in their homes, also made women particularly vulnerable to vice in the outside world.[33] And one of the most effective conduits of vice was female garrulousness, which having once beguiled Adam, now persuaded others to fall into temptation.[34]

These attitudes had far-reaching implications for women's lives and women's employment in particular. In effect, they worked to keep women out of occupations that required mobility and public exposure. This may explain the reasons given by the second-hand clothing dealers in prohibiting female street hawkers. They attributed women's sales abilities to their "seduction" of weak-willed female customers who succumbed to their sales pitch.[35] Surely, the guild took a different view of the male members of the trade who displayed similar skills.

Since women were considered flighty and incapable of complex reasoning, it also followed that they were meant to obey orders, not give them. Most Renaissance commentators subscribed to the Aristotelian notion that women are subject to the authority of males.[36] "They are madmen," says Giannozzo Alberti, "if they think true prudence or good counsel lies in the female brain." He adds, "all wives are thus obedient, if their husbands know how to be husbands."[37] A century later, Orazio Lombardelli, had this kind of admonition in mind when he instructed his new bride to be happy that God had granted her a husband such as he who would govern her in place of all others. Just as "the head adorns the body, the prince the city, the gem the ring, so the husband adorns the wife, and she should obey not only when he commands but when he doesn't."[38]

Because the subjection of women to men was seen as part of the natural order, men probably resented employment situations that placed women in superior positions. This worked to keep women out of occupations in which there were distinct workshop hierarchies. Undoubtedly, master's wives and female domestics helped out by cleaning the workshops, feeding the workers, stoking furnaces, and engaging in other secondary operations. They probably engaged in these tasks in greater numbers than appears from the written records. But although such work facilitated the functioning of their husband's or father's establishments, it also kept them apart from the ladder of advancement occupied by apprentices, journeymen, and masters in many of the crafts. Women's industrial and service occupations generally did not require them to have the extensive numbers of helpers required by workers in leather, stone, or metal crafts, among others. Theirs tended to be solitary jobs, and if help could be used, as was the case with silk throwsters, it was usually provided by other women.[39]

Yet another reason for the sexual segregation of labor in Florentine society was the large initial outlay of capital required for certain industries such as dye shops, foundries, or wood workshops. By the twelfth century, in Florence as in most of Mediterranean Europe, women were not granted equal shares of their patrimony with their brothers but were provided instead with a dowry that was usually much smaller. During their married years, their dowry was managed by their husbands and only upon becoming widows did they regain legal control over it, if the money had not been spent already. For most women, however, the amount of the dowry was not likely to suffice for both their daily maintenance and investment in trade and industry. Widowhood and poverty normally went hand in hand, and given women's lack of skills, they were not able through their own work to save enough to acquire the necessary equipment to launch themselves in a new occupation.[40]

This raises the issue of levels of wealth and pay differentials between men and women—a much neglected and particularly thorny subject among scholars concerned with premodern economies, because the wage data for this period are scarce and qualitatively different from those of modern times. According to the human capital theory, women should earn less because they did not attain the same skill level as men. Indeed, this is confirmed by the account books of Florentine textile manufacturers. While the piece rates paid weavers of both sexes did not vary for equal work, women were less well paid because they were employed more frequently in weaving cheaper, coarser cloths. A female weaver could make ten *braccia* of tafetta, a plain type of silk, in a week. For this she was paid approximately 70 soldi in the decade between 1610 and 1620. A skilled weaver, usually male, could weave three to four *braccia* of voided satin velvet a week, for which he received between 210 and 280 soldi.[41] In short, a skilled male weaver could expect to earn three to four times more than an unskilled female.

There were, however, other differences in pay scales that cannot be explained on the basis of human capital. For example, while tafetta weavers (mostly female), whose job required a certain amount of skill, made 70 soldi a week, totally unskilled male workers in the construction industry received an average daily wage of 20 soldi, which comes to 100 soldi in a five-day work week.[42]

The wage differences observed in these two low-skill occupations stem from the sexual segregation of labor itself. As women were restricted to a limited number of occupations, there was a relatively large supply of workers in the fields that were open to them. This "overcrowding," as some economists have called it, resulted in women's receiving lower wages and men's receiving higher wages than if sexual constraints to occupational mobility had not existed.[43] If then the economic value of urban women, as measured by cash wages, was low compared with that of men, it was not because they did not participate in the market economy but rather because they had fewer skills and because they were crowded into a smaller number of activities that were less well rewarded than those of men.

Rural Women

The restrictions on work faced by urban women were perforce different from those faced by women living in the country. For one, in rural Tuscany the agricultural family was to a large extent both the unit of production and of consumption. Wage labor was not very common. Secondly, because household tasks and the tasks of the farm could not be so easily separated, women naturally had provided a considerable portion of the labor force from time immemorial.

Yet, although female labor had always been important, we should nonetheless keep in mind that the extent of rural women's productive labor was closely related to the requirements of specific agricultural systems. In Tuscany, as elsewhere in Europe, these varied tremendously over short distances, as mountains, plains, rivers, and other geographic features helped determine the agricultural output. Some parts of Tuscany were almost entirely devoted to sheep raising, some to cereal cultivation or to mixed cropping that included viticulture and olive trees, and others added different crops ranging from flax to saffron. Institutional arrangements also differed widely. Some areas relied primarily on sharecropping, others on fixed rent tenancies, and still others on the family owned and operated farm. All of these factors had a bearing on how women were integrated into the agricultural work force, so that a valid generalization covering all these situations cannot be made. Neither is it possible to give a detailed account of the labor of country women throughout Tuscany because of the limitations of space as well as the obscurity that still shrouds the rural world of the Renaissance, the world in which the vast majority of people lived.

Given these limitations, to what extent can one find in the countryside a parallel to the growing economic function of urban women in the late Renaissance? Despite obvious geographic differences among agricultural landscapes, we can observe similarities in agricultural developments that helped engender a new role for women. In some areas of the Florentine state, there was a growth of *agricultural promiscua,* multicrop farming that aimed, among other things, to give landlords a larger share of commercial crops and to make a more profitable use of available land and labor.[44] Gradually less land was devoted to cereals and a larger share was planted with vines, olives, and mulberry trees for sericulture. The spread of these crops was related to a growth in demand for Tuscan wines, a change in tastes, as consumers switched from eating animal fats to olive oil, and to the growth of the Florentine silk industry in the sixteenth and seventeenth centuries.[45]

These new forms of land use, and especially those related to sericulture, had a profound impact on the role of women in the agricultural economy. Tuscan agriculture had always made use of labor-intensive techniques. But not all hands could be used for many of the time-consuming and important tasks. Most peasants, for example, did not own ploughs, so the cultivation of cereals depended on the use of the hoe (*vanga*)—a back-breaking, slow, and labor intensive method that was done most effectively by strong men. It has been estimated that a 25-acre farm devoted primarily to cereal cultivation, as was the case in much of Tuscany in the early Renaissance, required at least four to five men capable of using a *vanga*.[46] For each of them, however, the rural population contained approximately five women, children, and elderly men, most of whom were idle or underemployed during much of the agricultural cycle. Because such a large proportion of the land was devoted to cereals, both the amount of land that could be farmed and the total agricultural output of the early Renaissance were very limited.

The extension of viticulture and olive trees created new opportunities for the previously underemployed workers in the farm. Women could tie the vines and harvest the grapes as easily as men. In some tasks, however, such as pruning olive trees and terracing hillsides, men still had a comparative advantage. The major breakthrough in establishing a more productive system of agricultural labor finally came with the introduction of mulberry trees and sericulture. Mulberry trees were raised first in the Valdinievole and the territory of Pisa and Pistoia after the mid–fifteenth century and, in response to market demands and government efforts, spread rapidly to other parts of the state, including the Valdelsa and the Arno valley. Tuscan sericulture increased by three-quarters from 1440 to 1576, more than doubled in the following twenty-five years, and increased by two and one-half times between 1610 and the mid-seventeenth century.[47] In the last half of the 1600s, sericulture was a major agricultural activity in the Val di Nievole, Valle del Bisenzio, the Tuscan Romagna, the Val di Chiana, the Pratomagno, and parts of the Val d'Arno, with production reaching an average of 110,000 *libbre* of silk annually.

If cereal cultivation was male-labor intensive, sericulture was female and child intensive. Women and children gathered the leaves from the mulberry trees, which in many areas were kept suitably pruned to a small size. Women also raised the silk cocoons, as the English traveler Robert Dallington remarked during his Tuscan travels, when he saw peasant women hatching the silkworm eggs in their bosoms to supplement with their own bodies the insufficient warmth provided by the sun.[48] Raising silk worms was a very labor intensive process, but it took only a few weeks and, in contrast to the labor inputs for other agricultural tasks, it required no special physical attributes, only constant vigilance. Practically all members of a household could be utilized. Women and children therefore performed these tasks while the men engaged in other forms of labor on the farm. The next stage of silk preparation, processing cocoons into raw silk by reeling and spinning, was also in the hands of women, assisted by children or otherwise unoccupied members of the household. Probably planting and pruning mulberry trees and cutting wood for the fires required in reeling were the only tasks performed by able-bodied men.[49]

Sericulture thus constituted an important source of additional employment for Tuscan women and helped to link the household economy to the market place.[50] The introduction of this activity into the rural economy of the late Renaissance resulted in a more intensive use of society's labor resources. Just how intensive may be estimated from late sixteenth- and seventeenth-century production figures. In 1590, when Florence produced about 10,000 silk cloths annually, 12.5 percent of the raw silk came from Tuscany. To produce this amount required the full-time labor equivalent of approximately 1,560 workers to raise the cocoons over a 45-day season, 120 reelers over a 100-day season, and 70 spinners over a 200-day season. By the 1650s, when the Florentine silk cloth industry continued to produce the same number of cloths but got 75 percent of its silk from Tuscany, sericulture provided full-time employment for approximately 9,360 cocoon raisers, 740 reelers, and 420 spinners over similar work seasons.[51] In reality, a much larger number of women undoubtedly engaged in these occupations, as most did not work full days at making silk but rather added these tasks to their other chores. Sericulture thus had a profound impact on the lives of women as productive members of rural society. When we consider the low level of output of premodern agricultural systems, when one out of every three or four years could bring famine, we can appreciate the importance of the integration of female labor into the agricultural world. Every person who could work to enlarge the agricultural surplus, every person who was not dependent on the meager output of others, helped to keep rural society from the brink of catastrophe. By contributing to the rising agricultural output of the early modern period, the work of women helped to improve people's material life and their chances for survival.

Renaissance for Women

To conclude, both in the cities and in the countryside, women were gradually integrated into the workforce of Renaissance Tuscany. Despite formidable barriers related to the lack of skills and capital, to prejudice about where women could work without losing their honor, and to resentment on the part of male artisans, women became very active participants in the economy of the Renaissance city and its countryside. Indeed, one is tempted to reverse recently advanced arguments that the limited economic function of women helped bring an end to Tuscan economic growth by mid-sixteenth century and to argue instead that the failure of the economy to modernize in the early modern period was related to the very success with which women gained access to paid employment and to productive labor in the family farm.[52] If women had had more limited economic functions, perhaps there would have been greater incentive for the economy to turn to new industries that were more conducive to modernization. Too much importance having been attached already to the first notion, however, it would be equally wrong to attribute to the labor of women the major blame for the economic turn of events in post-Renaissance Tuscany. To understand the course of the Tuscan economy in the sixteenth and seventeenth centuries, many other aspects of economic life, about which we know all too little, need to be examined. Nevertheless, there is not much doubt, on the basis of the available evidence, that the participation of women in the labor force became increasingly significant in the late sixteenth century and continued to be so in the next century.

This raises a number of important issues for scholars working on the history of women in Renaissance times. The first is that of the relationship between ideology and behavior. From the mid-fourteenth through much of the seventeenth century, the rules governing the lives of Tuscan women were not significantly relaxed. Despite some tentative starts toward a reassessment of the notion of woman and her role in society, Renaissance thought continued to be tied to what Ian Maclean has called the "scholastic synthesis," which relegated women to a subordinate and dependent status. Yet, despite this relatively static ideology and the rules of behavior that they engendered, women managed to assert themselves in growing numbers in realms of economic activity from which they had been absent in the early Renaissance. How are we to explain this discrepancy? Surely, the importance of ideology cannot be denied. Renaissance women had to contend with it and to develop strategies, conscious or unconscious, for dealing with it. But if the rules that constrained their behavior closed off many options, they still left others open, and, as many of the essays in this volume reveal, women were very inventive in carving out for themselves meaningful, productive, and creative roles. We need, therefore, to look not only at the rules of society but also at how men and women understood them, implemented them, and often circumvented them.

Another question that arises from our study of Tuscan women is to what extent were they exceptional? Were they the only ones to surmount some of the economic constraints imposed on them or did women elsewhere in Renaissance and early modern Europe also increase their participation in the labor market? A precise answer is still premature because the economic life of women in Renaissance times is still largely uncharted territory. Some of the evidence presented by Richard Rapp on Venice suggests that while women may have found increasing employment in the sixteenth century because of the growth in that city's industrial base, they lost ground in the seventeenth century when some industries moved to the country-side.[53] The work of Merry Wiesner on women in Nuremberg suggests that in that city women were increasingly relegated to the margins of the labor force. And Alice Clark in her survey of the working life of English women argues that the development of capitalism in seventeenth-century England led to the exclusion of women from the skilled trades and from most forms of wage earning.

On the other hand, not all the evidence points in this direction. Rapp also suggests that in industries other than textiles the absence of women wage earners in Venice may be "a fiction of documentation . . . in a city where more than one of every ten households was headed by a woman it would be imprudent to discount their presence in the work force."[54] Equally important, evidence gathered in the last half century about the early forms of capitalism suggest that it is no longer possible to subscribe to Alice Clark's account of the usurpation of small-scale household production by merchants who organized large workshops separating work from the home and thereby turning independent artisans into wage earners and women into idle dependents.[55] Until the advent of the factory system, at a much later date, most work continued to be done in the home, even in England, the birthplace of the industrial revolution. There was therefore nothing inherent in the economic system that kept women from full participation in the labor force, as Clark and then Joan Kelly have previously argued. That large numbers of women in many parts of Europe in fact continued to participate is ample evidence that there is no simple link between the advent of capitalism and the declining role of women in the labor market. Clark's evidence itself subverts her argument. Notwithstanding guild restrictions and other constraints, her sketch reveals women actively engaged in many aspects of textile production, including weaving, as well as in the retail trades and in various crafts such as printing and chandlery.[56] Recent work on London's working women by Nancy Adamson reinforces this impression. Women were butchers, bakers, flaxdressers, and feltmakers, doing virtually all kinds of work alongside their husbands and fathers.

Moreover, widows often continued in these occupations and took on apprentices and journeymen. Legally, women could belong to the guilds, and although few did so independently, many London widows took advantage of the guild privileges accorded them and freely practiced their craft or trade within the city.[57]

On the Continent, women also appear frequently in the ranks of wage laborers and artisans, as can be seen in the work of Natalie Davis for Lyon and Martha Howell for Leiden.[58] They usually adjusted their labor to the workshop needs of fathers, brothers, or husbands, but independent artisans were by no means rare. Whether this was true for most European cities or whether such participation in market-related employment was more or less common in the Renaissance than in medieval times will have to await further research. It is worth remembering, however, that if in some places women were barred from certain occupations either because of the altered organization of production or because of guild restrictions, the impact of this was partly counterbalanced by the creation of new occupations and the growth in the total number of jobs linked to the market by the spread of a capitalist economy.[59]

Finally, there is the question of whether the availability of paid employment opportunities increased women's economic power. Here again our assessment must be very cautious. The wages of female workers were usually very meager. Most were fortunate if they could earn enough to keep themselves, let alone their children, above the margins of subsistence. Women, more often than men, were dependent on the handouts of charity institutions to supplement their wages. Yet, however limited the options and the rewards, would not the young wife augmenting the income of her artisan husband and aware of the importance of her contribution, assert herself more boldly in the management of her household than would the totally dependent wife? And wouldn't the husbands, fathers, and brothers of such women grant them a greater say in the important decisions affecting the family, knowing that its very survival depended on the additional income generated either directly or indirectly by the work of the female members of the household? To the extent that increased employment opportunities contributed to greater financial independence, women undoubtedly gained a small measure of economic power.[60] If we limit our assessment, then, to this one area of economic life, without implying that it covers all facets of women's economic experience or even all classes of women, then we can argue that in Florence, and perhaps in other cities as well, there was in the Renaissance, a renaissance for women.

Part Three

The Works of Women:
Some Exceptions to the Rule of Patriarchy

13

Catherine de' Medici as Artemisia: Figuring the Powerful Widow

SHEILA FFOLLIOTT

Designed to celebrate and draw attention to important events at court, sixteenth-century pageants were studied exhibitions of power. In triumphal entries, French kings were alternately hailed as Jupiter, Hercules, or Mars, whose attributes not only represented but reinforced their male sovereignty. Such self-presentation, masked in the mythology borrowed from classical culture, staged absolutist rule in narratives that spoke the discourses not only of political but of sexual power. If in the dynastic politics of the era, however, political and sexual power were hardly to be distinguished, so too, by accident, the fictive representation of power could provide the arena for an historical and real shift in actual power.

In 1559, after the treaty of Cateau-Cambrésis, Henri II of France and his Queen Catherine de' Medici planned festivities to celebrate the marriages of their daughters: Claude to the duke of Lorraine and Elizabeth (by proxy) to King Philip II of Spain.[1] The climactic event was the Tournament of Queens, a joust staged so that the king could demonstrate his renowned prowess in front of the foreign visitors and the three queens: Catherine de' Medici, queen of France; the dauphine, Mary, queen of Scots; and Elizabeth of Valois, the new queen of Spain. Following chivalric tradition Henri wore the colors of his lady, in this instance, the black and white of his mistress, Diane de Poitiers, who sat in the retinue of the queens. In the archaic ritual of the joust, the presentation of Henri as a martial, warrior king both called attention to the ancient foundation from which the monarchy sprang and emphasized the combative power of the individual who headed the state.

Against the wishes of Queen Catherine, whose astrologers had warned her of danger in the king's undertaking single combat, Henri's desire for self-display triumphed.[2] Even when, after several successful jousts, the queen repeated her pleas, he chose to ignore the warning and tilt again. This time his opponent's broken lance pierced his helmet and a splinter lodged in his eye socket. Ten days later he died of the abcessed wound. The martial image that Henri had insisted on projecting had ironically brought about his undoing. Suddenly and unexpectedly, Catherine de' Medici found herself in an uncomfortable and tenuous position: a widow in a foreign country at a court in which her husband's favorite, Diane de Poitiers, had clearly held a position superior to her own during his lifetime.

Catherine de' Medici's actions immediately following her husband's death showed that she had no intention of withdrawing from the center of power. Instead of retiring to the solitude of her chamber, she proceeded directly to the Louvre to see what needed to be done.[3] In the ritualized world that was the French court, the queen mother now needed her own iconography of power to articulate the active role she intended to play and to establish her with her public. This became even more critical following the death in 1560 of her eldest son, Francois II, who had been of legal age at the time of his father's death but whose own death brought about the succession of ten-year-old Charles IX. The situation called for a regent, but the queen mother faced an uphill battle; she had to make herself appear the most likely person to take charge of the government. France, because the Salic Law had been interpreted as prohibiting female succession to the throne, was unused to being ruled by women.[4] Catherine staged her campaign for the regency in two related ways: first, she carefully defined how she would appear in public; and second, she contrived her own official imagery. Both strategies were designed to be consonant with what was considered proper for a woman while also allowing the queen to assert herself.

All representations of Catherine de' Medici—portraits, medals, and illustrations of life at court—made from the time of Henri II's death until her own show her wearing black as a sign of her eternal mourning. The sincerity of her grief cannot be doubted; she was genuinely devoted to her husband. But more importantly, wearing a color of mourning underlined her status as widow; it forged a permanent link with her deceased husband. At the time, of course, colors other than black were acceptable signs of mourning: Diane de Poitiers, also a widow, wore black and white.[5] That Catherine chose black, then, is significant. Black worked for her on a number of levels.[6] It was, for example, the color worn by the strong-minded Catholic rulers of the period—Philip the Good, duke of Burgundy; Charles V; Philip II.[7] Catherine de' Medici's late husband had even acquired the custom while living as a hostage in Spain.[8] Catherine could thus declare herself Henri's widow while also presenting herself as cut from the same cloth as her contemporary male monarchs. By wearing black, she seemed Henri's virtual stand-in. This choice of color, moreover, made her stand out in a crowd, as numerous illustrations of the later Valois courts, notably the Valois Tapestries, demonstrate. One has only to glance at the representations of the assembled royal family wearing bright colors to see not only who dominates but also who appears to be the strongest and most serious person present.

In addition to planning her appearance at court functions in such a way as to convey a sense of her strength, Catherine de' Medici also sought to stage her newly fashioned persona in the works of art she commissioned. As Stephen Orgel has argued, "the age believed in the *power* of art—to persuade, transform, preserve."[9] Her selection of a striking color for public appearances made a direct statement about how Queen Catherine perceived herself; her association with an ancient prototype, chosen specifically to justify her pretensions, allowed her to present herself with the same narrative force as was provided by the mythological dramas used by her male predecessors.

Finding a suitable prototype for a woman ruler was not an easy matter: the queen could not, with proper decorum, simply assume those of her husband's pantheon. Nor would Juno, used previously to refer to Queen Catherine as consort in the orbit of her husband, or Minerva, be appropriate.[10] Juno never ruled in her own right and, thus, could not figure a new Catherine desirous of being considered competent to govern. Minerva, although renowned for courage and wisdom—desirable traits in a ruler—was neither widow nor mother and could not project the image now needed. Other female Olympians were equally ill-adapted. Diana, the chaste and powerful goddess of the moon, had provided the perfect cover for Diane de Poitiers and would be forever associated with her.[11] Venus too had been linked to Diane and would not, in any case, have conveyed the sense of authority required. In addition to other important associations, Catherine's wearing of black had blotted out Diane's noted use of black and white; Catherine's choice of imagery, too, had not only to promote her own status as widowed queen mother but also to expunge the memory of her late husband's powerful mistress.

Henri's death put an end to the strange *ménage à trois* consisting of himself, his queen, and Diane, a ménage even given formal recognition in a typically ambiguous Renaissance fashion in his device of H in which Cs or Ds or one of each—depending upon how you chose to read them—were interlaced.[12] The young Henri began his liaison with

Diane at the age of twelve, after his return from a lonely alienating four years spent as hostage in Madrid.[13] She was almost twenty years his senior, old enough to have been the mother he had barely known.[14] Henri became dauphin at the death of his jovial and lettered elder brother, who had been their father's favorite. Doubtless Henri, saturnine and martial, felt his father's disappointment and sought guidance from someone not in the close circle of the king but experienced nevertheless in the ways of the French court. Diane de Poitiers was such a person, while Catherine de' Medici, his young foreign bride and a favorite of François I, was not.

Given this unusual set of circumstances, the art surrounding Catherine needed to figure her in a radically redefined role. Since her only ties to the French throne were through her deceased husband and her male children, any imagery that would enhance her position as regent would have to be based on her status as a widowed mother. The dilemma of locating a classical model to authorize her power was solved by Nicolas Houel, a courtier, who in 1562 presented her with the *Histoire de la Royne Arthémise*.[15] Although never published, Houel's manuscript no doubt circulated at court. Catherine de' Medici's reaction to receiving it is unknown, but it bears her coat of arms on its binding and is catalogued at the Bibliothèque Nationale with the rest of her books. The question whether the Queen asked Houel to write the *Histoire* or whether he did it on his own, hoping to attract her attention, is unresolved.[16] The author's services, however, were retained at court, an indication that Catherine probably found his work useful.[17]

The *Histoire* is an idealized biography of Artemisia, queen of Caria in Asia Minor in the fourth century B.C. She was best known to the Renaissance, through Boccaccio's brief biography in *De claris mulieribus*, as the inconsolable widow of Mausolus. After his death she ruled Caria in her own right and supervised the building of the Mausoleum at Halicarnassus, a funerary monument so famous as one of the Seven Wonders of the World that it gave its name subsequently to an entire genre.[18] Artemisia, then, was celebrated as being something that none of the immortals could ever be: a widow.[19] She proved the perfect prototype for Catherine in that she both dramatically mourned the loss of her husband—the rightful monarch—and stood as an authoritative ruler in his stead.[20]

The ancient sources provide little information about the historical Artemisia; Houel created his lengthy biography by adding events that mirrored those of the life of Catherine.[21] Although the *Histoire* has been dismissed as a "roman fort insipide," when understood in the context of the time and situation in which it was written, it reveals the tensions inherent in the position of Renaissance women who sought to rule.[22] Its importance, then, lies in the very invention of the prototype's character and in the nature of Houel's argument. He makes it clear at the outset that Catherine should view Artemisia as a model and that he intends to instruct her in her new role: the Histoire "conforms to the time, the greatness, and the concerns of the Queen";[23] "She who reads it will derive great profit for it will teach how a Queen should govern a kingdom."[24] Houel, moreover, understands the special predicament of the female ruler: "A woman must be put to the proof to test her *vertu* so that it is clear to all around her that under the body and dress of a woman she has the understanding of a man sufficient for the administration of great affairs."[25] The underlying theme of the entire *Histoire* is that Artemisia was first and foremost an ideal woman; in addition, she possessed all the male virtues necessary to make a competent ruler. *Vertu* must be understood, of course, in its Renaissance sense as "courage or valor," deriving from the Latin *virtus* (from *vir*, man). Influenced by the humanist-inspired "mirror of princes,"[26] Houel's *Histoire* employs a strategy similar to that observed by Constance Jordan in Sir Thomas Elyot's *Defence of Good Women* (1540). Elyot's "theoretical defense is supported by evidence from history; the Syrian Queen Zenobia is both an exemplary wife and competent ruler."[27]

In the *Histoire*, Houel refers to related illustrations that, it is suggested, the queen will use as cartoons for tapestries to decorate one of her residences.[28] These highly finished drawings, attributed to Antoine Caron and others, depict the most important events of Artemisia's life. They form, with the accompanying sonnets composed by Houel himself, a book in their own right.[29] More importantly, unlike the manuscript *Histoire* that was intended primarily for private reading, the compositions of the fifty-nine drawings are directed at a public audience. There is no firm evidence to show that tapestries from the Artemisia cartoons were actually woven during Catherine de' Medici's lifetime. Since tapestry was the most expensive art of the period, her well-documented financial constraints probably forced her to spend her money elsewhere.[30] Artemisia did enter Catherine's pantheon, however, as revealed by the decorations of some of the triumphal entries staged after Henri's death.[31] The imagery invented in the drawings also made a sufficient impact on two later French queen-regents, Marie de' Medici and Anne of Austria, that they had tapestries made, attesting thereby to the success of Artemisia as a prototype.[32] Indeed, the fact that the drawings were so treasured as to be kept into the next century, illustrates the importance with which this collection was regarded.

Although not all the scenes include images of Artemisia, the proposed tapestries form the most extensive series to date chronicling the life of a woman. Like much of the art and architecture made for Catherine de' Medici, however, these also had a precedent in works made for Diane de Poitiers, who always managed to get there first. A small series of tapestries illustrating several episodes from the life of her immortal namesake Diana were made for her château at Anet.[33] Not only would the greater number of tapestries in Catherine's series far exceed Diane's, but the French name of Catherine's new prototype, Arthémise, would replace that of the goddess Diana's Greek name, Artemis, or Arthémise in French.[34] The effectiveness of this overkill cannot have been lost on Catherine de' Medici. While Henri II lived, Diane de Poitiers's position was unassailable; now not even her imagery could help her.

The Artemisia drawings show the antique queen in the variety of activities that reflect her wifely but royal duties: arranging for the funeral of her deceased husband, planning the construction of his funeral monument, supervising the education of her young son— invented by Houel to correspond to Charles IX—and administering the interim government. Houel's narrative invents episodes in the life of Artemisia to make it more closely parallel the life of Queen Catherine, but it is the artists who shape these episodes into visible expressions of the power structure of the court and the mysteries of the French monarchy. Although individual drawings are not dated, a number of them may postdate some of the *grandes fêtes* that the queen mother arranged to dramatize her young son's authority.[35] It is possible, therefore, that her arrangement of the *fêtes* with their placement of figures and activities—some of which were recorded in other drawings by Caron—had a direct effect on his work on the Artemisia drawings. If this is so, then Catherine, whose participation in the staging of the festivals is well documented, may have herself influenced the eventual Artemisia drawings. The same influence may be perceived in both.

Whereas her late husband had promoted the jousting matches that accidentally caused his death, Catherine instead chose to stage festivals in which an overlay of spectacle supplanted the actual fighting. Charles IX makes an appearance in the costume of a knight in the Bayonne *Fête* of 1565, but he does not really fight; iconography takes precedence over combat. While deemphasizing the potential violence, Catherine plays up the symbolic representation of power. The devaluation of violence in court spectacle was, of course, coherent with her policy of conciliation between warring religious factions, but her emphasis on symbolic as opposed to actual power coheres with her insistence on the mediating (because already mediated) nature of her own indirect power as queen mother.

Houel in the *Histoire* seeks to rationalize female rulership by arguing the case of an exceptional woman ruler—that is, an exception to the general rule of women's inherent inferiority. But Houel cites other female rulers as well, who furnish further evidence that the image of the female ruler—as of the male—could be exemplary.[36] In this, as Orgel has noted, it is the "*image* of the monarch that is crucial, the appearance of virtue, whether it accords with an inner reality or not."[37]

But what was the process involved in the creation of an iconography of female *virtù* on a grand scale in the visual arts? As there were few images of women in positions of authority to be found anywhere in the culture, what were the formal prototypes for the Artemisia drawings? What limitations were imposed by the decorum of gender on these representations of a powerful, authoritative female?

The first drawings in the series chronicle the funeral of Mausolus and the construction of the Mausoleum. In one drawing (fig. 1), Artemisia stands to the left of center, one step higher than the workmen who present to her a model for the Tomb of Mausolus. She places her left elbow on the shoulder of one of the workmen while her right hand rests on her hip, elbow jutting out in a manner similar to that seen in male figures of the period. An outstanding—and, in context, very interesting—example is Michelangelo's (seated) statue of Lorenzo de' Medici, duke of Urbino (Medici Chapel, Florence): Lorenzo was Catherine's father; he was also the man to whom Machiavelli—unfortunately for Catherine's reputation in France—had dedicated *The Prince*. The gesture of the relaxed, crooked arm shows self-assurance; it is the action of someone at ease about his or her status, denoting confidence and power. It is a gesture, moreover, that is never seen in a woman in a work of art from this period. Artemisia's placement of her left elbow on the shoulder of one of the workmen produces a sense of close camaraderie that is unusual between members of the opposite sex from clearly divergent classes. In the visual arts, appearance is all there is; capabilities, therefore, must be shown by gesture, posture, and glance. In the drawing, Artemisia's typically male posture and gestures make her appear not only clearly in charge of the situation but they also illustrate Houel's point in the *Histoire* that a woman ruler has to prove that she has the capabilities of a man underneath her female appearance.

Fig. 1. Antoine Caron, *Artemisia Viewing the Model for Mausolus's Tomb* (pen and ink with wash). Paris, Bibliothèque Nationale, Estampes, Rés. Ad 105, f. 39

Because the drawings were intended to serve as tapestry cartoons, the narratives are enclosed within elaborate decorative borders. The imagery of these borders differs slightly in each drawing, but all contain devices referring to Catherine and her grief. Like her change in prototype, new devices have now replaced her earlier optimistic and light-colored rainbow, which had been combined with the motto "I bring joy and gladness." In the border of the last drawing (fig. 2) in the Mausoleum series, back-to-back *K*s refer to her name in its Greek spelling (Katherine), calling attention, perhaps, to Artemisia's being a figure from ancient Greece. However, such classical accuracy has contemporary political points to make: the *K* is a letter less easily confused with the letter *D* when combined with other letters than the former *C* had been. The form of the letter *K* is similar to the letter *H* of her deceased husband, reminding the viewer that Catherine now stands for him. Furthermore, the cipher resembles a superimposed *I* over *X*, the Roman numerals of Catherine's son, Charles IX, who was the ruling king. This device, then, has the effect of amalgamating their joint rule. The scythes and broken mirrors refer to Henri's untimely early death, while the falling rain that does not douse the flames

Fig. 2. Antoine Caron, *Artemisia and Lygdamis View the Completed Mausoleum* (pen and ink with wash). Paris, Bibliothèque Nationale, Estampes, Rés. Ad 105, f. 43.

underscores the new Latin motto *ardorem testantur extincta vivere flamma* ("the glow lingers though the flame is gone").

While Artemisia is the largest and most compelling figure in the drawing, she appears at the extreme left margin, gesturing with her left hand toward the completed Mausoleum. Her young son stands in front of her echoing her gesture. The Mausoleum, placed in the center of the composition, is cut open to reveal the funerary monument of the earlier drawing. Ancient literary descriptions provided enough information for Renaissance architects to attempt reconstructions of the Mausoleum.[38] Caron's building conforms to the most famous of these descriptions, the one by Pliny, in many of its details, but it differs in one important respect: it is round even though Pliny clearly describes it as rectangular. Here again Houel and Caron are tailoring the known facts about Artemisia in order to create a prototype that refers directly to Catherine de' Medici.

One of the major focuses of the queen's artistic patronage after the death of Henri II was the creation of his funerary monument. She planned a dynastic chapel for the house of Valois that would hold not only the tombs of her husband and herself but also those of their children.[39] As a foreigner and a widow, she must have realized that her continued popularity with the French depended upon their perceiving her loyalty to France and its future through her devotion to her Valois family. The most concrete demonstration that she could make of her continued devotion to the memory of her husband, as well as of her hopes for the future of France, was this lavish monument with whose construction her name would invariably be associated. Not only would the monument itself serve to express this loyal desire but the illustration of its prototype in the series of tapestries chronicling the life of Artemisia would make its presence known wherever she chose to display them.

Catherine had intended the Valois Chapel to occupy a site on the north side of the abbey church of St. Denis, just west of the apse. While the French monarchy had long chosen St. Denis as a burial place, the Valois Chapel is the first independent burial chapel to be added to the church.[40] Its round form and placement specifically echo those of Roman imperial mausolea—such as the two appended to Old St. Peter's in Rome, one of which, in a position similar to that of the Valois Chapel at St. Denis, was known as the Chapel of the Kings of France.[41] By choosing to erect a funerary chapel in the traditional round form of an early Christian imperial mausoleum and by attaching it in like manner to the transept of St. Denis, Catherine and the architects in her employ appear deliberately to associate St. Denis with the older, specifically Roman church. The plan reaffirms her ancient connection with the French monarchy—in 1562 the duchy of Valois passed to her possession—while its form draws attention to Catherine's own origins in a Roman "papal" dynasty.[42] While the details of its decoration follow the ancient literary descriptions, Caron's drawing of Artemisia's Mausoleum makes it look like Catherine's round Valois Chapel. Although her energies are being channeled toward honoring the memory of her deceased husband, demonstrating thereby a concern for piety appropriate to females— funerary art was one of the main focuses for art patronage by women during this period[43]—Artemisia certainly appears to be in an authoritative position.

Caron's mannerist aesthetic permits elongating Artemisia's figure while giving her son the proportions of a miniature adult. These exaggerations suit the exigencies of the program, for the stature of Artemisia is emphasized without her losing in grace. She must both be an ideal woman—and she certainly appears beautiful in the drawings—and possess as well the virtues of the ideal (male) ruler. In

Fig. 3. Antoine Caron, *The Lesson in Horsemanship* (pen and ink with wash). Paris, Bibliothèque Nationale, Estampes, Rés. Ad 105, f. 31.

addition, the queen's position in the foreground makes her appear equal in height to the Mausoleum. Furthermore, while she appears at the left in an apparently marginalized position, she inhabits the entrance position for someone reading the drawing from left to right. This repeated pattern of representation—a marginalized figure who yet dominates the composition—appears again in the Valois Tapestries, also based on drawings by Antoine Caron, where Catherine's off-center figure still demands primary attention by its contrasting black color.[44]

Another important activity of Catherine as regent—as of any queen regent—was supervising the education of the young king.[45] In a drawing depicting her fulfillment of this responsibility, also attributed to Caron (fig. 3), Artemisia appears in her characteristic position on a raised platform at the left foreground, watching her son receiving a lesson in horsemanship. He is the center of attention, while she is shown from the back; her gesture, however, echoes that of the riding master, indicating her active participation in the proceedings. On the right a colossal statue of Hercules, frequently employed by French mythographers to refer to the sovereign, stands, representing, no doubt, the absent Henri II. Although Artemisia is present and alive,

Fig. 4. Antoine Caron, *The Lesson in Swordplay* (pen and ink with wash). Paris, Bibliothèque Nationale, Estampes, Rés. Ad 105, f. 32.

the scale of her figure is dwarted by that of the statue, whose position is further strengthened by its facing forward. The message is clear: Artemisia can supervise under the aegis of Hercules, who is himself the proper *exemplum* for the young king.

In another drawing (fig. 4), Artemisia stands at the same sidelines while her son receives a lesson in swordplay. This time her face is turned away, but it is echoed in the profile of another female figure on the right, a statue of Victory, bearing palms and crowns, symbols of military triumph. In both of these drawings illustrating the young king's military education, the symbolism of power and victory takes precedence over his own prowess, any claim to which would be incongruous with his age. As in the court festivals arranged by Catherine, symbolic representation of power overrides actual combat.

Artemisia's turn as if to discuss her son's progress with her attendants is similar to the illustrations of the queen's participation in his schoolwork. Such a representation grossly overstates the truth of Catherine's situation, however, for while Henri lived, Catherine's role in the education of their children was extremely limited. It was the letters of Diane de Poitiers to Jean d'Humières, administrator of the Maison des Enfants de France, that most often conveyed the king's

Fig. 5. Antoine Caron, *Les Placets: Artemisia Receiving Petitions* (pen and ink with wash). Paris, Bibliothèque Nationale, Estampes, Rés. Ad 105, f. 37.

wishes for the education of the royal children.[46] Catherine's correspondence was directed instead to Madame d'Humières, and she often had to ask for information about the health of her children, further chiding the woman for not sending word about her daughters as well as her sons.[47] In Henri's ménage, it was the mistress, not the mother, who oversaw the education of the Valois children. In the tapestries Artemisia-Catherine clearly takes charge.

Competent interim administration is the third general theme of the drawings. According to Houel, one of Artemisia's first acts upon taking charge of Caria was requiring provincial judges to hear all grievances from her people.[48] The drawing known as *Les Placets* (fig. 5) illustrates the relay of these petitions to Artemisia at her villa near the capital. Artemisia stands in her characteristic position to the left, acting on behalf of her son beside her. Scholars have remarked on the curious setting for the queen's activity: she stands in a portico in front of a fountain decorated with a sculpture that obviously depicts the statue of Diana at Anet, Diane de Poitiers's famous villa.[49] Instead of being a puzzle, this drawing repeats the pattern of Catherine's subtle appropriation of Diane's iconography as she, in the guise of Artemisia, takes over what had been Diane's strong position. Al-

Fig. 6. Antoine Caron, *The Estates-General* (pen and ink with wash). Paris, Bibliothèque Nationale, Estampes, Rés. Ad 105, f. 17.

though she could not force Diane to relinquish her own Anet, Catherine did make Diane cede to her the royal château at Chenonceau in exchange for that at Chaumont. Catherine then went on to make Chenonceau one of the major stages for her famous court festivals. In art, however, it appears that Catherine was able to supplant her rival entirely; Artemisia appears as chatelaine of Diane's own château.

Another example of the poetic license characteristic of the series shows Artemisia, again posed to one side with her son, in a drawing of the Carian version of the Estates-General (fig. 6). Caron's drawing is doubtless intended to refer to contemporary engravings that display the presumed disposition of personnages at the Assembly of Orleans in 1561. Caron has changed the viewpoint, however, from the head-on view typical of engravings designed simply to record the event, to a view that makes the composition less strictly formal, thereby creating a narrative of the ambiguities of shared power. The young king is at the center of the dais under a canopy, which has been turned at a right angle to the picture plane. The queen mother sits on his left. While Artemisia is a larger, more central, and more active figure than her son, he maintains his dominance by virtue of his position in front of her, his profile pose rendering him more hieratic in the tradition of ancient ruler portraits in relief; he is the *image* of the ruler. The nature of the queen's authority is made clear by the fact that she looks at him. If she can be larger and more pictorially central than her son, she all the while maintains her actual position to his side.[50] Her gesture presents her son, now larger proportionately to her, to the assembled crowd, as if referring to one of Catherine's first projects after Charles IX attained his majority—her arrangement of an extensive tour of the kingdom, billed as a means of presenting the realm to him.[51]

The composition of this drawing as a whole is a mannered reworking of that paradigmatic Renaissance assembly, Raphael's *School of Athens.* What had been the pivotal position of Plato and Aristotle under central arches in Raphael's composition is here occupied by two very minor figures. The obvious draw of the central vanishing point in a perspective composition is here made strangely insignificant; the "center" of attention has been shifted to the less obvious left foreground, Artemisia's established position.

In the Artemisia portraits, the queen watches and directs all events from the sidelines. This is in contrast to how François I, for example, had been depicted by Rosso Fiorentino in a fresco at Fontainebleau, *The Unity of the Realm.* Although the setting of the fresco is antique, the king himself, dressed in Roman armor, appears front and center. As the source of his power is direct and is seen to stem from antiquity, he himself can appear in his central function. Artemisia-Catherine, however, must rule indirectly. Her position on the side in the drawings allows her to appear strong while still within the parameters of decorum imposed by the actual political situation. When it is a matter of government, she is always shown with her son, never running things on her own.

Artemisia was an ideal prototype for a woman ruler because she possessed the virtues of a man while never losing the grace of a woman, following what Houel had said about an ideal female ruler in the *Histoire.* In the drawings Artemisia always appears tall, graceful, and beautiful, according to the contemporary canons of female beauty. She appears first the ideal woman, but her actions show her to possess the masculine virtues of a ruler as well. She acted as was expected of a woman, spending the rest of her days mourning her deceased husband. But in this marginalized position, she is shown to exercise great power. Artemisia was the epitome of a nonthreatening prototype, providing the perfect imagery for Catherine de' Medici in her quest to maintain the French monarchy—against all odds—in a period of extreme conflict.

14

Feminism and the Humanists: The Case of Sir Thomas Elyot's *Defence of Good Women*

CONSTANCE JORDAN

Sir Thomas Elyot's *Defence of Good Women,* published in 1540 and dedicated to Anne of Cleves, is one of many treatises on the status of women that appeared during the fifteenth and sixteenth centuries. These works were of various kinds: some were written for a popular audience, others for scholars; some were composed for wives and husbands, others were intended for teachers or the clergy.[1] Within this large body of writing, Elyot's *Defence* belongs to a special class. Like such works as Boccaccio's *De claris mulieribus* (1361) and Bruni's *De studiis and litteris* (1409), it is humanist in character and apologetic in purpose. Treatises of this class typically argue that the cardinal virtues, celebrated in antiquity and represented in classical philosophy and history, have been (and can be) as well exemplified by women as men. That is, they seek to establish a theoretical equality of virtue between the sexes, particularly emphasizing the qualities and attributes required for participation in civic life. Not all treatises on women by humanists take such a position. Some respect traditional notions concerning the subservient place of women in society and represent their capacity for intelligent action accordingly; that is, they restrict it to familial activities and specifically to the responsible performance of wifely duties. Others, more or less facetiously, insist on women's superiority to men—perhaps an indication of how difficult it was for persons accustomed to seeing creation as fixed in a hierarchical order to conceive of different creatures as equal in any respect. But many are dedicated to demonstrating that women can act as forcefully and decisively as men in those areas of endeavor—government, military action, scholarship, and the arts—generally thought to be the province only of men.[2] It is the emphasis of these treatises on the actual value of the secular and public lives of women, judged in relation to standards of male performance, that suggests the propriety of the term *feminist* to describe them.[3]

Humanist defenses of women generally consider three kinds of subject and tend to emphasize one more than the rest. They establish the excellence of women by referring to examples from history; they celebrate the full humanity of a wife in relation to her husband; or they argue for the humanist education of girls. In each case, there is likely to be a certain overlap of concern. Discussions of marriage offer examples of virtuous wives like those described in the *De claris mulieribus*; arguments for education insist that learning makes wives more tractable; chronicles of worthies dwell on the beneficial effects of education or the companionableness of a wife. Elyot's *Defence,* treating all three of these subjects, logically refutes Aristotle's notion of the inferiority of women and is supported by evidence from "experience," dramatically embodied in the Syrian Queen Zenobia who is a general, an exemplary wife, and a woman educated in philosophy and history.

The secular and more particularly the political character of these humanist defenses needs special recognition. The most generally acknowledged rules of feminine behavior required of women two principal virtues: silence and chastity. Of these, the first was the most decisive, for it prevented women from venturing outside their families and into public life. Humanists challenged these rules and in effect created others. Fascinated with examples of women who had taken part in the great drama of history, humanists compared them with men, praised their "virility," and entertained the possibility of a single standard for male and female virtue.

Boccaccio, whose *De claris mulieribus* is practically the first example of this genre, characterizes its difference from more traditional treatises on the subject of women and establishes in his preface to his work its area of concern—politics and history:

> However it seemed to me appropriate—and I would not wish to pass over the matter in silence—not to include with the ladies [in my treatise] any from sacred history, either Hebrew or Christian, except Eve. It seemed to me in fact that pagan and Christian ladies have little in common with each other, nor do they move on an equal footing. Ladies of sacred history, following in the paths and the rules of their holy Teacher, often, to attain true eternal glory, forced themselves to tolerate adversities almost beyond human comprehension. Pagan women, on the other hand, attained glory—and with

what a burning strength of spirit—either owing to a certain natural instinct; or, more probably, because they were driven by a spark of the fleeting splendor of this world; and sometimes beneath the blow of crushing fortune also faced most severe tests. The first, shining with the true inexhaustible light, not only live in a paradise well-earned, but also are noted here; for their virginity, chastity, sanctity, and virtue, and the indomitable constancy in chains and the tortures of the flesh and the punishments of tyrants they are described— as their merits require—in several works of holy men, famous for their sacred learning and their obvious majesty. The merits of the second, however, since they are published in no book—as I have said—nor remarked on by anyone, I have set myself to describe, as if to render them a just reward.[4]

Boccaccio's interest in proving the moral value of *pagan* women, enlightened by reason and moved by honor, sets him off from his contemporaries; his purposes are different from those of writers who praise women for their faith and morals, as does Christine de Pisan in her *Livre de la cité des dames* (1404),[5] or for their constancy in love, as does Chaucer in his half-facetious *Legend of Good Women* (1386). Boccaccio's emphasis on glory—not eternal glory but worldly glory—indicates how thoroughly he embraced the idea that women, like men, might have a part in civic life. They, too, might be enflamed by a "spark of the fleeting splendor of this world." By excluding from his defense examples of saints, martyrs, and patient Griseldas—types that other apologists frequently praise—Boccaccio institutes the character of humanist feminism.[6]

Political events may have contributed to the humanists' preoccupation with the notion of women as citizens rather than as daughters, wives, and mothers. Women had always held political power, in various ways and degrees, but in the Renaissance, with the consolidation of nation-states, women "governors" became conspicuous. How they were to be trained for the tasks they would have to undertake, and in what way they were to defer to men, were finally questions of national importance. Treatises like Boccaccio's, which drew attention to politically powerful women from antiquity to the recent past (in his dedication Boccaccio praises Joanna of Naples), stimulated feminist debate. What kind of education was appropriate to a queen or princess into whose hands royal power had passed? What kind of obedience did a ruling queen owe her husband? Could a woman lead troops in battle?

Moreover, such specific questions on the political status of women were raised in the context of general discussions on the benefits of various forms of government, on the obligations of magistrates, and on lawful resistance to authority. Treatises on these topics poured from the presses in Europe, especially in the sixteenth century, and among the concerns virtually all of them shared was the need to articulate the political responsibilities of classes of persons that by custom or nature or divine law were deemed to be subservient to other classes that were, by contrast, in authority. In the subordination of the woman to the man, most commonly instanced as that of the wife to the husband, writers saw mirrored an image of a possible kind of relationship between the governed and the governor. Aristotle's assertion that family life was the basis for the political order of the *polis* made it easy for political theorists to draw parallels between what was expected of women in the family and the obligations of persons classed as subordinates in the hierarchy of government. They frequently claimed that the good government of the family was the precondition for that which should obtain between ruler and people in the state as a whole. Wives were often characterized as minor magistrates who carried out the commands of their superiors; at the same time, they almost always had that right typically reserved for the people, that is, the right to resist the commands of an authority who abused his power. In short, the relationship of the woman to her family and to the larger communities in which she lived was politicized, in part because a *very few* women were in fact becoming "governors," in part because women as a class were seen to represent the earliest and most universal example of subordination to authority provided by human society, and it was with subordination and authority that contemporary political treatises were concerned.[7]

How urgent might be the need to demonstrate publicly the capacity of women to fulfill civic responsibilities can be gauged by briefly reflecting on the content of Elyot's *Defence* in relation to the circumstances of its publication. Its dedication to Anne of Cleves is clearly anomalous; that queen could not have regarded with anything less than dismay Elyot's principal example of a "good woman," the Syrian Queen Zenobia, whom he represents as a widow, defeated and a captive, and virtually under house arrest. The similarity of Elyot's Zenobia to Catherine of Aragon may well have occurred to her, but even if it did not, the fate of Zenobia was not one she could have wished for herself. The anomaly is partly resolved if an earlier date of composition and a different audience for the *Defence* is assumed, but this in turn raises another set of questions altogether more speculative.

Some readers have in fact identified Elyot's Zenobia with Catherine, largely on comparative grounds.[8] Like Elyot's Zenobia, a queen who exemplifies the "virile" virtues appropriate to a governor or prince, Catherine was educated in the humanist manner; by her defeat of James IV at Flodden she was known as a competent general; she was recognized as a skillful diplomat, versed in languages and knowledgeable in the affairs of state.[9] Moreover certain of the circumstances of Zenobia's life—as Elyot presents them—recall Catherine's. Zenobia is the prisoner of the Emperor Aurelianus and her movements through the city are restricted. In 1531, Henry ordered Catherine to prepare to seek a domicile apart; in 1533, she was removed under guard from Ampthill to Buckden in Huntingtonshire. Her route was lined with sympathetic subjects who must indeed have seen her as a "captive queen."[10] Finally, Elyot's Zenobia comes from "Surry"—a version of Syria not uncommon in sixteenth-century English texts but perhaps also a reference to Catherine's house in Richmond.

To understand Elyot's Zenobia as a figure for Catherine of Aragon places the question of Elyot's purpose in writing the *Defence* in a curious light. It transforms Elyot's treatise into a defense of one "exceptional" woman, Catherine herself. But would he have written such a treatise in 1540, five years after Catherine's death? To support the Zenobia-Catherine identification the reader must begin by assuming either that Elyot had some plausible reason for praising Catherine in 1540 (or late in 1539) or that he wrote the *Defence* at an earlier date when such praise might have been appropriate. Defenses of Catherine as Henry's wife, that is, treatises against the divorce, did in fact appear in England from 1529 to 1532. Elyot's *Defence* cannot be included in this group, however; it does not touch on the question of divorce.

A definitive account of the composition and publication of Elyot's *Defence* may not be possible on the available evidence. Certain well-established facts do, however, suggest a connection between *The Defence,* Catherine's divorce, and its aftermath—Henry's virtual imprisonment of her and of Mary. During the period of Catherine's separation from Henry and before her death, that is, from summer 1532 to January 1536, Elyot led a double life. Outwardly he complied with royal policy and even participated in Henry's government, but secretly he was a party to the conspiracy organized by Eustache Chapuys, the ambassador of Charles V, and supported by men who were prepared to welcome on English shores the forces of Charles V, depose Henry, and place Catherine on the throne as regent for Mary.[11]

Chapuys had sought to persuade humanists to write against the divorce in 1531 and earlier—he contacted Elyot about such a treatise in 1532—and it seems not unreasonable to assume that he might also have been interested in defenses of Catherine as regent after the divorce had occurred.[12] If the *Defence* is associated on stylistic and thematic grounds with Elyot's other dialogues, *Pasquil the Plaine* and *The Knowledge that Maketh a Wise Man,* written early in 1533 and in fact critical of Henry, the case for reading it as propaganda is further strengthened. Specifically it becomes an apology for Catherine as regent for Mary—her position were Chapuys's conspiracy successful. Persons disaffected with Henry and his new queen who might have been expected to rally behind Catherine in the event of an invasion must then be considered Elyot's intended audience and the *Defence* a device contrived to persuade them to accept Catherine's leadership. Moreover, if this too is assumed to be the case, as I believe it should be, Elyot's *Defence* can be seen to illustrate what seems to be a common feature of the literature of defenses of women as a whole, that is, the extent to which it is occasional, each defense motivated in some measure by a need to address a specific audience at a particular moment in history. In other words, the proposition that women possessed the masculine virtues, that they were competent to participate fully in civic life, is linked, frequently if not invariably, to historical situations in which it may be advantageously asserted by one party for the benefit of another.

Like *Pasquil the Plaine* and *The Knowledge that Maketh a Wise Man,* the *Defence* is in the form of a dialogue. It dramatizes an argument among three speakers: Candidus, the enlightened defender of women who adopts a Platonic position and insists that women are fit to participate in civic affairs; Caninius, their barking Aristotelian detractor; and finally Candidus's friend, Queen Zenobia, the captive of the emperor Aurelianus. Candidus's strategy is simple. He defeats Caninius by logically invalidating the criticisms of misogynists; he then confirms his position with "experience," or evidence from "history"; and, in conclusion, he adduces a living example of the truth of his opinion, the captive Queen Zenobia. Reliance on "experience" to support a feminist position is common to most defenses of women. Boccaccio, Castiglione, and others, denying denunciations of women based on received opinion, resort to examples of worthies as proof. Elyot's treatment of "example" is particularly effective in this case: by representing Zenobia as a character in a dialogue, a living voice, he endows her with a kind of "vital authority"—actually defined by Socrates who prefers conversation to writing for the communication of the truth—that an account of her life alone would not provide.[13] Zenobia offers Candidus a "perfyte conclusion" to his argument and by "the example of her lyfe vanquishethe the obstinate mynde of the frowarde Caninius" because her authority, vested in a palpable being, is difficult to deny.[14]

To support his attack on women, Caninius draws first on the complaints of poets (Boccaccio seems indicated, although he is not mentioned) and second on the works of Aristotle touching the subject of women—the two most conspicuous sources of misogynist literature available to Renaissance readers. He begins the debate by declaring that women are faithless, especially in love: in women there is "in the stede of fayth, falshode and trechery" (sig. B3). Candidus dismisses the point by asserting that it is one only poets make and they are not to be believed. He alludes to the dubious truth of all poetic statements (reminding Caninius that Plato expelled poets from his republic for spreading falsehood) and observes—and this is his principal point—that the poets who see in "al women most beastly conditions" are either ungrateful or disappointed lovers who, rejecting women or else rejected by them, revile them from spite. In effect he denies that the idea of women as faithless has a basis in observed fact and attributes it instead to compensatory fictions created by men to serve their own emotional needs. It is of theoretical importance that Candidus's reasoning here is based on the principle of induction rather than deduction. When humanists examined dogmatic concepts of womanhood by reference to "experience," they could reveal their inadequacies. Candidus's answer may actually have a source in a similar reply directed by Castiglione's Magnifico to Gasparo in *Il libro del cortegiano* (1528).[15] In its appreciation of psychological determinants it is certainly comparable to the explanation of the apparently natural submissiveness of women offered by Agrippa in his treatise *De nobilitate et praecellentia sexus foeminei* (1529).[16] Insights like these subverted the orthodox doctrine on women and allowed critics to see it as an effect of psychological and social forces rather than as objectively true.

In refuting Caninius's neo-Aristotelian misogyny, Candidus has a more difficult task. Caninius begins this phase of his attack by noting Aristotle's claim that women are a "worke of nature unperfecte" (sig. C3^r), a dictum he takes from the philosopher's discussion of reproduction in *The Generation of Animals*.[17] He continues by advancing correlative points:

They be weaker than men, and have theyr flesshe softer, lasse
heare on theyr visages, and theyre voyse sharper . . . And
as concernynge the soule, they lacke hardynes, and in peryles
are timerouse, more delycate than men, unapte to paynful-
nesse, except they be therto constrained, or steryd by wylfull-
nesse: And the wytte, that they have, is not substanciall but
apyshe . . .

(sig. C6, C6v)

These are opinions that Caninius discovered in the *History of Animals*.[18] And he concludes that women cannot govern: "In the partes of
wysedome and civile policy, they be founden unapte, and to have litell
capacitie" (sig. C6v), a view Aristotle expresses in the *Politics*.[19]

It would be difficult to overestimate the support Renaissance
misogynists derived from Aristotle. His notion of women as fundamentally inferior to men underlay the arguments of most learned
treatises limiting the activities of women to family life. His logic is
circular but it was rarely rejected on this account. He derives his
doctrine of the subordination of women from his belief that they are
morally weaker than men, but he in turn derives this notion of moral
weakness—which he correlates with such physical traits of the female
as smallness of size, softness of flesh, and need for sleep—from
women's subordinate place in the political economy.[20] Despite the
obvious flaw in this reasoning, commentators were generally reluctant
to challenge Aristotle's conclusions, which they saw repeatedly cor-
roborated in scripture, notably in Genesis where Eve's transgression
institutes the subordination of wives in accordance with the will of
God, and in St. Paul's epistles where women are forbidden to speak in
public (especially I Timothy 2: 11–12). Even such an ostensible
feminist as Vives could not renounce the main tenets of Aristotle's
antifeminism. In fact Vives's *De institutione foeminae christianae* (1523),
which argues for the humanist education of women, paradoxically
concludes with his condemnation of women in public life.[21] (Since the
purpose of humanist studies was to develop the talents and conscience
of the *citizen* rather than the contemplative, Vives's position is at least
theoretically self-contradictory.) Elyot's decision to assign Aristotle's
notions to a Caninius, a detractor of women, indicates a remarkable
willingness to contest the philosopher's authority.

Candidus responds to Caninius's citation of Aristotle with an
argument that he claims is equally Aristotelian. He points out that in
the *Economics* (which Renaissance scholars did not yet recognize as
spurious) the virtues proper to men and women are, although

different, yet directed to the same purpose; that is, these virtues are complementary. Paraphrasing his putative source, he asserts that nature made man "more strong and courageouse," the woman more "weake, fearefull and scrupulouse." Her "feblenesse" makes her "more circumspecte," his "strengthe" makes him more "adventurouse" (sig. C7, C7v). A man's nature is suited to "preparynge," the acquisition of goods, the woman's to "kepyng," their conservation (sig. D1). Yet when these occupations are compared, that of the woman is perceived to be of greater value; indeed, for being less associated with mere physical skills, her occupation is deemed more rational and therefore more characteristically human. Activities that call for circumspection exhibit "Reason," in its manifestations as "Discretion," "Election," and "Prudence," in contrast to those that exercise the body. Therefore, Candidus concludes, women are more reasonable and have stronger "wits" than men. This leads him to a final point. Because of her "economic" virtue of circumspection and the superior reason it requires, "a woman is not a creature unperfyte but as it seemeth is more perfyte than man" (sig. D4v). Here Candidus claims that women are not only equal but even superior to men.

This ingenious refutation of Caninius's neo-Aristotelian argument does not, in fact, derive from the pseudo-*Economics,* where the tasks of men and women are described as interdependent—men acquire, women preserve—but where neither is preferred as the more "reasonable."[22] Rather it echoes passages in the third book of *Il libro del cortegiano,* where the Magnifico hints that a comparison of the virtues of men and women (which he claims are "essentially" the same but "accidentally" different—"that in which one differs from the other is something accidental and not essential") would establish the greater intelligence of the women. According to the Magnifico, men are distinguished for their strength, but brute force is not estimable even in war. Women are known to be weak, but their frailty produces in them a mental alertness. Men acquire goods; women preserve them— by implication the worthier task. The Magnifico defeats Gasparo with the same logic that Candidus uses against Caninius: "there is no doubt that women, for being of softer flesh, are yet more mentally acute and have an intelligence, better attuned to speculation that men."[23] The two versions of the argument are different only in tone. Candidus is relentlessly serious, while the Magnifico plays with his audience. Overtly, however, both Candidus and the Magnifico commit themselves to the proposition that physical weakness entails a compensatory intellectual strength.

Having silenced Caninius, Candidus begins a counterattack and addresses directly the question of women in political life. His approach to this question, typical of defenses of women in general, is dictated by the contrasting treatments of the subject—women in politics—that appear in the *Republic* and the *Politics,* the humanists' principal sources of pro- and antifeminist argument. The latter work, insisting that women innately possess virtues only in a mode of subordination, unlike men who possess the same virtues in a mode of command, provides authority for limiting the activity of women to the family and for placing them under the rule of their husbands. Aristotle's model of the state imitates the configuration of power within the family: at its head is the class of men, representing the father; under it is the class of women, representing the father's wife and mother of his children; and beneath these classes are slaves, servants, and children. For Aristotle, the family is the fundamental unit of the state, which itself is an aggregate of families.

Many humanists found this model of government in the state and the family insusceptible to criticism: not only did it appear to correspond to what was recognized as natural law, it also received confirmation from scripture. Plato's notion of women as endowed with the same virtue as men achieved no significant acceptance by major humanists. They might base their arguments on Socrates' statement that the virtue in men and women is the same, but they did not accept the politics that Plato then constructs on this premise.[24] Why they did not pursue the notion of women as "guardians," rulers and governors of the state—an investigation that might have concluded in justifying in principle the right of women to govern men— is unclear. But their unwillingness to examine Plato's image of the female guardian must in part be a response to the very conditions in which Plato imagined the guardians would live, that is, with property and children in common.[25] Such a class would violate all Christian norms of social life and for this reason it could not be an element in a Christian politics.

To validate gynococracy, humanists took another approach, which is well illustrated in the *Defence.* They left questions of authority aside and concentrated rather on the evidence in history and what it might be seen to imply.[26] Some of the evidence cited as "example" is patently ridiculous. Most humanist defenses of women do not make any distinction between figures of myth (Dido), and women who are the subject of essentially historical accounts (Cleopatra) but consider them all equally convincing. This lack of discrimination must often have caused Renaissance readers (as it causes modern readers) to call into question *all* the evidence supplied in such defenses. It was not until humanists developed a sense of what is really acceptable evidence that they could begin to offer cogent arguments against assertions of the natural inferiority of women. In this respect, the question of evidence is like the question of psychological determinants. In both cases, received opinion can only be challenged by observations based either on actual experience or experience for which there is some valid or verifiable historical reference.

But proofs based on example have another even more serious shortcoming: they produce paradoxical arguments. The women who illustrate feminine excellence are noted for acting courageously and intelligently—in short, in a manner specified as virile. These women logically prove the worth of their sex by denying it: a strange form of defense. While it questions sexual stereotypes, that some women can do men's work, it also seems to confirm gender-related values, that everything female is inferior. The regularity with which these exemplary women are labelled "manly" finally undermines their rhetorical purpose. These limitations aside, however, the practical orientation of defenses that proceed by example did permit a consideration of how women perform tasks of government customarily assigned to men even if it excluded debate on more contentious matters of principle. An account (whether or not fictitious) of a woman who was successful in speaking in council or commanding an army obviously has bearing on the larger question of gynocoracy and tends to undermine theoretical denunciations of such government.

Candidus's perception of the place of women in political life is expressed in two propositions: "in armes women have been found of no lyttell reputation" (sig. D6v) and "the wyttes of women are apte . . . to wisedom and civile policie" (sig. D4v). These claims—that women have the capacity to perform in the two fields of endeavor crucial to the success of a Renaissance prince—are far-reaching although not unusual in humanist defenses of women.[27] (They are certainly implicit in the *De claris mulieribus* and *Il libro del cortegiano*.) If Candidus can substantiate them, he will have established the validity of the female governor. The notion that women could take part in active warfare was supported by instances in which this actually happened. Agrippa, for example, alludes admiringly to "La Pucelle" in his *De nobilitate*[28] and Castiglione to Isabella of Castile in *Il libro del cortegiano*[29] Yet popular and learned opinion was generally opposed to the practice. A woman's comparative lack of physical strength constituted a rational basis for limiting her part in war. In some cases the prospect of women at war was regarded with angry shock. Vives, for example, warns women that they cannot succeed at this deadly occupation: "Therfore you women that . . . go about to hurle downe townes afore you . . . lyght upon a hard rocke. Whereupon though you brouse and shake contres very sore, yet they scape and you perisshe."[30] The idea that women might be adept at "civile policie" was almost as often the object of criticism. The practice of "civile policie" naturally entailed the skilful use of rhetoric and oratory and in fact women were prevented from speaking in public, in accordance with the literature of classical antiquity and scripture. A correlative of Aristotle's conception of a woman as emotional was a belief that her judgment was likely to be faulty. She tended to speak a great deal but little to the point.[31] St. Paul simply forbade women to preach (speak in public), and this rule seems to have been associated in the popular imagination with Eve's role in persuading Adam to disobey God's commandment in paradise. Women were commonly viewed as garrulous; if they were also clever they might become dangerous. In one of the earliest humanist treatises on the education of girls, Bruni explicitly denies his students instruction in eloquence: "Rhetoric in all its forms—public discussion, forensic argument, logical fence, and the like—lies absolutely outside the province of women."[32] Vives is even more vehement: "As for eloquence I have no great care nor a woman nedeth it nat but she nedeth goodnes and wysedome." And he makes a precise connection between the study of oratory and the practice of government:

> Wene you it was for nothyng that wyse men forbad you rule and governaunce of contreis and that saynt Paule byddeth you shall nat speke in congragatyon and gatherynge of people? All this same meaneth that you shall nat medle with matters of realmes or cities. Your own house is a cite great inough for you; as for the abrode neither know you nor be you knowen.[33]

Despite these rules determining feminine behavior, many defenders of women, and particularly humanists, included in their work "examples" of women who excelled in both forbidden activities. Mythical figures are cited as the founders of various arts, and certain queens, both mythical and historical, are praised for their administrative and martial achievements. Women scholars, orators, and historians are described as paragons of intellectual virtue. A survey of these panegyrical accounts suggests the extent to which their writers—almost entirely male—saw fit to question the feminine paradigms that tended decisively to deny to women a part in public life.

Queen Zenobia is among the most frequently described of female worthies: she appears in Vives's *De institutione,* in Agrippa's *De nobilitate,* in Chaucer's "Monk's Tale," and in Lydgate's *Fall of Princes,* a popular paraphrase of Boccaccio's *De casibus virorum illustrium.* Boccaccio tells her story twice. In the *De casibus virorum,* he emphasizes her fame, thus fulfilling the purpose of that work: "and if great virtue rises then it must also fall. Not even Zenobia could escape this unscathed." He barely hints that her fall is due to her violation of norms of feminine behavior: "[Aurelius,] having thought it unsuitable that a woman possess part of the Roman Empire, took up arms against Zenobia."[34] In the *De claris mulieribus,* he eliminates the fortune theme and describes her simply in superlatives: most learned, most courageous, and so forth. He even manages to transform her catastrophic capture into a complimentary occasion: "Just as if he had conquered the greatest of generals and the fiercest enemy of the republic, Aurelius rejoiced in glory and kept her for a triumph and lead her to Rome with her sons."[35]

Elyot's Zenobia is in many respects the liveliest of these representations; she incarnates the central paradox so often generated by the introduction of humanist ideals into the context of an essentially Christian antifeminism largely shaped by the persistence of Aristotelian norms. She demonstrates to a greater degree than many of her counterparts the qualities conventional to women, but also, by contrast, those that distinguish humanist models. She duly conforms to the expectations of conservative readers by being modest, dutiful, temperate, patient, and obedient to her husband. Yet she is also unmistakably the product of a humanist imagination working (or playing) on the possibility that a woman can also attain a full measure of humanity.

Zenobia's education was characteristically humanist. She studied philosophy and history until she was twenty and did not marry before that time. Moreover she reports that her "lernynge was had of none honeste man in any derysyon" (sig. E3). Learned women were frequently thought to be disposed to levity and the charge was regularly denied by their defenders. Hyrde, for example assures his readers that an educated wife is more not less tractable[36]—a view also endorsed by More[37] and Erasmus.[38] Her widowhood allowed her to demonstrate her civic virtues (the product, she asserts, of her education); immediately realizing that her position as regent for her sons was precarious and that "I beinge a woman, shoulde nothynge be feared" (sig. E3) she took control of the state, making speeches, establishing laws (on the basis of her acquaintance with household

economy), inspecting fortifications, and even conquering territory by
the extraordinary means of moral suasion. She declares "[I] added
moche more to myne Empire, not soo moche by force, as by renoume
of juste and politike governaunce, whiche all men had in suche
admyration, that dyverse of our said ennemies. . .chase. . .to
remayne in our subjection than to retourne to theyr owne countryey"
(sig. E5) But her most daring and unusual trait—one that shows her
humanist origins more vividly than any other—is her real autonomy
in relation to her husband. Elyot is careful to express himself as
decorously as possible; nevertheless his message is clear. Zenobia
obeys her husband but only to a point. "Justice," she says, taught her
to give "due obedience" to her husband and restrained her from
"anythynge whiche [was] not semely" (sig. E1v). Furthermore she
declares that a wife must suit her will to her husband. But she also
insists that a wife is exempt from these constraints on her freedom if
what her husband wishes "may tourne them bothe to losse or
dyshonesty" (sig E2). That is, a wife must actually exercise her own
judgment. Here Elyot may well be remembering the spurious
Aristotle who cites Homer's instruction on marriage: "It is clear that
the poet is teaching husband and wife to dissuade one another from
whatever is evil and dishonorable while unselfishly furthering to the
best of their power one another's honourable and righteous aims."[39]
But Elyot's emphasis on what a wife must *not* do recalls the other
source on which he has already relied heavily: Zenobia's words echo
Ludovico's reply to Federico, who had asked whether a courtier
should obey a dishonorable command: "if [your lord] commands you
to do a dishonorable thing, not only are you not obligated to do it,
you are obligated not to do it, both on your own account and in order
to not to be the one to contribute shame to your lord."[40] In
concluding this part of the dialogue, Elyot does, admittedly, minimize
the radicalism of Zenobia's views. She ends her rules of marriage by
saying that a wife should dissemble her "disobedience": if she cannot
do her husband's "wyll, . . . than should she seme rather to give him
wise counsaile, than to appere disobedient or sturdy" (sig. E2). This
reservation does not, however, obscure the substance of her argument: like Castiglione's courtier, Elyot's wife must finally act as if she
had free will.

Both Agrippa and Erasmus stress the companionableness of a wife
and see marriage as a relationship of mutuality. Erasmus's remark that
an ill-behaved wife is due to an ill-behaved husband—"an evyll wyfe
is nat wont to chaunce but to evyll husbandes"—implies that if a
husband embarks on dishonorable conduct he can expect to find his

wife similarly engaged and in ways that may indeed appear disobedi-ent.[41] But no humanist, to my knowledge, gives a wife as much autonomy as Elyot does by casting her in an essentially political role. It is not accidental that here Elyot's Zenobia resembles Castiglione's courtier, because in a sense they confront the same problem.[42] Both wife and courtier function as advisors to persons to whom they owe affection and loyalty. Both must serve their "lord," but—and this is the crucial contribution that both works make to the concept of service—only if they are satisfied that his course of action is not one that will bring dishonor on him, his court, or his state.

Zenobia's obvious excellence, her modesty, and her competence confound Caninius who admits defeat. But the victory is Candidus's alone, for Zenobia, despite her virtue, remains the captive of the Emperor Aurelianus and among the conquered not the conquering. Her character has a certain pathos, and one is tempted to think that Elyot, who had nothing to say about courageous and intelligent women in any of his other works, wrote the *Defence* somewhat half-heartedly and perhaps to fulfill an obligation. Zenobia must nevertheless be recognized as fine example of a type, a representative of the powerful women of antiquity who first captured Boccaccio's imagination. Because he and later humanists perceived these women as free from the constraints imposed on the sex by convention, they could invest them with attributes answering to the rational criteria for public life that were in part the product of their own investigations. The pagan women celebrated in humanist defenses functioned collec-tively as the image of what might be possible if accepted social custom, shaped by Christianity and medieval scholasticism, were no longer to determine the nature and status of women in European society. They presented a fruitful enigma, a point of reference for the interesting doubts and difficult questions surrounding the accepted view of women as subordinate to men. The image itself—of a woman who is the virtuous equal of the man—is always an image of the culturally alien. The figures of Hippolyta, Semiramis, Dido, Camilla, and Artemisia, among others, are united not only by their virility but also by their barbarism. They are always on the enemy side; the writer imagines them as it were at the borders of the culturally constituted community to which his work is addressed, even as threatening the integrity of that community. But because they often brilliantly exemplify the nonbarbaric or civilized values of the writer's own society—as the male enemy does not (compare Artemisia with Xerxes or Camilla with Turnus)—they also invite sympathy. The conflict between attitudes—overt disapproval marked with fear on one hand

and occasional admiration on the other—is later epitomized in the great warrior maidens of Renaissance epic: Merediana, Antea, Marfisa, Bradamante, Clorinda, Britomart.

The historical assimilation of the concept of political equality between the sexes, a process begun in the fifteenth and sixteenth centuries, is partly indicated by the domestication of these characters during this period. The difference between the Merediana of the anonymous fifteenth-century *Orlando* and Ariosto's Bradamante a century later has nothing to do with their characters, which generally adhere to a chivalric type: they are remarkably similar in being courageous, resourceful, noble, passionate, and virile. They are distinguished only by their religion and national origin: the former, an infidel, comes from "Pagania," while the latter is Christian and French. The proliferation of the type in later epic (Spenser and Tasso) suggests that as the concept of the *donna operosa* became less strange, writers responded to a need to discriminate among possibilities. Ariosto's two female knights, Marfisa and Bradamante, and Spenser's comparable pair, Radigund and Britomart, represent each poet's analysis of the positive and negative elements of what was once a single image.

If, as I suggested earlier, the *Defence* is indeed an apology for Catherine as regent, many of its passages gain an additional interest. If it was designed principally to arouse popular support for the queen as head of state, its representation of Zenobia as a commanding general must have caused Henry some concern. He certainly thought Catherine capable of doing what Chapuys had planned for her, and early in 1535 he described to his council the sort of conflict that would ensue were Charles V to invade England: "The lady Catherine is a proud stubborn woman of very high courage. If she took it into her head to take her daughter's part she could quite easily take the field, muster an great army, and wage against me a war as fierce as any her mother Isabella waged in Spain."[43] As Henry knew, Isabella's wars had overturned the throne of Castile. He could not therefore have drawn a more alarming parallel to the possible outcome of his own struggle to maintain power than the events in Spain a generation earlier, events in which Catherine had a clear personal interest.

A less obvious but more important audience for the *Defence* might have been Catherine herself. As is established by Mattingly's brilliant biography of her, she continuously opposed on grounds both logical and emotional the projected invasion and insurrection. Legally, since she rested her case against Henry's divorce on the ground that her own marriage was legitimate, she could not behave in a way that might cast suspicion on her status as wife. Above all, this entailed obedience to her husband, a condition that participating in, inspiring, or even condoning a conspiracy to depose him would manifestly violate. The nature of her defense required that she, a wife, be at her husband Henry's command. Is it this paradoxical situation that Elyot's addresses when Zenobia qualifies the extent of a wife's obedience? If Zenobia's statements apply to Catherine, they praise the queen's refusal to allow Henry to commit an action that "maye tourne them bothe to losse or dyshonesty" and encourage her to continue in that refusal. Catherine also declined to support Chapuys's conspiracy on the ground that it would lead to shedding Christian blood.[44] Was Catherine's pacificism partly responsible for Elyot's emphasis on Zenobia's irenic interests, her use of persuasion not force, her adherence to a strategy of moral not literal warfare?

These are specific ways in which the *Defence* appears to speak to Catherine's condition. More broadly, the *Defence* may have been intended to educate Catherine to perceive herself as regent. Its emphasis on the secular life open to women, the moral duties of government that might be carried on by queens as well as kings, and the association of an independent judgment with early and prolonged training in philosophy and history would have constituted a covert appeal to Catherine's memories of her mother and her own childhood. It would have presented her with an image of womanhood in which were expressed Isabella's fortitude (so impressively recalled by Henry) and her belief in the value of a humanist education that Catherine in turn had insisted on giving her own daughter. It would, moreover, have stood in significant contrast to another humanist's defense of women, Vives's *De institutione,* one that Catherine knew well and had had written for Mary.[45] If Elyot knew it—and it is hard to imagine he did not—he could not have helped seeing it as deleterious to the cause he secretly espoused from 1532 to 1535. It expressed the views most likely to discourage Catherine from attempting to govern, even as regent; it would have made it difficult for her command troops, to speak in Parliament or council, in short to be a ruling queen. Vives's influence on Catherine was well known to be important, and Elyot might naturally have been concerned to provide Catherine with a model of femininity more aggressively political than that presented by Vives—a model specifically permitting her to "medle in matters of realms." These are, of course, only speculations. But one thing is sure. If Chapuys's plans had succeeded, Catherine would have had to take Elyot's model seriously.

15

Singing Unsung Heroines: Androgynous Discourse in Book 3 of *The Faerie Queene*

Lauren Silberman

In the beginning of the second canto of Book 3 of *The Faerie Queene,* Spenser transforms Ariosto's encomium of unsung heroines in the *Orlando Furioso* (20.1–3, 37.1.24) into a compliment for Elizabeth, the acknowledged mistress of "artes and pollicy." But masquerading as a conventional compliment to the monarch is, I think, a statement of genuine iconoclasm. Ariosto pays women a rather backhanded compliment. He poses as the honest historian of their achievements while calling attention to his own invention as a poet. The warrior maids Marfisa and Bradamante never existed outside his poem. There have been many renowned women, Ariosto assures us; it is just that somehow or other no one has ever heard of them. Spenser is after something very different. In revising Ariosto, he shifts emphasis from fictitious heroines to the false men who have suppressed the exploits of heroic women:

> Here haue I cause, in men just blame to find,
>   That in their proper prayse too partiall bee,
>   And not indifferent to woman kind,
>   To whom no share in armes and cheualrie
>   They do impart, ne maken memorie
>   Of their braue gestes and prowesse martiall;
>   Scarse do they spare to one or two or three,
>   Rowme in their writs; yet the same writing small
> Does all their deeds deface, and dims their glories all.
>
> But by record of antique times I find,
>   That women wont in warres to beare most sway,
>   And to all great exploits them selues inclind:
>   Of which they still the girlond bore away,
>   Till enuious Men fearing their rules decay,

> Gan coyne streight lawes to curb their liberty;
> Yet sith they warlike armes haue layd away,
> They haue exceld in artes and pollicy,
> That now we foolish men that prayse gin eke t'enuy.[1]
>
> (3.2.1–2)

The complex pun, that men "in their proper prayse too partiall bee," suggests that the improper partiality that leads men to disregard women produces only incomplete, partial praise of themselves. Spenser admits that sexuality affects the way people look at the world, which is radical enough; characteristic of male *parti pris* is the assumption of universality.[2] "Man and wife are one person under the law, and that person is the man." More than that, however, Spenser considers the *topos* of the unsung heroine not simply as an opportunity for irony but as a standing challenge to language itself. How does one write about a reality for which men have made no room in their writs? How does one challenge the assumptions of one's own culture? We who find ourselves faced with the latter problem have, I think, much to learn from Spenser's willingness and ability to be genuinely revisionary.[3]

When Spenser sets the "record of antique times" against men's "writing small," he taxes his poetic invention in both senses of the word *invention*. It requires great creative power to rediscover a world excluded from written records. Spenser fashions the *Legend of Britomart* in response to Platonic hierarchical dualism and Petrarchan poetics. Petrarchan poetry, which is based on the hierarchy of male poet and female love object, represents the quintessence of partial praise: it parts men and women and it enshrines male subjectivity in a specious transcendence.[4] The Petrarchan poet writes of a mistress who is unattainable so that his own perpetual longing provides subject matter for his poetry and the occasion for his assuming the vocation of poet. As the woman's active participation in the love relationship is denied, she is removed to the margins of the lyric, allowing the poet ample scope for expatiating on his own ability to make the absent beloved present in his verse. Britomart, who takes a very active role in a loving relationship, is an anti-Petrarchan heroine. Her warmth and vulnerability expose the essential sterility and self-absorption of Petrarchan lovesickness. And her uncertainty, as she falls in love with Artegall having seen nothing more than his image, about whether her love is true and destined to be fulfilled or whether it is a perverse and cruel delusion, shows up the too-pat Petrarchan strategy of making of the poet's own mental state the primary, objective reality.

Consider Spenser's famous image of artifice, Merlin's mirror: "For thy it round and hollow shaped was, / Like to the world it selfe, and seem'd a world of glas" (3.2.19, ll. 8–9).[5] This is generally considered a model of Spenser's own poetic enterprise, but what is less often remarked is that the world of glass is offered as an alternative model that Spenser goes on, in the next stanza, to contrast with a more conventional version of poetic enterprise:

> Who wonders not, that reades so wonderous worke?
> But who does wonder, that has red the Towre,
> Wherein th' Ægyptian *Phao* long did lurke
> From all mens vew, that none might her discoure,
> Yet she might all men vew out of her bowre?
> Great *Ptolomæe* it for his lemans sake
> Ybuilded all of glasse, by Magicke powre,
> And also it impregnable did make;
> Yet when his loue was false, he with a peaze it brake.
>
> (3.2.20)

Here Spenser suggests that, although the universal, androgynous poetics figured by the mirror seems unusual, is it not equally strange to accept without question a phallic image of artistic creation that will not stand up against woman's autonomy?

Spenser's world of glass and Ptolemy's tower differ, not only in shape but in the epistemology each embodies as well. The unexpectedly fragile tower reveals the hidden inconsistency of a dualistic world view; the world of glass offers a better model, based on the principle of *discordia concors*. Ptolemy's glass tower offers a virtual parody of the epistemological categories *subject* and *object,* and of the sexual values tacitly given those categories: the male subject and the female object. With his artifice, Ptolemy makes Phao a subject of perception—she can see from within her tower but cannot be seen—in order to make of her a private sexual object. Ptolemy obstructs the process of social interaction, where people are objects of others' perception and subjects of their own, in order to exercise power over Phao. Although she gets to be both subject and object, the categories are manipulated for Ptolemy's sexual advantage. In contrast, when Britomart looks into the magic mirror, Spenser gives us an image of woman-as-subject that is not a bad joke. And, in place of the epistemological shell game, where mutually exclusive categories of subject and object are switched around to serve the will to power, Spenser offers a model of subjective participation in the object. In Merlin's looking glass, the interdependence of subject and object effects a kind of truce: as the categories are not entirely separable, it is impossible to accord one or the other primacy:

> It vertue had, to shew in perfect sight,
> 　What euer thing was in the world contaynd,
> 　Betwixt the lowest earth and heauens hight,
> 　So that it to the looker appertaynd . . .
>
> 　　　　　　　　　　　　　　　(3.2.19 ll. 1–4)

The phrase *so that* is deliberately ambiguous: it is both the introduction of a result clause—the mirror could show sights in such a way that they pertained to the looker—and the equivalent of "provided that"— the mirror will reveal any sight, provided that it pertains to the looker. The double meaning keeps unclear to what extent the vision in the mirror is a subjective transformation of the object—that whatever appears in the mirror is distorted to pertain to the looker—and to what extent the pertinence of the object to the subject is a necessary precondition for the magic vision—that you can see anything you want, just as long as it pertains to you. The former is accounted a bad kind of subjectivity in Western culture when it is opposed to the virtue of objectivity or, if one has a Romantic sensibility, it is accounted a good kind for the freedom it gives.[6] Spenser's epistemology does not permit the reductive confidence of either idealized objectivity or of Romantic subjectivity. He proposes an engaged subjectivity in which admitting the danger of illusion is the price of vision. Spenser teases the reader about the traditional pejorative judgment of subjectivity when he describes Britomart's encounter with the magic mirror:

> One day it fortuned, faire *Britomart*
> 　Into her fathers closet to repayre;
> 　For nothing he from her reseru'd apart,
> 　Being his onely daughter and his hayre:
> 　Where when she had espyde that mirrhour fayre,
> 　Her selfe a while therein she vewd in vaine;
> 　Tho her auizing of the vertues rare,
> 　Which thereof spoken were, she gan againe
> Her to bethinke of, that mote to her selfe pertaine.
>
> 　　　　　　　　　　　　　　　(3.2.22)

The word *vaine* raises the specter that Britomart may be guilty of a morally dangerous vanity. She engages in a long dialogue with Glauce about whether or not she is worse than Narcissus to have fallen in love with the image of a handsome knight shown to her by the mirror as soon as she began innocently to speculate about her future husband.

Spenser's joke is that "vanity, self-love" is not the primary meaning of *vaine* in context. As long as Britomart sees her own face in the looking glass, its magic is vain: it does not work. She cannot be content to be the objective observer with no prior interest in what she sees; that is what is truly vain.

Britomart's very uncertainty about what she sees in the mirror supplies the *tertium quid,* the third term, the distributed middle, that mediates between subject and object and transforms binary opposition into the ternary form of *discordia concors.*[7] Britomart cannot know for sure whether Artegall is real or is, in fact, a subjective, Narcissistic fantasy. By seeking after the knight whose image she has seen in the mirror, as her nurse Glauce urges her to do, she risks being in love with a mere fantasy; this risk is the *discordia* of *discordia concors.* And the wounding that forms a recurring motif in Book 3 attests to this risk. Spenser's poetics are based on a theory of reading as an act of courage—braving the gap between subject and object—with both sexual and moral connotations of *courage* equally relevant.

For the rest of this paper, I shall focus on the two major episodes in Book 3 that most clearly and directly express Spenser's critique of Petrarchan poetics and Platonic metaphysics. First, I shall consider the House of Busirane, that master of Petrarchan sexual poetics. Then, I shall discuss the Gardens of Adonis, where Spenser develops his poetics of harmonious discord as a genuine revision rather than an expedient transformation of Platonic dualism of spirit and matter. Just as Spenser restores active female participation, excluded by Petrarchanism from love poetry, so he restores the female and the physical components of procreation in his version of the Gardens of Adonis. The Gardens of Adonis are an erotic parody of Plato's myth of spiritual origins set out in the *Meno* and *Phaedo,* which offers an image of evolving plenitude to replace the Platonic metaphysics of full presence.[8] Spenser criticizes Platonic dualism for substituting a will to power for genuine effort at understanding. Busirane's anti-Spenserian poetics exploits the Platonic model of dualism in that it depends on establishing binary oppositions—of reader and text, signifier and signified, subject and object, form and matter—that he can collapse for his own ends. He manipulates dualism in order to reap the benefits of duplicity, making a spurious object of Amoret the better to violate her integrity.

There is a kind of introduction to the House of Busirane in which Britomart comes upon Scudamore lying on the ground crying. She asks him what the problem is, and he explains what Busirane has done to his lady.[9] In many respects, Scudamore's problem is the key to what is wrong in the House of Busirane: the failure of courtly language to do justice to intersubjective reality. As Scudamore chivalrously blames himself for the injustice done his virtuous and innocent lady, his language betrays his failure to understand his own personal engagement in Amoret's plight. In his speech to Britomart, Scudamore admits more than he explicitly acknowledges:

> My Lady and my loue is cruelly pend
>   In dolefull darkenesse from the vew of day,
>   Whilest deadly torments do her chast brest rend,
>   And the sharpe steele doth riue her hart in tway,
>   All for she *Scudamore* will not denay.
>   Yet thou vile man, vile *Scudamore* art sound,
>   Ne canst her ayde, ne canst her foe dismay;
>   Vnworthy wretch to tread upon the ground,
> For whom so faire a Lady feeles so sore a wound.
>
> (3.11.11)

Scudamore's castigation of himself "for whom so faire a lady feeles so sore a wound" is a complex judgment. By punning on the preposition *for,* Spenser indicates the ambiguity of the relationship between Amoret's suffering and Scudamore. She feels a wound for his sake—because she will not betray him—and she feels a wound because of him—because of his failure to protect her. Scudamore acknowledges these two meanings, but there is yet a third significance of which he does not seem to be aware; namely, that Amoret feels a wound of desire for Scudamore. Here, again, wounding confirms the engagement of subject and object. Scudamore is blind to this because as a conventional lover, he appropriates all of the active role for himself. In so doing, he connives at Amoret's enforced passivity and, because he has assumed an impossible role, he prevents himself from acting at all. That Busirane's particular villainy—he has "pend" Amoret by imprisoning her and by penning her in language—has been permitted by Scudamore's misguided view of love suggests the dependence of Busirane's poetic strategy on psychological bias, specifically on Scudamore's characteristically male illusion of objectivity, which ironically blinds him to his own status as a sex object.

If it is Scudamore's own bias that aids Busirane, neither is it an accident that Amoret falls into Busirane's clutches: Busirane and Amoret are natural enemies. Scudamore reveals more about Amoret's role in her own predicament than he himself is able to acknowledge with his explanation, "All for she Scudamore will not denay." In context, the primary sense of *denay* is "abjure, say no to the claims of." That is, Busirane continues to torment Amoret because she will not deny her commitment to Scudamore. However, the secondary meaning, "say no to, withhold anything desired" suggests that Amoret is tormented because she will not deny Scudamore anything, not quite Scudamore's picture of wronged, passive innocence. Critics often want to interpret Amoret's problem as her own fear of marriage, but it makes much more sense to see her as the lady who says "yes" and thereby incurs the animosity of the Petrarchan poet.[10]

But even more is revealed about the source of Busirane's hostility. *Denay* is a special kind of word; one denays by uttering "nay." Word and meaning coincide, but only because the referent is so purely a speech act, is so completely defined by social interaction.[11] Busirane seeks to sequester Amoret from any social context in order to impose his own forms on her. He has "pend" her in both senses of the word. Geographic dislocation and rhetorical manipulation combine strategically in his assault on Amoret's chastity. That is to say, Busirane exploits and confounds dualities of form and content and of speaker and audience in order to disguise the place where the masque is occurring. Is it in Britomart's mind? Amoret's mind? Busirane's castle? The page of Spenser's text?

The masque of Cupid pits form against content in a double assault on both the audience and Amoret. After Ease disappears, twelve paired figures march out, each figure an allegorical representation of a word: Fancy, Desire, Doubt, Daunger, Dissemblaunce, Suspect, Griefe, Fury, Displeasure, and Pleasaunce. The apparent formal coherence of the masque persuades us that the pageant expresses a coherent meaning, but we are being invited to yield to force and call it understanding. If one looks closely at the individual figures, how each expresses its meaning, and how each relates to its companion figure, one sees a picture of extreme incoherence, systematic discontinuity masquerading as continuous allegory. For example, Doubt exemplifies doubt; Hope does not exemplify hope, but provokes it in others. Fancy is linked to its companion Desire through moralized genealogy: Fancy begets Desire. Suspect is defined in relationship to his partner Dissemblaunce: she laughs at him; he lowers at her. But, although Dissemblaunce dissembles, she does not fool Suspect; she just teases him. The iconography of those figures seems rich and complex, but the real poetic point of the masque lies in how the language comes to life the moment Amoret enters. The appearance of a flesh-and-blood woman among the walking allegories gives a genuine shock.

After all these there marcht a most faire Dame,
  Led of two grysie villeins, th'one *Despight,*
  The other cleped *Cruelty* by name:
  She doleful Lady, like a dreary Spright,
  Cald by strong charmes out of eternall night,
  Had deathes owne image figurd in her face,
  Full of sad signes, fearfull of liuing sight;
    Yet in that horror shewd a seemely grace,
And with her feeble feet did moue a comely pace.

Her brest all naked, as net iuory,
  Without adorne of gold or siluer bright,
  Wherewith the Craftesman wonts it beautify,
  Of her dew honour was despoyled quight,
  And a wide wound therein (O ruefull sight)
  Entrenched deepe with knife accursed keene,
  Yet freshly bleeding forth her fainting spright,
    (The worke of cruell hand) was to be seene,
That dyde in sanguine red her skin all snowy cleene.

At that wide orifice her trembling hart
  Was drawne forth, and in siluer basin layd,
  Quite through transfixed with a deadly dart,
  And in her blood yet steeming fresh embayd . . .
                                    (3.12.19–21)

Busirane's attempt to impose upon Amoret the conventions of courtly love is a forcible troping: he forces her to embody a metaphor, a profane version of the sacred heart, in order to alienate Amoret's chaste affection for Scudamore. Busirane assaults her integrity with those Petrarchan conventions that identify a woman with a heart and mind of her own as Cruel and Despiteous.[12] He uses the masque both to imprison Amoret among alien forms and to intrude foreign content into her mind. The motif of spoils plays on the metaphor of form as a garment: Amoret's breast is despoiled so that she may become the spoil of Cupid, his *objet trouvé,* the free floating sign of his power. At the opposite extreme, Busirane resorts to psychological warfare as the masque degenerates to a phantasmagoria:

There were full many moe like maladies,
  Whose names and natures I note readen well;
  So many moe, as there be phantasies
  In wauering wemens wit, that none can tell,
  Or paines in loue, or punishments in hell . . .
                                    (3.12.26, ll. 1–5)

The near-pun on the preposition *in* raises a genuine question about the location of the masque. Is the pageant the product of Amoret's sexual fears: does it represent the pain that naturally accompanies love? Or is the masque torture inflicted from without, like the punishments in hell?[13] Busirane abuses poetry in passing off his own cruelty as both an objective statement about love and as a representation of Amoret's subjective fears.

Busirane's duplicity will not withstand a second look, however, because language cannot be contained by his reductive categories. When the masque appears the next night, Britomart follows the figures back into the room from which they came and sees Amoret chained to a pillar and Busirane "figuring straunge characters of his art," (3.12.31, l. 2). The masque has been demystified, but not because its characters turn out to be nothing but a pack of tropes; the transformation of the masque into marks on the page is just another of Busirane's tricks. It is the continued presence of Amoret, her wounded heart still in her breast, that gives the lie to Busirane's dualism. All the signifieds turn into signifiers, all the masque figures are displaced, deferred, by Busirane's writing, with the exception of Amoret. Busirane's limited, phallic poetics can only pen Amoret. He can only confine her; he cannot move her psychologically. "A thousand charmes her formerly did proue; / Yet thousand charmes could not her stedfast heart remoue" (3.12.31, ll. 8–9). Busirane's charmes are merely incantations; they have no power to move the heart. Spenser's figure, Amoret, eludes Busirane because Spenser shows language eluding dualism. Spenser describes the weapon used by Busirane on Amoret as "The cruell steele which thrild her dying hart," (3.12.38.1). The word *thrild* can be taken in three separate senses, "pierced," "made thrall of," or "moved emotionally," Busirane can marshall only the first two of the three senses because his poetics make no allowance for another subjective consciousness, independent yet engaged. Spenser's exclamation, "Ah, who can loue the worker of her smart?" (3.12.31, l. 7) points up Busirane's failure both as lover and as poet, for the question is both rhetorical and real.[14] The rhetorical answer is, "no one." Amoret cannot love Busirane for his abuse of her; mere sadomasochism, the archetypal dualism, is rejected. An alternative to simple sadomasochism is suggested in the other answer to Spenser's question, "Ah, who can loue the worker of her smart?" The answer is Britomart. She loves Artegall, the worker of her smart.[15] She risks wounding to receive love. With her, subjective engagement transcends sadomasochism.

The transformation of dualism to *discordia concors* is mapped out in the Gardens of Adonis. Spenser's basic strategy is to rewrite Plato, specifically Plato's theory of recollection propounded in the *Meno* and *Phaedo;* he takes the Platonic myth of spiritual origins and makes it erotic, turning Plato's own terms against Plato in order to challenge the Platonic distinction between abstract ideas and concrete manifestation. Plato's theory of the heavenly origin of ideas is transformed in Spenser's myth to the image of heavenly influence, which combines austere astrophysics with extremely physical eroticism. Belphoebe and Amoret were conceived "through influence of th'heauens fruitful ray"; literal inflowing as well as spiritual emanation or action at a distance.

By positing immutable origins, Plato achieves a metaphysics of full presence. He opposes abstract and concrete, spirit and flesh, immortal and mortal in order to exalt the ideal over the mutable.[16] In shifting focus from heavenly origins to heavenly influence, Spenser emphasizes process and relationship over presence. Spenser seeks intellectual stability by examining the principles of mutability and the nature of the relationship between abstract principles and concrete reality. He revises Plato's binary opposition of abstract and concrete into paradox. Heavenly influence insures the purity of Belphoebe's conception, "vnspotted from all loathly crime / That is ingenerate in fleshly slime" (3.6.3, ll. 4–5); her conception has the purity of an intellectual idea. At the same time, the entire cosmos is shown to be sexual, which makes spiritual purity and fastidiousness seem a bit beside the point.

The Gardens of Adonis reveal the origins of Belphoebe's virtue, not by reproducing the Platonic myth of an immutable origin but by showing the reconciliation of abstract ideas to what is sensible, concrete, and mutable. Spenser transforms Plato's epistemological puzzle—how can we know something we do not already know—into a playful show of simultaneous ignorance and knowledge of the garden's geography. The narrator pretends to be uncertain whether Venus's particular *pied-à-terre* is Paphos, Cythera, or Gnidus while admitting. "But well I wote by tyrall, that this same / All other pleasant places doth excell," (3.6.29, ll. 6–7). Delicate hints of physiological punning and feminine geography bring Platonic idealism down to earth. The garden is a seminary—"the first seminarie / Of all things, that are borne to liue and die," (3.6.30, ll. 4–5)—in both senses of the word. It is both a seed plot and a place of education. In examining the principle of natural change, Spenser will not deny the possibility of learning. For Plato's metaphysics of full presence, which must reject learning as a sign of lack, Spenser substitutes an evolving plenitude, which allows active, complementary roles to both intellect and nature.

Spenser presents the essential harmony of intellect and nature, abstract and concrete in three contradictory descriptions of the garden, which together enact the maxim *harmonia est discordia concors*. As Donald Cheney observes, the garden appears, first as the womb of the natural world, then as the image of the natural world, and finally, as "a grove located on top of a 'stately Mount.' "[17] That can be taken further, however. The first version of the garden, metaphorical womb, represents the idea of generation that underlies the appearance of earthly mutability; the second version is the world as it appears to us; and the third version reconciles stable, intelligible form and changeable appearance in *discordia concors*.[18]

The first version of the Gardens of Adonis offers an allegory of generation in which the principle of earthly generation is expressed in cyclical metaphors of cosmic fecundity. This is a telling parody of Plato's myth of the origin of ideas because in it a generation myth explains the idea of generation and avoids the embarrassment of epistemology. The first version of the garden represents nature considered in the abstract without provision made for the constructing human mind. This is a garden that needs no gardener. The only shortcoming of this version of the garden is that its permanence, dispossessed of human consciousness, degenerates to the bloomin' buzzin' confusion of *Chaos*. The philosophical system grows more complicated and self-contradictory as the language becomes choked with arid abstractions. The decay, both of the poetry and the cosmology, is embodied in the decay of those curious "formes" that grow in the garden:

> The substance is not chaunged, nor altered,
>> But th'only forme and outward fashion;
>> For euery substance is conditioned
>> To change her hew, and sundry formes to don,
>> Meet for her temper and complexion:
>> For formes are variable and decay,
>> By course of kind, and by occasion;
>> And that faire flowre of beautie fades away,
> As doth the lilly fresh before the sunny ray.
>
> (3.6.38)

A number of critics have made extensive efforts to sort out the metaphysical ground of this passage.[19] Spenser's basic strategy seems to be to cross Plato with Aristotle, but, as in the Masque of Cupid, the real point is not philosophical but poetic, namely our aesthetic surprise and relief as that flower metaphor springs from the philosophical compost.

The welcome metaphor of the flower makes the transition to the second version of the garden. What follows is the same cycle of decay and regeneration given in the first version but this time seen from below, from the human perspective, where the pain of mortality accompanies aesthetic pleasure. Lovely things die and this saddens us. The problem with this version is that nature considered strictly as the world of appearances yields nothing of permanence unless one is prepared to lie about it. The only vision of eternity possible from this perspective is perpetuity, a spurious extension of familiar nature compounded of wishful thinking and rhetorical epanorthosis, or correction:

> All things decay in time, and to their end do draw.

> But were it not, that *Time* their troubler is,
>   All that in this delightful Gardin growes,
>   Should happie be, and haue immortall bliss:
>   For here all plentie, and all pleasure flowes,
>   . . . .
> There is continuall spring, and haruest there
>   Continuall, both meeting at one time:
>   (3.6.40, l. 9;41, l. 1–4;42, ll. 1–2)

Plenty is naïvely linked with pleasure, and the mutability that underlies the earthly process of generation is wished away.

The final version, the more circumscribed "stately Mount" within the garden proper, offers a poetic resolution to the problem of mutability. Here, the Spenserian version of the Venus and Adonis myth reconciles the mutable world of the senses with the peculiarly pliant form of poetry. As the father of all formes, Adonis figures the Platonic myth of origins. But the overt sexuality of Venus and Adonis subverts the neat, bloodless hierarchy of male-form, female-matter that those figures purport to represent. That Adonis is eterne in mutabilitie suggests both that he embodies the idea of change and that, as Venus's consort, he is sexually durable. The point of Spenser's revision of Ovid is just this reinclusion of banished sexuality in order to liberate poetic form. In Ovid, the myth of Venus and Adonis is a cautionary tale about poetic repression.[20] In warning Adonis to forgo hunting fierce beasts in favor of cony-catching, Ovid's decorative, fearful Venus dooms her lover by her own inadequacy as a love goddess. The boar as well as the rabbit belongs in the entourage of the true goddess of love. But, having been excluded from his rightful place, the boar returns as the agent of castration as well as the emblem of a repressed sexuality. Spenser transforms Ovid's paradox into one that is no less ferocious but is liberating in its ferocity. His Venus imprisons the boar "in a strong rocky Caue, which is they say / Hewen underneath that Mount" (3.6.48, ll. 8–9). The image promises Adonis's safety while figuring forth the *vagina dentata,* ultimate expression of Venus's fearsome power. The interchangeable hiearchies of male/female, form/matter, are resolved by the reader's courage in facing the threat to which hierarchy and exclusion attest. The text itself creates a reader who is anything but partial, who by a courage that is moral as well as sexual transcends the partiality Spenser attributes to men, who, when they write and when they read, praise only themselves.

16

Stella's Wit:
Penelope Rich as Reader of
Sidney's Sonnets

CLARK HULSE

As literary criticism has given up its focus on a self-referential text, the audience has reemerged as a creative partner with the artist. Too often, however, we speak of the audience as if it were monolithic, even ahistorical, or as something constructed from within the text. Readers, like writers, exist as real people, particular and historical. Just as the image of the writer within the text acts as a double for the real writer, partially disclosing, partially hiding his life and thoughts, so the image of the reader in the text interacts ironically with real readers, replicating or conflicting with their situations and reactions. When we measure our sense of the fictive audience of a poem against a real Renaissance audience, this interplay can help us to see how the creation of the poem was itself an act with consequences—personal, sexual, and political—within its literary culture.

Although English poetry of the Renaissance was written almost entirely by men, its audience was clearly both male and female. When a poet addressed a patron like the countess of Pembroke or her daughter Lucy, countess of Bedford, more was at work than mere convention or a desire for reward. By every evidence such women were well-educated, knowledgeable critics, able to make serious demands upon a poet, to respond—sometimes unpredictably—to his innovations, and to have a share in the determination of his meanings. While Sir Philip Sidney's sonnet sequence *Astrophil and Stella* is shaped, like any other poem of the period, by this general character-istic of the Elizabethan literary audience, it is unusual in that its original audience can be specified far more exactly: the sonnets form a record of a complex political and sexual relationship between two persons, Sir Philip Sidney and Penelope Devereux Rich. Sidney's editor William Ringler observes that Sidney "took considerable pains to indicate that the *Astrophil and Stella* poems were based upon personal experience," and he concludes: "That Sidney intended, that contemporaries believed, and that Lady Rich herself accepted the identification [of herself as Stella] is established by an overwhelming amount of evidence, as certainly as any historical fact can be."[1]

My argument is quite simple: that the historical audience, the ideal reader, and the principal reader described within the poems are all one person, Penelope Devereux Rich. From that obvious fact flows a series of consequences: that the poems themselves derive from her authority as well as his; that the love-game enacted in the sonnets is a struggle between her and Sidney for control not only over their relationship but over the poems as well; and that this struggle follows a pattern that characterizes the political milieu of the Elizabethan court.[2] Such poetry is ultimately a struggle for power between the reader and the writer, and in Penelope Rich, Sidney addresses a reader of unusual skill.

The standard argument is that Stella is a dummy reader, naive and uncritical, just a veil through whom Sidney addresses his more clever, subtle, and presumedly male, critical audience.[3] This gives us a sixteenth-century audience remarkably like a twentieth-century academic audience trained in New Critical assumptions about *personae*. The argument turns on an unhistorical and overly rigid dichotomy between court lady and critic. It would be a step closer to the truth simply to reverse the dichotomy and see the court "wits," the male critics, as a rhetorical blind for the real critic, Penelope Rich.

Indeed, in the *Defense of Poetry*, Sidney criticizes contemporary love poets who "so coldly apply fiery speeches that, if I were a mistress, they never would convince me, that they were in love."[4] Here Sidney contemplates the male reader entering into the poem only by imagining himself as a woman, and this strategy works most easily if that woman is a critic. Elsewhere Sidney tells us that "professors of learning" are by contrast the worst possible critics—and poets—because for them passion is a tool to show off their erudition. Stella-as-blind is exactly the kind of rhetorical dodge that Sidney is denouncing. Learning, he insists in the poems, produces wittiness, and wit leads to passion. Criticism is just the natural defence of a shy lover.

In the opening lines of the sequence, Sidney invokes a woman both clever and evasive:

> Loving in truth, and faine in verse my love to show,
> That she (deare she) might take some pleasure of my paine:
> Pleasure might cause her reade, reading might make her
>   know,

Knowledge might pitie winne, and pitie grace obtaine,
  I sought fit words to paint the blackest face of woe,
Studying inventions fine, her wits to entertaine.

$$(1.1-6)^5$$

Sidney assumes that the woman whom he addresses is highly skilled
in a rhetorical process in which the manipulation of an artificial
language is a necessary—and even desirable—first step toward a sexual
encounter.[6] Hence this first poem goes on to denounce false rhetoric
in a language embroidered with figures of *gradatio*, *anadiplosis*,
polyptoton, and *prosopopoeia*—all guaranteed to entertain her wits.
While some poems are addressed overtly to male courtiers, and a
larger number to Stella herself, this poem, like the sequence as a
whole, is written as if Stella were overhearing it. Number 45
comments directly on this process, as Stella is described weeping over
a story of lovers' grief and Astrophil resolves to address her in just
such an oblique way:

Then thinke my deare, that you in me do reed
  Of lover's ruine some sad Tragedie:
I am not I, pitie the tale of me.

$$(45.12-14)$$

This voice of self-abstraction is a device by which a private message
might be spoken in the presence of others. Privacy as we know it
simply does not exist in a Renaissance court, where every detail of life
may be subject to observation. Courting must be conducted more or
less in public and so requires a certain duplicity in language. Specifically, the practice of reciting poems in court assemblies requires that
the poem simultaneously convey a general meaning to the audience at
large and a special meaning to those few who understand.[7] The
language of the sonnets, then, is like the language of *imprese* and other
emblematic devices with which Sidney was so familiar. Astrophil and
Stella are not so much *personae*, masks or alternative or even fictive
selves, as they are synechdoches, heraldic devices by which Sidney
figures forth part of their identities and enigmatically veils the rest.

Even if the rhetorical structure of the poems will permit us to
imagine a real, critically-minded woman as the audience of the
sonnets, we still must ask if Penelope Rich is right for the job. Letters
to Philip's brother, Sir Robert Sidney, in 1597 describe Penelope Rich
lobbying the queen to get him a new office and acting as a conduit for
his letters. The letters that survive from her own hand, mostly written
around the fateful years of 1600 and 1601, show her to have had a

rather invertebrate but effective prose style, especially in what Francis Bacon called a "piquant" letter to the queen protesting the imprisonment of her brother, the earl of Essex.[8] On 21 February 1601, the night before his execution, the earl made his famous confession:

> And now I must accuse one who is most nearest to me, my sister who did continually urge me on with telling me how all my friends and followers thought me a coward, and that I lost all my valour. She must be looked to, for she hath a proud spirit.[9]

Given the situation Essex was in, one might discount the blame he throws on others, but interestingly, when one of the witnesses to this scene, Lord Howard of Effingham, wrote to Penelope's lover Charles Blount (by whom she had five illegitimate children), he calls Essex's confession a "weakness" and "unnaturalness," but doesn't question its accuracy. What upsets him, in fact, is the indiscretion whereby Essex "spared not to say something of her affection to you."[10] Then he encloses a letter to Blount from "your black eyes" and laments that he is no longer thirty.

This beautiful, vain, witty, and politically assertive Penelope Rich is universally attested to. A famous letter of St. Stephen's Day, 1595, describes how the christening of Robert Sidney's son was held up because Penelope, who was to stand godmother, had "a Tetter, that sodainly broke out in her faire whyte Forheade, which will not be well in 5 or 6 Dayes," and "my Lady *Riches* Desires are obeyed as Comandment. . . ."[11] None of this proves what the "real" Penelope Rich was like. What matters is the apparent discrepancy between these accounts and Astrophil's description of Stella as demure and high-principled. William Ringler suggests that Sidney just may not have known her very well.[12] Likewise, it is possible that she changed radically after Sidney's death. But a closer look at Stella will, I think, reveal that she is more like Penelope Devereux than it seems and that even the apparent dissimilarity is due to a consistent mechanism of distortion within the poems.

The most immediately visible mechanism of distortion is wit, both Astrophil's and Stella's. If the relationship between linguistic and political power is figured by the synechdoche of the text, then it is through wit that we can trace the relationship between language and erotic power. "Wit" has a wide range of meanings in the Renaissance, but in *Astrophil and Stella* just one is primary: wit is the disturbance of language by the force of erotic desire. Alongside the descriptions of

Penelope Devereux, we might place one of Sidney's sister Mary, the countess of Pembroke, by John Aubrey:

> [She] maried to Henry, the eldest son of William Earle of Pembroke; but this subtile old Earle did see that his faire and witty daughter-in-lawe would horne his sonne, and told him so, and advised him to keepe her in the Countery and not to let her frequent the Court.
>
> She was a beautiful Ladie and had an excellent witt, and had the best breeding that that age could afford. . . .
>
> She was very salacious, and . . . One of her great Gallants was Crooke-back't Cecill, Earl of Salisbury.
>
> In her time, Wilton House was like a College, there were so many learned and ingeniose persons. She was the greatest Patronesse of witt and learning of any Lady in her time. . . .
>
> Sir Philip Sydney was much here, and there was so great love between him and his faire sister that I have heard old Gentlemen say that they lay together, and it was thought the first Philip Earle of Pembroke was begot by him, but he inherited not the witt of either brother or sister.[13]

As fascinating as Aubrey's story may be, the point is not to describe Mary Sidney's sexual habits, for Aubrey is not a very reliable witness. The point is that in the rambling juxtapositions of Aubrey's prose, wit appears over and over as the connecting term between intellectual and sexual energy.

The narrative of *Astrophil and Stella* unfolds as a contest between the wits of Sidney and Penelope Rich, played out under the veil of synechdoche. Throughout the early poems, Sidney describes his passion in a series of political and military terms, saying that he is the horse on which Love rides to battle, or a land subjugated by Stella's beauty. This ceding of control is clearly a ruse that masks his counterploy, an attempt to gain control over her through the power of his witty conceits, especially the *blazon*, in which her body is dismembered and consumed as a critic consumes a text.[14]

Sidney's maneuver is a dangerous one, however, for his wit, in its alliance with desire, has run into a riot of the imagination that leads to a breakdown of language, to moods of silence and to outbursts of babbling. The power of passion to disorient language is illustrated by another story from Aubrey about another courtier-poet, Sir Walter Ralegh:

> He loved a wench well; and one time getting up one of the

Mayds of Honour up against a tree in a Wood ('twas his first Lady) who seemed at first boarding to be something fearful of her Honour, and modest, she cryed, sweet Sir Walter, what doe you me ask? Will you undoe me? Nay, sweet Sir Walter! Sweet Sir Walter! Sir Walter! At last, as the danger and the pleasure at the same time grew higher, she cryed in the extasey, Swisser, Swatter Swisser Swatter. She proved with child, and I doubt not but this Hero tooke care of them both, as also that the Product was more than an ordinary mortal.[15]

It is this particular juncture of "danger and pleasure" where ordinary language fails to say what one thinks it ought to say and says instead what one wants. Sidney's chaster wit remains in rhetorical control longer, submitting slowly to love's power:

> My best wits still their own disgrace invent:
>   My verie inke turnes straight to *Stella's* name;
> . . . .
> O let me prop my mind, yet in his growth
>   And not in Nature for best fruits unfit:
> 'Scholler,' saith *Love*, 'bend hitherward your wit.'
>   (19.5–6,12–14)

In its alliance with Love, Astrophil's wit has suffered the fate predicted by Machiavelli for the weak power that trusts itself to a strong neighbor. As he loses creative control over his text and becomes Love's scribe, the court "wits" appear, gossiping about Astrophil's "dearth of words, or answers quite awrie." Their gossip turns to the political situation in Holland, to Polish strife with Russia, and to the English presence in Ireland:

> These questions busie wits to me do frame;
>   I, cumbred with good maners, answer do,
>   But know not how, for still I thinke of you.
>   (30.12–14)

The collapse of his political venture is complete, both in foreign and domestic affairs.

Even as this sonnet marks the nadir of Astrophil's power, it proclaims the emergence of a new power in its last word, "you." This is the first time Stella is directly addressed in the sonnet sequence. She appears as his new audience at the very moment when he has reached a crisis with the old, and she is named repeatedly as the overt audience from this point on. The transition is marked by number 34, where Sidney conducts a dialogue with himself:

"Art not asham'd to publish thy disease?"
    Nay, that may breed my fame, it is so rare:
    "But will not wise men thinke thy words fond ware?"
Then be they close, and so none shall displease.
    "What idler thing, then speake and not be hard?"
What harder thing then smart, and not to speake?
Peace, foolish wit, with wit my wit is mard.
Thus write I while I doubt to write, and wreake
    My harmes on Ink's poore losse, perhaps some find
    Stella's great powrs, that so confuse my mind.

                                                    (34.5–14)

Astrophil resolves in effect to address a double audience, an outer one of the court dummy wits and an inner audience consisting of Stella and himself. His very babbling, from this point forward, will be a means of keeping his language "close." "What may words say, or what may words not say?" he asks in the first line of the next sonnet, and it is no surprise that the poem is one punning enigmatically on Stella's real name:

                            Fame
    Doth even grow rich, naming my Stella's name.
    Wit learns in thee perfection to express.

                                                    (35.10–12)

I am reminded by this of nothing so much as Elizabethan political correspondence, which faced exactly the same problem of communicating sensitive material by maintaining a layering of language. In his letters as lord deputy of Ireland, Philip Sidney's father Sir Henry Sidney consistently spoke of Penelope's father, earl of Essex, with respect. But when the line of communication to a political ally was secure, his language could be plainer. For instance, in February 1577, when rumors were flying that the elder Sidney had poisoned Essex, he wrote to Leicester denouncing the dead earl's "Mallyce" and swearing that "if *Essex* had lyved, you should have found hym as vyolent an Enemy, as his Hart, Power, and Cunyng would have sarved hym to have byn."[16]

When the line is less secure, or the enemies still alive, the language becomes "close," lest the message fall into the wrong hands. Interesting cases of this appear in the correspondence of Robert Sidney during his period as governor of Flushing in 1597–98. His trusty servant Roland Whyte kept him posted on the doings at court, employing a primitive cipher in which numbers were substituted for names. For instance, at a delicate point in maneuverings for supplies and offices for the conduct of the Dutch wars, Whyte wrote to Sidney that "n.n. says that 200 labours 1500 for 30, but yet does no good."[17] The passage means that Lady Rich reports that Cecil is lobbying the queen to appoint Lord Cobham governor of the Cinque-Ports. The point of the cipher is not to prevent disclosure, as it would have been penetrable to anyone familiar with court politics.[18] Rather, it loosens the reference between words and things and introduces enough ambiguity and enigma to allow the correspondents to dismiss its actual meaning as a misconstruction. Astrophil's playing on Stella's married name of "Rich" is just such an enigma and subject to just such denials.

Once Astrophil's linguistic confusion has become a means to close communication with the inner audience of Stella, he is confronted with the full extent of her power. She has made far more cunning alliances than he, joining forces with Virtue and Honor. Their combined power is enough to turn Astrophil's own weapons against him:

> My words I know do well set forth my mind,
> . . . .
> [But] when the breath of my complaints doth tuch
> Those daintie dores unto the Court of blisse,
> The heav'nly nature of that place is such,
>   That once come there, the sobs of mine annoyes
>   Are metamorphosed straight to tunes of joyes.
>   (44.1, 10–14)

This marks a crucial turn in the entire sonnet sequence, for at this point Stella becomes the virtual coauthor of the sonnets (not that she physically wields the pen—I mean that she exercises authority by her *virtú*). He may make the words, but she has the power to form her response to them and so to transform their meaning. Stella then appears in public as the performer of Astrophil's sonnets, replacing his voice with her own:[19]

> She heard my plaints, and did not only heare,
> But them (so sweete is she) most sweetly sing,
> With that faire breast making woe's darknesse cleare.
> A pretty case! I hoped her to bring
>   To feel my griefes, and she with face and voice

So sweets my paines, that my paines me rejoyce.
(57.9–14)

. . . .
                 in piercing phrases late,
Th'anatomy of all my woes I wrate,
Stella's sweete breath the same to me did reed.
   O voice, o face, maugre my speeche's might,
   Which wooed wo, most ravishing delight
Even those sad words even in sad me did breed.
(58.9–14)

Stella has read—or rather sung—the sonnets against themselves, turning the witty part of Astrophil's woe to sweetness and alienating both herself and him from their intended effect. If she has subverted the ideology of his poem, it is a subversion of their subversion of ideology, for she is winning him from his rebellious state to a reacceptance of honor and virtue. Hence Astrophil confesses himself "witt-beaten," and the wit that was the original vehicle of his rebellion "becomes a clog," of which Love will soon relieve him entirely.

Stella's victory is Pyrrhic, however, for in adopting his tool of poetic wit, she is vulnerable to the same countermaneuver. When Stella has spoken in her own poetic voice, displaying the "Muses' treasures" (60), Astrophil can then subject her logic to the test of rigor:

But this at last is her sweet breath'd defence:
   That who indeed infelt affection beares,
So captives to his Saint both soule and sence,
That wholly hers, all selfnesse he forbeares,
Thence his desires he learnes, his live's course thence.
   Now since her chast mind hates this love in me,
   With chastned mind, I straight must shew that she
Shall quickly me from what she hates remove.
   O Doctor *Cupid,* thou for me reply,
   Driven else to graunt by Angel's sophistrie,
That I love not, without I leave to love.
(61.3–14)

Once Astrophil has found out the conundrum at the heart of her argument, he has only to assume his guise of witlessness to see it as simple contradiction rather than transcendent paradox. Having broken Stella's logic, Astrophil then catches her in grammatical contradiction:

I crav'd the thing which ever she denies:

She . . . twise said, No, No.
> . . . Sing then my Muse,
>   For Grammer sayes (o this deare *Stella* weighe,)
>   For Grammer sayes (to Grammar who sayes nay)
> That in one speech two Negatives affirme.

> (63.12–14)

In this series of short, rapid steps, Astrophil has found in Stella's "angel's sophistrie" a deceptive intent, which implies a dangerous wittiness that in turn leads to the revelation of her erotic nature. The remnant of his own wit is released again as he breaks the power of syntax with his double parenthesis, disrupting the text with his own sophistry to open the window to passion.

When Stella tries again to speak, he treats her words as she has treated his:

> Why doest thou spend the treasures of thy sprite,
>   With voice more fit to wed *Amphion's* lyre,
>   Seeking to quench in me the noble fire,
> Fed by thy worth, and kindled by thy sight?
>   And all in vaine, for while thy breath most sweet,
> With choisest words, thy words with reasons rare,
> Thy reasons firmly set on *Vertue's* feet,
> Labour to kill in one this killing care:
>   O thinke I then, what paradise of joy
>   It is, so faire a Vertue to enjoy.

> (68.12–14)

Just as she used her power as reader to transform his grief to virtue, so he uses his power to turn her virtue to enjoyment. His strategy of reading her language against itself leads immediately to the famous sonnet in which he wins her heart "while vertuous course I take," but concludes, "No kings be crown'd but they some covenants make" (69). Sidney's subversion of sexual morality extends inevitably to the political, where all the cant of virtuous rule is revealed as a cover for Machiavellian practice. Rather than resume the play of wit, Sidney acknowledges the consequences of the standoff:

> Cease, eager Muse, peace pen, for my sake stay,
>   I give you here my hand for truth of this,
>   Wise silence is best musicke unto blisse.

> (70.12–14)

When prying into language threatens to reveal the secrets of state, it is far more prudent to be "close."

The balance of mutual subversion pushes their language to a new level of enigma in which meanings are increasingly unintelligible to the dummy audience of critics. The songs come thickly at this point, and much of the narrative is distanced into their third-person mode. As poems increasingly refer to narrative events, such as Stella's kiss—or another in which he bites her—the exact meaning of these events recedes into enigma, and we, as the dummy audience, are alienated from its enjoyment. As historically distant readers, our alienation is doubled; however much we may try to take the position of Stella, we are made, whether male or female, into male voyeurs, and our poetic enjoyment comes from glimpses caught through the curtain of the text.[20]

As Sidney's language becomes detached from us, it becomes a language of bliss, in which Sidney fleetingly plays with disclosure of private pleasures. Bliss arises from the continuous oscillation in the text between control and loss of control—or, more exactly, in moments where Astrophil gains control by surrendering it to Stella.[21] For instance, number 81 describes the kiss:

> O kisse, which soules, even soules together ties,
> By lines of *Love,* and only Nature's art:
> How faine would I paint thee to all men's eyes,
> Or of thy gifts at least shade out some part.
>   But she forbids, with blushing words, she sayes,
>   She builds her fame on higher seated praise:
> But my heart burnes, I cannot silent be.
>   Then since (deare life) you faine would have me peace,
>   And I, mad with delight, want wit to cease,
> Stop you my mouth with still still kissing me.
>
> (81.5–14)

The audience of "all men" is first asserted, then denied, and finally reasserted only if the subject of the poems is honorable. The basic address of the sonnet, however, is to the kiss, and so this possibility of honor is inherently rejected in favor of the two audiences, one private, female, and sensuous, the other public, male, and hypocritically moral. The dilemma created by Stella's contradictory behavior is now complete. She is offered control of the poems (for he "wants wit") only by ceding sexual control to Astrophil.

Stella's abandonment of virtuous behavior in favor of an external virtue of language coincides with the removal of the action of the poems from the court to the country—that is, from the presence of that epitome of virtue, the queen, to a realm of nature. What happens in the country is shrouded in enigma and contradiction. In the Fourth Song, Stella momentarily places herself in range of Astrophil's linguistic power:

> Your faire mother is a bed
> Candles out, and curtaines spread:
> She thinks you do letters write:
> Write, but first let me endite.
>
> (iv.37–40)

Each of his increasingly clever pleas is answered with Stella's refrain, "No, no, no, no, my Deare, let be." When the same answer meets his admission of defeat, however, its effect is reversed:

> Wo to me, and do you sweare
> Me to hate? But I forbeare,
> Cursed be my destines all,
> That brought me so high to fall:
> Soone with my death I will please thee.
> "No, no, no, no, my Deare, let be."
>
> (iv.49–54)

Stella's self-contradiction releases the stanza's puns and plays on "high," "fall," "death," and "please," turning it into as clear a statement of consummation as we can expect from a diplomatic poet. As an enigma this is not a difficult one to penetrate; it provides just the right degree of ambiguity and deniability.

   The principal difficulty in my account of what really happened is the Eighth Song, which gives us a different version of an identical interview—different, that is, only in its outcome:

> "Trust me while I thee deny,
> In my selfe the smart I try,
> Tyran honour doth thus use thee,
> Stella's selfe might not refuse thee . . ."
>
> (viii.93–96)

If the Fourth Song veiled itself in enigma, then this is the song of contradiction. While providing the socially necessary denial of the evidence of the Fourth Song, it demolishes the grounds for Stella's refusal even as it advances them. It begins with their mutual evasion of socially imposed restraints and ends once again in a subversion of the meaning of speech:

> Then she spake; her speech was such,
> As not eares but hart did tuch:
> While such wise she love denied,
> As yet love she signified.
>
> (viii.69–72)

To be told in this context that only "Tyran honour" refuses Astrophil, not Stella's self, is to adopt the language of libertine pastoral (specifically the "Golden Age" chorus from Tasso's *Amyntas*) in order to assert the repressive values of the court. Such honor is a mere social pretense, of no more weight than a king's covenant, and so it is no argument of refusal at all.[22]

Even as I claim that *Astrophil and Stella* is a poetry of enjoyment, the effect of Stella's half-refusal is devastating, both to the affair and to the language that describes it. Her invocation of "Tyran honour" reasserts the presence of a power greater than either of them, the hegemonic social order centered in the cult of chastity around the queen. Astrophil has attempted to rebel against that power, and briefly won Stella to join him, but the subversive moment is by its nature brief, unstable, offering only a glimpse of the desired end. In the first line after the consummation of the Fourth Song, he asks, "Alas, whence came this change of looks?" (86). In the Fifth Song he foresees Stella's incipient realliance with honor and counters with his own tyranny. It is she who commits treason, "Rebell by Nature's law, Rebell by law of reason" (v.63). Honor shall be *his* ally, for by his poetic speech he can defame her publicly. The cynical covenant of number 81 is offered again—unless she yields, he will expose her as the murderer of his heart, the witch who has entranced him, the devil who tempts him to leave the ways of heaven:

> You see what I can say; mend yet your froward mind,
> And such skill in my Muse you reconcil'd shall find,
> That all these cruell words your praises shall be proved.
>
> (v.88–90)

This final battle over who shall have "honor" for his ally marks the failure of the rebellion and the return of the whole affair to the sphere of the court, a move underscored by the shift of the action away from the country house. From that moment, the outcome is swift and predictable—poems on absence, on illness, a waning of passion, some poems of impenetrable enigma (93 and 94) for those of us ignorant of their occasion, balanced by others directed to the public audience. Their individual powers, even when conjoined, are too weak, too self-contradictory, to maintain themselves without a powerful ally, and the danger of such an ally is exactly as Machiavelli warned, the loss of independence.

The affair between Philip Sidney and Penelope Rich is from beginning to end conducted within the bounds of court politics, a game whose rules shape its every detail, down to its poetic language, even when there is nothing that we would normally call political at stake—nothing, that is, except the relationship between men and women. Every document associated with them attests to this, going back to the negotiations for a marriage match between them as a ground for ending the rivalry between their fathers. On 14 November 1576, Edward Waterhouse, who handled a series of extremely delicate matters for Sir Henry Sidney after the death of the first Earl of Essex (remember the rumors that were flying!), wrote to his master,

> the Lords do generally favour and furder [the young Earl of Essex, Penelope's brother] . . . And all thes Lords that wishe well to the Children, and, I suppose, all the best Sort of the *English* Lords besides, do expect what will become of the Treaty betwene Mr. *Phillip,* and my Lady *Penelope.* Truly, my Lord, I must saie to your Lordship, as I have said to my Lord of *Lecester,* and Mr. *Phillip,* the Breaking of[f] from this Match, if the Default be on your Parts, will turne to more Dishonour, then can be repaired with eny other Mariage in England.[23]

Though Penelope's father might wish that "God so move both theire hartes,"[24] any question of liking between them is entwined with their maneuverings for public honor, for favor, for power. The political alliance of the parents projected by Waterhouse is realized at last in the marriage of Penelope's mother to Sidney's uncle. It carries to the generation of the children with the sonnets and is reaffirmed with the marriage of Sidney's widow to Essex. And its remarkable permanence is attested to by the correspondence describing the mutual political activities of Penelope Rich and Robert Sidney fifteen years later.

The creation of the fictional poetry of *Astrophil and Stella,* then, is inseparable from the creation of an actual human relationship and from the shaping of the political arrangements of their society. It is hard to know at any moment, and pointless to ask, which is cause and which is effect. Still, it is possible to see emerging from the poetry a model for the power structure of the Elizabethan court, a model significantly at variance with the overt political ideology of Elizabethan England or recent literary theory of the ideology of the text. Each of these contemplates a hegemonic structure maintained by language, whether it is the personal power of the queen, ordained by the word of God and manifested in her pronouncements, or the hegemony of a means of production, maintained by the propagation of a dominant ideology.

This hegemonic model squares neither with my sense of the Renaissance, nor of *Astrophil and Stella,* nor of power itself. The courtier is a person with a certain inalienable status owing to his aristocratic birth, who nonetheless depends upon the crown for the enrichments of favor and office. The prince—in theory absolute—in practice works through intrigue to maintain a shifting coalition in support of her policies, all the while spewing out clouds of rhetoric about virtue and glory. In this system the individual has considerable room for maneuvering as he moves into and out of momentary alliances with his fellow players, adopting and dropping policies as it is convenient, as long as he pays lip service to the prince and her ideology. He works for the most part undisturbed by the aloof and secretive monarch but is always aware that she may at any moment whimsically intrude, juggling the rival factions and demanding that all dance in attendance about her, until she withdraws again behind her mythological screens to dangle favors and avoid decisions.

It is in such a world that Philip Sidney and Penelope Rich move, a many-sided world where there is one great power and several smaller ones, of which two concern us, one male and one female. Sidney approaches Penelope Rich first within the language of honor and virtue, the language in which he might praise the queen herself or with which a nonaristocratic sonneteer like Sam Daniel would address Sidney's sister. Yet within that language he weaves a code, a closed speech, in which he lays out his dangerous plot of rebellion under the very eyes of the ruler. Penelope briefly joins the revolt, but the alliance cannot maintain itself against the amassed powers of husband, friends, monarch, and morals, and they fall to arguing over who most enjoys the favor of that queen, Honor. Their league dissolved, each moves on to new intrigues, new plots (he to the Walsinghams, she to Mountjoy), their small morsels of linguistic, sexual, and political power intact. The nonhegemonic text they leave behind has three power centers, the poet, the reader, and the society around them, each pulling and tugging at the language of the poems to control their shape and meaning. It is to this complex and pluralistic transaction that we owe the richness of *Astrophil and Stella,* a piece of wit that is both product and producer of Elizabethan courtly culture.

17

Gender vs. Sex Difference in Louise Labé's Grammar of Love

FRANÇOIS RIGOLOT

> Le plus grand plaisir qui soit après amour, c'est d'*en* parler.
> (The greatest pleasure that comes after love is talking about
> it.)
>
> —*Le Débat de Folie et d'Amour.*[1]

There are a number of possible critical avenues to exploration of
sexual differences in literary discourse. The premise of this essay is
that Renaissance love discourse functions basically as a system of
thematic and linguistic patterns, long established by the male-oriented
theory and practice of *fin' amor,* and perceived as such by both male
and female readers and writers (writers being always the best readers,
"diligents lecteurs" *par excellence*).[2] I shall take for granted that, for
any Renaissance writer, the frame of reference is male oriented. To
put this point in the terms offered by Hans Robert Jauss's
Receptionästhetik, the "horizon of expectations" can be considered a
predirected process of perception that every particular poetic work
modifies or subverts to some extent.[3] On what Jauss calls the
"trans-subjective horizon" of reading, the lady ("Donna," "Dame")
is perceived—whether actually depicted as such or not—as the exclusive object of virtuous love (for instance: *Délie, Object de Plus Haulte
Vertu*).[4] As Jonathan Culler puts it in his discussion of Jauss's theory,
"a work does not have an inherent meaning; it does not speak, as it
were, it only answers."[5] Therefore, writers are compelled to rewrite
the inherited thematic and linguistic models with only a small degree
of modification (or, rather, an *apparent* small degree since, as we shall
see, a slight deviation can be potentially disruptive), for these models
have been codified by the only idealizing principles that are fully
acceptable to the reading public of courtly love and Petrarchist poetry.

Since Renaissance love discourse has been shared by male and female writers, it seems that one possible approach is to look for bizarre or incongruous elements in female-authored texts and find out if they can be interpreted as revealing sex differentiation. To paraphrase Michael Riffaterre, we would single out words or sentences that seem "less acceptable than their context" and try to solve the problems of their "ungrammaticality": "Ungrammaticality varies widely. It ranges from utter nonsense to obscurity to what are perceived as metaphors, but metaphors in which the semantic transfer seems somehow deviant."[6] For our purpose here, *ungrammaticality* will be used in a narrower sense; namely, grammatical deviations encountered by the reader in her or his initial, heuristic reading. In other words, difficulties may arise at many levels in comprehending literary texts referentially. Yet, certain elements of discourse are more likely to be subverted by the author's sex difference. Gender is obviously the most sensitive grammatical category to be affected. Thus I will try to focus the discussion on the possible *misuse* of gender forms as a sexually-coded index of self-expression.

Although I wish I could have taken my examples from other great female poets like Vittoria Colonna and Gaspara Stampa, I have concentrated exclusively on their French counterpart, Louise Labé, whose prose and verse production was composed roughly around 1550 and published in a single volume as her *Euvres* by Jean de Tournes, the best printer of Lyons in 1555. A few reminders may be appropriate at this point. Louise Labé (1524?–1566), also known as "la Belle Cordière," is, with Maurice Scève, the most famous poet of the so-called Ecole de Lyon that flourished in the mid-1550s. Labé's works, which I have recently edited for a Paris publisher, consist of four different types of pieces: (1) a dedicatory epistle to a female friend, Clémence de Bourges, which, interestingly enough, spells out a feminist platform for the future; (2) a mythological prose narrative in the form of a dialogue, *Le Débat de Folie et d'Amour*; (3) three love elegies, each over one hundred lines in length; and (4) twenty-four love sonnets, the first one in Italian and the other twenty-three in French. On the whole, it is an extremely erudite work, with many allusions to classical and Italian authors. Yet, to this day, it has remained a most readable literary document, as it manages to recreate the illusion of spontaneous experience, the forcefully pathetic expression of carnal love. As Sainte-Beuve wrote in 1845: "No matter how scholarly Labé's work may be, it speaks passionately to the reader of any time the language of her or his soul."[7]

The first type of ungrammaticality that we encounter in Labé's works has to do, not unexpectedly, with the textual expression of love. As lexicographers tell us, in the sixteenth century, when *Amour* is capitalized and personalized as Cupid, Venus's son, it always takes the masculine gender. In all other cases, *amour* is a feminine noun. This, of course, differs from modern grammar that requires a masculine *amour* in the singular and a feminine *amours* in the plural ("les belles amours").[8] Edmont Huguet's *Dictionnaire de la langue française du XVIe siècle* gives numerous examples of *amour* in the feminine singular. He quotes Lemaire de Belges, Marot, Rabelais, Calvin, Belleau, Desportes, and Montaigne; but he omits Louise Labé and, characteristically, all female writers.[9] Similarly, Littré's *Dictionnaire* explains that *amour* comes from Latin *amor,* masculine; it was feminine in Old and Middle French ("la fine amor, la fole amor") and followed the pattern of all other similar derivations that are still feminine in modern French (*la douleur,* from *dolor; la peur,* from *pavor*).

In Labé's works, many examples can be found that follow the general rule of *amour* as a feminine noun. In her *Débat de Folie et d'Amour,* when Jupiter asks about the duties of Love, *Amour* (that is, Cupid, the masculine god of love) talks at length about *Amour* (the feminine word used to designate the result of his actions):

AMOUR. La premiere chose dont il faut s'enquerir, c'est, s'il y ha quelque Amour *imprimée*: et s'il n'y en ha, ou qu'*elle* ne soit encor *enracinée, ou qu'elle* soit desja toute *usée,* faut songneusement chercher quel est le naturel de la personne aymée . . .

The first thing about which it is necessary to inquire is whether there is such a thing as Love innate. And if there is not, then in what does it have its roots, how may it be completely developed, how is it necessary to find out carefully the nature of the person loved . . .

Quell'Amour penses tu qu'elles t'ayent porté (les Dames que tu as aymées)?

What love do you think the women you have loved have felt?

Car cette affection de gaigner ce qui est au coeur d'une personne, chasse *la vraye et entiere Amour*: qui ne cherche son profit, mais celui de la personne, qu'*il* ayme (p. 63).

For that desire to win what is in the heart of anyone, drives
away love that is true and whole, love that seeks no profit for
itself but for the person that is loved (p. 29).

In this last sentence, Saint Paul's *sententia* is easily recognizable: "hē
agapē ou zētei ta heautēs," "Love does not seek its own profit" (1
Corinthians 13:5). It was popularized by Rabelais who used it, with a
comic rendition of Plato's *Androgyne,* to symbolize Gargantua's sense
of *agapē.*[10] Yet, what is striking in Labé's version of the Pauline
definition of love, is the ungrammatical use of the personal pronoun.
Whereas perfect *agapē* is conventionally described in the feminine as
"la vraye et entiere Amour" (Love true and whole), it is, immediately
after, referred to in the masculine in the relative clause: "qui ne
cherche son profit, mais celui de la personne qu'*il* ayme" (which seeks
not its own profit but the profit of the person *he* loves).

In the context of the *Débat,* this misuse of pronouns may be
explained by the fact that Amour is talking to Jupiter about Jupiter's
repetitively unsuccessful love affairs ("Masquerading as an animal
cannot make you loved . . . . Riches will enable you to possess
women who are avaricious, but to be loved by them, no!"). In this
case, we would have a kind of grammatical ellipsis in which, for the
sake of economy, the personal pronoun (*il*) would refer not to the
normal subject of the sentence but to the character addressed by the
speaker. On purely rhetorical grounds, this kind of *syllepsis* would be
unobjectionable. Yet, semantically, the switch from Pauline love to
Jovian *libido dominandi* is a total aberration. *Agapē,* "la vraye et entiere
Amour" is precisely presented by Amour as the negation of self-cen-
tered *philautia.* One has therefore to turn to other possible explanations for this ungrammaticality.

At this point, rather than offering an hypothesis to help resolve this
scrambled text, I would like to move to another example of grammatical deviation, closely related to gender unacceptability. This time, the
quotation will be taken from Labé's *Second Elegy.* Toward the end of
this poignant letter to the unfaithful love object, we read the following
lines:

> Ainsi, Ami, ton absence lointeine
> Depuis deus mois me tient en cette peine,
> Ne vivant pas, mais mourant d'*une Amour*
> *Lequel* m'occit dix mile fois le jour. (ll. 89–92)

> Thus, Friend, you have been away now for two
> months: I am so distressed; I don't live

anymore; I am dying of a [feminine] love
that [masculine] kills me ten thousand
times a day.

Critics have tried to resolve the ungrammaticality of lines 91–92, in
which a masculine relative pronoun (*Lequel*) is given a feminine
antecedent (*une Amour*). As early as 1824, Breghot du Lut explained
the difficulty away on the ground of so-called poetic license. Quite
simply, the reader should substitute *laquelle* for *lequel* and omit the
final *e* to keep the exact count of the ten-syllable line.[11] Similar
escapism pervades the most recent critical commentary on these lines,
which finds no alternative but to correct a "faulty" text.[12]

Critical defeatism is at its worst when it advances alteration of
self-proclaimed "errors" as a methodological principle. What modern
criticism may try to teach traditional philology is that, if the literary
text is a system of signs, the so-called textual errors may recur in
patterns that need to be accounted for, rather than eliminated.
Philologists may object that spelling norms for the vernacular are
rather elusive in the sixteenth century, that no serious criticism should
be based on orthography as it was all too often left to the whims of
printers. Yet the great Jean de Tournes, who published Labé's *Euvres*,
was no mere slop. As the most distinguished *imprimeur* in the Lyons of
the time, (with Leipzig, Lyons was, in the mid-sixteenth century, the
European capital of the book trade), his books were masterpieces of
clarity and precision. In addition, he was extremely careful to respect
the author's intentions about typography. Witness his professional
relationship with Jacques Peletier du Mans: Peletier's reformed spelling was adopted by de Tournes, who asked the great humanist and
poet to proofread many of his publications. Most likely, Labé's *Euvres*
were edited and corrected by Peletier himself.[13]

Therefore, it is tempting to identify this ungrammatical switch of
genders not as a typographical error but as a hermeneutic problem,
closely related to the intentionality of the text.[14] In line 91 of the
Second Elegy, Labé's persona as a female lover must use the conventional grammar to express the pangs of love. The French equivalent of
the Petrarchan cliché ("mourir d'amour") imposes itself upon writers
of both sexes with the power of a law. Ronsard will even coin a
maxim, with a play on the paronomastic qualities of *l'amour* and *la
mort*: "Car l'Amour et la Mort n'est qu'une mesme chose."[15] Thus,
line 91, "Ne vivant pas, mais mourant d'*une* Amour," obeys the laws
of conventional grammar because they are the very laws of conventional lyric poetry.

Yet—and this is my contention—love, which grammatically must be expressed in the feminine, must also be *un*grammatically masculine when, in a female-authored discourse, the love object becomes a man. In other words, I would like to identify the dramatic switch from line 91 "*une* Amour" to line 92 "*Lequel* m'occit" as a meaningful slip related to the existential problems of self-expression. I am perfectly aware of the difficulties inherent in this hypothesis. Rules of grammar have always been put under taboo: they are virtually untouchable even by mental patients. Yet, the great flexibility of the vernacular in the sixteenth century allowed for such bold plays on normative linguistic structures. The very notion of acceptability, so important today for normative grammar, was just as valid in Renaissance French; but there were no legal sanctions attached to syntactic deviations—no *Académie française*. The Pléiade poets' call for enrichment ("deffendre" and "illustrer") of the vernacular were geared exclusively toward the vocabulary; they left the syntax totally untouched.[16]

Characteristically the Pléiade poets were all men, and they centered their activities on the royal court, the growing source of power in a more centralized monarchy. Only the decentralized Lyons region allowed two major women poets to share in the love discourse of the Renaissance: Pernette du Guillet and Louise Labé.[17] My reading of lines 91–92 in the *Second Elegy* must therefore be, at least in part, referential: it is closely related to the status of the female writer, torn between a male-dominated grammar of love, which requires that *Amour* (the god of love) be masculine but *amour* (the poetic subject) be feminine, and a female wish to assert her independent *persona* both as subject of love and subject of poetry. The dramatization of this is practically emphasized by the conspicuous placement of "Lequel" (that is, the *Man* who kills me) at the beginning of a line, and by the choice of the emphatic *Lequel* over the regular pronoun *Qui*, which would not allow for a gender differenciation (*Qui* is both masculine and feminine).

If we return now to the dialogue between Cupid and Jupiter in the *Débat de Folie et d'Amour*, it is equally tempting to solve the problem of the ungrammatical *il*, referring to "la vraye et entiere Amour," along the same lines. The ungrammaticality of this *il* can be perceived as a transform of an *intertext*, closely related to the poet's textual experience as a female writer. This particular case of intertextuality carries definitely referential connotations. It corresponds more tightly to Julia Kristeva's theory of the *génotexte* than, for instance, to Michael Riffaterre's exclusively literary concept of intertextuality. When she writes that "true love does not seek its own profit, but the profit of the person *he* loves," Labé expresses something quite different from Saint Paul and Rabelais. In fact, she subverts the very definition of *brotherly* love, so prominent in the male-centered—not to say misogynous—worlds of Pauline and Rabelaisian *agapē*. Thus, "la personne, qu'il ayme" must be read as "la personne" (my feminine persona as lover-poet) "qu'il ayme" (writing a discourse in which the love subject is disturbingly masculine). It is no *intentional fallacy* to submit that, by inscribing the masculine *he* in a *sententia* (whose canonical form resists alteration and in which a *she* is expected), Labé reaffirms, in a devious but powerful way, her poetic identity as a feminine writer.

The question of poetic identity can be illuminated by another passage from the *Débat*, a passage that refers to Orpheus, the paradigm of lyric poets. In male-authored love poetry, Orpheus is generally represented as the exemplary male lover-poet, searching for Eurydice, his female beloved who is the sole object of his music and poetry. In the *Débat*, however, Labé has Mercury, the clever and eloquent messenger of the gods, compare the fate of women in love with Orpheus's pathetic quest to obtain the release of Eurydice from Hades:

> Combien en voy je, qui se retirent jusques
> aus Enfers, pour essaier si *elles* (les
> povrettes) pourront, comme jadis Orphée,
> revoquer leurs amours perdues? (98)

> How many do I see ready to go even to the
> Infernal Regions to try whether they—poor
> women!—might not, as Orpheus did once upon a time,
> recall their lost loves? (76)

Clearly, Labé disrupts a well-established mythological pattern. By becoming the model for feminine love, Orpheus loses his Virgilian and Ovidian status as a traditional male lover. His metamorphosis is pushed even one step further: his French name *Orphée* changes its masculine Greek ending (as in *le musée, le lycée*) into a typical feminine French form in *-ée* (as in *la fée, la mariée*). This *remotivation* of the mythical proper name is also a way of appropriating the classical paradigm into French culture; it is a typical humanistic practice, very much in keeping with the principles advocated in the *Deffence et Illustration*. Yet, contrary to the Pléiade manifesto, Frenchification and feminization are inseparable.

Now, we should remember at this point that Mercury was chosen in the *Débat* to defend Folly's interests against Cupid. Before the assembly of the gods, Mercury uses all the resources of rhetoric to prove that his female client is right and points to the gravest consequences for world order, should Folly be punished. The idea of going "even to the Infernal Regions" to recapture one's lost loves is characteristic of a Folly-inspired behavior. Mercury says so very clearly, immediately after the allusion to Orpheus: "Et en tous ces actes, quels traits trouvez vous que de Folie?" (98). (And in all these acts what traits do you find except those of Folly? [76–77]).

As I said before, lexical ungrammaticalities are usually considered unobjectionable. Even *syllepsis*, an unorthodox kind of grammatical agreement, falls within the limits of acceptability. Yet, the disruption of gender rules constitutes a much more serious attack against the political order of language: it is no longer Reason; it is Folly.

As Paolo Valesio has shown, contrary to medieval practice, there is a verbal aspect to the representation of madness in the Renaissance.[18] For instance, one way to make Orlando's speech "furioso" is by "mixing the images of high culture with the idiom of everyday life."[19] If, in French, *Folie* is both Folly and Madness, Labé uses the threatening features of gender disruption to provoke not an emotional disease but a linguistic (or semiotic) disease: a sort of foolish madness, because it shatters the formal equilibrium of male-dominated linguistic structures. Yet, it is a necessary madness, because it is the only kind of *intertextual overdetermination* that can impose itself upon the reader despite its unacceptability as normal usage. In Riffaterre's terms, Labé's intertextual "scrambling" aims at destroying traditional literary (male-oriented) conventions. But the referential *génotexte* is clear: gender scrambling is a devious yet indispensable way to reaffirm her identity as a female poet and lover, a feminine Orpheus.

Under these conditions, one might ask: of Amour (the masculine god) and Folly (the feminine goddess), which one will be the ultimate victor? This is precisely the question posed at the end of the *Débat* by Labé herself. After Apollo, who spoke for Cupid, and Mercury, Folly's advocate, have finished their speeches, Jupiter pronounces the following judgment:

> Pour la difficulté et importance de vos diferens, et diversité d'opinions, nous avons remis votre affaire d'ici à trois fois, sept fois, neuf siecles. Et ce pendant vous commandons vivre aimablement ensemble, sans vous outrager l'un l'autre (103).

> On account of the difficulty and importance of your differences and the diversity of opinions, we have postponed a decision from now for three times seven times nine centuries. And meanwhile we command you to live together in harmony, without injuring one another (84).

The debate between Love and Folly thus remains unresolved. Jupiter's last words of conciliation are in sharp contrast with Labé's own vibrant statements in favor of women, for instance in the dedicatory epistle to her friend, Clémence de Bourges (41–43). It is probably because Love and Folly have genders but no sex.

Although, throughout the *Débat*, *Amour* is referred to as a male character (*Mythologie oblige*) and *Folie* as a dame, a female character, Labé has been careful to avoid any rigid sexual characterization. She has given as many examples of true love and passionate madness among men as among women. In other words, she has not taken sides; she has been fair, just, impartial: like Jupiter *herself*. This is exemplified with striking clarity in the final lines of the judgment: "Et guidera Folie l'aveugle Amour, et le conduira par tout où bon *lui* semblera" (103). There are two possible translations to this sentence: (1) "And Folly will guide blind Cupid and will conduct him everywhere it seems good to *him* to go" (84), or (2), "And Folly will guide blind Cupid and will conduct him everywhere it seems good to *her* to go." Given the two possible genders of the indirect pronoun *lui*, both statements are equally acceptable. Semantically, Folly is the guide; yet, nobody knows who is entitled to give directions.

This ironical ending reinforces the fundamentally inconclusive issue of the debate. In Labé's discourse, the question "between Love and Folly, who will be the guide?" is also formulated as "between male and female, who will be the winner?" Contrary to Erasmus, there is no straight answer to this double question, not even an apparent *Praise of Folly*. Labé-Jupiter refrains from passing judgment (it is "postponed for three times seven times nine centuries"); and when she does pass judgment, she couches it in ambiguous language that defies any possible enforcement of the decision. In Rabelais's Abbey of Thélème there was only one rule: Fay ce que vouldras (Do what you will).[20] Labé's *theléma* (desire) is very similar: Fay ce que bon semblera (Do what seems right). But the one who "does" is not necessarily the one to whom it "seems right"; one may be male and the other female; one, Folly, and the other, Love. The whole interpretation of the *Débat* rests on a terrifying ambiguity. In the lack of gender differentiation lurks the lovable danger of madness.

I would like to return now to Labé's *Elegies* and reexamine the problems of gender ambiguity in the light of this discussion of the *Débat*. The *First Elegy* begins with a forceful evocation of *Amour*, the all-powerful victor of men and gods:

> Au tems qu'Amour, d'hommes et Dieus vainqueur,
> Faisoit bruler de sa flamme mon coeur,
> En embrasant de sa cruelle rage
> Mon sang, mes os, mon esprit et courage. . . .
>
> (107, ll. 1–4)

Not only Amour, but Phoebus-Apollo, the friend of green laurels ("ami des lauriers vers") has inflamed the poet with divine fury ("sa fureur divine," l.9); he has bestowed upon her the famous lyre on which Sappho herself sang her poetry in the Aegean island of Lesbos:

> Il m'a donné la lyre, qui les vers
> Souloit chanter de *l'Amour Lesbienne*:
> Et à ce coup pleurera de *la mienne*.
>
> (ll. 14–6)

It is interesting that the first poem of the *Ecriz divers*, published at the end of Labé's *Euvres* to praise her poetry, is precisely a Greek epigram celebrating Labé as a new Sappho. "The odes of harmonious Sappho," it begins, "had been lost over the centuries, but, lo and behold, Louise, our new poet, has given them back to us. . . ."(142)[21]

There is no doubt that "l'Amour Lesbienne" refers both to the antiquity of the passion and the modernity of its expression. Labé identifies with the paradigmatic persona of the female lover-poet. This identification is underlined by the mimetic use of the feminine rhyme: "la mienne / Amour Lesbienne" (my own kind of Sapphic love poetry). Yet, this epitomized expression of feminine love can change radically a few lines later, when Labé characterizes women's unrequited love as "dur Amour" (unfeeling, pitiless, *hard*-hearted love, l.59). Here, the enslavement that women are brought under is described in masculine terms: *Amour* is no longer feminine; it is *dur*, not *dure*. This sudden switch in gender determination is emphasized by the fact that "dur Amour" is, prosodically, the completion of a grammatical unit begun in the preceding line:

> Leur coeur hautein, leur beauté, leur lignage,
> Ne les ont su preserver du servage

De dur Amour. Les plus nobles esprits
En sont plus fort et plus soudain espris.

(ll. 57–60)

This kind of *enjambement*, which, a half-century later, will be frowned on by Malherbe, has the defiant force of a feminist manifesto. Before Hugo's famous "escalier / Dérobé", it carries a controversial statement—not so much about poetic techniques (run-on lines were widely used in the fifteenth and sixteenth centuries) as about the poet's right to self-expression. The harsh treatment inflicted by men upon the noblest women can indeed be expressed within a feminine *translatio studii*, namely Sappho's celebrated inheritance.

The misuse of gender to describe a situation of slavery can be read as a double provocation. Thematically and linguistically, "Amour lesbienne" is free and natural; it is grammatically and humanly acceptable. On the contrary, masculine "Dur Amour" is barbarous and uncouth; it is coarse and rough in form; it connotes slavery and, grammatically, un-naturalness. Paradoxically, Labé brings back "dur Amour" to its Latin origin (*amor durus, amor rudis*) as she attempts to renew very special ties with a Greek poetic tradition. This might be construed as another proof that Pauline and Rabelaisian *agapē* needs to be redefined from a feminine viewpoint. "L'amour vraye et entiere" (63) is to "dur Amour" (108) what *agapē* is to *eros*. Sappho knew this very well; and Labé's mission, as she expresses it in her letter to Clémence de Bourges, is to use her freedom ("ceste honneste liberté que notre sexe ha autre fois tant desirée") to show men all the wrong they did to women by depriving them of their share in culture ("montrer aus hommes le tort qu'ils nous faisoient en nous privant du bien et de l'honneur qui nous en pouvoit tenir," that is, "des sciences et disciplines," 41).

At the beginning of this paper, I proposed to explore the literary implications of sexual differenciation through the interpretation of gender deviations or ambiguities in speech patterns. Of course, as text-oriented criticism has told us, ambiguity is central to the poeticalness of literary discourse in general. As Jonathan Culler writes, summing up the structuralists' common practice and conviction, "By its very nature, poetic discourse is ambiguous and ironical, displays tension, especially in its modes of qualification."[22] Yet, within this general theory of poetic discourse, certain types of ambiguities can be attributed to the specific intertext poets have to struggle with: in Labé's case, male-coded conventions of Renaissance love poetry.

In this respect, it is interesting to compare Labé's performance with Pernette Du Guillet's, the other famous female poet of the Lyons circle. As Gillian Jondorf has remarked, Du Guillet is obviously uncomfortable with the traditional masculine style of Petrarchan discourse. For instance, she writes her poems with a "neutral voice" so that, taken out of context, her readers might assume that they were experienced and written by a male persona.[23] In contrast, Labé manages to work successfully and creatively within the context of a style overwhelmed and overworked by male poets without number. In Harold Bloom's language, Labé's daring "revisionism" asserts, in a devious way, her intellectual freedom through an unexpected yet radical reversal of the grammatical foundations of authority. In this sense too she is a "strong poet." "Le plus grand plaisir qui soit après amour, c'est d'*en* parler": the greatest pleasure that comes after love, is talking about *it*, about *him*, about *her*? Nobody will ever know.

18

City Women and Their Audiences: Louise Labé and Veronica Franco

ANN ROSALIND JONES

A study of two women poets should open by acknowledging that to be a woman writer at all during the sixteenth century was to be an exception. Although literacy throughout Europe increased throughout the Renaissance, to the extent that an urban literacy rate of 50 percent at the end of the sixteenth century has been estimated,[1] women's literacy was lower than men's—and to read is not necessarily to write. Indeed, women faced particular constraints as readers and as writers. Most educational theorists (Erasmus and Vives, for example) recommended that princesses and the daughters of aristocrats be taught to read and exposed to cautiously chosen classical and contemporary texts, but such girls undertook a humanist program further limited by what they could learn at home, through their brothers' tutors.[2] If they went on to write, gender expectations also shaped their choice of genres and their sense of an audience. Religious meditations and translations of religious texts were often undertaken by women (Margaret More, Marguerite de Navarre, Mary Sidney), but, unlike the humanist and courtly texts that male writers directed toward rulers and fellow citizens, women's literary production was typically described as intended only for the use of their families. Their themes and their audiences were *private*.[3]

Why this should have been so is suggested by the writers of conduct books, who said, over and over again, that a noblewoman's work was work in the home, in the house of her father and her husband. What women needed was not political theory or rhetoric but moral purity and modesty. In Francesco Barbaro's influential *De Re uxoria* (Paris, 1513; 1533), modesty is defined in relation to women's speech: "Let them reply modestly to their husbands when called upon . . . and when place and occasion offer, let them speak to the point so briefly that they may be thought reluctant rather than eager to open their mouths . . . By silence indeed women achieve the fame of eloquence."⁴ That paradoxical conclusion confirms that the outgoing civic orientation of humanism had its limits where women were concerned. Giovanni Bruto went further than Barbaro in his *La institutione di una fanciulla nata nobilmente* (Anvers, 1555). Revealing the male anxiety that met women's entry into the public sphere, he linked the reading and writing of love poetry directly to the likelihood of women's sexual misbehavior, adducing female figures from classical literature as negative examples:

> I am therefore of this advise, that it be not mete . . . for a Maiden to be . . . trayned up in learning of humayne arts, in whome a vertuous demeanor and honest behavior, would be a more sightlier ornament than the light or vaine glorie of learning . . . in such studies as yieldeth recreation . . . there is . . . daunger, that they will as well learn to be subtile and shameless Lovers, as connyng and skilful Writers, of Ditties, Sonnettes, Epigrames and Ballades. Let them be restrained to the care and governement of a familie, and teach them to bee envious in following those, that by true vertue have made little accoumpt of those, that to the prejudice of their good names, have beene desirous to bee reputed Diotimes, Aspaties, Sapphoes and Corinnes.⁵
>   (Thomas Salter's translation, London, 1579)

The discourses of the public world could only threaten the private virtue of the lady. Barbaro summed up the prevailing view in a symptomatic analogy: a woman's speech *was* a woman's body. Praising a Roman matron for withdrawing her bare arm from the sight of an admirer, he wrote, "It is proper, however, that not only arms but indeed also the speech of women never be made public; for the speech of a noblewoman can be no less dangerous than the nakedness of her limbs."

If, in spite of such strictures, women wrote love poetry—still, conceivably a private genre—the kinds of lyrics they produced were understandably circumscribed. Female-authored Neoplatonism might pass, because it emphasized the spiritual ascent of the lover and the superiority of the beloved in ways that presented no threat to ideologies of feminine chastity and masculine authority. Even so, it was a rare and tricky business for a woman to publish her writing. Pernette du Guillet's poems to Maurice Scève, for example (*Rymes,* Lyons, 1545), were irreproachably Neoplatonist, yet her printer claimed to make them public only at the insistence of her mourning husband, and he hedged them around with epigraphs commemorating her life-long chastity.[6] The case of Mary Wroth in England suggests that toleration of women's writing had not increased much by the beginning of the seventeenth century. When Wroth published her romance, *Urania* (1621), she was attacked by a courtier who suspected that one episode in the book alluded to his role in his daughter's forced marriage. Lord Denny wrote an insulting verse epistle to Wroth, in which he reproached her for behavior unsuited to a woman and advised her to stop writing for public consumption:

> Hermophradite in show, in deed a monster
>   As by thy works and words all men may conster
> Thy wrathful spite conceived an Idell book
>   Brought forth a foole which like the damme doth look.
>   . . . leave idle books alone
> For wise and worthyer women have written none.[7]

If she insisted on writing, he told her, she should turn to religious poetry, as her aunt Mary Sidney had done. Wroth withdrew her book from circulation.

Against such a system of beliefs and controls, Louise Labé (*Euvres*, Lyons, 1555) and Veronica Franco (*Terze rime*, Venice, 1575) stand out sharply. They published their writing themselves, and in their writing they presented themselves as public figures, seen and admired by men and speaking directly to them. So doing, they gained the support of the cultural elites of their cities, and they faced down detractors. In this paper, I focus on three questions about their entry into writing and publishing. What enabled them to depart from ideals of modesty and silence? What were their motives? And how did their gender, class, and ideological status inform their uses of lyric modes?

One striking point is that neither woman belonged to the aristocracy, the class to which early treatises on women's intellectual activity were most often dedicated. Louise Labé was the daughter of a rich ropemaker, who married her to another, Ennemond Perrin. Veronica Franco, the daughter of a courtesan, earned an often luxurious living as mistress to a series of Venetian noblemen and bourgeois. Neither were these women courtiers, for whom literary accomplishment was a means to economic and political advancement at urban and royal courts; composing ambassadorial Latin or a pageant in honor of the monarch belonged strictly to men at court.[8]

Yet for Labé and Franco, literary practice does seem to have led to social advancement. In her prefatory and autobiographical poems, Labé associated herself with the civic pride of Lyons, a center during the 1550s for international travel and publishing.[9] Her poetry was praised by the scholars, poets, and publishers of the Lyons coteries that have since been labeled the Ecole lyonnaise, the most influential literary grouping in France before the Pléiade. Labé herself applied for the royal imprimatur, rarely granted to women, for her book, and she prided herself on being read in Spain and Germany as well as France.[10] She framed her poems around the Petrarchan courtship of a noble-man–poet and companion to French churchmen in Rome, Olivier de Magny. De Magny adopted some of her lines in his poems, and he wrote a revealing comic ode to "Sire Aymon," whom he characterizes as a clumsy ropemaker who deserves neither the perfections of his lute-playing wife nor the company of the "brave captains and men of learning" whom she assembles in his house. The class snobbery of the poem leads to an unsettling mixture of conflicting modes, ending with an image of Aymon in a greasy apron, hard at work in his tower, but shifting back and forth between courtly compliments to the lady and ribald dismissals of her husband.[11] In de Magny's version of Labé, the woman poet is assigned a higher status than is her husband. The noble-man–poet represents her literary leanings, like her beauty, as setting her above the dreary bourgeois to whom she is so unfittingly bound.

Labé herself certainly aimed higher than Ennemond Perrin. She dedicated her book to Clémence de Bourges, the daughter of one of the most prestigious landowners of the region, and she concluded her book with twenty-four poems written by men in her honor. The eulogies are anonymous, but their vocabularies demonstrate the erudition and cosmopolitanism of their authors: one is an ode in Greek, comparing Labé to Sappho; another, in Italian, celebrates her as the greatest tourist attraction of Lyons.[12] Labé's biography, like-wise, suggests the advantages she gained by entering into the cultural elite of Lyons. She was violently criticized during a trial in Geneva at which her cousin accused her of leading her into lechery and finally to the murder of her husband, but Labé must have had protectors against this charge; she was never brought to trial herself. One of her biographers, Fernand Zamaron, conjectures that some of the hostility toward her arose out of class disapproval—that by cultivating the aristocracy of her city so openly, she offended the bourgeoisie.[13] In any case, a myth arose about her: she granted her favors to all the well-born men who frequented her house; she disguised herself in men's clothes and provided her own and other women's sexual services to the local clergy (this last was an invention of Calvin's, in an attack on an anti-Reform churchman of Lyons). Hostility to social climbing, suspicion of the sexuality of a woman who was also a poet,

Calvinist slander—all these shaped the myth, which reveals the opposition that confronted a woman with ambitions like Labé's.

Veronica Franco's relationship to her social and literary milieu was less ambiguous. Her mother was listed in Venetian records as her procuress; after a short-lived marriage to a doctor, Veronica began her own rise as a courtesan in the republic of Venice about 1562. Her poems had a frankly commercial purpose: as a display of wit and learning, they added to her desirability as a courtesan for the elite. Some of her texts, like Labé's, are patriotic, a theme that may be partly explained by the relatively high status of courtesans in Venice. They were prosecuted less often there than in Rome and Florence; indeed, the Venetian council saw them as an asset. The English traveler Thomas Coryat, in his 1608 account of his voyages, accounted for the great number of courtesans by paraphrasing Venetian gentlemen's realistic recognition of their function as preservers of aristocratic marriage: "they do graunt large dispensation and indulgence unto them . . . For they thinke that the chastity of their wives would be the sooner assaulted, and so consequently they should be capricornified (which of all the indignities in the world the Venetian cannot patiently endure) were it not for these places of evacuation."[14] He reported that the city supported a foundling home for the newborn children of courtesans, who were later put to work as galley rowers and courtesans themselves; and he added, "the revenues which they pay unto the Senate for their tolleration doe maintain a dozen of their galleys (as many reported to me in Venice) and so save them a great charge." The republic also exploited courtesans as a tourist attraction. A list of the "principal and most illustrious Venetian courtesans," including their addresses and fees, was common property in the city in the 1550s; the young Henri III of France met Franco in 1574 on the advice of officials who had shown him a catalogue of courtesans' portraits.[15]

To have entertained the French king was obviously a *coup* for Franco. She prefaced her *Lettere familiari* (1580) with two sonnets to him, and she worked his name into other letters and poems. She also established ties with several of the noble families of Venice, including the circle around Domenico and Marco Venier, and her connections with the Martinengo family of Bergamo led her to assemble a set of memorial poems, by various writers, for Estor Martinengo after his death.[16] She also sent a copy of her letters to Montaigne when he was staying in Venice in 1580. He was not impressed. But the speed with which she made the offering suggests the confidence she felt in her reputation as a courtesan of literary accomplishment.

Franco's use of poetry as self-advancement clarifies the derivation of the English word *courtesan* from *cortigiana,* the feminine form of *courtier* (*cortigiano*) in Italian. If the courtiers of the Renaissance increasingly needed the skills and graces of peacetime for political advancement, such skills and graces were also the stock in trade of courtesans. Singing, making music and witty conversation, familiarity with classical and modern literature—these were the accomplishments of the courtier, and they were also the accomplishments that distinguished the *cortigiana onesta* from the less well-paid prostitute (*puttana* or *meretrice*). Litrary testimony confirms the similarity between *cortigiane* and *cortigiani*: a courtesan character in a play by Guarini, for example, explains that her mother first tutored her in the liberal arts and then threw open the doors to all Vicenza, certain of rich rewards for her labor; Pietro Aretino claims in his satires that procuresses and pimps could quote Petrarch at the drop of a hat.[17] Montaigne noted that courtesans charged for conversation alone, and Coryat's warning to young Englishmen to resist the verbal blandishments of the Venetian courtesans establishes a striking parallel between the eloquence of courtiers and of their female counterparts: "Also, thou wilt find the Venetian Courtezan . . . a good Rhetorician, and a most elegant discourser, so that if she cannot move thee with all these aforesaid delights, she will assay thy constancy with a Rhetoricall tongue."[18]

In this statement, Coryat reverses the gender roles on which love poetry was conventionally based. Constancy was assumed as a feminine trait, to be admired or overcome by men's uses of rhetoric; for Coryat, men's chastity is endangered by women's manipulations of language, and to encounter a "public woman" is to risk the casuistries of a previously masculine discourse. Practically speaking, he was wrong; a man who had sought out a courtesan could hardly claim to be seduced by her rhetoric. But Coryat's remark, as ideology, provides a useful entry into the poems of Labé and Franco. They are indeed rhetoricians: they use their femininity as a basis for claims to doubly public reputations, regendering terms such as *gloire* and *fama* as support for the arguments they address to men. My argument is that the public nature of their ambitions—the desire to rise socially, to be defined through and benefit from ties with powerful men—led both poets to a contradictory rhetoric. It is a transgressive rhetoric in two senses: they refuse injunctions to chastity and silence, and they speak to and for women in ways that shift the man-woman focus of love poetry to new concerns and positions. But theirs is also a rhetoric shaped and contained by the constant presence of men as the ultimate critics—of women's beauty, of their merit as poets, of their present and future reputations.

Labé addresses her sonnets to a lover whose long silence suggests that he has abandoned her. But she is less interested in reproaching him than in persuading him to return. Maneuvering both inside and outside ideologies of the feminine, she deploys multiple strategies to win her beloved back. One strategy comes directly from male-authored love poetry: flattery. But while a male poet was likely to base his praises of the lady on her beauties as he alone perceived them, Labé turns such praises outward, incorporating the *topoi* of male humanists' mutual admiration into a defense of her merit as lover. In sonnet 10, she describes her beloved's poetic triumph in a ceremony of laureation that she witnesses as part of a crowd:

> Quand j'aperçoy ton blond chef couronné
> D'un laurier verd, faire un lut si bien pleindre,
> Que tu pourrois à te suivre contreindre
> Arbres et rocs: quand je te vois orné,
> Et de vertus dix mile environné,
> Au chef d'honneur plus haut que nul ateindre:
> Et des plus hauts les louanges esteindre:[19]

> When I see your blond head crowned
> With a green laurel, making a lute weep so skillfully
> That you could force
> Trees and rocks to follow you; when I see you decorated
> And encircled with ten thousand virtues,
> Attaining a peak of honor high than any other,
> And exceeding the praises of the worthiest men:

In this setting of public success, Labé's argument has a certain logic: why not add to your other merits the fame of loving me?

> Tant de vertus qui te font estre aymé,
> Qui de chacun te font estre estimé,
> Ne te pourroient aussi bien faire aymer?
> Et ajoutant à ta vertu louable
> Ce nom encore de m'estre pitoyable,
> De mon amour doucement t'enflamer?

> Could so many virtues, which make you loved,
> Which make every man hold you in high esteem,
> Not make you love, as well?
> Adding to your praiseworthiness
> The further fame of being pitiful toward me,
> Of gently catching fire from my love?

But her plea simultaneously challenges expectations of women, who were defined as most praiseworthy precisely to the extent that they were least accessible to men outside their families. Instead, Labé argues ingeniously that her love, acknowledged as the source of his, will bring honor to the man who links his name and fame to hers.

She makes the same argument more bluntly in her second elegy. Nothing could be further from the speechless modesty of Barbaro's ideal wife than Labé's invitation to her beloved to take advantage of his edge over the competition offered by her admiring international audience. Fearing that she has been displaced, she counters the claims of a rival with an assertion of her renown—which she disclaims in a highly unconvincing gesture of modesty:

> Si say je bien que t'amie nouvelle
> A peine aura le renom d'estre telle,
> Soit en beauté, vertu, grace et faconde,
> Comme plusieurs gens savans par le monde
> M'ont fait à tort, ce croy je, estre estimee . . .
>
> Goute le bien que tant d'hommes desirent:
> Demeure au but où tant d'autres aspirent:
> Et croy qu'ailleurs n'en auras une telle.
>
> (ll. 55–71)

> Yet I know that your new love
> Can hardly have a reputation like mine
> For the beauty, virtue, grace and eloquence
> For which many learned men, throughout the world,
> Have—wrongly, I think—made me admired . . .
>
> Enjoy the pleasure so many men desire,
> Rest at the goal to which so many aspire,
> And be assured, you'll never find my like elsewhere.

The citational and indirect quality in these and other appeals addressed by Labé to her beloved is striking. She never engages in a description of her own beauty. To do so would mean facing a possibly unsurmountable contradiction: to praise herself as seen from without, to speak as desired object and desiring subject at the same time. Instead, she mirrors herself in the words of men, by pointing to the sheer quantity and the discernment of her admirers. Yet this solution poses an acute problem for the humanist standards within which she frames her argument. "If I am admired for the same capacities as you are," she says to her beloved, "you should return my love." Such a logic would have scandalized Barbaro and Bruto; as a ploy of seduction, it was exactly what they were writing to prevent. Labé eroticizes the humanist celebration of the poet by refusing to accept the assumption that literary fame was an exclusively male preserve.

Less predictably, Labé establishes another group as an audience: the women of Lyons. Her publisher framed her poems to emphasize her typicality as a woman of her city; she is identified on the title-page as "Louise Labé, Lyonnoise." And in her famous dedication to Clémence de Bourges, she stresses their shared position as women on the brink of a better era:

> Estant le tems venu, Mademoiselle, que les severes loix des hommes n'empeschent plus les femmes de s'apliquer aus sciences et disciplines: il me semble que celles qui ont la commodité, doivent employer cette honneste liberté que notre sexe ha autre fois tant desirée, à icelles aprendre: & montrer aus hommes le tort qu'ils nous faisoient en nous privant du bien et de l'honneur qui nous en pouvoit venir: Et si quelcune parvient en tel degré, que de pouvoir mettre ses concepcions par escrit, le faire songneusement et non dédaigner la gloire.

> Since the time has come, Mademoiselle, when the harsh laws of men no longer prevent women from studying the arts and sciences, it seems to me that those who have the ability should take advantage of this honorable right to learning which our sex formerly wanted so much, and show men the wrong they did us by depriving us of the pleasure and honor which could have come to us from study. And if one woman succeeds to the extent of being able to set her ideas in writing, let her do it carefully and not reject fame.

Labé ends the preface by acknowledging social constraints on women, but she uses the convention of chaperonage wittily, to justify her appeal to Clémence as patroness: "Et pource que les femmes ne se montrent volontiers en publiq seules, je vous ay choisie pour me servir de guide" (And because women do not willingly show themselves alone in public, I have chosen you to act as my guide).

Yet the relationship Labé reaches for with a feminine and potentially feminist audience reveals strains as well as group spirit. She promises in her first elegy that she will pity (and perhaps act as a literary model for) all women in love, but she adds a condition: they must sympathize equally with her:

Dames, qui lirez [mes maux],
De mes regrets avec moy soupirez.
Possible, un jour je feray le semblable,
Et ayderay votre voix pitoyable
A vos travaus & peines raconter.

(ll. 43–47)

Ladies, who will read my woes,
Sigh with me over my laments.
Perhaps one day I'll do the same for you,
And help your pitiable voice
To tell the story of your suffering and pain.

A similar doubt surfaces in her third elegy, in which she claims that love can overcome anyone's resistance; she adds pointedly that she at least has been free of the vices of envy and gossip. Her exhortation to women to write (to *one* woman, as the phrasing of her dedication suggests) may likewise be a defense of her own writing. In 1555, Labé's appeals to women were partly a self-protective justification for her so far unusual individual ambition.

In her final sonnet, she pleads again that women not condemn her:

Ne reprenez, Dames, si j'ay aimé . . .
Si en pleurant, j'ay mon tems consumé,
Las que mon nom n'en soit par vous blamé . . .

Mais estimez qu'Amour, à point nommé,
Pourra, s'il veut, plus vous rendre amoureuses: . . .
Et gardez vous d'estre plus malheureuses.

Do not reproach me, ladies, if I have loved . . .
If I have wasted my days in weeping,
Alas, may my name not be censured by you . . .

But recognize that love, once named . . .
Could, if he likes, make you fall even more in love: . . .
And beware of being more unfortunate than I.

If in that last line, Labé seems to be making herself a mouthpiece for the kind of warning through which male-dominated societies have kept women under sexual control ("one step outside the boundaries and you will be doomed to misery"), she nonetheless disassociates herself from convention to the extent that it encourages women to condemn one another in support of "the harsh laws of men." Her appeal to women may be at once the most historically determined and the most utopian element in her poems: if she defends herself against women, she speaks to and for them as well. A male beloved and male readers were her primary audience, but her poems are also mediated through her situation as a woman adapting masculine discourses to her own needs. It is not surprising, then, that she was willing to declare sympathy for similar needs—for love outside arranged marriage, for education, for recognition—among her *concitoyennes* in Lyons.

Franco's *Terze rime* share Labé's orientation toward the public world.[20] But while Labé deprivatized the longings of the unrequited lover, Franco publicized actual sexual performance. Her self-advertisement is straightforward. All her *rime* are addressed to men, and she frames her first six poems as responses to poems written to her by men. Rima 1, a salutation by Marco Venier, praises her erotic and her poetic talents as related gifts:

> Venere in letto ai vezzi vi ravvisa,
> a le delizie che 'n voi tante scopre,
> chi da pietà vi trova non divisa;
> si come nel compor de le dotte opre
> de le nove Castalie in voi sorelle
> l'arte e l'ingegno a l'altrui vista s'opre.
> E così'l vanto avete tra le belle
> di dotta, e tra le dotte di bellezza,
> e d'ambo superate e queste e quelle.
>
> (ll. 127–35)

> Venus claims you as hers by your charming ways in bed,
> By the many delights discovered in you
> By the man who finds you willing to pity him,
> Just as, when you compose learned verses, the skill
> And wit you share with the nine Castalian sisters
> Is revealed to the view of others.
> So you are praised among beauties
> For your learning, and among learned women for your
>   beauty,
> And you rise above them both in both respects.

As the poem shifts from praise to seduction, Venier further blurs the distinction between writing and lovemaking. He bases his argument on a logic like Barbaro's: the woman who exposes herself to the world's notice and memory through her writing is one and the same as the woman who exposes herself to men's desire:

> A Febo è degno che si sodisfaccia

dal vostro ingegno; ma da la beltate
a Venere non meno si compiaccia:
le tante da lei grazie a voi donate
spender devete in buon uso, si come
di quelle, che vi diede Apollo, fate:
con queste eternerete il vostro nome,
non men che con gli inchiostri; e lento e infermo
farete il tempo, e le sue forze dome.

(ll. 151–59)

It's right that Phoebus should be contented
by your wit; but let Venus
be no less delighted by your beauty;
you should put the many graces she gave you
to good use, as you do
the gifts Apollo gave you.
With her gifts you will make your name eternal
no less than with your ink; and you will
slow down and weaken time, and conquer its power.

Although Franco appears to accept the terms of Venier's poem in her response, she also insists on reciprocity in the erotic bargain; and she separates writing from lovemaking by turning her answer to his compliments exclusively in the direction of Venus:

Aperto il cor vi mostrerò nel petto,
allor che'l vostro non mi celerete,
e sará di piacervi il mio diletto;
e, s'a Febo si grata mi tenete
per lo compor, ne l'opere amorose
grata a Venere più mi troverete.
Certe proprietati in me nascose
vi scovrirò d'infinita dolcezza,
che prosa o verso altrui mai non espose.

(ll. 46–54)

I will show you my heart, open in my breast,
as long as you do not hide yours from me,
and my delight will be to give you pleasure.
And if you think my writing makes me dear to Phoebus,
you will find me, in the works of love,
dearer still to Venus.
Certain qualities hidden in me
I'll reveal to you, with infinite sweetness,
which neither prose nor verse have ever shown another.

Franco sets Venier's poem at the beginning of her collection as testimony confirming the masculine admiration on which her livelihood depends. She adds to her acceptance of the erotic pact with Venier a defense of how she goes about her profession. Arturo Graf, in his study of Franco, confessed with some exasperation that he could make no sense of her counterrequest to Venier, but the lines seem clear enough if they are interpreted as Franco's repetition of an earlier appeal to Venier to write a memorial poem for the collection that she was assembling in honor of Estor Martinengo:

> E però quel, che da voi cerco adesso,
> non è che con argento over con oro
> il vostro amor voi mi facciate espresso;
> perchè si disconvien troppo al decoro
> di chi non sia più che venal, far patto
> con uom gentil per trarne anco un tesoro.
> Di mia profession non è tal atto;
> ma ben fuor di parole, io 'l dico chiaro,
> voglio veder il vostro amor in fatto . . .
> De le virtuti il mio cor s'innamora,
> e voi, che possedete di lor tanto,
> ch'ogni piu bel saver con voi dimora,
> non mi negate l'opra vostra in tanto,
> che con tal mezzo vi vegga bramoso
> d'acquistar meco d'amador il vanto.
>
> (ll. 94–111)

> But what I want from you now
> is not that you express your love to me
> with silver or with gold;
> for it is totally unfitting
> to anyone more than merely venal to make an agreement
> with a gentleman in order to take a fortune from him;
> such an act is unsuited to my profession.
> But rather than in words, I tell you outright,
> I want to see your love in deed . . .
> My heart is won by merit,
> and you, who possess so many of them
> that every loveliest kind of knowledge is lodged in you,
> do not deny me your effort in such a great cause;
> let me see you eager, in this way,
> to win with me the fame of being a lover.

Franco's request for payment in poetry rather than cash may look like a mystification of courtesanship, but the question is not so simple. More materially than for Labé, Franco's stock in trade was the recorded respect and literary cooperation of powerful men, and the circulation of verse epistles was one way in which she could document her status as private mistress and as an inspirer of poetry that went beyond the erotic.[21]

The wordgame she plays with Venier in this first poem may have been one of the easier requirements of her work as a courtesan. The career also made harsher demands on her: what for a client like Venier was her alluring fame could be attacked by her enemies as scandalous notoriety. In two of her longest poems, she defends herself against the satiric onslaught of a detractor. Written attacks on courtesans were common; they included signs hung on statues in public squares, and they could do real damage, since a courtesan's claim to high fees depended on her reputation for selectivity. In her sixteenth poem, Franco takes on a man who has called her a common whore (*puttana*).[22] To demonstrate her superiority to such a lowly category, she adopts the vocabulary of duelling to set up a contest, in words that display her familiarity with satiric debate:

> Prendete pur de l'armi omai l'eletta . . .
> La spada, che'n man vostra rade e fora,
> de la lingua volgar veneziana,
> s'a voi piace d'usar, piace a me ancora:
> e, se volete entrar ne la toscana,
> scegliete voi la seria o la burlesca,
> ché l'una e l'altra è a me facile e piana.
> Io ho veduto in lingua selvaghesca
> certa fattura vostra molto bella,
> simile a la maniera pedantesca:
> se voi volete usar o questa o quella . . .
> qual di lor più vi piace, e voi pigliate,
> ché di tutte ad un modo io mi contento,
> avendole perciò tutte imparate.
>
> (ll. 109–126)

> Take your choice of weapons, then . . .
> If you want to use the common Venetian tongue
> as the sword that strikes and pierces in your hand,
> that suits me equally well;
> and if you want to try Tuscan,
> choose a lofty or a lowly style,
> for one and the other are clear and easy for me.

I have seen admirable writings of yours
in rustic language,
and others in a learned vein:
If you want to use either one . . .
Choose whichever suits you best.
I am equally contented with them all;
I have learned them all, for this purpose.

By challenging her adversary to an exchange in city vernacular, regional dialect, and high or low style, Franco claims a linguistic and
rhetorical virtuosity far beyond what the less well-defended *puttana* or
the cloistered noblewoman of her time needed. At the same time, she
presents herself as ready not for a private duel with a lover (although
this is the basis for one of her wittiest poems, 13) but for a public
confrontation with an enemy of her profession. Her literary competitor, although an easy match for her verbally, is also an enemy to her
sex, and Franco begins by defining the contest as a defense of women
in general:

e le donne a difender tutte tolgo
contra di voi, che di lor sete schivo,
si ch'a ragion io sola non mi dolgo.

(ll. 79–81)

And I undertake to defend all women
agianst you, who are so contemptuous of them
that, rightly, I am not alone in resenting it.

In a later poem, 24, she speaks in defense of a more specific
category, her fellow courtesans: she takes to task a man who has tried
to beat a courtesan and threatened to disfigure her by slashing her face.
(Such attacks were common enough to have given rise to the
expression *dare la sfregia,* to give the scar.) The poem, an oration in
favor of women and courtesans alike and an invocation of the
chivalrous ritual on which their safety depended, sums up the
contradictions within which Franco maneuvers. On one hand, she is
exquisitely polite to the man she addresses, in order to demonstrate in
action the courtesy she is recommending to him:

basta che mi tegniate per amica,
come infatti vi son, si che in giovarvi
non sarei scarsa d'opra o di fatica.
Ed or ch'io mi conduco a ragionarvi

di quanto intenderete, a quel m'accosto,
che dè chi fa profession d'amarvi.

(ll. 19–24)

Only think of me as a friend,
as indeed I am, so much that I would spare
no task or effort to make you happy.
And so that now I am going to reason with you
so that you will understand, from my manner of approach,
how someone who claims to love you should behave.

Confronting but also disguising the man's possession of greater physical power and social license than hers or her fellow courtesans',
Franco uses beguiling rhetoric to convince him that force is inappropriate. On the other hand, her defense of women goes aggressively to
the center of ideologies of masculine superiority. Speaking to women,
she exclaims:

Povero sesso, con fortuna ria
sempre prodotto, perch ognor soggetto
e senza libertà sempre si stia!

(ll. 55–58)

Unhappy sex, always led about by cruel fortune
because you are always subject
and always deprived of liberty!

She goes on to argue that men and women have equal intellects and
indeed that women, from necessity, are sharper-witted than men.[23]
They tolerate men's cruelty only because they must, she says, in order
that "the human race continue to beautify the world." Altogether, she
leaves her male listener very little to pride himself on. Yet she ends the
poem on a note of gentle flattery and with the humbly offered advice
that he make peace with his victim and so be forgiven by all women.
However clearly Franco points out the injustice of men's power and
women's dependence on them, she frames her defense, as she must,
within the discursive possibilities generated by such gender relations.

Franco's patriotism also presents deep contradictions. She writes
several poems in what she describes as unwilling exile from Venice,
and in her twelfth, she advises a lover to dispense with praise for her
and to take on a greater topic, the city they both inhabit:

lodar d'Adria il felice almo ricetto,
che, benché sia terreno, ha forma vera
di cielo in terra a Dio cara e diletto.

(ll. 10–13)

Praise the blessed and gracious home of the Adriatic,
which, though earthly, has the true form
of heaven on earth, cherished and precious to God.

In this and other poems, she dwells on the golden and marble palaces,
the unvanquished past, the religious autonomy, and the international
renown of the city. A crude explanation for her contributions to the
celebration of Venetian civic pride would be that it permitted her to
align herself with the male elites who also praised the republic—and
this is certainly true. But the imagery traditionally associated with
Venice, "la donzella d'Adria" (the maiden of the Adriatic)—for
example, in the annual ceremony in which the doge threw a golden
ring into the lagoon as a symbol of the marriage of signorial power
with the sea—may also have offered Franco important imaginary
satisfactions. In one of her letters (22), she denounces the financial and
psychic insecurity of the life of a courtesan, in a vocabulary strikingly
different from the idealizing feminine symbolism on which her male
contemporaries based their praise of Venice as lady/sovereign city:

Troppo infelice cosa e troppo contraria al senso umano è
l'obligar il corpo e l'industria di una tal servitù che spaventa
solamente a pensarne. Darsi in preda di tanti, con rischio
d'esser dispogliata, d'esser rubbata, d'esser uccisa, ch'un solo
un dì ti toglie quanto con molti in molto tempo hai
acquistato, con tant'altri pericoli d'ingiuria e d'infermità
contagiose e spaventose; mangiar con l'altrui bocca, dormir
con gli occhi altrui, muoversi secondo l'altrui desiderio,
correndo in manifesto naufragio sempre delle facoltà e della
vita; qual maggiore miseria? quai richezze, quai commodità,
quai delizie posson acquistar un tanto peso? Credete a me: tra
tutte le sciagure mondane questa è l'estrema; ma poi, se
s'aggiungeranno ai rispetti del mondo quei dell' anima, che
perdizione e che certezza di dannazione è questa?[24]

Too miserable a thing it is, and contrary to human reason, to
force one's body and energy into such slavery, terrifying even
to contemplate; to expose oneself as prey to so many men,
with the risk of being despoiled, robbed or killed, or that one
man, one day, may take from you everything you have
acquired with many, over a long time, added to so many
other dangers of insult and contagious, frightful disease; to eat
with the mouth of another, to sleep with the eyes of another,
to move according to another's will, endlessly rushing toward the inevitable shipwreck of one's abilities and life; what

greater misery? what wealth, what comfort, what pleasure can make up for such a burden? Believe me, of all the world's misfortunes, this is the worst; and then, if you consider the needs of the soul as well as those of the world, what perdition and certainty of damnation!

If this warning summary of a courtesan's life is set against Franco's echoes of conventional personifications of Venice in her twelfth poem, the contrast suggests an understandable longing, an identification with an ideal of feminine purity, safety and privilege:

> Questa dominatrice alta del mare,
> quella vergine pura, inviolata,
> nel mondo senza esempio e senza pare.
>
> (ll. 22–24)

> This lofty lady, dominatress of the sea,
> a royal virgin, pure, inviolate,
> without parallel or equal in the world.

The city of Venice, like Lyons for Labé, provided Franco with a group identification and, at least in fantasy, an escape from the grimmer realities of women's positions within the gender boundaries of the late sixteenth century.

Several conclusions are suggested by this exploration of how urban settings and ambiguous class positions influenced two women poets in their use of the discourses that they found in place. One is that the various rhetorics of love poetry meant significantly different things to men and to women. Praises perhaps intended by Labé's male contemporaries as conventional compliment served, for her, to justify her less conventional amorous pleading as a woman; Franco's elegant and frankly erotic poems simultaneously elevated her status as a courtesan and de-idealized the love lyric as a genre. Both poets challenged the terms of masculine discourse by claiming a place for themselves amidst humanist glorification of worldly fame, by refusing the restriction of that fame to males. Their double-edged participation in cultural groupings toward which they experienced class and gender marginality sets off revealing resonances and contradictions among the conventions within which they lived and wrote. And, finally, their writing, as well as advancing their individual careers, began to transform and open out the modes of literary exchange.

Notes

Introduction

1. Jacob Burckhardt, *The Civilization of the Renaissance in Italy* (1860), authorized translation, from the 15th ed., by S. G. C. Middlemore (New York: Albert and Charles Boni, 1935), pt. 4, chap. 6, p. 389.

2. Arcangela Tarabotti, *La Semplicitá Ingannata o la tirannia paterna* (Leida: Gio. Sambix, 1654), p. 149; cited in Ginevra Conti Odorisio, *Donna e societá nel seicento: Lucrezia Marinelli e Arcangela Tarabotti* (Rome: Bulzoni Editore, 1979), p. 96, our translation. Tarabotti was born in 1604, was forced by her father to enter a convent when she was sixteen and remained there until her death in 1652. The *Semplicitá Ingannata*, evidently a youthful work, was circulated in manuscript but was published only after Tarabotti's death. For a good account of her life and works see E. Zanette, *Suor Arcangela Monaca del seicento veneziano* (Rome and Venice: Institutio per la collaborazione culturale, 1960).

3. See Margaret L. King, "Book-Lined Cells: Women and Humanists in the Early Renaissance," in *Beyond Their Sex: Learned Women of the European Past,* ed. Patricia H. Labalme (New York: New York University Press, 1980), pp. 66–90.

4. See Leonardo Bruni, *De Studiis et litteris,* trans. W. H. Woodward, in *Vittorino da Feltre and Other Humanist Educators: Essays and Versions* (Cambridge, 1879; reprint, ed. E. Rice, New York, 1963), p. 126; quoted in King, "Book-Lined Cells," p. 77. Burckhardt writes that Renaissance women "had no thought for the public" (*Civilization,* p. 391); to prove this point, he cites a male writer (Antonio Galaseo) advising a woman (Bona Sforza) to perform her proper task of pleasing men by being "prudent and sober" and "despising the vulgar" (p. 391, n. 7).

5. In her seminal essay "Did Women Have a Renaissance?" (*in Becoming Visible: Women in European History,* ed. Renate Bridenthal and Claudia Koonz [Boston: Houghton Mifflin, 1977]), Joan Kelly-Gadol argues that "a new division between personal and public life made itself felt as the state came to organize Renaissance society, and with that division the modern relation of the sexes made its appearance" (p. 160). See also Jean Ehlstain, *Public Man, Private Woman: Women in Social and Political Thought* (Princeton: Princeton University Press, 1981).

6. Burckhardt's view of the "equality" of men and women in the Renaissance, which derives in large part from an uncritical reading of humanist texts, appears also in Hannelore Sach's *The Renaissance Woman,* trans. Marianne Herzfield (New York: McGraw Hill, 1971); see esp. the chapter on "Upbringing and Education of Young Girls," pp. 14–19. As Joan Kelly-Gadol observes, Burckhardt's view "has found its way into most general histories of women" (e.g., Mary Beard's *Woman as Force in History,* 1946), and also "dominates most histories of Renaissance women" (e.g., E. Rodocanachi's *La femme italienne avant, pendant et apres la Renaissance,* 1922); see Kelly-Gadol, "Did Women Have a Renaissance?" pp. 137–64; her discussion of Burckhardt's influence is on p. 161, n. 1.

7. The quotation, from a letter written by Nogarola to Guarino Veronese reproaching him for having exposed her to mockery, is taken from King, "Book-Lined Cells," p. 72; see also King's "The Religious Retreat of Isotta Nogarola (1418–1486): Sexism and its Consequences in the Fifteenth Century," *Signs: Journal of Women in Culture and Society* 3 (Summer 1978): 807–22; and her "Thwarted Ambitions: Six Learned Women of the Italian Renaissance," *Soundings: An Interdisciplinary Journal* 59 (Fall 1976): 280–304.

8. According to Marx, "the capitalist era dates from the sixteenth century," although "we come across the first sporadic traces of capitalist production as early as the fourteenth or fifteenth centuries in certain towns of the Mediteranean" (*Capital: A Critique of Political Economy,* vol. 1, trans, Ben Fowkes [New York: Vintage, 1977], p. 876). In his *Studies in the Development of Capitalism* (1947; rev. ed., New York: International Publishers, 1963), Maurice Dobb followed Marx in dating the "opening phase" of capitalism not in the twelfth century, as Henri Pirenne did, but rather "in the latter half of the sixteenth and the early seventeenth century" (p. 18). For the debate engendered by Dobb's book, see *The Transition from Feudalism to Capitalism,* Introduction by Rodney Hilton, essays by Paul Sweezy, Christopher Hill, Eric Hobsbawm, and others (1976; reprint, London: Verso Editions, 1978). See also Etienne Balibar's chapter, "Elements for a Theory of Transition," in Louis Althusser and Etienne Balibar, *Reading Capital* (1968), trans. Ben Brewster (London: New Left Books, 1970), pp. 273–308.

9. The phrase appears often in titles and subtitles of books influenced by the work of social historians known as *Annalistes,* after the journal founded by Marc Bloch and Lucien Febvre in 1929 and entitled, since 1946, *Annales: economies, societés, civilisations.* For a discussion of the Annalistes' concern with "long term" patterns of change (*conjunctures*), see Peter Burke's introduction to *Economy and Society in Early Modern Europe: Essays from Annales* (New York: Harper Torchback, 1972), pp. 1–10.

10. See Ephraim Lipson, *The Economic History of England,* 3 vols. (1915–31; 3d. ed., London: A. and C. Black, 1937), 2:xxvi, "The fundamental feature of capitalism is the wage system under which the worker has no right of ownership in the wares which he manufactures: he sells not the fruits of his labour but the labour itself—a distinction of vital economic significance." See Dobb, *Studies,* pp. 7–10, for a discussion of the debates about the meaning of the term *capitalism.* Since Dobb's book was published, a number of economic historians have continued to define capitalism as an "entrepreneurial" activity that predates the sixteenth century; see, e.g., *The Cambridge Economic History of Europe,* vol. 5, *The Economic Organization of Early Modern Europe,* ed. E. E. Rich and C. H. Wilson (Cambridge: Cambridge University Press, 1977), p. 460.

11. This sentence is adapted from Mary Wiesner's essay in this volume; for further bibliographical references, see her note 4.

12. Lawrence Stone, "The Rise of the Nuclear Family in Early Modern England: The Patriarchal Stage," in *The Family in History,* ed. Charles E. Rosenberg (Philadelphia: University of Pennsylvania Press, 1975), pp. 13–57. The quotations are from pp. 13–14. An expanded version of this essay appears in chap. 4 of Stone's *The Family, Sex and Marriage in England, 1500–1800* (London: Weidenfeld and Nicolson, 1977). See also his chap. 5, "The Reinforcement of Patriarchy" and, in addition, Joan Kelly-Gadol, "Family Life: A Historical Perspective," in *Household and Kin,* ed. Amy Swerdlow (Old Westbury, N.Y.: Feminist Press, 1981), pp. 1–45; Roger Thompson, *Women in Stuart England and America: A Comparative Study* (London and Boston: Routledge & Kegan Paul, 1974), esp. chap. 7, "The Family"; and Joan W. Scott, *Women, Work and Family* (New York: Holt, Rinehart & Winston, 1978), all with further references.

13. Stone, *The Family, Sex and Marriage,"* p. 151.

14. See Hamilton, *The Liberation of Women: A Study of Patriarchy and Capitalism* (London: George Allen and Unwin, 1978), p. 18.

15. See Hamilton, *Liberation,* pp. 15–16 for a critique of Marx's and Engels' accounts of changes in the structure of the family. Marx briefly discusses the "dissolution" of the "Christian-Germanic form of the family" that accompanied the rise of large-scale industry in *Capital,* trans. Fowkes, 1:620–621; Engels discusses the effects of the nineteenth-century factory system on the family in *The Condition of the Working Class in England,* ed. W. O. Henderson (Oxford: Blackwell, 1958), p. 164. For a perspective on family history that coincides with Hamilton's in emphasizing the Renaissance as a period of crucial change, see Philippe Ariès, "From the Medieval to the Modern Family," in *Centuries of Childhood,* trans. Robert Boldick, (New York: Knopf, 1962). Unlike Hamilton, Ariès stresses change in the educational system as a major cause for changes in the nature of the family.

16. Hamilton, *Liberation,* p. 92.

17. Michael Walzer notes that London's population probably tripled between the accession of Elizabeth and the death of James (*The Revolution of the Saints* [Cambridge: Harvard University Press, 1964], p. 201). According to Lawrence Stone, women who entered the agricultural and servicing labor markets in England during the sixteenth and seventeenth centuries "were everywhere paid at a rate which was one quarter that of men" ("The Rise of the Nuclear Family," p. 50); in France, according to Natalie Zemon Davis, unskilled female workers received wages that ranged from a half to two-thirds of men's (*Society and Culture in Early Modern France* [Stanford: Stanford University Press, 1975], p. 71).

18. Quoted from Christopher Hill, *Society and Puritanism in Pre-Revolutionary England* (New York: Schoken, 1964), p. 262.

19. The quotation is from Hill's *Society and Puritanism,* p. 262. For discussions of English women on welfare see Hamilton, *Liberation* p. 93; and Alice Clark, *The Working Life of Women in the Seventeenth Century* (New York: Harcourt Brace, 1920), pp. 69–91. On new theories and practices of welfare aid in Renaissance France, see Natalie Zemon Davis, "Poor Relief, Humanism, and Heresy," in *Society and Culture,* pp. 17–64.

20. Hamilton's argument, it should be noted, focuses only on English women and relies heavily on Alice Clark's evidence that women as a group were adversely affected by the development of capitalism; see Judith Brown's essay in this volume for an alternative view of the issue.

21. See Joan Kelly-Gadol, "Did Women Have a Renaissance?" p. 148.

22. Perry Anderson, *Lineages of the Absolutist State* (1974; London: Verso Editions, 1979), p. 128.

23. On Elizabeth's strategies of controlling the institution of marriage and her own position as the most valuable object in the marital "system of exchange," see, in addition to the essay by Louis Montrose in this volume, Leonard Tennenhouse, "Representing Power: *Measure for Measure* in Its Time," in *The Forms of Power and the Power of Forms,* ed. Stephen Greenblatt, *Genre* 15, nos. 1/2 (1982), pp. 139–56.

24. Ruth Kelso, *Doctrine for the Lady of the Renaissance* (1956; reprint, Urbana: University of Illinois Press, 1978), p. 3. See also Allison Heisch, "Queen Elizabeth and the Persistence of Patriarchy," *Feminist Review* 4 (Feb. 1980): 45–56.

25. For a useful discussion of a notion of ideological production that goes beyond the "reflection" theory of older Marxist critics, see Roisin McDonough and Rachel Harrison, "Patriarchy and Relations

of Production," *Feminism and Materialism: Women and Modes of Production* (London: Routledge & Kegan Paul, 1978), pp. 11–41.

26. For Rubin's discussion of the "sex-gender" system—a phrase she considers more analytically useful than other terms (notably *patriarchy* and *mode of reproduction*) frequently used to designate a sexual order relatively autonomous from that of the economic "base"—see "The Traffic in Women," *Toward an Anthropology of Women,* ed. Rayna R. Reiter (New York: Monthly Review Press, 1975), pp. 156–210, esp. pp. 150, 161. The definition of the sex-gender system quoted in our text is from Louis Montrose's essay in this volume.

27. With the exception of Clark's book, most serious studies of women in the Renaissance period published before 1970 focus not on the sex-gender system but rather, as Joan Kelly-Gadol observes, on "exceptional women." See her "Suggestions for Further Reading," in "Did Women Have a Renaissance?", pp. 163–64.

28. For a useful discussion of feminist approaches to the canon, see Christine Froula, "When Eve Reads Milton: Undoing the Canonical Economy," *Critical Inquiry* 10 (Dec. 1983): 321–47. See also Judith Fetterly, *The Resisting Reader: A Feminist Approach to American Fiction* (Bloomington: Indiana University Press, 1971).

29. Paul Ricoeur, *Freud: An Essay in Interpretation,* trans. Denis Savage (New Haven: Yale University Press, 1970), p. 28.

30. See Kelly-Gadol, "The Social Relations of the Sexes: Methodological Implications of Women's History," *Signs* 1 (Summer 1976): 810–23; the quotation is from pp. 810–11.

31. Kelly-Gadol, p. 817. She cites a similar argument by Natalie Zemon Davis for research on *both* sexes: "It seems to me that we should be interested in the history of both women and men, that we should not be working only on the subjected sex any more than a historian of class can focus exclusively on peasants. Our goal is to understand the significance of *sexes,* of gender groups in the historical past. Our goal is to discover the range of sex roles and of sexual symbolism in different societies and periods, to find out what meaning they had and how they functioned to maintain the social order or to promote its change" (Address to the Second Berkshire Conference on the History of Women, October 1975; cited in Kelly-Gadol, "Social Relations of the Sexes," p. 817).

32. Jehlen, "Archimedes and the Paradox of Feminist Criticism," *Signs* 6 (Summer 1981); 575–601; the quotation is from p. 585. For responses to Jehlen, see *Signs* 8 (Autumn 1982); 160–76. For a related debate see Peggy Kamuf, "Replacing Feminist Criticism" and Nancy K. Miller, "The Text's Heroine: A Feminist Critic and Her Fictions," *Diacritics* 12 (1982); 42–53.

33. In *Woman's Estate* (1971; reprint, New York: Vintage, 1973), Juliet Mitchell surveys the treatment of women in works of socialist

theory, including Engels' famous book, *The Origin of the Family, Private Property and the State* (1884); she concludes that in the works of Marx, Engels, and most of their twentieth-century followers, the problem of women's social roles remains "dissociated from or subsidiary to, a discussion of the family," which is "in its turn subordinated as merely a precondition of private property" (p. 80). Gayle Rubin's discussion of Marxist treatments of women is more complete than Mitchell's; Rubin cites many articles, mostly published since 1969, which attempt to analyze the specific role played by women (particularly housewives) in capitalist economy; see "The Traffic in Women: Notes on the Political Economy of Sex," esp. pp. 160–69. Nonetheless, Rubin argues persuasively that Marxist theoretical discussions of women, both classical and recent, have failed to address the specific questions posed by "the realm of human sex, gender, and procreation"; in most Marxist work, Rubin writes, "the concept of [the sexual realm as] the second aspect of material life has tended to fade into the background, or to be incorporated into the usual notions of the material life" (p. 166).

34. Sir Robert Filmer, *Patriarcha and Other Political Works,* ed. Peter Laslett (Oxford: Basil Blackwell, 1949); quoted in Stone, *The Family, Sex and Marriage,* p. 152. On patriarchalism as a political ideology see Gordon Schochet, *Patriarchalism and Political Thought* (New York: Basic Books, 1975); R. W. K. Hinton's two-part article, "Husbands, Fathers, and Conquerers," in *Political Studies* 15 (1967): 291–300, and *Political Studies* 16 (1968): 55–67; and Jean Ehlstain's chapter, "Patriarchalism and the Liberal Tradition," in *Public Man, Private Woman,* pp. 100–46.

35. Stone, *The Family, Sex and Marriage,* p. 152.

36. As Kelly-Gadol notes, "the major Renaissance statement of the bourgeois domestication of women was made by Leon Battista Alberti in Book 3 of *Della Familgia* (c. 1435)," which freely adapts Xenophon's description of women's place in the household sphere in the *Oeconomicus* ("Did Women Have a Renaissance?" p. 161, n. 2). Stallybrass's discussion of the "enclosure" of women draws on Elias, *The Civilizing Process: The History of Manners* (1939; English trans., 1978) and Mikhail Bakhtin, *Rabelais and His World* (1965; English trans. 1968). As Stallybrass observes, however, neither of these authors specifically addressed issues of gender.

37. The quotation, from Wyatt's poem "Stond whoso list," is taken from *The Collected Poems of Sir Thomas Wyatt,* ed. Kenneth Muir (Cambridge: Harvard University Press, 1949), p. 164.

38. Barbaro's statement, from his *De re uxoria,* is taken from the essay by Ann Jones in this volume; see her note 4.

39. For a useful survey of debates about women in Renaissance medical, legal, and theological texts see Ian Maclean, *The Renaissance*

Notion of Women: A Study in the Fortunes of Scholasticism and Medical Science in European Intellectual History (New York: Cambridge University Press, 1980). See also Linda Woodbridge, *Woman and the English Renaissance: Literature and the Nature of Womankind, 1540–1620* (Urbana: University of Illinois Press, 1984) and, for a fuller and more critical discussion of theories about women than Maclean offers, Hilda Smith, "Gynecology and Ideology in Seventeenth Century England," in *Liberating Women's History: Theoretical and Critical Essays,* ed. Berenice A. Carroll (Urbana: University of Illinois Press, 1976), pp. 97–114.

Chapter 1: Fatherly Authority

The argument I present here represents a reworking of material drawn from *James I and the Politics of Literature: Jonson, Shakespeare, Donne, and Their Contemporaries* (Baltimore: Johns Hopkins University Press, 1983). I am grateful for many suggestions I have received about my argument, and I have acknowledged specific debts at appropriate spots.

1. All citations in my text are drawn from *The Political Works of James I,* ed. Charles H. McIlwain (Cambridge: Harvard University Press, 1918).

2. Gordon Schochet's *Patriarchalism in Political Thought* (New York: Basic Books, 1975) traces the recurrent patriarchal claims to authority. It is important to add, of course, that the repetition of a rhetorical formula is not evidence of the same configuration of power. The material conditions of family life, for instance, would affect the meaning of the claims, which is not to say, on the other hand, that the terms and the "facts of life" would be related to each other transparently.

3. All citations in my text are drawn from *Patriarcha and Other Political Works,* ed. Peter Laslett (Oxford: Basil Blackwell, 1949).

4. *Political Studies* 15 (1967): 298.

5. James added to Divine Right theory "the identification of indefeasibility with hereditary succession by primogeniture in the legitimate line," Elton claims in "The Divine Right of Kings," *Studies in Tudor and Stuart Politics and Government,* 2 vols. (Cambridge: Cambridge University Press, 1974), 2:203.

6. *The Family, Sex and Marriage in England 1500–1800* (New York: Harper & Row, 1977), p. 152.

7. Alan Sinfield, *Literature in Protestant England 1560–1660* (Totowa, N.J.: Barnes & Noble, 1983), p. 66.

8. All citations drawn from *The Complete Works of Shakespeare,* ed. David Bevington (Glenview, Ill.: Scott, Foresman, 1980).

9. All citations from Ben Jonson, *The Complete Masques,* ed. Stephen Orgel (New Haven: Yale University Press, 1969).

10. *Van Dyck: Charles I on Horseback* (London: Allen Lane, Penguin Press, 1972), p. 70.

11. Ian Donaldson has reminded me of the poignant moment at the close of Milton's last sonnet, "Methought I saw my late espoused Saint," with its rich resonances in Homer, Dante, and Virgil. In the elaboration of the "gap," I pursue some questions raised by Hugh Craig and for which I remain grateful; for the analogy with *sacra conversazione*, I am thankful for a comment by L. D. Ettlinger.

12. Louis Althusser, "Ideology and Ideological State Apparatuses (Notes towards an Investigation)," in *Lenin and Philosophy*, tr. Ben Brewster (New York: Monthly Review Press, 1971), p. 164.

13. Dobson was Van Dyck's successor as favored painter at the court of Charles I; for his history, see Malcolm Rogers, *William Dobson 1611–1646* (London: National Portrait Gallery, 1983). The Streatfeild portrait is a late work and, as Rogers remarks, "it is not impossible to see in Dobson's late works (several of them unfinished), and in the tired and insecure glances of his sitters, an index of Royalist fortunes at the time" (p. 19).

14. B. L. Harl. Ms. 6987, fol. 180; *The Poems of James VI of Scotland*, ed. James Craigie, 2 vols. (Edinburgh: Wm. Blackwood & Sons, 1955, 1958), 2:177.

15. The picture could be described, in Alan Sinfield's words (in *Literature in Protestant England*), as poised between the conflicting claims of patriarchy and mutual affection (according to Stone, the direction that family relations take in the succeeding century). As Sinfield points out, protestantism attempted to install the mutuality of love within a patriarchal frame: "It is quite feasible to see the idea of mutuality in sexual relations *both* as a progressive break, at least in the long term, *and* as involved, perhaps contradictorily, in an immediate regressive tendency" (p. 66).

16. See Walter Liedtke, *Flemish Paintings in the Metropolitan Museum of Art*, 2 vols. (New York: Metropolitan Museum of Art, 1984), 1:177. Liedtke argues for a 1639 date on the basis of style, and he thinks that the blue sash and the knot, with its suggestion of male attire (a scabbard for a sword), confirm the identity of the child as Peter Paul; as curator of Flemish paintings, Liedtke has retitled the painting to reflect his argument—until 1984, it was known as 'Rubens, his wife, and their child.'

17. *The Letters of Peter Paul Rubens*, ed. and trans. Ruth S. Magurn (Cambridge: Harvard University Press, 1955), p. 415.

18. Ibid., p. 370.

19. See "High and Low: The Theme of Forbidden Knowledge in the Sixteenth and Seventeenth Centuries," *Past and Present* 73 (1976): 28–41.

Chapter 2: The Absent Mother in *King Lear*

I am grateful to David Leverenz and Louis Adrian Montrose for their sensitive comments on drafts of this essay.

1. This and all subsequent quotations are taken from the Arden edition of *King Lear*, ed. Kenneth Muir (Cambridge: Harvard University Press, 1952).

2. See Ilza Veith, *Hysteria: The History of a Disease* (Chicago: University of Chicago Press, 1965).

3. As Veith (ibid.) shows, during the Middle Ages, hysteria had ceased to be known as a disease and was taken as a visible token of bewitchment. Jordan wrote his treatise to argue for a distinction between the two. Both his work and the pamphlet by Samuel Harsnett denouncing the persecution of witches (from which Shakespeare took much of Poor Tom's language) have the effect of pointing up parallels between hysteria and witchcraft as deviant kinds of behavior associated with women, which are then used to justify denigrating women and subjecting them to strict control. In her essay on the literary and social forms of sexual inversion in early modern Europe whereby women took dominant roles and ruled over men, Natalie Zemon Davis notes that such female unruliness was thought to emanate from a wandering womb and comments, "The lower ruled the higher within the woman, then, and if she were given her way, she would want to rule over those above her outside. Her disorderliness led her into the evil arts of witchcraft, so ecclesiastical authorities claimed . . ." See "Women on Top," in *Society and Culture in Early Modern France* (Stanford, Calif.: Stanford University Press, 1975), p. 125. Hilda Smith notes that a gynecological text published in 1652 calls the entire female sexual structure "The Matrix," subordinating female sexuality to its reproductive function; see her "Gynecology and Ideology in Seventeenth Century England," in *Liberating Women's History*, ed. Berenice Carroll (Urbana: Illinois University Press, 1976), pp. 97–114. For a theory of hysteria as a disorder that "makes complex use of contemporaneous cultural and social forms," see Alan Krohn, *Hysteria: The Elusive Neurosis* (New York: International Universities Press, 1978).

4. Dianne Hunter, "Psychoanalytic Intervention in the History of Consciousness, Beginning with O," *The (M)Other Tongue: Essays in Feminist Psychoanalytic Interpretation*, ed. Shirley Nelson Garner, Claire Kahane, Madelon Sprengnether (Ithaca, N.Y.: Cornell University Press, 1985). Freud suggests that attachment to the mother may be "especially intimately related to the aetiology of hysteria, which is not surprising when we reflect that both the phase and the neurosis are characteristically feminine." "Female Sexuality" (1931), *Standard Edition* 21:223–45.

5. Gayle Rubin, "The Traffic in Women: Notes on the 'Political

Economy' of Sex," in *Toward An Anthropology of Women*, ed. Rayna Reiter (New York: Monthly Review Press, 1975), pp. 184–85.

6. C. L. Barber, "The Family in Shakespeare's Development," in *Representing Shakespeare: New Psychoanalytic Essays*, ed. Murray Schwartz and Coppélia Kahn (Baltimore: Johns Hopkins University Press, 1980), pp. 199.

7. See my article, "Excavating 'Those Dim Minoan Regions': Maternal Subtexts in Patriarchal Literature," *Diacritics* (Summer 1982), 32–41, which contains a much condensed version of this essay. The idea of a maternal subtext was first suggested to me by Madelon Gohlke's essay, " 'I wooed thee with my sword:' Shakespeare's Tragic Paradigms," in *Representing Shakespeare: New Psychoanalytic Essays* (Baltimore: Johns Hopkins University Press, 1980). She writes of a "structure of relation" in which "it is women who are regarded as powerful and men who strive to avoid an awareness of their vulnerability in relation to women, a vulnerability in which they regard themselves as 'feminine' " (p. 180).

8. *The True Chronicle Historie of King Leir and His Three Daughters*, in *Narrative and Dramatic Sources of Shakespeare*, ed. Geoffrey Bullough, 7 vols. (New York: Columbia University Press, 1973), 7:337–402.

9. In his brilliant and wide-ranging essay in this volume, " 'Shaping Fantasies:' Figurations of Gender and Power in Elizabethan Culture," Louis Adrian Montrose explicates the patriarchal ideology threaded through *A Midsummer Night's Dream*, whereby the mother's part in procreation is occluded and men alone are held to "make women, and make themselves through the medium of women." He interprets this belief as "an overcompensation for the *natural* fact that men do indeed come from women; an overcompensation for the cultural facts that consanguineal and affinal ties *between* men are established through mothers, wives, and daughters."

10. Murray Schwartz explored this idea in a series of talks given at the Center for the Humanities, Wesleyan University, February–April 1978.

11. Lawrence Stone's *The Family, Sex, and Marriage in England, 1500–1800* (New York: Harper & Row, 1978) offers a picture of Elizabethan filial relationships which is both highly suggestive for readings of Shakespeare and much at variance with him; see especially pp. 151–218. For a convenient summary of Stone's account of the Elizabethan patriarchal family, see his essay, "The Rise of the Nuclear Family in Early Modern England," in *The Family in History*, ed. Charles E. Rosenberg (Philadelphia: University of Pennsylvania Press, 1975), pp. 25–54.

12. Adrienne Rich, *Of Woman Born: Motherhood as Experience and Institution* (New York: W. W. Norton, 1976; reprint, Bantam, 1977);

Dorothy Dinnerstein, *The Mermaid and the Minotaur: Sexual Arrangements and Human Malaise* (New York: Harper & Row, 1976); Nancy Chodorow, *The Reproduction of Mothering: Psychoanalysis and the Sociology of Gender* (Berkeley and Los Angeles: University of California Press, 1979). My article, "Excavating 'Those Dim Minoan Regions,' " mentioned above is in part a review of these books.

13. Sigmund Freud, "Female Sexuality" (1931), *Standard Edition* 21:228.

14. Robert Stoller, "Facts and Fancies: An Examination of Freud's Concept of Bisexuality," in *Women and Analysis: Dialogues on Psychoanalytic Views of Feminity*, ed. Jean Strouse (New York: Grossman, 1974), p. 358.

15. For a reading of Shakespeare in light of this differentiation and the ideology connected with it, see my *Man's Estate: Masculine Identity in Shakespeare* (Berkeley and Los Angeles: University of California Press, 1981).

16. See reviews by E. P. Thompson, *Radical History Review* 20 (Spring-Summer 1979): 42–50; Alan MacFarlane, *History and Theory* 18 (no. 1, 1979): 103–26; Randolph Traumbach, *Journal of Social History* 13 (no. 1, 1979): 136–43; Richard T. Vann, *Journal of Family History* 4 (Fall 1979): 308–15.

17. Lawrence Stone, *The Crisis of the Aristocracy, 1558–1641*, abridged ed. (New York: Oxford University Press, 1967), p. 271.

18. This and the following paragraph appear in *Man's Estate*, pp. 13–14.

19. Quoted from *Political Works of King James I*, ed. C. H. McIlwain (Cambridge: Harvard University Press, 1918), p. 307; cited in Lawrence Stone, "The Rise of the Nuclear Family," p. 54.

20. "An Homily of the State of Matrimony," in *The Two Books of Homilies Appointed to be Read in Churches*, ed. John Griffiths (Oxford, 1859), p. 505.

21. David Leverenz, *The Language of Puritan Feeling: An Exploration in Literature, Psychology, and Social History* (New Brunswick: Rutgers University Press, 1980), p. 86. Leverenz gives a fuller and more psychologically astute interpretation of childrearing than does Stone. Though he is specifically concerned with the Puritan family, he relies on the same sources as Stone—Elizabethan and Jacobean manuals of childrearing and domestic conduct, holding that "almost any point made in Puritan tracts can be found in non-Puritan writings" (p. 91).

22. Lynda Boose, "The Father and the Bride in Shakespeare," *PMLA* 97 (May 1982): 325–47.

23. For a subtle and lucid account of pre-oedipal experience, see Margaret S. Mahler, Fred Pine, and Anni Bergman, *The Psychological Birth of the Human Infant: Symbiosis and Individuation* (New York: Basic Books, 1975), pp. 39–120.

24. Sigmund Freud, "On Narcissism" (1914), *Standard Edition* 14:69–102.

25. Sigmund Freud, "The Theme of the Three Caskets," *Standard Edition* 12:289–300.

26. Stone, *Marriage, Sex, and the Family*, pp. 106–109.

27. John Bowlby, *Attachment and Loss*, 2 vols. (New York: Basic Books, 1969).

28. *Batman upon Bartholeme* (1582), cited in the Arden edition, p. 118. "The kind life-rend'ring pelican" was a familiar image of Christ in the Middle Ages, wounding herself with her beak to feed her children. Even today, the blood bank of the city of Dublin, administered by an organization called "Mother and Child," is known as "the Pelican." (I am indebted to Thomas Flanagan for this information.)

29. Stephen J. Greenblatt, "Lear's Anxiety," *Raritan Review* (Summer 1982), 92–114.

30. Marianne Novy, "Shakespeare and Emotional Distance in the Elizabethan Family," *Theatre Journal* 33 (October 1981):316–26.

31. See C. L. Barber, "The Family in Shakespeare's Development: Tragedy and Sacredness," in *Representing Shakespeare: New Psychoanalytic Essays*, for the idea that "the very central and problematical role of women in Shakespeare—and the Elizabethan drama generally—reflects the fact that Protestantism did away with the cult of the Virgin Mary. It meant the loss of ritual resource for dealing with the internal residues in all of us of the once all-powerful and all-inclusive mother" (p. 196).

32. Stanley Cavell, "The Avoidance of Love," in *Must We Mean What We Say?* (Cambridge: At the University Press, 1976).

33. This reading of the play suggests that Shakespeare departed from his sources and let Cordelia die because he wanted to confront as starkly as possible the pain of separation from the mother.

Chapter 3: Prospero's Wife

This chapter was first published in *Representations* no. 8 (Fall 1984):1–13. © 1984 by The Regents of the University of California. Reprinted by permission of The Regents.

1. Line references throughout are to the Arden edition, edited by Frank Kermode. In this instance, I have restored the folio punctuation of line 59.

2. Murray M. Schwartz and Coppélia Kahn, eds, *Representing Shakespeare* (Baltimore: Johns Hopkins University Press, 1980).

3. *The New Yorker*, 1 March 1982, p. 53.

4. "So Rare a Wonder'd Father: Prospero's *Tempest*," in *Representing Shakespeare*, p. 48.

5. Coppélia Kahn makes this point, following a suggestion of Harry Berger, Jr., in "The Providential Tempest and the

Shakespearean Family," in *Representing Shakespeare*, p. 238. For an alternative view, see the exceptionally interesting discussion by Joel Fineman, "Fratricide and Cuckoldry: Shakespeare's Doubles," in *Representing Shakespeare*, p. 104.

6. The charge that he was David Rizzio's child was current in England in the 1580s, spread by rebellious Scottish Presbyterian ministers. James expressed fears that it would injure his chance of succeeding to the English throne, and he never felt entirely free of it.

7. C. H. McIlwain, *Political Works of James I* (Cambridge: Harvard University Press, 1918), p. 24.

8. From the 1603 speech to parliament; McIlwain, *Political Works*, p. 272.

9. *Metamorphoses*, 7:197–209, apparently at least partly refracted through Golding's English version.

10. Kermode and most editors read "entertained," but I have restored the folio reading, which seems to me unexceptionable.

11. "'Wife' or 'Wise'—*The Tempest* I. 1786," *University of Virginia Studies in Bibliography* 31 (1978).

Chapter 4: *A Midsummer Night's Dream* and the Shaping Fantasies of Elizabethan Culture

A longer and more extensively documented version of this essay has been published as " 'Shaping Fantasies': Figurations of Gender and Power in Elizabethan Culture," *Representations* 44 2 (Spring 1983):61–94, © 1983 by The Regents of the University of California. I am grateful to Stephen Greenblatt and the editorial board of *Representations*, and to the University of California Press, for permission to republish that essay in the present shortened and revised form.

1. Quoted from manuscript in A. L. Rowse, *The Case Books of Simon Forman* (London: Weidenfeld and Nicholson, 1974), p. 31.

2. Excerpts from Forman's autobiography are printed in Rowse, *Case Books*; see especially pp. 273, 276.

3. See C. L. Barber, "The Family in Shakespeare's Development: Tragedy and Sacredness," in *Representing Shakespeare*, ed. Murray M. Schwartz and Coppélia Kahn (Baltimore: Johns Hopkins University Press, 1980), pp. 188–202; quotation from p. 196.

4. André Hurault, Sieur de Maisse, *Journal* (1597), trans. and ed. G. B. Harrison and R. A. Jones (Bloomsbury: Nonesuch Press, 1931), pp. 25–26.

5. "Extracts from Paul Hentzner's Travels in England, 1598," in *England as seen by Foreigners in the Days of Elizabeth & James the First*, ed. William Brenchley Rye (1865; reprint, New York: Benjamin Blom, 1967), pp. 104–5.

6. Sir Robert Naunton, *Fragmenta Regalia* (written ca. 1630;

printed 1641), ed. Edward Arber (1870; reprint, New York: AMS Press, 1966), p. 51.

7. I use the term *patriarchal* advisedly, to describe a specific household organization in which authority resides in a male "head" who is husband, father, and the master of servants and apprentices. Lawrence Stone links the early modern patriarchal family to the centralization of political authority, in *The Family, Sex and Marriage in England 1500–1800* (New York: Harper & Row, 1977), pp. 123–218. Also see Gorden J. Schochet, *Patriarchalism in Political Thought* (New York: Basic Books, 1975), pp. 37–98.

8. See *The Letters and Epigrams of Sir John Harington,* ed. N. E. McClure (Philadelphia: University of Pennsylvania Press, 1930), p. 122.

9. All quotations from *A Midsummer Night's Dream (MND)* follow *The Arden Shakespeare* edition of *MND,* ed. Harold F. Brooks (London: Methuen, 1979), and are cited in the text by act, scene, and line.

10. Paul A. Olson, "*A Midsummer Night's Dream* and the Meaning of Court Marriage," *ELH* 24 (1957):95–119.

11. See Gayle Rubin, "The Traffic in Women: Notes on the 'Political Economy' of Sex," in *Toward an Anthropology of Women,* ed. Rayna R. Reiter (New York: Monthly Review Press, 1975), pp. 157–210. For an introduction to the construction of one gender in European intellectual history, see Ian Maclean, *The Renaissance Notion of Woman* (Cambridge: Cambridge University Press, 1980).

12. William Painter, *The Palace of Pleasure* (1575), ed. Joseph Jacobs, 3 vols. (1890; reprint New York: Dover, 1966), 2:159–61. Further page citations will be to volume 2 of this edition. For a sense of the ubiquity of Amazonian representations in Elizabethan culture, see the valuable survey by Celeste Turner Wright: "The Amazons in Elizabethan Literature," *Studies in Philology* 37 (1940):433–56. My interest in the play's relationship to Amazon myth was kindled by the work of Page duBois. See her *Centaurs and Amazons* (Ann Arbor: University of Michigan Press, 1982).

13. *The Faerie Queene* is quoted from the often-reprinted *Oxford Standard Authors* edition of Spenser's *Poetical Works,* ed. J. C. Smith and E. de Selincourt (Oxford: Oxford University Press, 1912), and is cited by book, canto, and stanza. In quotations from this and other Elizabethan texts, I have silently modernized obsolete typographical conventions.

14. *An Elizabethan in 1582: The Diary of Richard Madox, Fellow of All Souls,* ed. Elizabeth Story Donno, Hakluyt Society, 2d series, no. 47 (London: Hakluyt Society, 1977), p. 183.

15. See Linda T. Fitz, " 'What Says the Married Woman?' Marriage Theory and Feminism in the English Renaissance," *Mosaic* 3 (Winter

1980):1–22, who suggests that "the English Renaissance institutionalized, where it did not invent, the restrictive marriage-oriented attitude toward women that feminists have been struggling against ever since . . . The insistent demand for the right—nay, obligation—of women to be happily married arose as much in reaction against women's intractable pursuit of independence as it did in reaction against Catholic ascetic philosophy" (pp. 11, 18). For a recent and balanced discussion of marriage and family in the early modern period (and a critique of the work of Lawrence Stone), see Keith Wrightson, *English Society 1580–1680* (London: Hutchinson, 1982), pp. 66–118. On the concept of woman as property in English social and legal history, see Keith Thomas, "The Double Standard," *Journal of the History of Ideas* 20 (1959):195–216.

16. See Joan Bamberger, "The Myth of Matriarchy: Why Men Rule in Primitive Society," in *Woman, Culture and Society,* ed. Michelle Zimbalist Rosaldo and Louise Lamphere (Stanford: Stanford University Press, 1974), pp. 262–80; esp. pp. 266, 277.

17. This paragraph is much indebted to J. A. Barnes, "Genetrix : Genitor :: Nature : Culture?" in *The Character of Kinship,* ed. Jack Goody (Cambridge: Cambridge University Press, 1973), pp. 61–73. On Elizabethan embryological notions, see Audrey Eccles, *Obstetrics and Gynaecology in Tudor and Stuart England* (London: Croom Helm, 1982); and Angus McLaren, *Reproductive Rituals: The perception of fertility in England from the sixteenth century to the nineteenth century* (London: Methuen, 1984), esp. pp. 13–29. As McLaren emphasizes, Galenic embryological theories, rather than Aristotelian ones, were predominant in the sixteenth century; in Galenic medicine, "both sexes were presented as contributing equally in conception and accordingly both had to experience pleasure" (*Reproductive Rituals,* p. 17). In *MND,* and in other plays of the Shakespearean corpus, one may detect a tension between Aristotelian and Galenic perspectives.

18. For a review and analysis of the play's sources and analogues, see Brooks's *Arden* edition, pp. lvii–lxxxviii; 129–53; and the notes, passim. D'Orsay W. Pearson, " 'Vnkinde' Theseus: A Study in Renaissance Mythography," *English Literary Renaissance* 4 (1974):276–98, surveys Theseus's "classical, medieval, and Renaissance image as an unnatural, perfidious, and unfaithful lover and father" (p. 276).

19. See Winfried Schleiner, "*Divina virago*: Queen Elizabeth as an Amazon," *Studies in Philology* 75 (1978): 163–80.

20. *The Discovery of the Large, Rich, and Beautiful Empire of Guiana* (1596), ed. Sir Robert H. Schomburgk, Hakluyt Society, 1st ser., no. 3 (1848; reprint, New York: Burt Franklin, n.d.). References will be to this edition.

21. See Natalie Zemon Davis, *Society and Culture in Early Modern*

France (Stanford: Stanford University Press, 1975), p. 130. Davis's own argument is that inversion phenomena may not only act as safety valves that renew the existing structures but as sources of cultural innovation and social change.

22. In the *Letter* to Ralegh that was printed with the first three books of *The Faerie Queene* in 1590, Spenser writes that, "considering [Elizabeth] beareth two persons, the one of a most royall Queene or Empresse, the other of a most vertuous and beautiful Lady" (*Poetical Works*, p. 407), it is necessary to allegorize her various qualities in various fictional personages. On the legal, political, and dramatic aspects of the doctrine that the queen had a body politic and a body natural, see Marie Axton, *The Queen's Two Bodies* (London: Royal Historical Society, 1977).

23. The extant text is putatively a transcription made on the occasion of the Queen's speech by her chaplain, Dr. Lionel Sharp, and first printed in *Cabala: Mysteries of State and Government in Letters of Illustrious Persons* (London, 1654); quoted in Paul Johnson, *Elizabeth I: A Study in Power and Intellect* (London: Weidenfeld & Nicholson, 1974), p. 320. Other representations of the event are discussed in Schleiner, "*Divina Virago*."

24. Sir Robert Cecil to Sir John Harington, 29 May 1603, printed in John Harington, *Nugae Antiquae,* 3 vols. (1779; reprint, Hildesheim: Georg Olms, 1968), 2:264.

25. See J. E. Neale, *Elizabeth I and Her Parliaments 1559–1581* (New York: St. Martin's Press, 1958), pp. 49, 109. Neale prints the full texts of these speeches.

26. *In Felicem Memoriam Elizabethae* (ca. 1608), in *The Works of Francis Bacon,* ed. James Spedding, et al., 15 vols. (Boston: Brown and Taggard, 1860), 11:425–42 (Latin text), 443–61 (English trans.); quotation from p. 450. Future page citations will be to vol. 11 of this edition.

27. The policy and iconography of the royal cult are studied in Frances A. Yates, *Astraea* (London: Routledge & Kegan Paul, 1975), pp. 29–120, 215–19; Roy Strong, *Portraits of Queen Elizabeth I* (Oxford: Clarendon Press, 1963); Roy Strong, *The Cult of Elizabeth* (London: Thames & Hudson, 1977). Also see E. C. Wilson, *England's Eliza* (1939; reprint, London: Frank Cass, 1966), for the literary idealizations of the queen; and Louis Adrian Montrose, " 'Eliza, Queene of Shepheardes,' and the Pastoral of Power," *English Literary Renaissance* 10 (1980):153–82, on pastoral metaphors and royal power.

28. I quote the printed text of the Kenilworth entertainment (1576) from *The Complete Works of George Gascoigne,* ed. J. W. Cunliffe, 2 vols. (Cambridge: Cambridge University Press, 1910), 2:107, 120.

29. George Peele, *The Aragynment of Paris* (printed 1584), ed. R. Mark Benbow, in *The Dramatic Works of George Peele,* C. T. Prouty,

gen. ed. (New Haven, Conn.: Yale University Press, 1970), lines 1172–73. See Louis Adrian Montrose, "Gifts and Reasons: The Contexts of Peele's *Araygnement of Paris*," *ELH* 47 (1980):433–61.

30. Described in Sir William Segar, *Honor Military, and Civill* (1602), pp. 107–200; reprinted in John Nichols, *The Progresses and Public Processions of Queen Elizabeth*, 3 vols. (1823; reprint, New York: Burt Franklin, 1966), 3:41–50; quotation from Nichols, 3:46.

31. The change suffered by the flower—from the whiteness of milk to the purple wound of love—juxtaposes maternal nurturance and erotic violence. To an Elizabethan audience, the metamorphosis may have suggested not only the blood of defloration but also the blood of menstruation—and, perhaps, the *menarche*, which manifests the sexual maturity of the female, the advent of womanhood and potential motherhood. An awareness that the commonest Elizabethan term for the menses was *flowers* (see *Oxford English Dictionary*, s.v. "flower," sense 2.b) adds a peculiar resonance to certain occurences of the word and of floral imagery in Renaissance texts. This is especially the case in *MND*, in which flowers are conspicuously associated with female sexuality, with moisture, and with the moon. The imagery of Shakespeare's text insinuates that, whatever its provenance in horticultural lore, Oberon's maddening love juice is a displacement of vaginal blood: a conflation of menstrual blood—which is the sign of women's generative powers and of their pollution, their dangerousness to men—with the blood of defloration—which is the sign of men's mastery of women's bodies, of their generative powers and of their dangerousness.

32. The text of the Sudely entertainment was printed in *Speeches Delivered to Her Majestie this Last Progresse* (1592), and reprinted in *The Complete Works of John Lyly*, ed. R. Warwick Bond, 3 vols. (Oxford: Clarendon Press, 1902), vol. 2, pp. 477–84. For a detailed analysis, see Montrose, " ' Eliza, Queene of Shepheardes'," pp. 168–80.

33. Reprinted in Nichols, *Progresses and Public Processions*, 2:312–29. Further page references will be to vol. 2 of this edition. See Louis Adrian Montrose, "Celebration and Insinuation: Sir Philip Sidney and the Motives of Elizabethan Courtship," *Renaissance Drama*, n.s. 8 (1977):3–35.

34. W. Waad to Sir Robert Cecil, 3 June 1600, printed in *Calendar of the Manuscripts of . . . The marquis of Salisbury . . . preserved at Hatfield House*, 18 vols. (London: HMSO, 1883–1940), 10:172–73.

35. For a subtle consideration of these issues, see Stephen Greenblatt, *Renaissance Self-Fashioning* (Chicago: University of Chicago Press, 1980); Greenblatt discusses Elizabeth's self-fashionings on pp. 165–69, 230. The processes by which the queen is fashioned by her subjects I explore further in "The Elizabethan Subject and the Spenserian Text," in *Literary Theory and Renaissance Texts*, ed. Patricia

Parker and David Quint (Baltimore: Johns Hopkins University Press, forthcoming 1986).

Chapter 5: Puritanism and Maenadism in *A Mask*

1. Spenser's "Epithalamion" is exemplary in this respect.

2. All quotations of Milton are taken from *The Poetry of John Milton,* ed. John Carey and Alastair Fowler (London: Longmans, 1968).

3. See Charles Segal, *Dionysiac Poetics and Euripides' Bacchae* (Princeton, N.J.: Princeton University Press, 1982).

4. I should note that while my essay emphasizes those aspects of Dionysian rite and myth that tended to liberate women, other aspects served patriarchal culture. "Dionysus," writes Segal, "in his birth from Zeus's 'immortal fire' and 'male womb' acts out a fantasy of the male's independence from the female cycles of menstruation and birth, with their attendant uncleanness, and achieves that independence from the female which recurs wishfully throughout early Greek culture" (p. 181).

5. See Marcel Detienne. *Dionysos Slain,* trans. Mirielle and Leonard Muellner (Baltimore: Johns Hopkins University Press, 1979), chap. 3.

6. See Albert Henrichs, "Greek Maenadism from Olympias to Messalina," *Harvard Studies in Classical Philology* 82 (1978):121–60.

7. Roberta Hamilton, *The Liberation of Women: A Study of Patriarchy and Capitalism* (London: George Allen & Unwin, 1978).

8. Quoted by David Aers and Bob Hodge, " 'Rational Burning': Milton on Sex and Marriage," *Milton Studies* 13 (1979):3–33, *q.v.*

9. Quoted in Hamilton, *Liberation of Women,* p. 66.

10. There has been some controversy over this point, which turns primarily on whether the marriage of Cupid and Psyche (1004–1011) fortells an earthly or heavenly marriage for the Lady. I prefer the former interpretation, as does Tillyard. The generally hymeneal associations of the masque form aside, the notion of perpetual virginity would seem inappropriate to the masque's occasion. The Egertons, one assumes, hoped that their daughter Alice would wed some day. Of course, Cupid and Psyche are cut from the Bridgewater version, as is almost all of the Spirit's final song. Yet even lines 887–890 of the Bridgewater version (966–69 in the 1637 text) celebrate the virtues of earthly generation:

Noble Lord, and Lady bright,
I have brought ye new delight,
Here behold so goodly grown
Three fair branches of your own.

A Mask, it seems to me, must be read as describing a virginal *rite de passage,* which prepares the Lady for a chaste married life. I will return to this point later.

11. "Chastity and purity of life consist either in sincere virginity, or in faithful matrimony." William Baldwin, *A Treatise of Morall Philosophie* (1547), enlarged by Thomas Palfreyman (1620; reprint, Gainesville, Fla.: Scholars' Press, 1967), p. 246. I am not suggesting that there is anything unusual about Milton's usage: *chastity* is a common synonym for *virginity.*

12. I am not suggesting a direct influence, for the simple reason that the outburst of radical thought on sex and matrimony did not occur until the 1640s, whereas *A Mask* was written in 1634. Then, too, Milton's being still unmarried meant that he had not considered these questions with the seriousness that he would after 1642. Nevertheless, as I will go on to suggest, there is a remarkable ideological and poetic continuity between *A Mask,* the twelfth sonnet (ca. 1646), and *Paradise Lost* on all of the issues discussed here. Spenser had already found it necessary to navigate the difficult course from virginity to chastity; the ideological contradictions were already in place, although a revolutionary culture had not yet released them.

13. See Ilza Veith, *Hysteria: The History of a Disease* (Chicago: University of Chicago Press, 1965), pp. 130–31 and passim.

14. Nathaniel H. Henry, "Who Meant License When They Cried Liberty?" *MLN* 66 (1951): 509–13.

15. Early on, the chorus of Asian maenads sings,

It is wise to withold one's heart and mind
    from men who think themselves superior.
      Whatever the multitude,
    the ordinary people, take as normal and practice, this would
      I accept.
                (G. S. Kirk, trans. [Cambridge:
      Cambridge University Press, 1979], lines 427–33.)

Even in Hellenic and Hellenistic culture, however, maenadism does not seem to have been entirely democratic. "It seems very unlikely that maenadism was ubiquitous in Greek lands, or that in places where it existed admission was invariably open to every woman who wanted to be a maenad: at least in Athens, Delphi, and perhaps Thebes maenadism was restricted to selected groups of women" (Henrich "Greek Maenadism," p. 153). Apparently, women often bought contracts for the right to lead maenadic bands.

16. See Christopher Hill, "The Uses of Sabbatarianism," in *Society and Puritanism in Pre-Revolutionary England* (New York: Schocken, 1964), pp. 145–218. Maryann Cale McGuire also treats the "sports

controversy" at length in the first chapter of her book, *Milton's Puritan Masque* (Athens: University of Georgia Press, 1983).

17. Quoted in Hill, "Uses of Sabbatarianism," pp. 193–94.

18. Ibid., pp. 184–85.

19. See Christopher Hill, "Puritans and the 'Dark Corners of the Land,' " in *Change and Continuity in Seventeenth Century England* (Cambridge: Harvard University Press, 1975). The *literal* setting of Milton's masque was Ludlow castle, which was near the Welsh border but still in England. Yet the masque's occasion would seem to demand at least an oblique reference to the Earl of Bridgewater's new status as Lord President of Wales. The pacification of this "dark corner" forms one important element of what is a symbolically overdetermined landscape.

20. This discussion is heavily indebted to Leah Sinanoglou Marcus, "The Occasion of Ben Jonson's *Pleasure Reconciled to Virtue,*" *SEL* 19 (1979): 271–93.

21. Quoted in ibid., p. 278.

22. See ibid., passim.

23. See lines 321–25. The shepherds are allowed an antic dance at the end of the masque, but even this chastened festivity is soon dismissed by Thyrsis: "Back, shepherds, back; enough your play" (957).

24. Apparently, country sports were often as abandoned as their opponents claimed. Manslaughter and unwanted pregnancies were not infrequent results, as Hill has documented, adding, "We must be very careful not to sentimentalize ye olde morrice dances of Merrie England" ("Uses of Sabbatarianism," pp. 190–91).

25. Natalie Zemon Davis, "Women on Top: Symbolic Sexual Inversion and Political Disorder in Early Modern Europe," reprinted in *The Reversible World: Symbolic Inversion in Art and Society* (Ithaca, N.Y.: Cornell University Press, 1978), pp. 147–90.

26. *The Minor Poems of John Lydgate,* ed. H. N. MacCracken (London: E.E.T.S., 1934), pp. 675–82. Information on the masque's performance from Stephen Orgel, *The Jonsonian Masque* (Cambridge: Harvard University Press, 1965), p. 20.

27. John Steadman cites some interesting classical and medieval sources that held that Maenadic rites, including *sparagmos,* took place in Britain. "A Mask at Ludlow: Comus and Dionysiac Revel," in *Nature into Myth: Medieval and Renaissance Moral Symbols* (Pittsburgh: Duquesne University Press, 1979), pp. 213–40.

28. See Davis, "Women on Top," pp. 151–57.

29. Henry, "Who Meant License," p. 512.

30. These two fears (of women and of the mob) are not unrelated and indeed had a basis in social reality. Writes Davis, "In England in the early seventeenth century . . . a significant percentage of the rioters against enclosure and for common land were female" (176).

31. *For the Honor of Wales* was a direct rewriting of *Pleasure Reconciled to Virtue,* emended to eliminate Comus (whose satiric resemblence to dissolute courtiers cut too close for James's taste) and to celebrate Prince Charles's recent investiture as Prince of Wales (Marcus, "The Occasion of Jonson's *Pleasure,*" pp. 291–93):

> [I]n place of *Pleasure Reconciled to Virtue*'s heroic triumphs over the dangerous opposites of puritanism and popery, *For the Honor of Wales* offers humor and palliatives: the satire against overfeasting and drinking is abandoned for praise of plain Welsh food and drink, and an invitation to James to feast in Wales; instead of an antimasque of boasting pygmies, which the Welsh claim to scorn, there are dances to the music of the "ancient Welse [*sic*] harp" by proper British men and women. (p. 291)

"In Wales," suggests Jonson, "the king . . . will . . . find humble devotion to himself and his family, proper preservation of the old pastimes he encouraged through the *Book of Sports,* and measured feasting of the sort he recommended in the *Basilikon Doron*" (ibid., pp. 291–92).

Milton's revisionary technique simply collapses Jonson's two masques into one. By reviving Comus he also revives Jonson's satire against the court; and by implanting him in Wales, he attacks Jonson's implication that there is anything "measured" or "proper" about Welsh festivity.

32. In the eleventh sonnet, Milton defends the cacophonous title of *Tetrachordon* by comparing it favorably with the sound of Scots names:

> Why is it harder sirs than Gordon,
> Colkitto, or Macdonnel, or Galasp?
> Those rugged names to our like mouths grow sleek
> That would have made Quintillian stare and gasp.

In the manuscript, Milton originally wrote "barbarian" in place of "rugged." Further, the reference to Quintillian concerns his warning (*Institutes,* 1.5.8) against allowing barbarous foreign words infect the purity of Latin. Milton apparently considers the Celtic tongue barbarous even when it is used by his allies.

33. In *The Bacchae,* by contrast, the foreign emerges as dominant, or at least manages to unsettle the dominance of the native. G. S. Kirk argues that the play's descriptions of foreign lands partly reflect the interests of "the sophistic movement[, which] evinced a strong preoccupation with comparative ethnology and the collection of

details about foreign lands and customs, partly with the intention of showing that "law" is a relative concept" (p. 26 note). Dionysus, who is both a foreigner and a sophist, complements his political assault on Thebes with an epistemological assault on the transcendence of the Greek *logos*. "The contrast between . . . the joyful ecstasy of Dionysus and the traditional wisdom (*sophia,* 189) of the city of which the old men are the repository . . . [is an] aspect of the larger antithesis between the far and the near" (Segal, Dionysiac Poetics, p. 88). Dionysus undermines Pentheus's authority partly by deconstructing his claims to knowledge.

Sophist ethnology was revived for the Renaissance by Montaigne's essay *Of Cannibals* and by *The Tempest,* which not only drew on Montaigne but which provided, in Caliban, a literary model for Milton's Comus. Milton suppressed the radical implications of ethnological relativism, however, partly in order to inscribe a transcendental Christian *logos* and partly out of Prostestant nationalism. Yet the ethnocentrism of *A Mask* had already been prepared for by Jonson, who regularly filled his antimasques with pygmies, Indians, and other "barbarians" who were then symbolically tamed and subjugated by the power of the monarch.

34. In Philostratus's description of Comus, the concept of liminality becomes quite literal, for Comus is represented as standing at the doorway or threshold of the *thalamos* or marriage chamber. His position there, I think, is meant precisely to question the sanctity of limits, just as his followers do when they engage in transvestitism. The figure of Comus at the threshold was taken up by Renaissance illustrators, appearing in Cartari's *Images of the Gods of the Ancients* and in Blaise de Vignere's French translation of Philostratus's *Images.* See the illustrations in *The Jonsonian Masque* or in Steadman, *Nature into Myth.*

35. Hill, *The World Turned Upside Down: Radical Ideas during the English Revolution* (New York: Penguin, 1975), p. 320.

Chapter 6: Dalila's House

1. A basic statement of the position here argued can be found in Lévi-Strauss, "The Family," in *Man, Culture, and Society,* ed. Harry Shapiro (London: Oxford University Press, 1971), p. 347: "we should be careful to distinguish the *fact* of the division of labor between the sexes, which is practically universal, from the *way* according to which different tasks are attributed to one or the other sex, where we should recognize the same paramount influence of cultural factors . . ." Thus Lévi-Strauss argues that the fact of the sexual division of labor is "a device to institute a *reciprocal* state of dependency between the sexes" (p. 348; my italics).

2. Roberta Hamilton, *The Liberation of Women* (London: George

Allen & Unwin, 1978), p. 24. In the pioneering work on the subject, *The Origin of the Family, Private Property, and the State* (New York: International Publishers, 1952), Friedrich Engels argues that in premodern societies, "The division of labor between the two sexes is determined by quite other causes than by the position of women in society" (p. 113). While other aspects of Engel's theory have been disputed, it has been generally accepted that there is no *necessary* relation between division of labor and sexual subjection. On the question of women and labor in the seventeenth century, the most detailed study remains that of Alice Clark, *Working Life of Women in the Seventeenth Century* (New York: Harcourt, Brace & Howe, 1920).

3. See, for example, Immanuel Wallersten, *Historical Capitalism* (London: Verso Editions, 1983), p. 25: "What was new under historical capitalism was the correlation of division of labor and valuation of work. Men may often have done different work from women . . . but under historical capitalism there has been a steady devaluation of the work of women (and of the young and old), and a corresponding emphasis on the value of the adult male's work."

4. Annette Kuhn, "Structures of Patriarchy and Capital in the Family," in *Feminism and Materialism: Women and Modes of Production* (London: Routledge & Kegan Paul, 1978), p. 55. See also the essay in the same volume by Rosin McDonough and Rachel Harrison, "Patriarchy and Relations of Production," pp. 12–41. Engels's thesis concerning the rise of private property and the subjection of women is now very familiar. It has been revised and updated by Karen Sacks, "Engels Revisited," in *Women, Culture, and Society,* ed. Michelle Rosaldo and Louise Lamphere (Stanford: Stanford University Press, 1974). On the separation of household and occupation, see Max Weber, *Economy and Society,* 3 vols., ed. Gunther Roth and Claus Wittich, trans. Ephraim Fischoff et al. (New York: Bedminister Press, 1968), 1:375.

5. All quotations from Milton's poetry are cited from *John Milton: Complete Poems and Major Prose,* ed. Merrit Hughes (Indianapolis: Odyssey Press, 1957). On the Puritan concept of vocation, see the typical work by William Perkins, *A Treatise of Vocations, or Callings of Men* (1603), where the several senses of vocation or calling are set out. Both Perkins and the annotators of the Geneva Bible read the Samson story as an allegory of vocation. Perkins writes, "Samson's strength lay not in his haire (as men commonly think) but because he went out of his calling, by breaking the vow of a Nazarite when he gaue occasion to Dalilah to cut off his haire, therefore he lost his strength" (p. 728). On Judges 16:25, the Geneva annotation has: "Thus by God's just judgments they are made slaves to infidels, which neglect their vocation; in defending the faithful."

6. I am using the term *misrecognition* in the sense employed by

Pierre Bourdieu and Jean-Claude Passeron, in *Reproduction in Educa-tion, Society, and Culture,* trans. Richard Nice (London: Sage Publica-tions, 1977). Misrecognition, as defined by Richard Nice, refers to "the process by which power relations are perceived not for what they objectively are but in a form which renders them legitimate in the eyes of the beholder" (p. xiii). Bourdieu's concept of misrecognition is to be distinguished from Lacan's in that it is not concerned with any psychogenesis. In fact, the sexual division of labor, the form by which power relations between men and women have been maintained since the early modern period, comes to be misrecognized precisely as a psychical conflict (between higher and lower drives in the male). At a later point, I will suggest a psychological reading of *Samson Agonistes,* but I should emphasize that such a reading concerns the level of misrecognition in the drama.

7. Milton acknowledges the possibility of this opposition in a curiously direct way when he praises the sexual division of labor in *Paradise Lost* 9:232–34: "for nothing lovelier can be found / In woman than to study household good, / And good works in her Husband to promote." It would appear at first that Eve is instituting the sexual division of labor in the scene of the quarrel, a reading compatible with the rationale of her argument about labor. In fact the moment is much more complex than that because both she and Adam stand on both sides of the divide between feudal and bourgeois conceptions of labor. While Adam adopts an idealized conception of labor as an autotelic activity unrelated to survival and therefore external to economy, he also invokes, in the passage quoted, the sexual division of labor. That division, which in the real world could be articulated only in relation to production, is made somehow prelapsarian. Eve, on the other hand, although she proposes a rationalized, economic conception of labor, also seems to be recalling a more Medieval equality of male and female labor. Alice Clarke, in *Working Life of Women in the Seventeenth Century,* argues that domestic work in pre-modern times was more equally distributed between men and women, even the care of children. As for the family industry typical of many households: "No equation arose as to the relative value of their work, because the proceeds became the property of the family, instead of being divided between individuals" (p. 294). This does not imply an absence of subjection but an absence of conjunction with the sexual division of labor. On the subject of women in the Renaissance household, Louis B. Wright, in his study, *Middle Class Culture in Elizabethan England* (Chapel Hill: University of North Carolina Press, 1935), p. 218, quotes the advice to wives in the very popular and typical poem of Samuel Rowlands, *The Bride:* "haue domestique cares / Of priuate business for the house within, / Leaving her husband vnto his affaires." Wright points to the abundance of prose and verse guides to

domestic life that became available to middle-class households in the sixteenth and seventeenth centuries, evidence of increased interest in codifying and regulating domestic relations for social and pragmatic as well as ethical reasons. Not surprisingly, these guidebooks are more and more directed to regulating the behavior of housewives.

8. On the organization of classical culture into *polis* and *domus,* see Hannah Arendt, *The Human Condition* (Chicago: University of Chicago Press, 1958), pp. 22–78; also Jean Elshtain, *Public Man, Private Woman* (Princeton, N.J.: Princeton University Press, 1981), pp. 44–54.

9. In *The Doctrine and Discipline of Divorce,* Milton speaks of "the household estate, out of which must flourish forth the vigor and spirit of all publick enterprizes": *Complete Prose Works of John Milton,* 8 vols. Ed. Douglas Bush, et al. (New Haven, Conn.: Yale University Press, 1959), 2:247. In his annotation to the Yale edition of *Doctrine and Discipline of Divorce,* Ernest Sirluck notes the precedent of William Perkins's *Christian Oeconomie,* where marriage is said to be "the fountaine and seminarie of al other sorts and kinds of life, in the Common-wealth and in the church." On the historical matrix of the word *private,* very useful is Raymond Williams's brief essay in *Keywords* (New York: Oxford University Press, 1976), pp. 203–4, particularly the following comment: "Private . . . in its positive sense, is the record of the legitimization of a bourgeois view of life: the ultimate generalized privilege, however abstract in practice, of seclusion and protection from others (*the public*); of lack of accountability to 'them': and of related gains in closeness and comfort of these general kinds." Also useful is Richard Sennet's study of privatization, *The Fall of Public Man* (New York: Vintage Books, 1978).

10. I would note especially the following phrases: "Purple the sails, and so perfumed that / The winds were lovesick with them . . . Her gentlewomen, like the Nereides, / So many mermaids / . . . the silken tackle . . . From the barge / A strange invisible perfume hits the sense / of the adjacent wharfs." (2.2.192–219) Quotations from Shakespeare's *Antony and Cleopatra* are from the Signet edition of Barbara Everett (New York: New American Library, 1964).

11. From this point on, I also adopt the analytic distinction between the phallus and the penis, as argued by Jacques Lacan in "The Signification of the Phallus," *Ecrits,* trans. Alan Sheridan (New York: W. W. Norton, 1977), pp. 282–91. On the usefulness as well as the difficulty of the distinction, see the comments of Jean Laplanche and J. B. Pontalis in *The Language of Psycho-Analysis,* trans. Donald Nicholson-Smith (New York: W. W. Norton, 1973), pp. 312–14.

12. See the essay on "Fetishism," *Standard Edition of the Complete Psychological Works of Sigmund Freud,* 24 vols., trans. and ed. James Strachey (London: Hogarth Press, 1964), 21:152–153.

13. Such heightened femininity characterizes the female monarch about whom Milton seems to have had rather ambivalent feelings—Elizabeth. His ambivalence is obvious in his remark in *The Readie and Easie Way* about Elizabeth's reluctance to "give way so much as to Presbyterian reformation" during her reign (Y. E., 7:382). In her private life, however, he considers her a good Protestant.

14. I will argue later that Samson's relation with Dalila recapitulates certain aspects of the Oedipus complex, where the human subject is primally constituted by identification with the parent of the same sex. See especially "The Dissolution of the Oedipus Complex," S. E., 19:171–79.

15. In his presentation of Dalila as a ship, Milton is evidently remembering also a well-known sermon of Robert Wilkinson, *The Merchant Royall* (London: Felix Kingston, 1607), on the subject of marriage: The wife "is like a ship indeed, for first whosoever marries, ventures; he ventures his estate, he ventures his libertie, yea many men by marriage adventure their soules too" (p. 8).

16. On Puritan marriage doctrine, I have followed the study of James Turner Johnson, *A Society Ordained by God: English Puritan Marriage Doctrine in the First Half of the Seventeenth Century* (Nashville, Abingdon Press, 1970). Moderation of appetite within marriage seems to be the point of Milton's distinction betwen fallen and unfallen sexuality in *Paradise Lost*.

17. Consider the following statement from "Truth and Power," in *Power/Knowledge*, ed. Colin Gordon (New York: Pantheon Books, 1980), p. 120: "The result was a sexualising of the infantile body, a sexualising of the familial domain. 'Sexuality' is far more of a positive product of power than power was ever repression of sexuality."

18. On the pervasion of the domestic realm by an intensified eroticism, the argument of Lawrence Stone's *The Family, Sex, and Marriage in England 1500–1800* (New York: Harper & Row, 1977) is worth considering. I am not entirely comfortable with Stone's thesis of "affective individualism," which seems to require a dubious lack of affective bonding before the period of revolutionary change. But this requirement is necessary only because the concept of affect sounds in some way quantifiable. Stone's argument might be accepted in a modified form in the context of Foucault's history of a "rational technology of correction," which appropriated affective bonds to its purposes of regulation and so encouraged their intensity.

19. On this point, Milton's advanced position should be stressed. See, for example, Ian Maclean, in *The Renaissance Notion of Woman* (Cambridge: Cambridge University Press, 1980), p. 66, on Milton's singular defense of divorce. By "advanced" I mean only that Milton extrapolates further than his contemporaries the implications of contradiction in the family. This contradiction is easier to see in the

development of physical privacy, primarily in the architectural innovations of the corridor and the private bedroom. So far from
providing a space for the free indulgence of sexual activity, these
innovations are adjunct to the increasing regulation of "private"
behavior. See Norbert Elias, *The Civilizing Process, Vol 1: The History
of Manners*, trans. Edmund Jephcott (New York: Pantheon Books,
1978), pp. 161–91; and Lawrence Stone, *The Family, Sex, and Marriage*, pp. 169–72.

20. Judges 16:16 says very simply: "And it came to pass, when she
pressed him daily with her words, and urged him, so that his soul was
vexed unto death . . ."

21. See Lacan's *Ecrits*, p. 291: "The fact that femininity finds its
refuge in this mask . . . has the curious consequence of making virile
display in the human being itself seem feminine." Luce Irigaray makes
an interesting related observation about male homosexuality in *Ce
sexe qui n'en est pas un* (1977): "When the penis itself becomes simply
a means of pleasure among men, *the phallus loses its power.*" In *New
French Feminisms*, ed. Elaine Marks and Isabelle de Courtivon (New
York: Schocken Books, 1981), p. 108.

22. "Private parts" began to supercede "privy parts" in the early
modern period, probably in response to whatever pressures, linguistic
or ideological, that drove the term *privy* into obsolescence. If *privy
parts* names the genitalia by association with the excretory function,
the privy, the word *private* has the advantage of somewhat distancing
that function in favor of the sexual, as well as reassociating the
genitalia with newer senses of privacy. Of course we can only
conjecture about causes at this level of particularity. The OED records
the first use of *private* to signify genitalia in 1634, but that usage must
have been current by 1600 in order for the following exchange in
Hamlet to take place:

HAMLET: Then you live about her [Fortune's] waist,
              or in the middle of her favors.
GUILDENSTERN: Faith, her privates we.

                               (2.2.232–34)

23. The association of the female with the tongue is merely
traditional antifeminism and is itself the evidence of subjection by
silencing. A typical diatribe of the seventeenth century is the anonymous *Anatomy of a Womans Tongue* (1638), which compares the
woman's tongue variously to a salve, a poison, a serpent, a fire, a
thunder. Reprinted in *The Harleian Miscellany*, 4 vols. (London, 1800),
2:183–93. In Renaissance medical texts, the garrulity of women is said
to be a result of hysteria (in the root sense). See Ian Maclean, *The
Renaissance Notion of Woman* (Cambridge: Cambridge University
Press, 1980), p. 41. The question of female speech was of renewed and

sometimes critical importance to Milton's Puritan contemporaries because, as Keith Thomas has shown, certain aspects of the intensely patriarchal Puritan ideology came into conflict with the more antinomian implications of the Radical Sectarians. In some of these sects, the right of women to speak in church, or even to prophesy, was claimed. See "Women and the Civil War Sects," in *Crisis in Europe 1550–1650*, ed. Trevor Aston (London: Rutledge & Kegan Paul, 1965), pp. 317–40.

24. Norbert Elias, *The Civilizing Process*, p. 186.

25. For a general comment, see *The History of Sexuality*, p. 127: "We must return, therefore, to formulations that have long been disparaged; we must say that there is a bourgeois sexuality, and that there are class sexualities. Or rather, that sexuality is originally, historically bourgeois, and that, in its successive shifts and transpositions, it induces specific class effects."

26. Milton was of course unhappy with the "divorce at pleasure" interpretation of his tracts and expressed his unhappiness unequivocally in Sonnet 12. For a discussion of the issues involved in the reception of the divorce tracts, see Christopher Hill, *Milton and the English Revolution* (New York: Penguin Books, 1979), pp. 130–136.

Chapter 7: Patriarchal Territories

1. Marcel Mauss, "Techniques of the Body," *Economy and Society* 2 (1973):73.

2. Pierre Bourdieu, *Outline of a Theory of Practice*, trans. Richard Nice (Cambridge: Cambridge University Press, 1977), 94.

3. Ibid., 95.

4. M. Bakhtin, *Rabelais and His World*, trans. Helene Iswolsky (Cambridge, Mass.: MIT. Press, 1968).

5. Norbert Elias, *The History of Manners*, vol. 1 of *The Civilizing Process*, trans. E. Jephcott (New York: Pantheon, 1978).

6. Ibid., xiv.

7. Ibid., 80.

8. Ibid., 145.

9. F. A. Youngs, Jr. *The Proclamations of the Tudor Queens* (Cambridge: Cambridge University Press, 1976), 163, 164.

10. Bourdieu, *Outline of a Theory*, 95.

11. Youngs, *The Proclamations*, 167.

12. William Gouge, *Of Domesticall Duties* (London, 1622), 345, 284.

13. William Whately, *A Bride-Bush* (London, 1617), 36.

14. Ibid., 43.

15. Robert Snawsel, *A Looking Glasse for Married Folkes*, quoted in Kathleen M. Davies, "The Sacred Condition of Equality—How Original Were Puritan Doctrines of Marriage?," *Social History* 5 (1977):567.

16. Bakhtin, *Rabelais*, 26.

17. Ralph Houlbrooke, *Church Courts and the People during the English Reformation, 1520–1570* (Oxford: Oxford University Pess, 1979), 80.

18. Benedetto Varchi, *The Blazon of Jealousie*, trans. R. Toste (London, 1615), 28.

19. Francesco Barbaro, *On Wifely Duties,* trans. B. G. Kohl, in *The Earthly Republic: Italian Humanists on Government and Society*, ed. B. G. Kohl, R. E. Witt, with E. B. Welles (Pennsylvania: University of Pennsylvania Press, 1978), 205.

20. Samuel Rowlands, *Uncollected Poems (1603–1617)*, intro. by F. O. Waage, Jr. (Gainesville: Scholars' Press, 1970), 102.

21. Quoted in Jean Seznec, *The Survival of the Pagan Gods* (Princeton: Princeton University Press, 1972), 101. Seznec also quotes Alciati's imitator, La Perrière, who wrote in *Emblèmes* (ed. 1599):

> La tortue dit que femme n'aille loing.
> Le doigt levé, qu'à parler ne s'avance,
> La clef en main dénote qu'avoir soing
> Doibt sur les biens du mary par prudence. (p. 102)

22. See V. G. Kiernan, "Private Property in History," in *Family and Inheritance: Rural Society in Western Europe, 1200–1800*, ed. J Goody, J. Thirsk, and E. P. Thompson (Cambridge: Cambridge University Press, 1976), 367.

23. *The Laws Respecting Women*, foreword by S. R. Bysiewicz (New York: Oceana Publications, 1974), 65.

24. Varchi, *The Blazon*, 19.

25. C. Marlowe, *The Massacre at Paris*, 4.5.4–9, in *Christopher Marlowe: The Complete Plays*, ed. J. B. Steane (Harmondsworth: Penguin, 1969), 568–69.

26. Wye Saltonstall, *Picturae Loquentes* (Oxford: Blackwell, 1946), 8.

27. Ibid., 8

28. Ibid., 1.

29. Roy Strong, *Portraits of Queen Elizabeth I* (Oxford: Clarendon Press, 1963), 75–76 and plate XV.

30. Ibid., plate E32.

31. Victor Morgan, "The Cartographic Image of the Country in Early Modern England," *Transactions of the Royal Historical Society*, fifth series, 29 (1979):134, 136–37.

32. Quoted in Stuart Clark, "Inversion, Misrule and the Meaning of Witchcraft," *Past and Present* 87 (1980):107.

33. *An Order for Prayer and Thanksgiving (necessary to be used in these dangerous times)* (London, 1594), sig. A4.

34. Mary Douglas, *Purity and Danger* (London: Routledge and Kegan Paul, 1969), 35.

35. Quoted in Clark, "Inversion," 117.

36. Nicholas Breton, "Elogy of Queen Elizabeth" in *A Mad World By Masters*, vol. 2, ed. U. Kentish-Wright (London: Cresset, 1929), 5, 7.

37. See A. Bartlett Giamatti, *The Earthly Paradise and the Renaissance Epic* (Princeton: Princeton University Press, 1969), 11.

38. John King, *The Fourth Sermon Preached at Hampton Court* (London, 1606), 4.

39. J. A. Sharpe, "The History of Crime in Late Medieval and Early Modern England: A Review of the Field," *Social History* 7 (1982):200.

40. For an analysis of the relation of *imperium* to *dominium*, see Gordon J. Schochet, *Patriarchalism and Political Thought: The Authoritarian Family and Political Speculation and Attitudes* (Oxford: Blackwell, 1975), passim.

41. See Jean Bodin, *The Sixe Bookes of a Commonweale*, trans. R. Knolles (1606), reprinted ed. Kenneth D. McRae (Cambridge, Mass.: Harvard University Press, 1962) and Sir Robert Filmer, *Patriarcha and Other Political Works*, ed. Peter Laslett (Oxford: Blackwell, 1969).

42. Filmer, *Patriarcha*, 229.

43. John Aylmer, *An Harborowe for Faithfull and Trewe Subjects*, quoted in Schochet, *Patriarchalism*, 45.

44. Edmund Tilney, *A Brief and Pleasant Discourse of Duties in Mariage* (London, 1568), sig. E1.

45. Joel Samaha, "Gleanings from Local Criminal-Court Records: Sedition Amongst the 'Inarticulate' in Elizabethan Essex," *The Journal of Social History* 8 (1975):69.

46. F. Bacon, "On the Fortunate Memory of Elizabeth. . . ." and Sir John Harrington, *The Letters. . . .*, both quoted in Stephen Greenblatt, *Renaissance Self-Fashioning: From More to Shakespeare* (Chicago: University of Chicago Press, 1980), 166, 169.

47. Shirley Ardener, "Introduction: The Nature of Woman in Society," in *Defining Females*, ed. S. Ardener (New York: John Wiley, 1978), 41.

48. Quotations from *The Duchess of Malfi* and *The White Devil* are from *The Works of John Webster*, ed F. L. Lucas (Oxford: Oxford University Press, 1937).

49. Joan Kelly-Gadol, "Did Women Have a Renaissance?" in *Becoming Visible: Women in European History*, ed. Renate Bridenthal and Claudia Koonz (Boston: Houghton Mifflin, 1977), 159.

50. Thomas Coryat, *Coryats Crudities* (London, 1611), sig. a4.

51. Kenneth Burke, "Othello: An Essay to Illustrate a Method," *The Hudson Review* 4 (1951):166–67. But see also Stephen Greenblatt's fine essay, "The Improvisation of Power," in *Renaissance Self-Fashioning*.

52. Ibid., 181.

53. Francis Thynne, *Emblemes and Epigrames*, ed. F. J. Furnivall (London: N. Trübner, 1876), 35.

54. All quotations from *Othello* are from *The Riverside Shakespeare*, ed. G. Blakemore Evans et al. (Boston: Houghton Mifflin, 1974).

55. Susan Snyder, "*Othello* and the Conventions of Romantic Comedy," *Renaissance Drama*, n.s, 5 (1972):128.

56. J. L. Vives, "The Instruction of a Christian Woman," trans. Richard Hyrde, in *Vives and the Renascence Education of Women*, ed. Foster Watson (London: Edward Arnold, 1912), 114.

57. Ruth Kelso, *Doctrine for the Lady of the Renaissance* (Urbana: University of Illinois Press, 1956), 24.

58. E. Le Roy Ladurie, *Carnival in Romans*, trans. Mary Feeney (New York: George Braziller, 1979), 214.

59. Ibid., 254.

60. Ibid., 223–24.

61. Burke, *Othello*, 185.

62. Bourdieu, *Outline of a Theory*, 170.

63. See Ian Maclean, *The Renaissance Notion of Woman* (Cambridge: Cambridge University Press, 1980), 28–46; Hilda Smith, "Gynecology and Ideology in Seventeenth-Century England," in *Liberating Women's History*, ed. Berenice A. Carroll (Urbana: University of Illinois Press, 1976).

64. H. Krämer and J. Sprenger, *Malleus Maleficarum*, in *Witchcraft in Europe 1100–1700: A Documentary History*, ed. A. C. Kors and E. Peters (Philadelphia: 1972), 121.

65. Natalie Zemon Davis, "Women on Top: Symbolic Sexual Inversion and Political Disorder in Early Modern Europe," in *The Reversible World*, ed. Barbara B. Babcock (Ithaca: Cornell University Press, 1978), 154, 155.

66. Ibid., 177, 179, 176. For "Lady Skimmington," see also Buchanan Sharp, *In Contempt of all Authority: Rural Artisans in the West of England 1586–1660* (Berkeley: University of California Press, 1980), 97–105.

67. Bakhtin, *Rabelais*, 26.

Chapter 8: The Other and the Same

1. Francois Rabelais, *Gargantua*, édition critique V. L. Saulnier, Textes Littéraires Français (Geneva, Droz, 1970), p. 60. In other editions this is considered chapter 8. For all translations of Rabelais in this text, see J. M. Cohen, *The Histories of Gargantua and Pantagruel* (New York: Penguin Books, 1955).

2. See Jerome Schwartz, "Scatology and Eschatology in Gargantua's Androgyne Device," *ER* 14 (1977): 265–75. For Erasmus's letter see Johan Huizinga, *Eramus and the Age of Reformation* (New York: Harper & Row, 1957), p. 248.

3. See M. A. Screech, "Emblems and Colours: The Controversy over Gargantua's Coulours and Devices (*Gargantu* 8, 9, 10)," in *Mélanges d'histoire du XVIe siècle, offerts à Henri Meylan* (Lausanne: Bibliothèque historique vaudoise, 1970), pp. 65–80. Also Nan Cooke Carpenter, "Rabelais and the Androgyne" in *MLN* 68 (1953): 452–57. Jerome Schwartz, in an article called "Aspects of Androgyny in the Renaissance" in *Human Sexuality in the Middle Ages and the Renaissance*, ed. D. Radcliff-Umstead (Pittsburgh: Center for Medieval and Renaissance Studies, University of Pittsburgh, 1978), pp. 121–31, remarks: "The medallion may then be interpreted as a fusion of two apparently irreconcilable opposites: sexual love and Pauline charity. Here again a Renaissance writer chooses the Androgyne theme as the vehicle for the synthesis of contraries, reconciling fleshly *eros* and Pauline *agape*. What greater expression of Renaissance optimism than this?" (p. 125).

4. Thomas M. Greene, *Rabelais: A Study In Comic Courage* (Englewood Cliffs, N.J.: Prentice-Hall, 1970), p. 39.

5. Plato, *The Collected Dialogues, Including the Letters*, ed. E. Hamilton and H. Cairns (Princeton, N.J.: Princeton University Press, 1961); "Symposium," p. 542 (189e–190).

6. Schwartz, "Scatology and Eschatology," pp. 265–275.

7. Raymond Marcel, ed. and trans., *Marsile Ficin: Sur le Banquet de Platon ou de l'Amour* (Paris: les Belles Lettres, 1956), p. 169 (Latin text). For the English translation see S. R. Jayne, *Marsilio Ficino's Commentary On Plato's Symposium* (Columbia: University of Missouri Press, 1944), p. 155.

8. Schwartz, "Scatology and Eschatology", pp. 271–72.

9. Plato, *Collected Dialogues*, p. 545 (193a). The comic fable narrated by Aristophanes turns out to be tragic after all, describing a humanity without recourse to hope for transcendence. This, perhaps, is the meaning of Socrates' argument at the end of the *Symposium* (223d): "Socrates was forcing them to admit that the same man might be capable of writing both comedy and tragedy . . ."

10. Schwartz, "Scatology and Eschatology," p. 275.

11. Ibid., p. 273. See also note 32.

12. For examples of the positive symbolic value accorded the androgyne, see Mircea Eliade, *Mephistopheles and the Androgyne*, trans. J. M. Cohen (New York: Sheed and Ward, 1965), esp. pp. 103–17. See also C. G. Jung, *Mysterium Coniunctionis: An Inquiry into the Separation and Synthesis of Psychic Opposites in Alchemy*, trans. R. F. C. Hull (Princeton, N.J.: Princeton University Press, 1970). Examples of hermaphroditism as a derogatory concept can be found in Plato, Ovid, and Dante (as cited in the text) as well as in contemporary contexts, such as *Herculine Barbin: Being the Recently Discovered Memoirs of a 19th Century French Hermaphrodite*, trans. R. McDougall, intro.

Michel Foucault (New York: Pantheon Books, 1980), and Anais Nïn, *Delta of Venus: Erotica* (New York: Bantam Books, 1978), "Artists and Models", pp. 35–59.

13. Publius Ovidius Naso, *Metamorphoses*, vol. 1 (Cambridge: Harvard University Press, 1971), book 4, lines 315–88.

14. Ibid., book 4, lines 375–79. For the English translation, see Rolfe Humphries, *Ovid: Metamorphoses* (Bloomington: Indiana University Press, 1972), p. 93.

15. Ibid., book 4, lines 380–86; Humphries, p. 93

16. Giovanni di Garlandia, *Integumenta Ovidii*, ed. Fausto Ghisaberti (Messina-Milano, 1933); Petro Berchiori, "Ovidius Metamorphoseos Moralizatus", in *Studii Romanzi* vol. 23 (Roma, 1933), pp. 87–132; Johannus de Virgilio, "Allegorie Librorum Ovidii Metamorphoseos," in *Giornale Dantesco*, appendix.

17. Dante Alighieri, *Il Purgatorio*, in *The Divine Comedy*, vol. 2, ed. and trans. John D. Sinclair, ed. and trans. (New York: Oxford University Press, 1961), pp. 340–41, lines 82–84.

18. Marie Delcourt, *Hermaphrodite: mythes et rites de la bisexualité dans l'antiquité classique* (Paris: P.G.F., 1958), p. 68: "L'androgyne occupe les deux pôles du sacré. Pur concept, pure vision de l'esprit, elle apparaît chargée des plus hautes valeurs. Actualisée en un être de chair et de sang, elle est une monstruosité, et rien de plus." Eliade, *Mephistopheles and the Androgyne*, says, "if a child showed at birth any signs of hermaphroditism, it was killed by its own parents. In other words, the actual, anatomical hermaphrodite was considered an aberration . . . Only the ritual androgyne provided a model, because it implied not an augmentation of anatomical organs but, symbolically, the union of the magicoreligious powers belonging to both sexes" (p. 100).

19. Michel de Montaigne, *Essais, Livre I*, ed. A. Micha (Paris: Garnier-Flammarion, 1969), pp. 239 and 241. All translations will be taken from Donald M. Frame, *The Complete Essays of Montaigne* (Stanford, Calif.: Stanford University Press, 1965).

20. Plato, *Collected Dialogues*, "Symposium," p. 544, 191–92e.

21. Ida Nelson, *La sottie sans souci: essai d'interprétation homosexuelle* (Paris: Honoré Champion, 1977), p. 38.

22. Ibid.

23. Frédéric Godefroy, *Lexique de l'ancien francais* (Paris: Honoré Champion, 1971), p. 536.

24. Nelson, *La sottie sans souci*, pp. 169, 171, 190. See, for example, under the lexical entry "Teste Verte ou Teste Creuse ou Teste Ligière," where the proximity of the words *teste* and *verte* or *vert* may be seen to constitute a homosexual word game (p. 169). Nelson also suggests that the reference to thirst in the name "Pantagruel" carries homosexual connotations.

25. Ibid., p. 242. For a study of word play, particularly homophonic wordplay, in the Middle Ages, see Roger Dragonetti, *La vie de la lettre au moyen age (Le Conte du Graal)* (Paris: Seuil, 1980). Although we might expect more homophony in an oral culture than in the sixteenth century, an argument can be made for the persistence of certain characteristics of such an oral culture in Renaissance texts. On this subject consult Elizabeth Eisenstein, *The Printing Press as an Agent of Change: Communications and Cultural Transformation in Early-Modern Europe*, 2 vols. (Cambridge: At the university press, 1979), especially the introduction.

26. See Rabelais, *Pantagruel*, ed. V. L. Saulnier, chap. 14, p. 115. I have discussed these chapters in two articles: "Damning Haughty Dames: Panurge and the Haulte Dame de Paris (*Pantagruel* 14)," *Journal of Medieval and Renaissance Studies* 15 (1, Spring 1985): 57–67; and "The 'Instance' of the Letter in *Pantagruel* 15: Woman in the Text of Rabelais," *French Forum*, "The Incomparable Book: Rabelais and His Art" (Lexington: University Presses of Kentucky, forthcoming).

27. Michel Beaujour, *Le Jeu de Rabelais* (Paris: Herne, n.d.); see chap. 5, "Thélème," pp. 89–106.

28. I have treated the problem of Thélème as utopia more extensively in "Rabelais's 'Abbaye de Thélème': Utopia as Supplement," *Esprit Créateur* 25 (1, Spring 1985):73–87.

29. *Gargantua* (T.L.F.), chap. 55, pp. 304–5.

30. See M. A. Screech, *The Rabelaisian Marriage: Aspects of Rabelais's Religion, Ethics, and Comic Philosophy* (London: Edward Arnold, 1958).

31. See M. A. Screech, édition critique, *Le Tiers Livre* (Geneva: Droz, 1964), chaps. 30, 31, 32, and *Le Quart Livre*, ed. R. Marichal (Geneva: Droz, 1947), chaps. 18–25. For an excellent study of the theory of woman in the Renaissance, see Ian Maclean, *The Renaissance Notion of Woman, A Study in the Fortunes of Scholasticism and Medical science in European Intellecutal Life* (Cambridge: Cambridge University Press, 1980).

32. *Essais*, book 1, p. 234.

33. Ibid., p. 236.

34. V. L. Saulnier, ed., *Pantagruel*, chap. 9, p. 54.

35. Ultimately, the explicit rendering in Montaigne's text of some of the erotic problems submerged in Rabelais's figure, thus in retrospect illuminating the latter's semiotic obscurity, may point to a more generalized and symptomatic effacement (or silencing) of women in Renaissance discourse. This is a suggestion for further exploration and elaboration.

36. Plato, *Collected Dialogues*, "Symposium." See pp. 560–61, 290a–e.

37. Montaigne, *Essais*, book 1, pp. 236 and 237.

38. See K. Rahner and H. Vorgrimler, *Dictionary of Theology*, 2d ed. (New York: Crossroad, 1981), p. 65: "Charity."

39. *The Holy Bible*, King James version, I Corinthians 11:3–10.

40. Ibid., 14:34.

41. See Shoshana Felman's commentary on Luce Irigaray in "Women and Madness: The Critical Phallacy", *Diacritics* (Winter 1975), pp. 2–10. She notes that: "Theoretically subordinated to the concept of masculinity, the woman is viewed by man as *his* opposite, that is to say, as *his* other, the negative of the positive, and not, in her own right, different, other, Otherness itself. Throughout the Platonic metaphors which will come to dominate Western discourse and to act as a vehicle for meaning, Luce Irigaray points out a latent design to exclude the woman from the production of speech, since the woman, and the Other as such are philosophically subjugated to the logical principle of Identity—Identity being conceived as a solely *masculine* sameness, apprehended as *male* self-presence and consciousness-to-itself. The possibility of a thought which would neither spring from nor return to this masculine Sameness is simply unthinkable" (p. 3).

42. One is tempted to see in the passage an imaginative emblem of Lacan's Imaginary, with man caught in the mirror-phase of self-contemplation. See Jacques Lacan, *Ecrits I* (Paris: Seuil, 1966), pp. 83–97, "Le stade du miroir comme formateur de la fonction du Je."

Chapter 9: Usurpation, Seduction, and the Problematics of the Proper

1. Although virtually all of Derrida's writing is concerned with a critique of the discourses of Western philosophical thought, the metaphor of violence is used most extensively, to describe the operations of signification and reference in relation to political domination, in an essay on Claude Lévi-Strauss's *Tristes Tropiques* entitled "La violence de la lettre: de Lévi-Strauss à Rousseau." See Jacques Derrida, *De la grammatologie* (Paris: Les éditions de Minuit, 1967), pp. 149–202. For the English translation from which I shall quote in my text see "The Violence of the Letter: From Levi-Strauss to Rousseau" in *Of Grammatology*, trans. Gayatri Chakravorty Spivak (Baltimore: Johns Hopkins University Press, 1976), pp. 101–40. Two more essays by Derrida, in problematizing the notion of "man" as it has been used to ground various humanisms, are highly pertinent to subsequent deconstructive attempts to investigate the notion of "woman": "Les fins de l'homme" and "signature événement contexte" in *Marges de la philosophie* (Paris: Les éditions de Minuit, 1972), pp. 129–64 and 365–93. These two essays appear in English as "The Ends of Man" and "Signature Event Context" in *Margins of Philosophy*, trans. Alan Bass (Chicago: University of Chicago Press, 1982), pp. 109–36 and

307–30. "Les fins de l'homme" briefly renews the investigation of the structural solidarity of military and economic violence with "linguistic violence" (p. 162 in French; 135 in English).

"Woman" is demarcated from "man" by Derrida, and her discursive position investigated, in *Spurs: Nietzsche's Styles / Eperons: Les styles de Nietzsche.* trans. Barbara Harlow (Chicago: University of Chicago Press, 1979) and in an interview conducted with Derrida by Christie V. McDonald: "Choreographies," *Diacritics* 12 (no. 2, 1982): 66–76. Two French feminist theoreticians, Hélène Cixous and Luce Irigaray, draw especially fruitfully upon deconstructive thought. The excerpts from their work in Elaine Marks and Isabelle de Courtivron, eds., *New French Feminism: An Anthology* (Amherst: University of Massachusetts press, 1980; Shocken Books, 1981) provide good representative examples. The feminist theoretician who has most forcefully argued the case, however, is Gayatri Chakravorty Spivak, whose critique of Derrida's *Spurs* greatly informs my account in this paper of the difficulties involved in deriving a feminist approach from deconstruction. See her "Displacement and the Discourse of Woman," in *Displacement: Derrida and After,* ed. Mark Krupnick (Bloomington: Indiana University Press, 1983), pp. 169–95.

2. Spivak, "Displacement and the Discourse of Woman," passim.

3. Derrida, *Spurs,* pp. 59–65 and 103–5.

4. Spivak, "Displacement," pp. 170 and 173–74.

5. Ibid., p. 184. The term "missed encounter," however, is drawn from Shoshana Felman, *The Literary Speech Act: Don Juan with J. L. Austin, or Seduction in Two Languages,* trans. Catherine Porter (Ithaca, N.Y.: Cornell University Press, 1983), p. 85. Felman's splendid treatment of language and seduction includes a reading of Molière's *Don Juan* parallel at several points to my reading of *Richard III,* though the two readings have very different points of departure. It was first published in French as *Le scandale du corps parlant: Don Juan avec Austin ou la séduction en deux langues* (Paris: Editions du Seuil, 1980).

6. Felman, pp. 76–77.

7. Ibid., p. 77.

8. These epithets and phrases are cited from the following critical studies: In order—Larry S. Champion, "Myth and Counter-Myth: The Many Faces of Richard III," in *A Fair Day in the Affections: Literary Essays in Honor of Robert B. White, Jr.,* ed. Jack D. Durant and M. Thomas Hester (Raleigh, N. C.: Winston Press, 1980), p. 50; Richard P. Wheeler, "History, Character and Conscience in *Richard III,*" *Comparative Drama* 5 (Spring 1971): 320 and 319, respectively; William B. Toole, "The Motif of Psychic Division in 'Richard III' " in *Shakespeare Survey: An Annual Survey of Shakespearian Study and Production,* vol. 27, ed. Kenneth Muir (Cambridge: At the university press, 1974), p. 25; R. G. Moulton, *Shakespeare as a Dramatic Artist*

(Oxford, 1893), p. 96, and A. P. Rossiter, "Angel with Horns: The Unity of Richard III," in *Angel with Horns and Other Shakespearean Lectures* (London: Longmans, Green, 1961), p. 16, cited in Edward I. Berry, *Patterns of Decay: Shakespeare's Early Histories* (Charlottesville: University of Virginia, 1975), p. 77, identify Richard as artist and actor respectively; Rossiter "Angel with Horns," p. 15; E. M. W. Tillyard, *Shakespeare's History Plays* (New York: Macmillan Co., 1946), p. 211; Nicholas Brooke, *Shakespeare's Early Tragedies* (London, 1968) cited in Champion, "Myth and Counter-Myth," p. 51; Rossiter, "Angel with Horns," p. 21.

9. All citations from Shakespeare's *Richard III* are from *The Tragedy of King Richard the Third,* ed. William Aldis Wright (Oxford: Clarendon Press, 1880). Quotations are identified by act, scene, and line number in my text except for the women's epithets for Richard which, in order not to render my page unreadable, I list here as follows: 4.4.139; 1.3.246; 1.3.229; 1.2.147; 1.3.216, 289; 1.2.102; 1.3.144; 1.3.228; 1.3.242; 1.2.184; 1.3.221; 4.4.52–53.

10. Derrida, *De la grammatologie,* p. 149. *Of Grammatology,* p. 101.

11. Ibid., p. 164. English translation, p. 112.

12. In the French text: "Nommer, donner les noms qu'il sera éventuellement interdit de prononcer, telle est la violence originaire du langage qui consiste à inscrire dans une différence, à classer, à suspendre le vocatif absolu. Penser l'unique *dans* le système, l'y inscrire, tel est le geste de l'archi-écriture: archi-violence, perte du propre, de la proximité absolue, de la présence à soi, perte en vérité de ce qui n'a jamais eu lieu, d'une présence à soi qui n'a jamais été donné mais rêvée et toujours déjà dédoublée, répetée, incapable de s'apparaître autrement que dans sa propre disparition" (pp. 164–65).

13. In "signature évenement contexte" Derrida makes this point a little differently, focusing on language's iterability. See p. 375.

14. Derrida, *Of Grammatology,* p. 112. In the French text: "Elle révèle en effet la première nomination qui était déjà une expropriation, mais elle dénude aussi ce qui des lors faisait fonction de propre" (p. 165).

15. Ibid., p. 165. English translation, p. 112.

16. Francesco Petrarca, *Canzoniere,* ed. Gianfranco Contini (Torino: Giulio Einaudi editore, 1968), p. 3. I quote, and Richard nearly quotes, line 11 of the opening sonnet.

17. For an extensive treatment of the theoretical understanding of the self as a linguistic construct as it is implicitly and explicitly worked out in the *Canzoniere,* see my book, *Petrarch's Poetics and Literary History* (Amherst: University of Massachusetts Press, 1980).

18. Madonne M. Miner, " 'Neither mother, wife, nor England's queen': The Roles of Women in Richard III," in *The Woman's Part: Feminist Criticism of Shakespeare,* ed. Carolyn Ruth Swift Lenz, Gayle

Greene, and Carol Thomas Neely (Urbana: University of Illinois Press, 1980), p. 35, and Irene G. Dash, *Wooing, Wedding, and Power: Women in Shakespeare's Plays* (New York: Columbia University Press, 1981), esp. pp. 196–98, but her entire chapter "The Paradox of Power: The *Henry VI–Richard III* Tetralogy," which focuses on Margaret, creates a powerful sense of the difference it makes and has made to read or receive this play in its usual lopsided form, with the female voices consciously or unconsciously suppressed. Other books and articles that focus on female characters in *Richard III* include Juliet Dusinberre, *Shakespeare and the Nature of Women* (London: Macmillan, 1975); Harold Brooks, "Unhistorical Amplifications: The Women's Scenes and Seneca," *Modern Language Review* 75 (October 1980): 721–37; Carole McKewin, "Shakespeare Liberata: Shakespeare, the Nature of Women, and the New Feminist Criticism," *Mosaic* 10 (Spring 1977): 157–64.

19. I am, of course, alluding again to the Marks and de Courtivron anthology.

20. Murray Krieger, "The Dark Generations of Richard III," in *The Design Within: Psychoanalytic Approaches to Shakespeare,"* ed. M. D. Faber (New York: Science House, 1970), p. 365–66.

21. Coppélia Kahn, *Man's Estate: Masculine Identity in Shakespeare* (Berkeley and Los Angeles: University of California Press, 1981), pp. 47–66 passim.

22. See Champion, "Myth and Counter-Myth," p. 52 and Wheeler, "History, Character, and Conscience in Richard III," p. 320 for presentations of "The Tudor myth of history" and "a divine moral plan" respectively. See also Berry, *Patterns of Decay,* p. 93 for a literary hisorical reading of Richard's role as analogous to that of the Antichrist, and Krieger, "The Dark Generations of Richard III," p. 364, for a sophisticated discussion of "the deadly weight of history" as a force opposed to Richard, a position that still, to my mind, dissimulates the connection between Richard's self-making and the play's performance of that self's undoing—the point being that the making and the unmaking may be seen as two ways of looking at the same thing.

23. This is the one point at which I take exception to Madonne Miner's otherwise groundbreaking article. See esp. Miner, "The Rules of Women in Richard III," p. 48. Our difference on this matter re-enacts one of the fundamental divergences between continental European and American feminism. For one of several good accounts of this quarrel, see Alice Jardine, "Gynesis," *Diacritics* 12 (no. 2): 54–65.

24. Richard's deformity, in other words, is *not* the ground for his actions that he comes to claim that it is. Its meaning for him is determined by the fundamental rhetorical operations I have just been

detailing. Biological destiny is no more determining in his case than it is in women's. The use that he makes of his hump, if that's what it is, is wonderfully consistent with his sexism.

25. For accounts of the tradition of reading scene 2 as credible or not, see esp. Berry, *Patterns of Decay,* pp. 73–78. See also Denzell S. Smith, "The credibility of the Wooing of Anne in Richard III," *Papers on Language and Literature* 7 (Spring 1971): 199–202; and Donald R. Shupe, "The Wooing of Lady Anne: A Psychological Inquiry," *Shakespeare Quarterly* 29 (1978): 28–36. Aside from its introductory remarks, the Shupe article is an account of a modern psychology experiment suggested to the author by Shakespeare's text.

26. The view that scene 2 displays Richard's brilliance is relatively ubiquitous, as I have mentioned (See above, n. 8). For a slightly different reading of the nature of his manipulativeness, see Phillip Mallet, "Shakespeare's Trickster-Kings: Richard III and Henry V," in *The Fool and the Trickster: Studies in Honour of Enid Welsford,* ed. Paul V. A. Williams and D. S. Brewer (Cambridge: Rowman and Littlefield, 1970), pp. 64–82.

27. V. N. Volosinov in *Marxism and the Philosophy of Language,* trans. Ladislav Matejka and I. R. Titunik (New York: Seminar Press, 1973) generalizes that "Language reflects, not subjective, psychological vacillations, but stable social interrelations among speakers" (p. 118). His discussion of the "real unit of language" as "not the individual, isolated monologic utterance but the interaction of at least two utterances—in a word, dialogue" (p. 117) accords suggestively with my understanding of the subversion in scene 2 of the notion (held by its two dramatic personae, among others) that its language represents two separate subjectivities.

Chapter 10. The Beauty of Woman

1. L. B. Alberti, *On Painting and Sculpture,* ed. and trans. C. Grayson (London: Phaidon, 1972), pp. 60–63 (*On Painting,* bk. 2, pp. 25–26).

2. *Lucian,* Loeb Classical Library, trans. A. M. Harmon, 8 vols. (London: W. Heinemann, 1925), 4:257–95. The dialogue opens by doubling the paradoxical play on the rival claims of words and images when Lycinus states that the woman he has seen is so beautiful that she strikes the viewer dumb.

3. Alberti, *On Painting and Sculpture,* pp. 94–97.

4. H. Wethey, *The Paintings of Titian; vol 2, The Portraits* (London: Phaidon, 1971), pp. 95f., no. 27. This is obviously the kind of portrait Catherine de' Medici had in mind when, on receiving a portrait of Elizabeth I, she observed that if the queen were as beautiful as she had heard, then she needed the service of better painters.

5. P. Rossi, *L'Opera completa del Parmigianino,* Classici dell'Arte Rizzoli, 101 (Milan: Rizzoli, 1980), p. 102, no. 55.

6. See S. J. Freedberg, *Parmigianino, His Works in Painting* (Cambridge: Harvard University Press, 1950), pp. 214f., for the possible interpretation of Barri's description of "L'innamorata, chiamata l'Antea del Parmigianino," to mean that she was both the courtesan and the painter's mistress. Freedberg provides a summary of the continuing debate over her identity, but his own argument that she cannot be Antea (because at the time Antea was older than she appears in the painting and because Parmigianino could not have had her sit for him) does not settle the matter. On p. 120 he agrees that the figure represented would be the sort of woman of whom Parmigianino could have been the lover.

7. This is the case, for example, with the traditional interpretation of Raphael's portraits of *La Fornarina,* and *La Donna Velata.* For an important discussion of these works (and others associated with this tradition), see D. A. Brown and K. Oberhuber, "*Monna Vanna* and *Fornarina:* Leonardo and Raphael in Rome," *Essays Presented to Myron P. Gilmore,* ed. S. Bertelli and G. Ramakus, 2 vols., Villa I Tatti Monographs (Florence: La Nuova Italia 1977), 2: 25–86.

8. Wethey, *The Paintings of Titian,* pp. 81f., no. 14. On 2 May, 1536, the Duke wrote "direte al Titiano . . . che quel'retratto di quella Donna che ha la veste azura, desideriamo che la finisca bella circa il Tutto et con il Timpano," for which see D. von Hadeln, "Zum Datum der Bella Tizians," *Repertorium fur Kunstwissenschaft,* 32 (1909): 69–71.

9. J. Pope-Hennessy, *The Portrait in the Renaissance,* the A. W. Mellon Lectures in the Fine Arts, Bollingen Series 35, vol. 12 (Princeton, N.J.: Princeton University Press), p. 144.

10. Wethey, *The Paintings of Titian,* p. 23. He also draws attention to the popular view that Eleanora Gonzaga della Rovere, duchess of Urbino, modeled for the *Venus of Urbino* and for the so-called *Girl in the Fur Coat.* While dismissing this tradition, he does believe that the latter subject was the model for the former.

11. Wethey, *The Paintings of Titian,* pp. 106f., no. 48, states "It is generally thought that *La Bella* and the *Venus of Urbino* represent the same model." Elsewhere, on p. 23, however, he seems to challenge the identification of her with *La Bella* because he finds the latter more beautiful. In the sale of Charles I's collection, as Wethey records, the *Girl in the Fur Coat* was called "Tytzians Mrs after Ye Life by Tytsian."

12. C. Hope, *Titian* (London: Jupiter Books, 1980), pp. 81f.

13. Ibid., p. 82.

14. B. Castiglione, *The Book of the Courtier,* trans. C. Singleton (Garden City, N.Y.: Doubleday, 1959), pp. 81–83.

15. *Rime*, 77 and 78. Neroccio de' Landi's *Portrait of a Young Woman*, National Gallery of Art, Washington, D. C., and Domenico Ghirlandaio's *Giovanna degli Albizzi*, Sammlung Thyssen-Bornemisza, Lugano, should be considered in the context of these sonnets.

16. The Narcissus myth also lies at the heart of Petrarch's ahistorical performative rhetoric, for which see, e.g., M. R. Waller, *Petrarch's Poetics and Literary History* (Amherst: University of Massachusetts Press, 1980), pp. 93–104. I would propose that the whole issue of the problematization of "I" that Waller raises in the context of Petrarch lies at the heart of many Renaissance portraits of beautiful women. For the case of Leonardo da Vinci's portrait of Ginevra de' Benci see below.

17. *Rime*, 19 and 20, in P. Bembo, *Prose e Rime*, ed. C. Dionisotti (Turin: UTET, 1966), pp. 521f. Lorenzo de' Medici also writes in response to the two sonnets by Petrarch in his *Rime*, 29, 70 and 71, and his contribution to the modification of the problem, alluded to below, is a significant one that requires a lengthier discussion than is possible here.

18. For Petrarch's legacy of fragmentation with specific reference to this, see N. J. Vickers, "Diana Described: Scattered Woman and Scattered Rhyme," *Critical Inquiry* 8 (1981): 265–79.

19. G. Pozzi, "Il ritratto della donna nella poesia d'inizio Cinquecento e la pittura di Giorgione," *Lettere Italiane* 31 (1979): 3–30. Pozzi in turn refers to my "On Beautiful Women. Parmigianino, *Petrarchismo*, and the Vernacular Style," *The Art Bulletin* 58 (1976): 374–94. Pozzi concentrates on the short form of the description of female beauty provided by lyric poetry, whereas I also discuss the influence of the extended *effictio* of the romance. The two are intimately connected, but in this paper I too have chosen to concentrate on the *paragone* arising out of painting's response to lyric metaphor.

20. Pozzi, "Il Ritratto della donna," pp. 23f. For the various identifications of the sitter see Pozzi, n. 6, and Pope-Hennessy, *The Portrait in the Renaissance*, p. 226.

21. Pozzi, pp. 23f., n.6; see also H. Wethey, *The Paintings of Titian*, vol. 3, *The Mythological and Historical Paintings* (London: Phaidon, 1975), pp. 184f., no. 37, for further bibliography.

22. Pozzi, pp. 24f.

23. F. R. Shapley, *Catalogue of the Italian Paintings, National Gallery of Art*, 2 vols. (Washington, D. C., 1979), 1: 251–55, and J. Walker, "*Ginevra de' Benci* by Leonardo da Vinci," in *National Gallery of Art: Report and Studies in the History of Art*, 1967, pp. 1–38. Walker's identification is based on that by E. Möller, "Leonardos Bildnis der

Ginevra dei Benci," *Münchner Jahrbuch der bildenden Kunst* 12 (1937–38): 185–209.

24. *Rime,* 359.

25. Translation from R. Durling, *Petrarch's Lyric Poems* (Cambridge: Harvard University Press, 1976), p. 557.

26. On love and memory in the *Rime sparse* see the discussion by Durling, ibid., pp. 18–26.

27. The correspondingly inanimate, melancholy face of Ginevra has prompted a good deal of romantic explanation. Walker's study is no exception, but does, in fact, provide the material for an interpretation of the work in the context suggested here. This is in the form of the poems by Cristoforo Landino, Alessandro Braccesi, and Lorenzo de' Medici, variously addressed to the chaste, beloved Ginevra, and to Bernardo Bembo (who played Petrarch to Ginevra's Laura). In Landino's eighth poem, for example, *forma* and *decor* are the parents of Love, to which the noble heart of the virtuous Bembo must submit. In a remarkable inversion of the expected relationship between the lover-beholder and the beloved, Lorenzo likens Ginevra to Eurydice. In his interpretation of all this, however, Walker considers the portrait only in relation to its presumed historical context, not to the broader critical one.

28. See I. A. Richter, *Paragone: A Comparison of the Arts by Leonardo da Vinci* (London: Oxford University Press, 1949), for a discussion of the whole debate; see also, *Lionardo da Vinci: Das Buch von der Malerei nach dem Codex Vaticanus (Urbinas) 1270,* ed. H. Ludwig, 3 vols., Quellenschriften für Kunstgeschichte und Kunsttechnik des Mittelalters und der Renaissance (1822; repr. Osnabrück: O. Zeller, 1970), 1: 28, no. 18.

29. See, for example, Leonardo's statement, ibid., p. 31, no. 19: "Tolgasi un poeta, che descriva le bellezze di una donna al suo innamorato, e tolgasi un pittore, che la figuri, vedrassi, dove la natura volgera piu il giudicatore innamorato." Directly challenging the notion of the silence of the beautiful image, Leonardo also claims that paintings are understood "come se parlassino," for which see ibid., p. 30, no. 18.

30. *Rime,* 39, "Sonnetto fatto a piè d'una tavoletta dove era ritratta una donna."

31. For the writings of Firenzuola, Pino, Luigini, and others, see Cropper, "On Beautiful Women."

32. Benedetto Varchi, for example, read into Petrarch's and Bembo's sonnets a justification for the superiority of painting over sculpture, for which see his *Della Maggioranza e nobiltà delle arti, Disputa prima,* in *Trattati d'Arte del Cinquecento fra Manierismo e Controriforma,* ed. P. Barocchi, 3 vols. (Bari: Laterza, 1960), 1: 40.

33. *Dialogo della Pittura,* ed. P. Barocchi, ibid., pp. 172f.

34. L. Mendelsohn, *Paragoni: Benedetto Varchi's "Due Lezzioni" and Cinquecento Art Theory* (Ann Arbor: UMI Research Press, 1982).

Chapter 11: Spinsters and Seamstresses

The research for this paper was carried out in six archives in southern Germany and France—the city archives of Memmingen, Nuremberg, Frankfurt, Munich, and Strasbourg, and the Württemberg state archives in Stuttgart. As each archive has its own system of organizing material, I have given references in the form by which the items may be most easily found. Anyone familiar with the joys of working in archives will understand why these are not regular or systematic. All translations are my own. I am grateful to the Deutsche Akademische Austauschdienst and the American Council of Learned Societies for their support in this study.

Some of the material in this chapter originally appeared in *Working Women in Renaissance Germany,* copyright © 1986 by Rutgers, The State University.

1. Quoted in Luise Hess, *Die deutschen Frauenberufe des Mittelalters,* Beiträge zur Volkstumforschung, Bd. 6 (Munich: Neuer Filser, 1940), p. 11.

2. Georg Steinhausen, *Deutsche Privatbriefe des Mittelalters* (Berlin: Weidmann, 1907) pp. 57, 82, 125.

3. Karl Bücher, *Die Frauenfrage im Mittelalter* (Tübingen: Laupp, 1910), p. 69; Helmut Wachendorf, *Die wirtschaftliche Stellung der Frau in den deutschen Städten des späteren Mittelalters* (Quackenbrück: Trüte, 1934), pp. 147–48; Rudolph Wissell. *Das alten Handwerks Recht und Gewohnheit* (Berlin: Colloquium, 1971), p. 445; Sibylla Harksen, *Die Frau im Mittelalter* (Leipzig: Edition Leipzig, 1974), p. 28; Sheila Lewenhak, *Women and Work* (New York: St. Martin's Press, 1980), p. 112.

4. Alice Clark, *Working Life of Women in the Seventeenth Century* (London: Routledge, 1919); Hans Medick, "The proto-industrial family economy: the structural function of household and family during the transition from peasant society to industrial capitalism," *Social History* 1 (1976):291–315; W. Secombe, "The Housewife and Her Labour under Capitalism," *New Left Review* 83 (1974):3–24; Eli Zaretsky, *Capitalism, the Family and Personal Life* (New York: Harper & Row, 1976).

5. Clark, *Working Life of Women in the Seventeenth Century*; Martha Howell, "Women's Work in Urban Economies of Late Medieval Northwestern Europe: Female Labor Status in Male Economic Institutions," ph.D. dissertation, Columbia University, 1979; Judith Brown, "A Woman's Place Was in the Home; Woman's Work in Renaissance Tuscany," below in this volume.

6. Natalie Davis, "Women on Top," in her *Society and Culture in*

Early Modern France (Stanford, Calif.: Stanford University Press, 1965), p. 126. Also by Davis, "City Women and Religious Change", in ibid., p. 94. Joan Kelly, "Early Feminist Theory and the *Querelle des Femmes* 1400–1789," *Signs* 8 (no. 1, Autumn 1982): 23.

7. Frankfurt Stadtarchiv, Bürgermeisterbücher, 1600, fols. 50b, 81b; Memmingen Stadtarchiv, Ratsprotokollbücher, December 4, 1603; October 15, 1604; June 12, 1612; July 20, 1618; Munich Stadtarchiv, Ratsitzungsprotokolle, 1608, fol. 238.

8. Joan Kelly-Gadol, "Did Women Have a Renaissance?" in *Becoming Visible: Women in European History,* ed. Renate Bridenthal and Claudia Koorz (New York: Houghton Mifflin, 1977), pp. 137–64; Eric Midelfort, *Witchhunting in Southwestern Germany, 1562–1684* (Stanford, Calif.: Stanford University Press, 1972); Donald Kelley, *The Beginning of Ideology* (Cambridge: At the university press 1981); Ian MacLean, *The Renaissance Notion of Woman* (Cambridge: Cambridge University Press, 1980); Margaret King, "Thwarted Ambitions: Six Learned Women of the Italian Renaissance," *Soundings* 59 (no. 3, 1976): 284.

9. Kelly-Gadol, "Did Women Have a Renaissance?" p. 160.

10. Olwen Hufton, "Women and the Family Economy in 18th Century France," *French Historical Studies* 9 (1975): 1–23; Louise Tilly and Joan Scott, *Women, Work and Family* (Chicago: University of Chicago Press, 1978).

11. Natalie Davis, "Women in the Crafts in Sixteenth-Century Lyon," *Feminist Studies* 8 (no. 1, Spring 1982): 47–80; Lyndal Roper, "Urban Women and the Household Workshop Form of Production: Augsburg 1500–1550," (unpublished paper); Susan Karant-Nunn, "Continuity and Change: Some Effects of the Reformation on the Women of Zwickau," *Sixteenth Century Journal* 12 (no. 2, 1982): 17–42; Grethe Jacobsen, "Women's Work and Women's Role: Ideology and Reality in Danish Urban Society, 1300–1550," *Scandinavian Economic History Review* 31 (no. 1 1983): 3–20; Heide Wunder, "Zur Stellung der Frau im Arbeitsleben und in der Gesellschaft des 15.–18. Jahrhundert: Eine Skizze," *Geschichtsdidaktik* 3 (1981): 239–51; Judith Brown and Jordan Goodman, "Women and Industry in Florence," *Journal of Economic History* 40 (1980): 73–80. Merry E. Wiesner, "Paltry peddlers or essential merchants? Women in the distributive trades in Early Modern Nuremberg," *Sixteenth Century Journal* 9 (no. 2. Summer 1981): 3–14.

12. Karl Bücher, *Die Berufe der Stadt Frankfurt im Mittelalter* (Leipzig: B.G. Teubner, 1914).

13. Munich Stadtarchiv, Steuerbücher, 1410–1500.

14. Annette Winter, "Studien zur sozialen Situation der Frauen in der Stadt Trier nach der Steuerliste von 1364," *Kurtrierisches Jahrbuch* (1975): 20–45.

15. Gustav Schmoller, *Die Strassburger Tucher und Weberzunft: Urkunden und Darstellung* (Strasbourg: Trübner, 1879), pp. 32–37.

16. B. Kreutzer, "Beiträge zur Geschichte des Wollengewerbes in Bayern," *Archiv für vaterländische Geschichte* 20 (1897): 241.

17. Schmoller, *Die Strassburger Tucher und Weberzunft*, p. 446.

18. Hess, *Die deutschen Frauenberufe des Mittelalters*, p. 71.

19. Eugen Nübling, *Ulms Baumwollweberei im Mittelalter* (Leipzig: Duncker and Humblot, 1890), p. 67.

20. A Frankfurt tailors' ordinance printed in Karl Bücher and Benno Schmidt, *Frankfurter Amts und Zunfturkunden bis zum Jahre 1602* (Frankfurt: Bauer, 1914), p. 513, even allows widows who married nontailors to continue in their craft as long as they made a special payment.

21. Found in many sixteenth century guild ordinances in all city archives.

22. See Memmingen Stadtarchiv, 451, no. 3 (1613).

23. Frankfurt Stadtarchiv, Zünfte, Ugb. C-59, Gg no. 3.

24. Schmoller, *Die Strassburger Tucher und Weberzunft*, p. 510.

25. Claus-Peter Clasen, *Die Augsburger Weber: Leistung und Krisen des Textilgewerbes um 1600* (Augsburg: Mühlberger, 1981), p. 23.

26. Munich Stadtarchiv, Steuerbücher.

27. Frankfurt Stadtarchiv, Zünfte, Ugb. C-58, no. Z.

28. Munich Stadtarchiv, Gewerbeamt, no. 2730.

29. Frankfurt Stadtarchiv, Zünfte, Ugb. C-58, no. Z.

30. Wissell, *Das alten Handwerks Recht und Gewohnheit*, p. 258; Frankfurt Stadtarchiv, Zünfte, Ugb. C-33, no. Aaa (1688).

31. Wissell, *Das alten Handwerks Recht und Gewohnheit*, p. 262.

32. As did Frankfurt wool weavers (1455) and Frankfurt stonemasons (1521), quoted in Bücher and Schmidt, *Frankfurter Amts und Zunfturkunden bis zum Jahre 1602*, p. 87.

33. See the 1653 case in Strasbourg, quoted in Schmoller, *Die Strassburger Tucher und Weberzunft*, pp. 307–9.

34. Bücher and Schmidt, *Frankfurter Amts und Zunfturkunden bis zum Jahre 1602*, p. 280.

35. Frankfurt Stadtarchiv, Zünfte, Abteil II, nos. 56 and 62.

36. Such as Nuremberg (1519) and Heilbronn (1513), quoted in Hess, *Die deutschen Frauenberufe des Mittelalters*, p. 28.

37. Strasbourg Hosenstrickerordnung, quoted in Schmoller, *Die Strassburger Tucher und Weberzunft*, p. 304; Memmingen Stadtarchiv, 441, no. 3 (1632).

38. Munich Stadtarchiv, Gewerbeamt, no. 1020.

39. Schmoller, *Die Strassburger Tucher und Weberzunft*, p. 541.

40. Ernst Mummenhoff, "Frauenarbeit und Arbeitsvermittlung," *Vierteljahresschrift für Soziale- und Wirtschaftsgeschichte*, 19 (1926): 157–65.

41. Frankfurt Stadtarchiv, Zünfte, Ugb. C-36, no. Cc (1649).
42. Wissell, *Das alten Handwerks Recht und Gewohnheit,* p. 441; F. G. Mone, "Die Weberei und ihre Beigewerbe von 14.–16. Jhd.," *Zeitschrift für Geschichte des Oberrheins* 9 (1858): 174.
43. Strasbourg, Archives municipales, Statuten, vol. 28, fol. 361.
44. Wissell, *Das alten Handwerks Recht und Gewohnheit,* p. 452.
45. Wachendorf, *Die wirtschaftliche Stellung der Frau,* p. 57.
46. Stuttgart, Württembergische Hauptstaatsarchiv, Landwirtschaft, A-58, no. 2, Bü. 19.
47. Clasen, *Die Augsburger Weber,* pp. 130–32.
48. Ibid., pp. 132–33.
49. Memmingen Stadtarchiv, Ratsprotokollbücher, February 7, 1539.
50. Munich Stadtarchiv, Ratsitzungsprotokolle, 1527; Memmingen Stadtarchiv, 471, no. 1 (1640).
51. Memmingen Stadtarchiv, Ratsprotokollbücher, October 29, 1554.
52. Munich Stadtarchiv, Ratsitzungsprotokolle, 1559, fol. 133.
53. Memmingen Stadtarchiv, 441, no. 3 (1632); Schmoller, *Die Strassburger Tucher und Weberzunft,* p. 346 (1603).
54. Memmingen Stadtarchiv, 441, no. 3 (1662).
55. Frankfurt Stadtarchiv, Zünfte, Abteil II, 52, no. 65 (1648).
56. Munich Stadtarchiv, Steuerbücher, 1590–1660.
57. Munich Stadtarchiv, Gewerbeamt, no. 2120 (1613).
58. Memmingen Stadtarchiv, Ratsprotokollbücher, September 1, 1620.
59. Clasen leaves it as a question: "Dürften sie den Webstuhl selbst betrieben, obwohl sie doch das Weben selbst gar nicht gelernt hatten?" (Clasen, *Die Augsburger Weber,* p. 59).
60. Frankfurt Stadtarchiv, Bürgermeisterbücher, 1595, fol. 5.
61. Memmingen Stadtarchiv, Ratsprotokollbücher, 8 Feb. 1581.
62. Strasbourg, Archives municipales, Statuten, vol. 21, fol. 186.
63. Clark, *Working Life of Women in the Seventeenth Century,* p. 19.
64. Mummenhoff, "Frauenarbeit und Arbeitsvermittlung."
65. Memmingen Stadtarchiv, 405, no. 12.
66. Memmingen Stadtarchiv, 422 (1605); Frankfurt Stadtarchiv, Zünfte, Ugb. C-36, no. Cc (1649); Nuremberg Stadtarchiv, QNG no. 68/I, 441: 68/II, nos. 674, 847, 853; 68/III, nos. 1093, 1107.
67. Strasbourg, Archives municipales, Akten der XV, 1607, fol. 147; 1618, fol. 119, Frankfurt Stadtarchiv, Bürgermeisterbücher, 1600, fol. 271; 1610, fol. 45.
68. Strasbourg, Archives municipales, Akten der XV, 1619, fols. 74, 179; 1633, fols. 88, 232; 1665, fols. 15, 83. Frankfurt Zünfte, Ugb. D-25, no. P, no. 2 (1692); Ugb. C-59, Cc (1639).
69. Memmingen Stadtarchiv, October 29, 1554. Strasbourg, Ar-

chives municipales, Akten der XV, 1572, fol. 72; 1628, fols. 173, 254; 1636, fols. 117, 175; 1640, fols. 118, 170. Strasbourg, Archives municipales, Akten der XXI, 1606, fol. 95. Frankfurt Stadtarchiv, Zünfte, Ugb. D-24, L4 (1698).

70. Susan Esterbrook Kennedy, *If All We Did Was to Weep at Home: A History of White Working Class Women in America,* (Bloomington: Indiana University Press, 1979); Alice Kessler-Harris, *Out to Work: A History of Wage Earning Women in the United States* (New York: Oxford University Press, 1982).

71. Frankfurt Stadtarchiv, Zünfte, Ugb. C-32, No. R, no. 1 (1663); Wachendorf, *Die wirtschaftliche Stellung der Frau,* p. 57 (reporting on Basel); Munich Stadtarchiv, Gewerbeamt, no. 2730.

72. Frankfurt Stadtarchiv, Zünfte, Abteil II, 62, fol. 240–244. Nuremberg Stadtarchiv, QNG no. 68/II, 663; 68/III, 1108. Howell, "Women's Work," pp. 215–20. Wachendorf, *Die wirtschaftliche Stellung der Frau,* p. 63.

Chapter 12: A Woman's Place Was in the Home

I thank Carl Degler, Richard Goldthwaite, Carolyn Lougee, Richard Roberts, and the members of the Stanford Social Science History Workshop for their criticisms on earlier drafts of this essay.

1. Joan Kelly-Gadol, "Did Women Have a Renaissance?" in *Becoming Visible: Women in European History,* ed. Renate Bridenthal and Claudia Koonz (Boston: Houghton Mifflin, 1977), p. 139.

2. Ibid.

3. Kenneth Arrow, "Economic Dimensions of Occupational Segregation: Comment," in *Women and the Workplace. The Implications of Occupational Segregation,* ed. Martha Blaxall and Barbara Reagan (Chicago: University of Chicago Press, 1976), p. 236.

4. Although David Herlihy would not necessarily agree that women of rank lost power, his conclusions about lower-class women are in accord with Kelly's. See, for example, David Herlihy, "Deaths, Marriage, Births, and the Tuscan Economy," in *Population Patterns in the Past,* ed. R. D. Lee (New York: Academic Press, 1977), p. 163. Kelly's statement appears in "Early Feminist Theory and the *Querelle des Femmes,* 1400–1789," *Signs: Journal of Women in Culture and Society* 8 (Autumn 1982): 7.

5. Louise A. Tilly and Joan W. Scott, *Women, Work and Family* (New York, 1978); Natalie Zemon Davis, *Culture and Society in Early Mordern France* (Stanford: Stanford University Press, 1975); Olwen Hufton, "Women and the Family Economy in Eighteenth-Century France," *French Historical Studies* 9 (Spring 1975): 1–22. The view on Italian women has been forwarded by Herlihy in "Deaths, Marriages, and Births."

6. Herlihy, "Death, Marriages, Birth," p. 163.

7. Natalie Zemon Davis, "Women in the *Arts Mecaniques* in Sixteen-Century Lyon," in *Mélanges en hommage de Richard Gascon,* ed. Jean-Pierre Gutton (Lyon: Presses universitaires, 1980).

8. Alfred Doren, *Studien aus der Florentiner Wirtschaftsgeschichte,* vol. 1: *Florentiner Wollentuchindustrie* (Stuttgart: J. G. Cotta, 1901), pp. 277–79.

9. Florence Edler de Roover, "Andrea Banchi, Florentine Silk Manufacturer and Merchant in the Fifteenth Century," *Studies in Medieval and Renaissance History* 3 (1966): 245–56.

10. David Herlihy and Christiane Klapisch-Zuber, *Les Toscans et leurs familles* (Paris: Ecole des etudes en sciences sociales, 1978), pp. 582–83.

11. Based on data from fourteen wool company account books for weavers, spanning the years 1458–1504 (four books) and 1553–1618 (ten books). The silk company account books that are extant are all from the seventeenth century, but the contrast with the evidence from the fifteenth-century account books examined by de Roover is so marked that one can only infer that a major shift toward the employment of females occurred in the sixteenth century, and most probably after 1537 when the Florentine political situation once more allowed the silk industry and the economy to flourish.

12. Data and tables appeared originally in Judith Brown and Jordan Goodman, "Women and Industry in Florence," *Journal of Economic History* 40 (no. 1, March 1980): 78–80.

13. Ibid., p. 78; Pietro Battara, *La popolazione di Firenze alla metà del '500* (Florence: Rinascimento del libro, 1935), p. 33.

14. Since there are no figures for the seventeenth-century Florentine population by age and sex, I have used the proportions recorded in the Catasto of 1427. As we are dealing with an open and unstable population, obviously, these proportions can change over time, but because I am lumping large age categories together, it is unlikely that the proportions would vary by very much. According to the Catasto, close to 50 percent of the population (46 percent—a likely underenumeration) was female and 20 percent of those were under age six and over seventy-nine. See Herlihy and Klapisch, *Les Toscans,* pp. 326–92, 660–63. With a total Florentine population of 61,000 in 1661, the closest population figure to 1663, we thus arrive at the estimate of the working age female population as follows:

$$\frac{61,000}{2} - (30,500 \times .20) = 24,400$$

The population of female workers is obtained by adding the female wool and silk workers in Tables 1 and 2 and assuming, on the basis of the proportions obtained from the 1631 census, that they amounted to 80 percent of all working women. Thus:

$$\frac{(473 + 11,782) \times 100}{80} = 15,319$$

The percentage of working women out of the working age female population is therefore calculated as follows:

$$\frac{15,319 \times 100}{24,400} = 63$$

15. This could be accomplished by assuming, on the basis of a population similar to that of 1427, that only women between the ages of seven and sixty-nine were employable, and that the wool and silk workers surveyed in 1663 represent 75 percent of all working women.

16. For a fuller version of this argument, see Brown and Goodman, "Women and Industry," pp. 75–76. A similar argument for the sustained performance of the craft and industrial sector of the Florentine economy until 1740 has been advanced by Paolo Malanima, "Firenze tra '500 e '700: l' andamento dell'industria cittadina nel lungo periodo," *Società e storia* 1 (no. 2, 1978): 231–56.

17. The data do not support other explanations such as increased celibacy or falling real incomes. See Brown and Goodman, "Women and Industry," p. 79.

18. See Merry Wiesner's essay in this volume above; also Alice Clark, *Working Life of Women in the Seventeenth Century,* (1919; reprint, New York: Augustus M. Kelly, Bookseller, 1968), pp. 103–4. The relation between guild control and women's participation emerged at a workshop, "Laboring Women in Early Modern Europe," held during the Berkshire Conference on the History of Women, Vassar, June 1981. The cities examined were Florence, Leyden, London, Lyon, and Nuremberg.

19. Lorenzo Cantini, *Legislazione Toscana, 1532–1775* (Florence: Pietro Fantsini e figlio, 1800–1808), vol. 1, pp. 102, 206–7, 366; vol. 3, pp. 214, 392; vol. 4, pp. 173–74; 369–70; vol. 9, p. 28.

20. Much to the discomfort of Florentine textile manufacturers, the Medici grand dukes encouraged the growth of textile industries in Pisa, Prato, and elsewhere in the dominion. They also allowed foreigners to join partnerships with Florentines, invited Florentine textile workers who had fled the state to resettle in the city, and encouraged the immigration into the state of other potential workers such as Portuguese and Jews. See Judith Brown, "The Political Economy of Cosimo I de' Medici," in *Firenze e la Toscana Medicea nell' Europa del 500* (Florence: Olschki, ed., 1984).

21. "Et seducunt mulieres ad dampnum virorum." Alfred Doren, *Le arti fiorentine,* trans. G. B. Klein (Florence: Felice le Monnier, ed., 1940), p. 203.

22. Archivio di Stato, Florence. *Università dei Linaioli, 3:*" Statuti," 1578, fol. 39.

23. Jacob Mincer and Solomon Polacheck, "Family Investment in Human Capital: Earnings of Women," *Journal of Political Economy* 82 (March 1974): 76–111; Gary S. Becker, *Human Capital: A Theoretical and Empirical Analysis with Special Reference to Education* (New York: Columbia University Press, 1964) Id. A Theory of the Allocation of Time," *Economic Journal* 75 (September 1965): 493–517; Id., "A Theory of Marriage: Part 1," *Journal of Political Economy* 81 (July 1973): 813–46. A survey and critique of the human capital and other approaches appears in Francine D. Blau and Carol L. Jusenius, "Economists' Approaches to Sex Segregation in the Labor Market: Appraisal," in *Women and the Workplace,* ed. Blaxall and Reagan, pp. 181–99. Blau and Jusenius's critique attacks the human capital theory not on the basis of commission but of omission for not taking into account other social factors such as prejudice. One of the few attempts to discredit the human capital theory on its own grounds is J. L. Medoff and K. G. Abraham, "Are Those Paid More Really More Productive? The Case of Experience," *Journal of Human Resources* 16 (Spring 1981):186–216. The attempt, however, fails because it is based on untenable assumptions about the adequacy of productivity appraisals in the work situation that they analyze. Recent work by Barry Eichengreen, based on detailed employment data of late nineteenth-century workers, convincingly demonstrates that both the amount and the quality of human capital acquired by workers have a decisive influence on the work and the wages received by men and women. See Barry Eichengreen, "The Experience and Earnings of Men and Women at the End of the Nineteenth Century," unpublished ms., Department of Economics, Harvard University.

24. Dennis Romano, "Artisan Networks in Early Renaissance Venice," paper presented at the 98th Annual Meeting of the American Historical Association, San Francisco, 1983; and Davis, "Women in the *Arts Mecaniques.*" In England and other parts of France, where women married later, there was a different perception of the marketability of women's skills; see Tilly and Scott, *Women, Work, and Family,* p. 38. There are no systematic studies of the occupational endogamy of Florentine women, but both the census of 1631 and guild records suggest that many women married men in crafts other than their own.

25. Brown and Goodman, "Women and Industry," p. 79.

26. A.S.F., *Miscellanea Medicea,* 311, ins. 8.

27. Some of these jobs, especially cleaning, also required some

muscular effort, but while this might result in fewer women engaged in such work and in lower wages for those that did, it should not have resulted in their total absence from those tasks if there had been no other barriers to entry.

28. E. Rodocanachi, *La femme italienne, avant, pendant et après la Renaissance* (Paris, 1920), p. 322. The most notable exception to this domestication of women is the emergence of women in commedia dell'arte roles. Kathleen M. Lea, *Italian Popular Comedy* (Oxford: Clarendon Press 1934).

29. Diane Owen Hughes, "The Death of Mourning: Controls on Ritual Life in the Italian Commune," unpublished ms., Dept. of History, University of Michigan.

30. St. Bernardino of Siena, "Della donna onesta," in *Prediche volgari*, ed. Ciro Cannarozzi (Pistoia: Alberto Pacinotti, 1934), 1:407. Similarly, several decades later Leon Battista Alberti argued that "The woman's character is the jewel of her family," in *I Libri della famiglia*, trans. Renee New Watkins as *The Family in Renaissance Florence* (Columbia: University of South Carolina Press, 1969), p. 213.

31. Ibid.

32. Baldesar Castiglione, *The Book of the Courtier*, trans. Charles Singleton (New York: Anchor Press, 1959), p. 241. Women's propensity to vice is a theme that runs through the sermons of moralists like St. Bernardino, who counsel women, "Don't go trotting off now here, now there, stay at home and and don't go off amusing yourself." St. Bernardino, "Comme debba vivere la donna in questo mondo e massimamente le vergini," *Prediche*, 5:223. Alberti also argues, "Women . . . are almost all timid by nature, soft, slow, and therefore most useful when they sit still and watch over our things. It is as though nature thus provided for our well-being, arranging for men to bring things home and for women to guard them. The woman as she remains locked up at home should watch over things by staying at her post, by diligent care and watchfulness." *Della famiglia*, pp. 207–8.

33. Ian Maclean, *The Renaissance Notion of Woman* (Cambridge: Cambridge University Press, 1980), pp. 20–22.

34. Ibid., pp. 15–16.

35. Doren, *Arti fiorentine*, p. 203.

36. Maclean, *Notion of Woman*, p. 50.

37. Alberti, *Della famiglia*, p. 210. Similarly, according to St. Bernardino, "It is up to the husband, who is wiser, to counsel and teach his wife that which she ought to know, rather than for her to counsel her husband . . . In her soul the wife is the equal of her husband, but in the flesh, the husband is superior to the wife, who must obey him in all things that are permitted and honest." *Prediche volgari*, 1:42.

38. Cited in Ruth Kelso, *Doctrine for the Lady of the Renaissance* (Urbana: University of Illinois Press, 1956), p. 96.

39. Scholars have yet to examine the all-female workshop in Renaissance Italy. Undoubtedly it existed, but how prevalent it was and how it functioned is not known.

40. The spread of the dotal system in the eleventh and twelfth centuries is analyzed by Diane Owen Hughes, "From Brideprice to Dowry in Mediterranean Europe," *Journal of Family History* (no. 3, Fall 1978): 262–96. For a discussion of widowhood and poverty, see Herlihy and Klapisch, *Les Toscans,* pp. 337–38.

41. Jordan Goodman, "The Florentine Silk Industry in the Seventeenth Century" (Ph.D. diss., London School of Economics, 1977), pp. 207–8.

42. Wage data for construction workers are problematic because the sources are discontinuous and because of seasonal fluctuations. The daily wage cited represents an average. For a fuller discussion, see Richard Goldthwaite, *The Building of Renaissance Florence* (Baltimore: Johns Hopkins University Press, 1981), pp. 317–31; also "Il movimento dei prezzi in Toscana dal 1520 al 1620," *Giornale degli economisti e annali di economia,* n. s. 26 (1967), table 4. Women were generally excluded from the Florentine construction industry except in times of crisis, as occurred in 1630–31, when the government employed them in large public works projects. The wages they received for such tasks as hauling stones and rubble were considerably lower than those of men, partly reflecting the lower productivity of women in this type of work; A.S.F., *Fabbriche medicee,* 126, fol. 127v.

43. Gary Becker, *The Economics of Discrimination* (Chicago: University of Chicago Press, 1957); Barbara R. Bergmann, "The Effect on White Incomes of Discrimination in Employment," *Journal of Political Economy* 79 (March 1971): 294–313; Id., "Occupational Segregation, Wages and Profits When Employers Discriminate by Race or Sex," *Eastern Economic Journal* 1 (April 1974): 103–10.

44. One of the best introductions to the agrarian life of this period is Giorgio Giorgetti, *Contadini e proprietari nell'Italia moderna: Rapporti di produzione e contratti agrari dal secolo XVI a oggi* (Turin: G. Einaudi, ed., 1974).

45. Federigo Melis, "Produzione e commercio dei vini italiani (con particolare riferimento all Toscana) nei secoli XIII–XVIII, *Annales cisalpines d'histoire sociale,* pp. 107–33; Id, "Note sulle vicende storiche dell'olio d'oliva (secoli XIV–XVII)," in *Dell'olio e della sua coltura* (Florence, Cassa di Risparmio di Firenze, 1972), pp. 11–21; Goodman, "Florentine Silk Industry," passim.

46. Carlo Pazzagli, *L'agricoltura toscana nella prima meta dell' 800* (Florence: Olschki, ed., 1973), pp. 165–78.

47. A.S.F., *Pratica Segreta,* 10 ins. 16; Goodman, "Florentine Silk Industry," p. 87.

48. Robert Dallington, *Survey of the Great Dukes State of Tuscany,* (London, 1605), p. 33.

49. For a fuller discussion of these agricultural tasks see Judith C. Brown, *In the Shadow of Florence: Provincial Society in Renaissance Pescia* (New York: Oxford University Press, 1982), pp. 80–82.

50. Edward Shorter, on the contrary, argues that until the eighteenth century women's spheres in rural households were largely removed from contact with the market economy: *The Making of the Modern Family* (New York: Basic Books, 1975).

51. For a fuller discussion of the amount of labor required to make silk and the length of the work seasons in particular tasks, see Brown, *Renaissance Pescia,* pp. 84–85. The actual amount of Tuscan raw silk produced in the 1590s can only be estimated from official reports stating the proportion of Tuscan silk used in the Florentine silk cloth industry. As we know the actual amount and the geographic sources of the silk used in several years in the 1650s, it is possible to calculate the amount of silk produced in the 1590s by assuming that in both periods there was a constant proportion between silk and cloth output. J. Goodman has kindly supplied the data for the 1650s.

52. The argument that Tuscan economic decline was partly related to the limited economic function of women has been advanced by Herlihy, "Deaths, Marriages, Births," p. 163. In contrast, the opposite conclusion is necessarily implied in Paolo Malanima's argument that the Florentine economy declined because sericulture, added to the cultivation of other crops, made such full use of rural Tuscany's labor supply, both male and female, that it reduced the incentive to develop the Florentine as well as the Tuscan economy in a direction that was more conducive to modernization. *La decadenza di un'economia cittadina: L'industria di Firenze nei secoli XVI–XVII* (Bologna: Il Mulino, 1982), p. 107.

53. Richard T. Rapp, *Industry and Economic Decline in Seventeenth-Century Venice,* (Cambridge: Harvard University Press, 1976), pp. 27–29.

54. Ibid., p. 29.

55. Clark, *Working Life of Women,* pp. 295–96.

56. In addition to the many examples of female workers in textiles and other occupations, Clark admits that her absence of information on women does not prove that they were rarely employed. The mid-nineteenth century account of the condition of handloom weavers quoted in her book testifies to the continued importance of female workers in that occupation throughout the centuries. Ibid., pp. 105; other crafts are cited in pp. 150–234.

57. Nancy Adamson, paper presented at the Berkshire Conference on the History of Women, Vassar, 1982.

58. Davis, "'Women in the *Arts Mecaniques*;" Martha C. Howell and Robert Duplessis, "Reconsidering the Early Modern Urban Economy: The Cases of Leiden and Lille," *Past and Present* 94 (1982): 49–84; also Martha C. Howell, paper presented at the Berkshire Conference on the History of Women, Vassar, 1982.

59. Carlo M. Cipolla, *Before the Industrial Revolution: European Society and Economy, 1000–1700,* 2d ed. (New York: W.W. Norton, 1980), pp. 204–47; Jan de Vries, *The Economy of Europe in an Age of Crisis, 1600–1750* Cambridge: University Press, 1976).

60. The most dramatic evidence of the increased power of working women is the decline in their mortality rates during the modern period. Data on American, English, and Swedish working women in the nineteenth century show that their mortality rates fell sharply in comparison to nonworking women, bourgeois women, or even males of all classes. This trend has been convincingly linked to their ability to command better treatment and better food within their families. Although evidence of this sort has not been gathered for sixteenth- and seventeenth-century Italian women and may not exist, it would not be surprising to find similar results for later centuries. See Sheila Johansson, "Deferred Infanticide: Excess Female Mortality During Childhood," *Infanticide in Animals and Man,* ed. G. Hausfater and S. Hrdy (New York: Aldine Publishing, 1984), pp. 463–74.

Chapter 13: Catherine de' Medici as Artemisia

Funding for this research was provided by the National Endowment for the Humanities and by the Office of Research and Advanced Study at George Mason University. Considerable work was accomplished while the author was a Visiting Scholar at the Center for Research on Women, Stanford University. Part of this paper was read at the 1983 meeting of the College Art Association/Women's Caucus for Art. The author would like to thank the following for their help and advice in completing this study: Pamela Askew, Sylvie Béguin, John Bender, Malcolm Campbell, John F. D'Amico, Shepard Krech III, Deborah Marrow, Nancy Roelker, Claire Richter Sherman, Nicola M. Sutherland, and the editors of this collection.

1. Roy Strong, *Art and Power: Renaissance Festivals 1450–1650* (Berkeley and Los Angeles: University of California Press, 1984), p. 98. The marriage of Elizabeth of Valois and Philip II of Spain was provided for in the treaty. Jousts were a common feature of marriage celebrations.

2. Ivan Cloulas, *Catherine de Médicis* (Paris: Fayard, 1981), pp. 119–21, and Eugene Defrance, *Catherine de Médicis, Ses Astrologues et Ses Magiciens-envoûteurs* (Paris: Mercure de France, 1911), p. 87, state

that the night before the tourney she had a nightmare in which she saw her husband lying wounded. Nostradamus, in his *Centuries* published in 1555, and Luca Gaurico, writing from Venice in 1552, had both made predictions that were interpreted as warning the king against undertaking single combat. See also L. Cimber and L. F. Danjou, eds., *Archives Curieuses de l'Histoire de France,* vol. 3 (1834–1840), p. 307.

3. Cloulas, *Catherine de Médicis,* p. 126, notes how the queen departed from the normal French practice of staying for forty days in the palace in which the King had died.

4. Claire Richter Sherman," The Queen in Charles V's 'Coronation Book': Jeanne de Bourbon and the 'Ordo ad Reginam Benedicendam,' " *Viator: Medieval and Renaissance Studies* 8 (1977): 258, in which she discusses "the myth of the Salic Law." Marion Facinger, "A Study of Medieval Queenship: Capetian France, 987–1237," *Studies in Medieval and Renaissance History* 5 (1968): 3–47, describes the role of the queen in France in the Middle Ages. For an enlightening survey of attitudes toward women in positions of power in all strata of society, see Natalie Zemon Davis, "Women on Top," in *Society and Culture in Early Modern France* (Stanford, Calif.: Stanford University Press, 1975), pp. 124–51.

5. When widowed Mary, queen of Scots and Louise de Lorraine wore white. See Anne Hollander, *Seeing through Clothes* (New York: Viking Press, 1975), pp. 373–74.

6. See, for example, Victor Turner's discussion of the multivalence of meanings of black in Ndembu ritual in *The Forest of Symbols* (Ithaca: Cornell University Press, 1967), p. 71.

7. Hollander, *Seeing through Clothes,* p. 367; Jane Schneider, "Peacocks and Penguins: the Political Economy of European Cloth and Colors," *American Ethnologist* 5 (1978): 426. Black was also a color chosen by Elizabeth I.

8. This is another example of the multivalence of meanings of a particular color or colors; some attribute Henri II's choice of costume to his desire to match Diane de Poitiers's black and white.

9. Stephen Orgel, *The Illusion of Power: Political Theater in the English Renaissance* (Berkeley and Los Angeles: University of California Press, 1975), p. 40.

10. Sarah B. Pomeroy, *Goddesses, Wives, Slaves, and Whores: Women in Classical Antiquity* (New York: Schocken Books, 1975), p. 8: "The goddesses of Olympus appear in myth never to have had more than narrowly-restricted functions . . . on the other hand, gods enjoyed a wider range of activities. The goddesses are archetypal images of human females as envisioned by males. The distribution of desirable characteristics among a number of females rather than their concentration in one being is appropriate to a patriarchal society." See also

Jean Chartrou, *Les Entrées Solonnelles et Triomphales à la Rénaissance, 1484–1551* (Paris: Presses Universitaires, 1928), p. 51, for references to Pallas/Minerva for Catherine; William McAllister Johnson, "Prolegomena to the Ulysses Gallery," (Ph.D. diss., Princeton University, 1968), p. 197c, for references to Catherine as Juno and p. 225 for Catherine as Minerva; Léon de Laborde, *La Rénaissance des Arts à la Cour de France* (Paris, 1855), p. 201, discusses the enamel by Léonard Limousin (Louvre no. 242) showing the court of Henri II as an assembly of gods with the king as Jupiter, Catherine de Medici as Juno, and Diane de Poitiers as Venus.

11. Françoise Bardon, *Diane de Poitiers et le Mythe de Diane* (Paris: Presses Universitaires de France, 1963).

12. Phillipe Erlanger, *Diane de Poitiers* (Paris: Gallimard, 1955), p. 134; Cloulas, *Catherine de Médicis,* p. 65; and Mariana Jenkins, "The Imagery of the Henri II Wing of the Louvre," *Journal of Medieval and Renaissance Studies* 7 (1977):95—all refer to the convenient ambiguity of the cipher, but none alludes to the possible inclusion of both the *C* and *D,* the *C* being attached to the right—or legitimate—and the *D* to the left—or illegitimate—side of the *H.*

13. Erlanger, *Diane de Poitiers,* p. 30. He was only seven when he went as hostage with his older brother in exchange for their father the king.

14. Queen Claude, first wife of François I, died in 1523 when the future Henri II was only four.

15. This manuscript, in the black binding of the queen's personal library, is today in the Bibliothèque Nationale, Paris, (manuscripts, fonds français, 306). Its full title is *Histoire de la royne Arthémise, contenant quatre livres, recuillé de plusieurs autheurs, en laquelle sont contenues plusieurs singularitez dignes de remarque touchant l'antiquité.* For information on Nicolas Houel, see Jules Guiffrey, "Nicolas Houel, Apothicaire Parisien, Fondateur de la Maison de la Charité Chrétienne et Premier Autheur de la Ténture d'Arthémise," Mémoires de la Societé de l'Histoire de Paris et de l'Ile-de-France (1898), pp. 179–220; Gustave Lebel, "Une lettre oubliée de Nicolas Houel," *Bulletin de la Societé des Historiens de l'Art Français* (1923) pp. 40–44; S. E. Lepinois, *Nicolas Houel* (Dijon, 1911); Antoine de Laborde, *Nicolas Houel, Fondateur de la Maison de la Charité Chrétienne* (Paris: Societé des Bibliophiles Françaises, 1937); Natalie Zemon Davis, "Printing and the People," *Society and Culture,* p. 215.

16. Guiffrey, "Nicolas Houel," p. 185, quotes Houel's contemporary, La Croix du Maine, who reports that he composed the *Histoire* on the express order of the queen mother and spent a great deal of money to get it illustrated. He said that he did not know what, if any, recompense was ever received.

17. He wrote another book, this one about the patronage activities

of French queens. Nicolas Houel, *Les mémoires et récherches de la devotion, pieté, et charité des illustres Roynes de France, ensemble les églises, monasteres, hospitaux, et collèges qu'elles ont fondez et edifiez en divers endroit de ce Royaume*, Paris, 1586. For information about his activity as director of the charity, see Frances Yates, "Religious Processions in Paris, 1583–84," *Astraea* (Harmondsworth: Penguin Books, 1977), pp. 173–207.

18. For information on the historical Artemisia, see Giovanni Boccaccio, *Concerning Famous Women*, trans. Guido A. Guarino (New Brunswick, N.J.: Rutgers University Press, 1963), p. 123; Diodorus Siculus, XIX. 11–51; Pausanius. IX, 7. Valerius Maximus IV. 6

19. For a discussion of the powerful role of the widow in early modern Europe, see Nancy Lyman Roelker, "Widowhood and Rational Domesticity: Modes of Independence for Women in Early Modern Europe," *Journal of Family History* 7 (1982):376–78.

20. Artemisia had been proposed before as a proper prototype for a French regent-widow, Anne de Beaujeu, by Jean LeMaire de Belges (see Walter Cahn, *Masterpieces: Chapters on the History of an Idea* (Princeton, N.J.: Princeton University Press, 1979), pp. 49–50); he also discusses Artemisia in his *Couronne Margaritique*, written for the dowager duchess of Savoy in 1549.

21. Some of the ancient authorities that Houel mentions having consulted are: Caesar, Cicero, Diodorus Siculus, Herodian, Herodotus, Horace, Macrobius, Martial, Ovid, Pliny the Elder, Plutarch, Seneca, Strabo, Suetonius, Tacitus, Thucydides, Valerius Maximus, Varro, Virgil, Vitruvius, and Xenophon. Some of the modern ones are François de Billon, Boccaccio, Guillaume Budé, and Ronsard. Conspicuous by their absence are Christine de Pizan, Erasmus, and Machiavelli.

22. I have discussed elsewhere the significance of the *Histoire* as a guide for a woman ruler, "Ideal Woman or Ideal Ruler: Thoughts on the Dilemma of the Renaissance Queen," at the Renaissance Society of America Annual Meeting, 1985.

23 Houel, *Histoire*, 9r, "Cet histoire conforme au temps et à la grandeur et aux affaires de la Royne."

24. Houel, *Histoire*, 6v, "L'histoire aporte grand proufit aux grandes dames"; 8v, "Ceulx qui seront lectures de cet histoire, auront grand proufit"; 12r. "L'enseigner comme une royne doibt gouverner un royaume."

25. Houel, *Histoire*, 38r, "Veritablement il fault qu'on aue faict une preuve bien grande de sa vertu, et que les hommes qui ont eslêve auyont eu asseurances comme soubs le corps et habit d'une femme elle avoyt un entendement viril prenoyant estre susfisante pour l'administraãon de grandes affaires." This language is similar to that employed by Michelangelo in the first line of a poem he wrote to

Vittoria Colonna, "A man, a god inside a woman." See *Complete Poems and Selected Letters of Michelangelo*, trans. Creighton Gilbert, ed. Robert N. Linscott (New York: Random House, Vintage Books, 1963), p. 131.

26. David D. McNeil, *Guillaume Budé and Humanism in the Reign of Francis I* (Geneva: Droz, 1975); Claude Bontems, "L'Institution du Prince de Guillaume Budé," in *Le Prince dans la France des XVIe et XVIIe Siècles*, (Paris: Presses Universitaires de France, 1965), p. 4; Erasmus, *The Education of a Christian Prince*, ed. Lester K. Born (New York: Octagon Books, 1965); François de Billon, *Le fort inexpugnable de l'honneur du sexe feminin* (Paris, 1555).

27. Constance Jordan, "Feminism and the Humanists: The Case of Sir Thomas Elyot's *Defence of Good Women*, *Renaissance Quarterly* 36 (1983): 182, and following in this volume.

28. The queen was an avid patron of various art forms. For painting, see Jean Ehrmann, *Antoine Caron* (Geneva: Droz, 1955); for sculpture, see Malcolm Campbell and Gino Corti, "A Comment on Prince Francesco de Medici's refusal to Loan Giovanni Bologna to the Queen of France," *Burlington Magazine* 115 (1973): 507–12 and Charles de Tolnay, *Michelangelo: The Final Period* (Princeton, N.J.: Princeton University Press, 1960), 5: 228; for architecture, see Anthony Blunt, *Philibert de l'Orme* (London: Zwemmer, 1958), pp. 88–107; and for garden design, see W. Howard Adams, *The French Garden* (New York: Braziller, 1979). She also commissioned works in the decorative arts and was a renowned orchestrator of court festivals and ballets; see Frances Yates, *The Valois Tapestries* (London: Routledge & Kegan Paul, 1959), pp. 51–70, and Strong, *Art and Power*, pp. 98–125.

29. Maurice Fenaille, *Etat general de la Manufacture des Gobelins depuis son origine jusqu'à nos jours*, 1600–1900 (Paris: Hachette, 1923), 1:109–60; Sylvie Béguin, "La Suite d'Arthémise," *L'Oeil* 38 (1958): 32; William McAllister Johnson and Geneviève Monnier, "Caron Antiquaire: A Propos de quelques dessins du Louvre," *Revue de l'Art* 14 (1971): 23; Ulrika von Haumeder, *Antoine Caron: Studien zu seiner 'Histoire d'Arthémise*," Ph.D. diss., Heidelberg, 1976.

30. Edmond Bonaffé, *Inventaire des meubles de Catherine de Médicis* (Geneva: Droz, 1973), p. 12. See also Gerardina Ijsselsteyn, *Tapestry: The Most Expensive Industry of the XVth and XVIth Centuries* (The Hague: Van Goor, 1969).

31. See, for example, Pierre Champion, *Catherine de Médicis présente à Charles IX son Royaume, 1564–1566* (Paris: Editions Bernard Grasset, 1937) and Victor E. Graham and W. McAllister Johnson, *The Royal Tour of France by Charles IX and Catherine de Medici, Festivals and Entries, 1564–1566* (Toronto: University of Toronto Press, 1972).

32. Fenaille, *Gobelins*, p. 113, cites several tentures woven during the reigns of Henri IV and Marie de' Medici and Louis XIII and Anne

of Austria. See also Madeleine Jarry, "Tapisseries inédits de la Tenture d'Arthémise," *L'Oeil* 220 (1973): 6 and Deborah Marrow, *The Art Patronage of Maria de' Medici* (Ann Arbor: UMI Research Press, 1982), p. 60.

33. Fenaille, *Gobelins*, pp. 60–67.

34. Béguin, "La Suite," p. 33.

35. Johnson and Monnier, "Caron Antiquaire," p. 22.

36. Those cited include: Olympias, mother of Alexander; Julia Mamaea, mother of Alexander Severus; Zenobia, queen of Palmyra; Frédégonde, mother of King Clotaire II; Blanche de Castille, mother of and regent for St. Louis; Jeanne de Navarre, Isabeau de Bavière, and Anne de Beaujeu.

37. Orgel, *Power*, p. 42.

38. Pliny the Elder, *Natural History*, 36.4.30–40; Vitruvius, *The Ten Books on Architecture*, 2.8.10–16. See also William B. Dinsmoor, "The Mausoleum at Halicarnassus," *American Journal of Archaeology* 12 (1908): 141, where he discusses various attempts to reconstruct the building.

39. Louis Dimier, *Le Primatice* (Paris: Michel, 1958), p. 5; Anthony Blunt, *Art and Architecture in France, 1500–1700* (Harmondsworth: Penguin, 1957), p. 55; A. de Boislisle, "La Sépulture des Valois à Saint-Denis," *Mémoires de la Societé de l'Histoire de Paris et de l'Ile-de-France* 3 (1876): 241, gives some archival documentation and the arguments surrounding the attributions to various architects of the design of the building. The work of Thomas Lersch, "Die Grabkapelle der Valois" (Ph.D. diss., Munich, 1964), was unavailable to me. One must await its publication for definitive arguments about the documentary history of the building.

40. Sumner M. Crosby, *The Abbey of St. Denis* (New Haven, Conn.: Yale University Press, 1942), I: 49.

41. Richard Krautheimer, *Corpus Basilicarum Christianarum Romae* (Vatican City: 1977), 5: 185; P. Fiel, "La *Pietà* di Michelangelo e la Cappella di S. Petronilla in San Pietro," *Illustrazione Vaticana* 4 (1933): 753; Charles de Tolnay, *The Youth of Michelangelo*, vol. 1 (Princeton: N.J.: Princeton University Press, 1948) p. 164.

42. Nicola M. Sutherland, "Catherine de Medici and the Ancien Régime" (London: The Historical Association, 1966), p. 5: "Her mother, Madeleine de la Tour d'Auvergne, comtesse de Boulogne . . . descended, on her father's side, from the ancient dukes of Aquitaine and the counts of Auvergne. Her mother, Jeanne de Bourbon-Vendôme, was a direct descendant of Saint-Louis, and a princess of the blood. [Catherine was] related to many members of the French nobility, in particular the dukes of Montpensier and Guise." Belittling her lineage was a frequent activity of her enemies and detractors, among them her daughter-in-law, Mary, queen of Scots,

who called her the *"marchande Florentine."* See Jean Hippolyte Mariéjol, *Catherine de Médicis* (Paris: J. Tallandier, 1979), p. 96.

43. Charles V's aunt, Margaret of Austria, regent of the Netherlands, supervised the building of a large funerary chapel at the church of Brou. See Cahn, *Masterpieces*, pp. 49–50, where he cites additional bibliography.

44. Yates, *Tapestries*, pp. 3–35.

45. Claire Richter Sherman, "Taking a Second Look: Observations on the Iconography of a French Queen, Jeanne de Bourbon (1338–1378)," in *Feminism and Art History: Questioning the Litany*, ed. Norma Broude and Mary D. Garrard (New York: Harper & Row, 1982), p. 114.

46. Cloulas, *Catherine de Médicis*, p. 76.

47. For an example of Catherine's correspondence, see Hector de la Ferrière-Percy, *Lettres de Catherine de Médicis* (Paris: Imprimerie Nationale, 1880), vol. 1, 1533–1563, p. 62.

48. Houel, *Histoire*, 62v, 63r.

49. Béguin, "La Suite", p. 26.

50. Orgel, *Power*, p. 10, discusses the significance of the place of royal personnages in the English Renaissance theater.

51. Champion, *Présente*, and Graham and Johnson, *Royal Tour*.

Chapter 14: Feminism and the Humanists

The material in this chapter was originally published in *Renaissance Quarterly* 36, no. 2 (1983):181–201.

1. Critical studies on the subject of women in the Renaissance are now numerous and increasing. I cite here only a few of the most comprehensive. For a general survey see Ruth Kelso's seminal *Doctrine for the Lady of the Renaissance* (Urbana: University of Illinois Press, 1956); and Ian Maclean, *The Renaissance Notion of Woman* (Cambridge, 1980). For women in France see Lula McDowell Richardson, *The Forerunners of Feminism in French Literature in the Renaissance from Christine of Pisa to Marie de Gournay* (Baltimore: Johns Hopkins Studies in Romance Literature and Languages, vol. 12, 1929). The English scene has been recently covered by Linda Woodbridge, *Women in the English Renaissance: Literature and the Nature of Womankind, 1540–1640* (Urbana: University of Illinois Press, 1984). For an analysis of three important treatises of the late *quattrocento* and a useful bibliography of defenses of women published in Italy in the sixteenth century, see Conor Fahy, "Three Early Renaissance Treatises of Women," *Italian Studies* 11 (1951): 30–55. See also E. Rodocanachi, *La Femme Italienne à l'époque de la Renaissance* (Paris: Hachette, 1904). For essays on women in political and intellectual life during this period, see *Beyond Their Sex: Learned Women of the European Past*, ed. Patricia H. Labalme (New York: New York University Press, 1980).

2. I use the term *humanist* loosely, to identify writers who refer in their treatises on women to Greek and Roman histories for *exempla* and to Aristotle for theories of the *polis* and the family, who focus on civic and political rather than religious and spiritual values, and who are concerned to promote the standing of women as citizens of the state, at least to some degree. Humanists who took a conservative position are among the most well known and in general active earlier in the period: Francesco Barbaro, Alberti, Poggio Bracciolini, Lodovico Dolce, Alessandro Piccolomini, and Vives. The most facetious defender of women is François Billon, but see also Christoforo Bronzini. The majority of treatises arguing for the civic virtue of women and their participation in the *vita activa* are written by Italians: notably, Bruni da Pistoia, Julio Cesare Capaccio, Galeazzo Capella, Castiglione, Luigi Dardano, Angelo Firenzuolo, Cornelio Lanci, Lucretia Marinelli, Girolamo Ruscelli, Sperone Speroni, Tasso, Trissino, and Bernardo Trotto. In England, the defense of women in public life was frequently an aspect of the succession debates; see especially David Chambers, Lord Ormond who writes a defense of ruling queens (specifically for Mary queen of Scots) modeled on that of John Leslie. John Aylmer answers John Knox's earlier attack on ruling queens. Agrippa of Nettesheim writes a defense of women, apparently inspired by Margaret of Austria. Pierre de la Primaudaye and Jean de Marconville argue for women in France. Moderata Fonte writes a treatise insisting on the superiority of women that is not obviously facetious; like Agrippa, she exposes some of the means by which the social subordination of women causes them to appear inherently inferior to men. Many of these defenses are clearly intended to complement women patrons, but their arguments seem to me to have an interest independent of their intentions.

3. None of these writers argues for anything like what today might be termed "the rights of women," political or economic. What they do insist on is th~~~ ~~women possess~~ the same kinds of virtues— intellectual and moral capac̄i̅t̅i̅e̅s̲ ̲ ̲ ̲ ̲ ̲ ̲ ̲ ̲ ̲ ̲ ̲ ̲ ̲ ̲ ̲ ̲̲̅ ̅p̅r̅o̅o̅f̲ the fact that women perform as men do when they are not ̄r̄e̲s̲t̲r̲i̲c̲t̲e̲d̲ household activities by law, social custom, or education.

4. "Attamen visum est, ne omiserim, excepta matre prima, his omnibus fere gentilibus nullas exsacris mulieribus hebreis christianisque miscuisse; non enim satis bene conveniunt, nec equo incedere videntur gradu. He quippe ob eternam et veram gloriam sese fere in adversam persepe humanitati tolerantiam coegere, sacrosancti Preceptoris tam iussa quam vestigia imitantes; ubi ille, seu quodam nature munere vel instinctu, seu potius huius momentanei fulgoris cupiditate percite, non absque tamen acri mentis robore, devenere; vel, fortune urgentis inpulsu, non nunquam gravissima pertulere. Preterea he, vera et indeficienti luce corusce, in meritam eternitatem

non solum clarissime vivunt, sed earum virginitatem, castimoniam, sanctitatem, virtutem et, in superandis tam concupiscentiis carnis quam suppliciis tiramnorum invictam constantiam, ipsarum meritis exigentibus, singulis voluminibus a piis hominibus, sacris literis et veneranda maiestate conspicuis, descriptas esse cognoscimus; ubi illarum merita, nullo in hoc edito volumine speciali—uti iam dictum est—et a nemine demonstrata, describere, quasi aliquale reddituri premium, inchoamus." Boccaccio, *De claris mulieribus*, ed. Vittorio Saccaria, in *Tutte le Opere*, 10, ed. Vittore Branca (Verona: Mondadori, 1967), pp. 26–28 (my translation).

5. Christine models her work on Boccaccio's *De claris mulieribus* but eliminates its humanist perspective. See Richardson, *Forerunners*, pp. 13–32. She is, on the other hand, highly sensitive to the social situation of contemporary women in other of her works, notably *Lavision*.

6. As acute readers of the *De claris mulieribus* have realized, it is in fact a highly ironic work, whose portraits of female worthies betray more often than confirm the high ideals of its prologue. This does not deny the polemical value of that passage, however, which declares the value of women in the civic life.

7. The question whether or not women had a Renaissance, first posed and answered (in the negative) so brilliantly by Joan Kelly Gadol, is a highly complicated one. The literature of the defenses suggests that during the sixteenth century, women (like men) who were members of the bourgeoisie acquired larger scope for all kinds of activities, both economic and social. Conceived of as a class within the state, however, women in general experienced a kind of repression; they exemplified an anomalous political entity, a subordinate who was nevertheless equal to her superior in certain respects, and as their condition became more precisely articulated, the definition of what constituted feminine nature became comparatively more rigid and allowed for less flexibility than it had had in earlier periods when the need to propose theories of the state and ideal government was less urgent. The noble or gentlewoman of the twelfth and thirteenth centuries, profiting from a relatively stable hierarchical society in which the relations between governor and governed were not in the process of reformulation, seems to have had in practice a greater social, political and economic power than her sixteenth-century counterpart. Yet the "defensive" treatment of women in the context of sixteenth-century political debates also had a liberating effect, for it made redundant discussions of femininity as a chiefly spiritual phenomenon and initiated others that employed the terms and reflected the values characterizing the narration of history per se. For Gadol's position, see her "Did Women Have a Renaissance?" in *Becoming*

Visible: Woman in European History, ed. Renate Bridenthal and Claudia Koonz (Boston: Houghton Mifflin, 1977), pp. 139–64.

8. See Stanford E. Lehmberg, *Sir Thomas Elyot: Tudor Humanist* (Austin: University of Texas Press, 1960; reprint, New York: Greenwood Press, 1969), p. 176; see also Foster Watson, *Vives and the Renascence Education of Women* (New York: Longmans, Green and Co., 1912), pp. 308–13.

9. Garrett Mattingly, *Catherine of Aragon* (Boston: Little, Brown and Company 1941), pp. 137–41, 157–62, 174–75, 203–19.

10. Mattingly, *Catherine*, pp. 335, 374–75.

11. "It is clear that Elyot sympathized with Catherine's cause, and he continued to give Chapuys information and support for a number of years. In 1543, Chapuys went so far as to include Elyot among those who would join a Spanish-led conspiracy to rid England of her 'heretic' king. Elyot's policy was dangerous; had Chapuys not kept his secrets unusually well, Elyot might have been tried for treason, and another head might have rolled on Tower Green. No man could safely serve two masters if one of them was Henry VIII." Lehmberg, *Elyot*, p. 108. The fullest account of the conspiracy is given in Mattingly, *Catherine*.

12. For Chapuys's contacts with Elyot, see Paul Friedman, *Anne Boleyn* (London, 1884), 1: 151; he cites Vienna Archives, P.C, 227, iii fols, 42 and 50.

13. Socrates defines the spoken word as "an intelligent word graven in the soul of the learner, which can defend itself, and knows when to speak and when to be silent." Of this "the written word is properly no more than an image." *Phaedrus*, 276; in *The Dialogues of Plato*, ed. B. Jowett (London, 1892; reprint, New York: Random House, 1939), 1:279.

14. Sir Thomas Elyot, *The Defence of Good Women* (London, 1540), sig. A3. Subsequent quotations from this work—in which I have written our abbreviations and modernized the use of *i/j*, *u/v*, and *vv*—will be noted in the text of this essay. My thanks to the Huntington Library for permission to quote from this edition of the *Defense*. The treatise is also available as edited by Edwin Johnston Howard (Oxford, Ohio: Anchor Press, 1940).

15. "Io . . . ho . . . conosciuti . . . molti, li quali, vedendosi aver in vano tentato e speso il tempo scioccamente, rocorrono a questa nobil vendetta e dicono aver avuto abondanzia di quello che solamente s'hanno imaginato; e par loro che il dir male e trovare invenzioni, acciò che di qualche nobil donna per lo vulgo si levino fabule vituperose . . ." *Il libro del cortegiano*, ed. Bruno Maier (Turin: Unione Tipographico, 1964), bk. 3, pt. 62, p. 396.

16. "For anon as a woman is borne even from her infancy, she is kept at home in ydelnes, and as thoughe she were unmete for any

hygher busynesse, she is permitted to know no farther than her nedle and her threede. And than whan she commeth to age, able to be married, she is delyvered to the rule and governance of a jelous husband, orels she is perpetually shutte up in a close nounrye. And all offyces belongynge to the commonweale, be forbydden theym by the lawes . . . And thus by these lawes the women being subdewed as it were by force of armes, are constrained to give place to men, and to obeye theyr subdewers, not by no naturall, no divyne necessitie or reason, but by custome, education, fortune, and a certayne tyrannical occasion." *Of the nobilitie and excellencie of womankynde* (London, 1542), sig. F8, F8v, G1, G1v.

17. The female child is the result of a deviation from the human norm which is male, *Gen. An.* 4.3.767b; trans. A. L. Peck (Cambridge, Mass.: Harvard University Press, 1943), pp. 400–401; and she is "as it were a deformity, though one which occurs in the ordinary course of nature," *Gen. An.* 4.6.775a; pp. 460–61. Cf. Gaspara to the Magnifico: "quando nasce una donna, è diffetto o error della natura e contra quello che essa vorrebbe fare." *Cortegiano,* bk. 3, pt. 11, p. 352. For a study of the views of Aristotle on women, see Susan Moller Okin, *Women in Western Political Thought* (Princeton, N.J.: Princeton University Press, 1973), pp. 73–96; and Maryanne Cline Horowitz, "Aristotle and Woman," *Journal of the History of Biology* 9 no. 9 (1979):183–213.

18. "Hence woman is more compassionate than man, more easily moved to tears, at the same time more jealous, more querulous, more apt to scold and to strike. She is, furthermore, more prone to despondence and less hopeful than the man, more void of shame and self-respect, more false of speech, more deceptive, and of more retentive memory. She is also more wakeful, more shrinking, more difficult to rouse to action, and requires a smaller quantity of nutriment." *Hist. An.* q.i. 608b; trans. D'Arcy Wentworth Thompson (Oxford: Clarendon Press, 1910), no pagination.

19. "Hence there are by nature various classes of rulers and ruled. For the free rules the slave, the male the female, and the man the child in a different way. And all possess the various parts of the soul, but possess them in different ways; for the slave has not got the deliberative part at all, and the female has it, but without full authority, while the child has it, but in an undeveloped form . . . Hence it is manifest that all the persons mentioned have a moral virtue of their own, and that the temperance of a woman and that of a man are not the same, nor their courage and justice, as Socrates thought, but the one is the courage of command, and the other that of subordination, and the case is similar with the other virtues." *Politics,* trans. H. Rackham (Cambridge, Mass.: Harvard University Press, 1972), 1.5.5–8; 1260a; p. 63. See also the pseudo-*Economics*: "[In matters outside the family]

let it be her aim to obey her husband; giving no need to public affairs, nor desiring any part in arranging the marriages of her children . . . a woman of well-ordered life should consider that her husband's uses are as laws appointed for her own life by divine will, along with the marriage state . . ." trans. G. Cyril Armstrong (Cambridge, Mass.: Harvard University Press, 1947), 3.1.400–403. See also the *De anima,* 3.5.430a21.

20. See Okin, *Women,* pp. 83–86. Gordon Schochet, however, notes that Aristotle distinguishes between the organization of the *polis* and the household, and also between political justice and household justice, *Patriarchalism and Political Thought* (New York: Basic Books, 1975), pp. 21–24.

21. *A very frutefull and pleasant boke called the instruction of a Christen woman* (London, 1540), sig. E2r, E2v; U2v.

22. "And so with this purpose in view Divine Providence has fashioned the nature of man and of woman for their partnership. For they are distinguished from each other by the possession of faculties not adapted in every case to the same tasks but in some cases for opposite ones, though contributing to the same end. For Providence made man stronger and woman weaker, so that he in virtue of his manly prowess may be more ready to defend the home, and she, by reason of her kind nature, more ready to keep watch over it; and while he brings in fresh supplies from without, she may keep safe what lies within." *Ec.* 1.3; Armstrong translation, pp. 332, 333. For the general influence of the *Economics* on Renaissance treatises on women, see Maclean, *Notion,* 4.5.5, 4.5.6, 4.5.7.

23. "Quello in che l'uno dall'altro son differenti è cosa accidentale e non essenziale . . . non è dubbio che le donne, per esser più molli di carne, sono ancor più atte della mente e de ingegno più accommodato alle speculazioni che gli omini." *Cortegiano,* bk. 3, pt. 3, 353.

24. *Meno* 71–73, Jowett translation, 1.349–52.

25. *Republic* 5.454–57, Jowett translation, 1.715–19. See also Okin, *Women,* pp. 40–43.

26. Plutarch sets a precedent in his introductory remarks to the *Mulierum virtutes.* On the importance of historicism in demolishing the authority of paradigms of femininity see Maclean, *Notion,* 6.2.3.

27. Whether a woman could wage a war was obviously a critical question. Cf. Machiavelli: "Uno principe non avere altro obietto, nè altro pensiero, nè prendere cosa alcuna per sua arte, fuora della guerra e ordin e discipline di essa; perchè quella è sola arte che si espetta a chi comanda . . ." *Machiavelli's The Prince,* ed. and trans. Mark Musa (New York: St. Martins Press, 1964) 1.14.120.

28. "Howe moche doo the Frenchemen prayse a yonge damsell, whiche beinge descended of a lowe image, toke upon her after the manner of the Amazons, to leade the forward of the army; and she

fought so valiantly, and hadde soo good chaunce, that the French men beleved verily, that by her prowesse, they recovered the relm of France out of the Englisshe mens handes." *Of the nobilitie,* sig. F2, F2v.

29. "A lei sola si po dar l'onore del glorioso acquisto del regno di Granata; ché in cosi lunga e difficil guerra contra nimici ostinati. . .mostrò, sempre col consiglio e con la persona propria tanta virtù, che forse a'tempi nostri pochi prìncipi hanno avuto ardire non che di imitarla, ma pur d'averle invidia." *Cortegiano,* bk 3, pt. 35, p. 386.

30. *Instruction of a Christen woman,* sig. U2v.

31. " 'Silence gives grace to woman' though that is not the case likewise with a man." *Politics,* 1.5.508; 1260a, ed. cit., p. 65.

32. Lionardo Bruni, *De studies et litteris,* trans. William Harrison Woodward, in *Vittorino da Feltre and other humanist educators* (Cambridge: Cambridge University Press, 1897), pp. 124, 126.

33. *The instruction of a Christen woman.* sig. E2, E2v. Later he reverses himself and declares he will not condemn eloquence, E2v. But the tenor of the treatise as a whole is negative.

34. "et si multa sit virtus adscendenti tunc quoque cadendum est. A quo nec Zenobia immunis evadere potuit." "[Aurelius] indignum ratus foeminam Romani partem Imperii possidere in Zenobiam arma convertit." *De casibus illustrium virorum,* a facsimile edition of the Paris edition of 1520. (Gainesville, Fla.: Scholars Facsimiles & Reprints, 1962), 8:192.

35. "Ex quo non aliter quam si maximum superasset ducem et acerrimum rei publice hostem, Aurelianus gloriatus est eamque triumpho servavit et adduxit cum filiis Roman." *Tutte le Opere,* 100:414.

36. See Hyrde's preface to Margaret More's translation of Erasmus's *Precatio domenica, A devout treatise upon the pater noster* (London, n.d.), sig. A4, A4v. This preface was written in 1524 for Frances Brandon, daughter of Charles Brandon, duke of Suffolk and his wife Mary, daughter of Henry VII.

37. See "Letter to his daughters," 1524; quoted in Foster Watson, *Vives and the Renascence Education of Women* (New York: Longmans, Green, 1912), p. 179.

38. Erasmus praises More's school for young women in a letter to John Faber; quoted in Watson, *Vives and the Renascence Education of Women,* p. 178. He also praised Catherine for her learning on several occasions; see Garrett Mattingly, *Catherine,* pp. 181–84, who cites Allen 3:602; 9:401.

39. *Ec.* 3.4; Armstrong translation, p. 414.

40. "pero se esso vi comandasse che faceste un tradimento, non solamente non sete obligato a farlo, ma sete obligato a non farlo e per

voi stesso, e per non esser ministro della vergogna del signor vostro."
Cortegiano, bk. 2, pt. 23, pp. 225, 226.

41. *A ryght frutefull epystle devysed by the moste excellent clerke Erasmus in laude and prayse of matrymony* (London, n.d.), D2v. This is a translation by Rychard Tavernour of the *Encomium matrimonii*, published in 1534. Erasmus's words are echoed by Agrippa: "for an evill wife never happeneth but to an evil husband" who further counsels "And let not [thy wife] be subject unto the, but let her be with the in all trust and counsayle, and let her be in thy house, not as a drudge, but as a maistresse of the house . . ." *The Commendation of Matrimony* (London, 1534), sig. C3r, C6v. This is a translation, by David Clapham, of the *De sacramento matrimonii declamatio*, 1526. For a different view see Vives, *The office and dutie of an husband* (London, n.d.) sig. N6r. The theological and philosophical background to the rule of obedience for a wife is briefly presented in Maclean, *Notion* 2.7.5, 2.8.1, 2.9.1.

42. In his article "Politics and the Praise of Women: Political Doctrine in the Courtier's Third Book," in *Castiglione: the Ideal and the Real in Renaissance Culture,* ed. Robert Hanning and David Rosand (New Haven: Yale University Press, 1982), pp. 29–34, Dain A. Trafton argues that in book 3 Castiglione actually evolves a basis for the political life of the courtier who is represented there in the collective image of the numerous ladies celebrated by the Magnifico.

43. Mattingly, *Catherine*, p. 405; who cites Cal. SP Span. 5, 430.

44. Mattingly, *Catherine*, p. 302; who cites Cal. SP Span. 4, 2 688. (V.A.). See also pp. 404–5; Cal. Span. IV, ii, 291, 554, 596.

45. Vives came to England in 1523 and remained for five years, lecturing at Oxford and gracing Henry's court. Catherine had commissioned him to write the *De institutione*, which he brought with him to England. Mattingly guesses that Catherine, having realized that Mary might one day rule, was concerned to have her trained to her part, *Catherine*, pp. 186–89. But if so, the treatise itself, with all its prohibitions against women in government, would have disappointed and perhaps alarmed her.

Chapter 15: Singing Unsung Heroines

1. All quotations from Spenser are taken from *The Poetical Works of Edmund Spenser,* ed. J. C. Smith (Oxford: Clarendon Press, 1909).

2. For example, consider Paul de Man's characterization of the ontological self in "Ludwig Binswanger and the Sublimation of the Self," in *Blindness and Insight: Essays in the Rhetoric of Contemporary Criticism* (New York: Oxford University Press, 1971), pp. 36–50. For a discussion of the role of gender in interpretation, see Annette Kolodny, "A Map for Rereading: Or Gender and the Interpretation of Literary Texts," *New Literary History* 11 (1980): 451–67.

3. Spenser is revising the patriarchal practice of relegating the female to the margins of culture and, with her, all those aspects of the human condition—emotion, physicality, mortality, subjectivity, vulnerability—that the culture did not, at a given moment, want to confront. An important part of Spenser's interest in chronicling the legend of Britomart and developing an anatomy of love in Book 3 is to restore wholeness to men and to language. The political implications of these discursive practices are well beyond the scope of this paper. Certainly (the highly problematic) Book 5 provides a very different view of female rule in regard to all women who are not Elizabeth.

4. See John Freccero, "The Fig Tree and the Laurel: Petrarch's Poetics," *Diacritics* 5 (Spring 1975): 34–40; and Giuseppe Mazzotta, "The *Canzoniere* and the Language of the Self," *SP* 75 (1978): 271–76.

5. Kathleen Williams has an extended discussion of Merlin's mirror in *Spenser's* Faerie Queene: *The World of Glass* (London: Routledge & Kegan Paul, 1966), pp. 93–96.

6. Gerald Graff considers this issue in *Literature against Itself: Literary Ideas in Modern Society* (Chicago: University of Chicago Press, 1979), esp. pp. 31–62.

7. For a discussion of Renaissance notions of *discordia concors,* see Edgar Wind, *Pagan Mysteries in the Renaissance* (1958; 2d ed., New York: W. W. Norton, 1968), pp. 81–96.

8. I borrow terms such as "Platonic metaphysics of full presence" from Derridean criticism without meaning to ally myself with any particular critical school and certainly without claiming that Spenser's poetic practice illustrates the theories of Jacques Derrida or anyone else. Discussion of linguistic self-consciousness—how an author's text reflects on the nature of its own language—in earlier texts, particularly in allegorical ones, sometimes seems tantalizing like deconstructive criticism. For a particularly felicitous application of contemporary literary theory to Ovid, the reader is urged to see John Brenkman, "Narcissus in the Text," *Georgia Review* 30 (1976): 293–327. Such a consideration of literary theory is well beyond the scope of this paper. I suspect, however, that the differences between the deconstructionist project and Spenser's undertaking are apt to be as interesting as the similarities. In particular, unlike the deconstructionists, Spenser is willing to risk mystification in order to construct the subject.

9. Kathleen Williams analyzes Scudamore's personal culpability at some length in *Spenser's World of Glass*. See esp. pp. 105–7, 134–37.

10. See, for example, James Nohrnberg, *The Analogy of* The Faerie Queene (Princeton, N.J.: Princeton University Press, 1976), pp. 474–78.

11. The notion of the speech act comes from J. L. Austin, *How To Do Things with Words* (1962; 2d ed., Cambridge: Harvard University

Press, 1975). Barbara Johnson discusses the ambiguous role of performative language in "Poetry and Performative Language: Mallarme and Austin," in *The Critical Difference: Essays in the Contemporary Rhetoric of Reading* Baltimore: Johns Hopkins University Press, 1980), pp. 52–66.

12. In *Heroic Love: Studies in Sidney and Spenser* (Cambridge: Harvard University Press, 1968), p. 123, Mark Rose observes that "Cruelty" and "Despight" refer to the role Amoret is made to play.

13. Critics who locate the pageant inside Amoret's head tend to see Busirane as trying to frighten Amoret with a distorted or reductive vision of sexuality that plays on her fears of marriage. Versions of this interpretation are given by Janet Spens, *Spenser's* Faerie Queene: *An Interpretation* (1934; reprint, New York: Russell, 1967), p. 105; A. C. Hamilton, *The Structure of Allegory in* The Faerie Queene (Oxford: Clarendon Press, 1961), pp. 145–46; William Nelson, *The Poetry of Edmund Spenser* (New York: Columbia University Press, 1963), p. 230; Thomas P. Roche, *The Kindly Flame: A Study of the Third and Fourth Books of Spenser's* Faerie Queene (Princeton, N.J.: Princeton University Press, 1976), pp. 473–75. Harry Berger, Jr., in "Busirane and the War Between the Sexes: An Interpretation of *The Faerie Queene* III. xi.xii," *ELR* 1 (1971): 99–121, shows a much greater appreciation of the role of the imagination in Amoret's plight. For a discussion of the element of fictionmaking in the Masque of Cupid, see Isabel MacCaffrey, *Spenser's Allegory: The Anatomy of Imagination* (Princeton, N.J.: Princeton University Press, 1975), pp. 107–17.

14. Paul de Man, "Semiology and Rhetoric," in *Textual Strategies: Perspectives in Post-Structuralist Criticism,* ed. Josué Harari (Ithaca, N.Y.: Cornell University Press, 1979), pp. 121–40.

15. Alpers makes a similar point, p. 402.

16. John Brenkman considers the issue of Platonic hierarchies in relation to the *Symposium* in "The Other and the One: Psychoanalysis, Reading, the Symposium," in *Literature and Psychoanalysis. The Question of Reading: Otherwise,* ed. Shoshana Felman, Yale French Studies, Nos. 55–56 (New Haven: Yale University Press, 1977), pp. 396–456.

17. Donald Cheney, *Spenser's Images of Nature: Wild Man and Shepherd in "The Faerie Queene,"* (New York: Yale University Press, 1966), pp. 126–30.

18. Owen Barfield treats the issue of familiar vs. inferred nature in *Worlds Apart* (Middletown, Conn.: Wesleyan University Press, 1963), esp. in the mock-Platonic dialogue, pp. 65–68. See also Harry Berger, Jr., "Spenser's Gardens of Adonis: Forces and Form in the Renaissance Imagination," *UTQ* 30 (1961): 128–49.

19. On the philosophical background of the Gardens of Adonis, see Frank Kermode, *The Sense of an Ending: Studies in the Theory of Fiction*

(London: Oxford University Press, 1966), pp. 67–89; Rosalie Colie, *Paradoxica Epidemica: The Renaissance Tradition of Paradox* (Princeton, N.J.: Princeton University Press, 1966), pp. 335–49; Humphrey Tonkin, "Spenser's Garden of Adonis and Britomart's Quest," *PMLA* 88 (1973): 408–17; Fred L. Milne, "The Doctrine of Act and Potency: A Metaphysical Ground for Interpretation of Spenser's Garden of Adonis Passages," *SP* 70 (1973): 279–87. In *The Kindly Flame,* Thomas Roche makes some judicious comments about the difficulties of assigning a piece of poetry to any particular philosophy.

20. Ovid, *Metamorphoses,* (10.503–59).

Chapter 16: Stella's Wit

1. William A. Ringler, Jr., ed. *The Poems of Sir Philip Sidney* (Oxford: Clarendon Press, 1962), pp. 440, 436; cf. Hoyt H. Hudson, "Penelope Devereux as Sidney's Stella," *Huntington Library Bulletin* 7 (1935): 89–129.

2. For parallel discussions of the literary and sexual politics of Elizabethan sonnets, see Ann Rosalind Jones and Peter Stallybrass, "Courtship and Courtiership: The Politics of *Astrophil and Stella,*" *Studies in English Literature,* 24 (1984), 53–68; Richard C. McCoy, *Sir Philip Sidney: Rebellion in Arcadia* (New Brunswick, N.J.: Rutgers University Press, 1979), pp. 69–109; Arthur F. Marotti, " 'Love is not Love': Elizabethan Sonnet Sequences and the Social Order," *ELH* 49 (1982): 396–428; and Clark Hulse, "Petrarchan Rhetoric," chap. 2 of *Metamorphic Verse* (Princeton, N.J.: Princeton University Press, 1981). All, unfortunately, leave Stella in the realm of the symbolic.

3. The position is first formulated by Hallett Smith in *Elizabethan Poetry* (Cambridge: Harvard University Press, 1952), pp. 146–53. While Smith phrases his argument about the two audiences with great subtlety and sensitivity to the text, it often becomes rigidly antibiographical in later hands. For a reasonable compromise between the claims of biography and fiction, see A. C. Hamilton, *Sir Philip Sidney: A Study of His Life and Works* (Cambridge: Cambridge University Press, 1977), pp. 79–86.

4. Sir Philip Sidney, *A Defence of Poetry,* ed. Jan van Dorsten (Oxford: Oxford University Press, 1966), pp. 69–70.

5. Sir Philip Sidney, *Astrophil and Stella,* 1.1–6; all citations are to Ringler's edition. In line 2 I adopt the reading of Ringler's copytext, the 1598 folio (98), which Ringler has rejected in favor of "the deare She," the reading of all other substantive texts except for the Bright manuscript, which reads "thee (deer ⟨ ⟩he." Ringler's choice is correct according to the principles of his edition, in which the reading of any two of the three text groups (X, Y, Z) is preferred over the third (p. 456). In this case, all Y and Z texts, plus one X text (Fraunce's *Arcadian Rhetorike*) concur on "the deare She." Ringler concludes, however,

that the X group as a whole probably derives from a manuscript owned by the countess of Pembroke (p. 449), who oversaw the production of the 1598 folio. Hence the 98 reading, in which Astrophil dramatically sighs and repeats himself at the mere mention of Stella, may represent the sonnet as it was presented to Sidney's immediate audience. Interestingly, the Bright manuscript, with its even more dramatic and direct reading, seems also to have originated within the Sidney family.

6. In *"Astrophil and Stella*: Pure and Impure Persuasion," *English Literary Renaissance* 2 (1972): 100–15, Richard Lanham argues that Sidney's purpose is to "bed the girl." He adds, "There is no Astrophil in the poem except as a name . . . He was not trying to hide the truth so much as follow a convention which masked the truth under flimsy pretext . . . I am not saying that the sequence cannot survive extraction from its biographical matrix. It can and has. But why extract it when it obviously gains from being left as the anomalous artifact, half art and half life, which it was?" (p. 108).

7. John Stevens analyzes the "game of love" as it was practiced at the beginning of the century in *Music and Poetry in the Early Tudor Court* (Cambridge: Cambridge University Press, 1961), pp. 154–202. Dorothy Connell draws on Stevens for her portrayal of Sidney as a "courtly maker" in *Sir Philip Sidney: The Maker's Mind* (Oxford: Clarendon Press, 1977), chap. 3. While it is no doubt true that the rise of print led to a gradual shift from orality to literacy in the late sixteenth century, leading in turn to a divorce between music and lyric poetry, there is evidence of a reassertion of manuscript circulation and coterie performance at court and the Inns of Court in the period 1580–1610, as a reaction to the growth of the public literary audience served by print.

8. Cyril Falls, "Penelope Rich and the Poets: Philip Sidney to John Ford," *Essays by Divers Hands: Transactions of the Royal Society of Literature,* n.s. 28 (1956): 131 [includes text of letter].

9. Quoted in G. B. Harrison, *The Life and Death of Robert Devereux, Earl of Essex* (London: Crowell, 1937). p. 319.

10. Quoted by Falls, p. 133.

11. Rowland Whyte to Sir Robert Sidney, in *Letters and Memorials of State* [by members of the Sidney family], ed. Arthur Collins, 2 vols. (London: T. Osborne, 1746), 1: 385.

12. Ringler, ed., p. 446.

13. John Aubrey, *Aubrey's Brief Lives,* ed. Oliver Lawson Dick (London: Secker and Warburg, 1960), pp. 138–39.

14. For the Petrarchan basis of the *blazon* as a device of control, see Nancy J. Vickers, "Diana Described: Scattered Women and Scattered Rhyme," *Critical Inquiry* 8 (1981): 265–79.

15. Aubrey, pp. 255–56.

16. Collins, *Letters and Memorials of State,* 1:88.

17. Collins, *Letters and Memorials of State,* 1:147.

18. A genuinely dangerous communication would be transmitted orally by a trusty messenger, or, if even this was imprudent, encoded by a one-time-only cipher.

19. Ringler, ed., pp. 566–68, lists musical settings for various sonnets by Sidney and for the songs in *Astrophil and Stella.* No Renaissance settings of sonnets from *Astrophil and Stella* survive. See also Connell, p. 70n; and Frank J. Fabry, "Sidney's Poetry and Italian Song-Form," *English Literary Renaissance* 3 (1973): 232–48.

20. Hence my position is diametrically opposed to that of Gary F. Waller in "Acts of Reading: The Production of Meaning in *Astrophil and Stella,*" *Studies in the Literary Imagination* 15 (1982): 23–35. Waller wishes to "consider the whole tradition of readers, from Greville or Dyer or Mary Sidney, or even Penelope Rich, to readers in 1982, and beyond—without privileging any." Precisely by privileging Penelope Rich as a reader, Sidney polarizes the field in which other readers act, giving their interpretations a sexual-political tension that Waller's reading would neutralize.

21. Cf. David L. Miller, " 'The Pleasure of the Text': Two Renaissance Versions," *New Orleans Review* 2 (1982): 50–55. Miller locates cruxes in *Astrophil and Stella* (especially 76) that alternatively offer "modest" and "wanton" readings to the audience, creating, in Roland Barthes' words, an "intermittance . . . which is erotic."

22. It may be significant that in the 1591 quarto and the Houghton manuscript (texts that elsewhere delete sensitive material), Stella's reply does not appear (Ringler, ed., pp. 541–42). See also Jean Robertson's discussion (in "Sir Philip Sidney and Lady Penelope Rich," *Review of English Studies,* n.s. 15 (1964): 296–97) of Sidney's deathbed struggle of conscience over "a Vanitie wherein I had taken delight, whereof I had not ridd my selfe. It was my Ladie Rich."

23. Collins, *Letters and Memorials of State,* 1:147.

24. Walter Bourchier Devereux, *Lives and Letters of the Earls of Essex,* 2 vols. (London: John Murray, 1853), 1:138–40.

Chapter 17: Gender vs. Sex Difference in Louise Labé's Grammar of Love

1. Louise Labé, *Oeuvres complètes,* ed. F. Rigolot (Paris: Flammarion, 1986), p. 76. The page reference for all quotations will be given in parentheses in the text. Edwin Marion Cox's translation of the *Débat* will be used with a fair degree of modification (London: Williams & Norgate, 1925), page number in the text. All other translations are mine.

2. I do not feel obliged to reconstruct these patterns since they have been brought out by much traditional criticism.

3. "Literary History as a Challenge to Literary Theory," in *New Directions in Literary History,* ed. R. Cohen (Baltimore: Johns Hopkins University Press, 1974).

4. This is the title of Maurice Scève's famous work, usually considered as the first French *canzoniere* (Lyons: Sulpice Sabon, 1544).

5. Jonathan Culler, *The Pursuit of Signs* (Ithaca, N.Y.: Cornell University Press, 1981), p. 54.

6. "Intertextual Scrambling," *Romantic Review* 68 (May 1977): 197.

7. "Qu'importe qu'elle ait été docte, puisqu'elle a été passionnée et qu'elle parle à tout lecteur le langage de l'âme?" *Revue des deux mondes,* 15 mars 1845, reprinted in *Portraits contemporains* (Paris: Michel Lévy, 1871), vol. 5. p. 37.

8. *Amours, délices,* and *orgues* are the only three French nouns which change from masculine to feminine as they turn from singular to plural. Some dictionaries and grammars state that there is no fixed usage for the gender of *armours* in the plural. Cf. M. Grevisse, *Le Bon Usage* (Gembloux: J. Duculot, 1975), pp. 212–13.

9. Edmont Huguet, *Dictionnaire de la langue française du XVIe siècle* (Paris: Champion, 1925), vol. 1.

10. *Gargantua,* ed. Calder-Screech (Geneva: Droz, 1970) chap. 7, p. 60 (see also the discussion above in this volume by Carla Freccero).

11. *Evvres de Lovize Labé Lionnoize* (Lyons: Perrin & Durand, 1824), p. 187, n. 123.

12. Labé, *Oeuvres complètes,* ed. Enzo Giudici (Geneva: Droz, 1981), p. 170, n. 29.

13. Cf. Nina Catach, *L'Orthographe française à l'époque de la Renaissance* (Geneva: Droz, 1968), p. 224ff.

14. For a discussion of these problems, see my "Intentionalité du Texte et Théorie de la *persona,*" *Michigan Romance Studies* 1 (1980): 186–207.

15. "For Love and Death are but one same thing": *Second Livre des Sonnets pour Hélène* (1578), 55, line 14.

16. Cf. Grahame Castor, *Pléiade Poetics* (Cambridge: Cambridge University Press, 1964). "Excellence of invention was held to be the most important factor in the achievement of those qualities . . . which the 16th century prized" (p. 189).

17. Marguerite de Navarre is, of course, a very special case, given her social position and connections with the royal court. As Natalie Z. Davis writes, in the first half of the sixteenth century, the image of the learned, wealthy, and well-born lady was strongly established. Yet, "reading and writing for women of the *menu peuple* was more likely to be ridiculous, a subject for farce. All this shows how extraordinary was the achievement of Louise Labé, the one low-born female poet of

16th-century France." *Society and Culture in Early Modern France* (Stanford, Calif.: Stanford University Press, 1975), p. 73.

18. "The Language of Madness in the Renaissance," *The Yearbook of Italian Studies* 1 (1970): 199–234.

19. Ibid., p. 210.

20. *Gargantua,* ed. Calder-Screech, chap. 55, p. 302.

21. *Ecriz de divers poëtes / A la louenge de Louise Labé,* in the 1555 and 1556 original editions of Labé's *Euvres.*

22. Jonathan Cruller, *Structuralist Poetics* (Ithaca, N.Y.: Cornell University Press, 1975), p. 162.

23. Gillian Jondorf, "Petrarchan Variations in P. du Guillet and L. Labé," *MLN* 71 (no. 4, 1976): 766–78.

Chapter 18: City Women and Their Audiences

1. For research into the still problematic area of literacy in the Renaissance, see Elizabeth Eisenstein, *The Printing Press as an Agent of Change* (Cambridge: Cambridge University Press, 1979), pp. 60–66; Natalie Zemon Davis, "Publishing and the People," in *Society and Culture in Early Modern France* (Stanford, Calif.: Stanford University Press, 1975); and David Cressy, *Literacy and the Social Order: Reading and Writing in Tudor and Stuart England* (Cambridge: Cambridge University Press, 1980).

2. For an analysis of the mixture of liberalism and restrictiveness in humanist educational theory as exemplified by Vives, see Gloria Kaufman, "Juan Luis Vives on the Education of Women, 1523," *Signs* 3 (no. 4, Summer 1978): 891–97. Ruth Kelso devotes two chapters, "Training" and "Studies," to ideas about education for women in her survey of conduct books, *Doctrine for the Lady of the Renaissance* (Urbana: University of Illinois Press, 1956; reprint, 1978). For a study of early seventeenth-century limits on education for women, see Dorothy Gies McGuigan's account of the career of Elena Cornaro, "To Be a Woman and a Scholar," *LSA Magazine,* Fall 1978 (University of Michigan: College of Literature, Science, and the Arts).

3. Ruth Kelso plausibly suggests that the emphasis on modesty, obedience, and withdrawal from the world exemplifies a Renaissance tendency to assign residual Christian duties to women while reserving new humanist justifications for worldly ambition to men (*Doctrine,* p. 25). A similar contradiction is identified by Margaret King in "The Religious Retreat of Isotta Nogarola: Sexism and Its Consequences in the Fifteenth Century," *Signs* 3 (no. 4, Summer 1978). King argues that pressures toward feminine reticence help to explain the Veronese scholar's eventual withdrawal from the public life of Verona and Venice. See also Janis Butler Holm, "The Myth of a Feminist Humanism," *Soundings,* 68 (no. 4, Winter 1984).

4. *De Re uxoria,* trans. in *The Earthly Republic: Italian Humanists on*

Government and Society, ed. Benjamin Kohl et al. (Philadelphia: University of Pennsylvania Press, 1978), p. 203.

5. Quoted in Kelso, *Doctrine,* p. 59.

6. See Antoine du Moulin's preface, in Pernette du Guillet, *Rymes,* ed. Victor Graham (Geneva: Droz, 1968).

7. Quoted by Josephine Roberts in "An Unpublished Literary Quarrel Concerning the Suppression of Mary Wroth's *Urania,*" *Notes and Queries* 222 (December 1877): 533.

8. Recent studies of the roles of humanists and courtiers as defenders and beneficiaries of ducal and royal patronage, to which I am indebted for my interpretation of women's somewhat different ambitions, include Lauro Martines, *Power and Imagination: City-States in Renaissance Italy* (New York: Alfred A. Knopf, 1979); Daniel Javitch, *Poetry and Courtliness in Renaissance England* (Princeton, N.J.: Princeton University Press, 1978); Stephen Greenblatt, *Renaissance Self-fashioning: from More to Shakespeare* (Chicago: Chicago University Press, 1980); and Arthur Marotti, " 'Love is not Love:' Elizabethan Sonnet Sequences and the Social Order," *ELH* 49 (Summer 1982): 396–428. A very useful analysis of literary salons is Carolyn Lougee's *Le Paradis des femmes: Women, salons, and social stratification in seventeenth-century France* (Princeton: Princeton University Press, 1976).

9. Two studies of the socioeconomic energy of Lyons as a spur to cultural production are Lucien Romier, "Lyons and Cosmopolitanism at the Beginning of the French Renaissance," in *French Humanism, 1470–1600,* ed. Werner Gundesheimer (New York: Harper & Row, 1969), and Natalie Zemon Davis, "City Women and Religious Change," in *Society and Culture.*

10. In her second elegy, Labé claims that she is read in Spain ("La terre . . . que Calpe et Pyrenée / Avec la mer tiennent environnée") and in Germany ("Du large Rhin les roulantes areines"), ll. 63–66. Her *Débat de Folie et d'Amour* was translated in England by Robert Greene and republished three times (1584; 1587, 1593, 1604).

11. Oliver de Magny, *Les Odes amoureuses de 1599,* ed. Mark Whitney (Geneva: Droz, 1964), pp. 132–36.

12. Fernand Zamaron includes a chapter on the poems written in honor of Labé in *Louise Labé: Dame de la franchise* (Paris: Nizet, 1968), pp. 124–48.

13. See Zamaron's chapter, "La Réputation de l'écrivain et de la femme," in *Louis Labé,* p. 66.

14. *Coryat's Crudities* (1611; reprint, Glasgow, James MacLehose for the University of Glasgow, 1905), 1:402–3. Coryat's observations are summarized and related to other travelers' tales by Fernando Henriques, *Prostitution in Europe and the New World* (London: Macgibbon and Kee, 1963), p. 78.

15. For a rich survey of Venetian courtesanship and a biography of

Franco, see Arturo Graf, "Una Cortigiana fra mille," in *Attraverso il Cinquecento* (Turin: Chiantore, 1926), pp. 174–284.

16. Georgina Masson recounts this and other anecdotes about Franco in the final chapter of her lively but sometimes overcredulous *Courtesans of the Italian Renaissance* (London: St. Martins Press, *1975).*

17. Graf, "Una Cortigiana fra mille," p. 188.

18. Coryat, *Crudities,* p. 405.

19. *Euvres complètes de Louise Labé,* ed. Enzo Giudici (Geneva: Droz, 1981), p. 150.

20. Veronica Franco, *Terze rime e sonetti,* ed. Abdelkader Salza, *Scrittori d'Italia* (Bari: Laterza, 1913), 52: 235.

21. The practical value to courtesans of associating with well-known humanists is exemplified in the legal triumph of Tullia d'Aragona, who was called into court in Florence in 1547 on the charge of disobeying a sumptuary law that required courtesans to wear a yellow veil. Her reputation as a poet, combined with the support for which she appealed to Benedetto Varchi, persuaded Cosimo de Medici to intervene on her behalf. He wrote on Varchi's petition, perhaps ironically, "Fasseli gratia, come poetessa" (Be merciful to her, as a poet). Unlike Franco's poem to Venier, the eulogy of Tullia's literary and philosophical talents written by Cosimo's minister suppresses any reference to her profession (Masson, *Courtesans of the Italian Renaissance,* pp. 119–21).

22. Tita Rosenthal, in a recent Yale dissertation, identifies Franco's attacker as Maffeo Venier and argues for much of Franco's poetry as a courtesan's self-defense ("Veronica Franco: The Courtesan as Poet in Sixteenth-Century Venice," 1985).

23. Similar arguments for women's intellectual equality (and even superiority) to men had been made by Christine de Pisan in *Le Trésor de la cité des dames* (1405) and by Cornelius Agrippa in *De nobilitate et praecellentia foeminei sexus* (1532). Franco, however, may have been an early participant in a rising wave of woman-authored defenses of women, typified by Modesta Pozzo in *Il merito delle donne* (1590) and Lucrezia Marinella (*Le Nobiltà et Eccellenze delle Donne* [1590]). See Adriana Chemello, "La Donna, il modello, l'immaginario: Moderata Fonte e Lucrezia Marinella," in *Nel Cerchio della luna: Figure di donna in alcuni testi del XVI secolo,* ed. Marina Zancan (Venice: Marsilio, 1983).

24. Veronica Franco, *Lettere,* ed. Benedetto Croce (Rome: Ricciardi, 1949), p. 38.

Selected Bibliography

The following selected bibliography is intended to provide readers with titles that will, at the very least, allow them to pursue further titles. Needless to say, any compilation touching on so many disciplines makes no pretense of exhaustive coverage. Moreover, in the interest of readability, such a list must be subdivided into categories that at times, regrettably, fail to reflect the interdisciplinary nature of the works cited. Three editorial principles here applied should be noted: first, in most cases where multiple articles in anthologies merited inclusion, the volumes—not the individual essays—have been indicated; second, in fields where extensive bibliography exists and has already been compiled (Shakespeare studies, for example) we have chosen not to repeat previous labor but rather to point our readers to it; and finally, we have not included primary texts, although we do indicate several anthologies of primary materials. Our categories are the following:

1. Bibliographies; Anthologies of Primary Texts
2. General
3. Literary Criticism
4. Art
5. Education
6. Religion
7. Law
8. Witchcraft
9. Medicine
10. Marriage and the Family
11. Work
12. Politics

1. Bibliographies; Anthologies of Primary Texts

Bornstein, Diane, ed. *Distaves and Dames: Renaissance Treatises for and about Women*. Delmar, N.Y.: Scholars' Facsimiles and Reprints, 1978.
———, ed. *The Feminist Controversy of the Renaissance*. Delmar, N.Y.: Scholars' Facsimiles and Reprints, 1980.

Clive, H. P. *Marguerite de Navarre: An Annotated Bibliography*. London: Grant & Cutler Ltd., Research Bibliographies & Checklists, 1983.

Frey, Linda, Marsha Frey, and Joanne Schneider. *Women in Western European History: A Select Chronological, Geographical, and Topical Bibliography from Antiquity to the French Revolution*. Westport, Conn.: Greenwood, 1982.

Gartenberg, Patricia, and Nena Thames Whittemore. "A Checklist of English Women in Print, 1475–1640." *Bulletin of Bibliography and Magazine Notes* 34 (Jan.–March 1977):1–13.

Goreau, Angeline, E., ed. *The Whole Duty of a Woman: Female Writers in Seventeenth Century England*. Garden City, N.Y.: Dial Press, 1985.

Goulianos, Joan, ed. *By a Woman Writt: Literature from Six Centuries by and about Women*. Indianapolis: Bobbs-Merrill, 1973.

Greco, Norma, and Ronaele Novotny. "Bibliography of Women in the English Renaissance." *University of Michigan Papers in Women's Studies* 1 (June 1974):30–57.

Guillerm, Luce, Jean-Pierre Guillerm, Laurence Hardoir, and Marie-France Piéjus, eds. *Le Miroir des femmes, I: moralistes et polémistes au XVIe siècle*. Lille: Presses Universitaires de Lille, 1983.

Hafton, Owen. "Women in History: Early Modern Europe." *Past and Present* 101 (1983):125–41.

Hageman, Elizabeth H., and Josephine A. Roberts. "Recent Studies in Women Writers of Tudor England." *English Literary Renaissance* 14 (Autumn 1984):409–39.

Henderson, Katherine Usher, and Barbara F. McManus, eds. *Half Humankind: Contexts and Texts of the Controversy about Women in England, 1540–1640*. Urbana and Chicago: University of Illinois Press, 1985.

Irwin, Joyce. "Society and the Sexes." In *Reformation Europe: A Guide to Research*, edited by Steven E. Ozment. Saint Louis: Center for Reformation Research, 1982.

Kanner, Barbara. *The Women of England: From Anglo-Saxon Times to the Present: Interpretive Bibliographical Essays*. Hamden, Conn.: Archon Books, 1979.

King, Margaret L., and Albert Rabil, eds. *Her Immaculate Hand: Selected Works by and about the Women Humanists of Quattrocento Italy*. Binghamton, N.Y.: Center for Medieval and Early Renaissance Studies, State University of New York at Binghamton, 1983.

Mahl, Mary R., ed. *The Female Spectator: English Women Writers before 1800*. Bloomington, Ind.: Indiana University Press, 1977.

Parker, Franklin, and Betty Parker, eds. *Women's Education, A World View: Annotated Bibliography of Books and Reports*. Westport, Conn.: Greenwood, 1981.

Rowton, Frederic. *The Female Poets of Great Britain*. Facsimile of the

1853 edition, edited by Marilyn L. Williamson. Detroit: Wayne State University Press, 1981.

Travitsky, Betty, ed. *The Paradise of Women: Writings by Englishwomen of the Renaissance.* Contributions in Women's Studies, no. 22. Westport, Conn.: Greenwood Press, 1981.

Utley, Francis Lee. *The Crooked Rib: An Analytical Index to the Argument about Women in English and Scots Literature to the End of the Year 1568.* Columbus: Ohio State University, 1944.

Wiesner, Merry E. *Women in the Sixteenth Century: A Bibliography.* Sixteenth Century Bibliography, no. 23. Saint Louis: Center for Reformation Research, 1983.

2. General

Albistur, Maïté, and Daniel Armogathe. *Histoire du féminisme français: du moyen âge à nos jours.* Paris: Des Femmes, 1977.

Arthur, Marilyn B. "Early Greece: The Origins of the Western Attitude toward Women." *Arethusa* 6 (1973):7–58.

Ascoli, Georges. "Essai sur l'histoire des idées féministes en France du XVIe siècle à la Révolution." *Revue de Synthèse historique* 12 (1906):25–57.

Axton, Marie. *The Queen's Two Bodies: Drama and the Elizabethan Succession.* London: Royal Historical Society, 1977.

Bergeron, David M. "Women as Patrons of English Renaissance Drama." In *Patronage in the Renaissance,* edited by Guy Fitch Lytle and Stephen Orgel, 274–90 Princeton: Princeton University Press, 1981.

Bomli, Petronella Wilhelmina. *La Femme dans l'Espagne du siècle d'or.* The Hague: M. Nijhoff, 1950.

Bridenthal, Renate, and Claudia Koonz, eds. *Becoming Visible: Women in European History.* Boston: Houghton Mifflin, 1977.

Brown, Judith C. *Immodest Acts: The Life of a Lesbian Nun in Renaissance Italy.* New York: Oxford University Press, 1986.

Brustein, Robert. "The Monstrous Regiment of Women: Sources for the Satiric View of the Court Lady in English Drama." In *Renaissance and Modern Essays,* edited by G. R. Hibbard, 35–50. New York: Barnes and Noble, 1966.

Bruyn, Jan de. "The Ideal Lady and the Rise of Feminism in Seventeenth-Century England." *Mosaic* 17 (1984):19–28.

Camden, Charles Carroll. *The Elizabethan Woman.* Houston, Tex.: Elsevier Press, 1952. Revised edition. Mamaroneck, N.Y.: P. P. Appel, 1975.

Crandall, Coryl. "The Cultural Implications of the Swetnam Anti-Feminist Controversy in the Seventeenth Century." *Journal of Popular Culture* 2 (1968):136–48.

Crawford, Patricia. "Attitudes to Menstruation in Seventeenth-Century England." *Past and Present* 91 (1981):47–73.

Darmon, Pierre. *Mythologie de la femme dans l'ancienne France.* Paris: Seuil, 1983.

Davis, Natalie Zemon. *Society and Culture in Early Modern France.* Stanford: Stanford University Press, 1975.

———. *The Return of Martin Guerre.* Cambridge: Harvard University Press, 1983.

Einstein, Lewis. *Tudor Ideals.* New York: Russell and Russell, 1962.

Fahy, Conor. "Three Early Renaissance Treatises on Women." *Italian Studies* 11 (1956):30–55.

Fitzmaurice-Kelly, Julia. "Woman in Sixteenth-Century Spain." *Revue hispanique* 70 (1927):557–632.

Grimal, Pierre, ed. *Histoire mondiale de la femme.* Vol. 2. Paris: Nouvelle Librairie de France, 1965.

Hamilton, Roberta. *The Liberation of Women: A Study of Patriarchy and Capitalism.* London and Boston: George Allen and Unwin, 1978.

Hill, Christopher. *The World Turned Upside Down: Radical Ideas during the English Revolution.* New York: Viking Press, 1972.

Hoffmann, Paul. *La Femme dans la pensée des Lumières.* Paris: Editions Ophrys, 1977.

Hogrefe, Pearl. *Tudor Women: Commoners and Queens.* Ames, Iowa: Iowa State University Press, 1975.

———. *Women of Action in Tudor England.* Ames, Iowa: Iowa State University Press, 1977.

Kamen, Henry. *The Iron Century: Social Change in Europe, 1550–1660.* New York: Praeger Publishers, 1972.

Kelly (-Gadol), Joan. "Notes on Women in the Renaissance and Renaissance Historiography." Part 2 of *Conceptual Frameworks for Studying Women's History,* 1–11. Bronxville, N.Y.: Sarah Lawrence Publications, 1976.

———. "Did Women Have a Renaissance?" In *Becoming Visible: Women in European History,* edited by Renate Bridenthal and Claudia Koonz, 139–64. Boston: Houghton Mifflin, 1977.

———. *Women, History, and Theory: The Essays of Joan Kelly.* Chicago: University of Chicago Press, 1984.

Klapisch-Zuber, Christiane. *Women, Family, and Ritual in Renaissance Italy.* Translated by Lydia G. Cochrane. Chicago: University of Chicago Press, 1985.

Le Roy Ladurie, Emmanuel. *Les Paysans de Languedoc.* Paris: Ecole Pratique des Hautes Etudes and Mouton, 1966.

Lougee, Carolyn C. *"Le Paradis des Femmes": Women, Salons, and Social Stratification in Seventeenth-Century France.* Princeton: Princeton University Press, 1976.

MacLean, Ian. *The Renaissance Notion of Woman: A Study in the*

Fortunes of Scholasticism and Medical Science in European Intellectual Life. Cambridge Monographs on the History of Medicine. Cambridge: Cambridge University Press, 1980.

Martines, Lauro. "A Way of Looking at Women in Renaissance Florence." *Journal of Medieval and Renaissance Studies* 4 (Spring 1974):15–28.

Maulde de Claviere, R. de. *The Women of the Renaissance: A Study of Feminism.* Translated by George H. Ely. New York: G. P. Putnam's Sons, 1905. Reprint. Folcroft, Pa.: Folcroft Library Editions, 1978.

Montaigu, Henry. *La Guerre des dames: la fin des féodaux.* Paris: Olivier Orban, 1981.

Monter, E. William. "Women in Calvinist Geneva, 1550–1800." *Signs* 6 (Winter 1980):189–209.

Notestein, Wallace. "The English Woman 1580–1650." In *Studies in Social History Presented to G. M. Trevelyan,* edited by J. H. Plumb, 69–107. London: Longmans, Green and Co., 1955. Reprint. Freeport, N.Y.: Books for Libraries Press, 1969.

Odorisio, Ginevra Conti. *Donna e società nel seicento: Lucrezia Marinelli e Arcangela Tarabotti.* Rome: Bulzoni Editore, 1979.

O'Faolain, Julia, ed. *Not in God's Image: A History of Women in Europe from the Greeks to the Nineteenth Century.* New York: Harper and Row, 1973.

Orgel, Stephen. *The Illusion of Power: Political Theater in the English Renaissance.* Berkeley and Los Angeles: University of California Press, 1975.

Plowden, Alison. *Tudor Women, Queens and Commoners.* New York: Atheneum, 1979.

Pozzi, Giovanni. "Il Ritratto della donna nella poesia d'inizio Cinquecento e la pittura di Giorgione." *Lettere Italiane* 31 (1979):3–30.

Prior, Mary, ed. *Women in English Society, 1500–1800.* London and New York: Methuen, 1985.

Radcliff-Umstead, Douglas, ed. *The Roles and Images of Women in the Middle Ages and Renaissance.* University of Pittsburgh Publications on the Middle Ages and the Renaissance, vol. 3. Pittsburgh: University of Pittsburgh Center for Medieval and Renaissance Studies, 1975.

————, ed. *Human Sexuality in the Middle Ages and Renaissance.* University of Pittsburgh Publications on the Middle Ages and the Renaissance, vol. 4. Pittsburgh: University of Pittsburgh Center for Medieval and Renaissance Studies, 1978.

Rat, Maurice. *Dames et bourgeoises amoureuses ou galantes du XVIe siècle.* Paris: Plon, 1955.

Rodocanachi, Emmanuel P. *La femme italienne avant, pendant et après la Renaissance*. Paris: Hachette, 1922.

Rogers, Katharine M. *The Troublesome Helpmate: A History of Misogyny in Literature*. Seattle and London: University of Washington Press, 1966.

Rose, Mary Beth, ed. *Women in the Middle Ages and the Renaissance: Literary and Historical Perspectives*. Syracuse: Syracuse University Press, 1985.

Rowbotham, Sheila. *Hidden from History: Rediscovering Women in History from the Seventeenth Century to the Present*. New York: Vintage, 1976.

―――. *Women, Resistance, and Revolution*. New York and London: Pantheon Books, 1972.

Ruggiero, Guido. *The Boundaries of Eros: Sex Crime and Sexuality in Renaissance Venice*. New York and Oxford: Oxford University Press, 1985.

Sachs, Hannelore. *The Renaissance Woman*. Translated by Marianne Herzfield. New York: McGraw-Hill, 1971.

Savoye-Ferreras, Jacqueline. *La Situation ambigüe de la femme au XVe siècle*. Paris: Ediciones Hispano-Americanas, 1966.

Schleiner, Winfried. "*Divina virago*: Queen Elizabeth as an Amazon." *Studies in Philology* 75 (1978):163–80.

Shapiro, Susan C. "Feminists in Elizabethan England." *History Today* 27 (November 1977):703–11.

Smith, Hilda L. *Reason's Disciples: Seventeenth-Century English Feminists*. Urbana: University of Illinois Press, 1982.

Springer, Marlene, ed. *What Manner of Woman: Essays on English and American Life and Literature*. New York: New York University Press, 1977.

Stenton, Doris. *The English Woman in History*. New York: Macmillan, 1957.

Thomas, Keith. "The Double Standard." *Journal of the History of Ideas* 20 (April 1959):195–216.

Thompson, Roger. *Women in Stuart England and America: A Comparative Study*. London and Boston: Routledge and Kegan Paul, 1974.

Warnicke, Retha M. *Women of the English Renaissance and Reformation*. Contributions in Women's Studies, no. 38. Westport, Conn.: Greenwood Press, 1983.

Weinstein, Minna F. "Reconstructing Our Past: Reflections on Tudor Women." *International Journal of Women's Studies* 1 (March–April 1978):133–40.

Wrightson, Keith. *English Society 1580–1680*. London: Hutchinson, 1982.

Yates, Francis A. *Astraea: The Imperial Theme in the Sixteenth Century*. London and Boston: Routledge and Kegan Paul, 1975.

3. Literary Criticism

Bamber, Linda. *Comic Women, Tragic Men: A Study of Gender and Genre in Shakespeare.* Stanford: Stanford University Press, 1982.

Berent, Eberhart. "Frauenverehrung und Frauenverachtung in der Dichtung des frühen Barock." In *Studies in Germanic Languages and Literature,* edited by Robert A. Fowkes and Volkmar Sander, 21–34. Reutlingen: Hutzler, 1967.

Berger, Harry. "Busirane and the War Between the Sexes: An Interpretation of *The Faerie Queene* III.xi.xii." *English Literary Renaissance* 1 (1971):99–121.

Bernard, Robert W. "Feminist Rhetoric for the Renaissance Woman in Marguerite de Navarre's *Heptaméron.*" *Chimères* 15, no. 2 (Spring 1982):73–89.

Boose, Lynda E. "The Father of the Bride in Shakespeare." *PMLA* 97 (May 1982):325–47.

Brownlee, Marina Scordilis. "Wolves and Sheep: Symmetrical Undermining in Day III of the *Decameron.*" *Romance Notes* 24, no. 3 (1984):1–5.

Bruyn, Lucy de. *Woman and the Devil in Sixteenth Century Literature.* Tisbury: Compton Press, 1979.

Cotton, Nancy. *Women Playwrights in England, c. 1363–1750.* Lewisburg, Pa.: Bucknell University Press; and London and Toronto: Associated University Presses, 1980.

Dash, Irene G. *Wooing, Wedding, and Power: Women in Shakespeare's Plays.* New York: Columbia University Press, 1981.

El Saffar, Ruth. *Beyond Fiction: The Recovery of the Feminine in the Novels of Cervantes.* Berkeley: University of California Press, 1984.

Erickson, Peter, and Coppélia Kahn, eds. *Shakespeare's 'Rough Magic': Renaissance Essays in Honor of C. L. Barber.* Newark, Del.: University of Delaware Press, 1985.

———. *Patriarchal Structures in Shakespeare's Drama.* Berkeley: University of California Press, 1985.

Falks, Cyril. "Penelope Rich and the Poets." In *Essays by Divers Hands, Being the Transactions of the Royal Society of Literature of the United Kingdom,* edited by Angela Thirkell, 123–37. Oxford: Oxford University Press, 1956.

Feugère, Léon Jacques. *Les Femmes poètes au XVIe siècle.* Paris: Didier, 1860. Reprint. Geneva: Slatkine, 1969.

Freccero, Carla. "Damning Haughty Dames: Panurge and the Haulte Dame de Paris (*Pantagruel* 14)." *Journal of Medieval and Renaissance Studies* 15 (Spring 1985):57–67.

———. "The 'Instance' of the Letter: Woman in the Text of Rabelais." In *The Incomparable Book: Rabelais and his Art,* edited by Raymond La Charité. Lexington, Ky.: French Forum, 1986.

Fritz, Angela McCourt. "The Novel Women: Origins of the Feminist

Literary Tradition in England and France." In *New Research on Women at the University of Michigan*, edited by Dorothy McGuigan, 20–46. Ann Arbor: University of Michigan, Center for Continuing Education of Women, 1974.

Froula, Christine. "When Eve Reads Milton: Undoing the Canonical Economy." *Critical Inquiry* 10 (December 1983):321–47.

Gagen, Jean Elizabeth. *The New Woman: Her Emergence in English Drama, 1600–1730.* New York: Twayne Publishers, 1954.

Giamatti, A. Bartlett. "A Prince and Her Poet." *The Yale Review* 73 (1984):321–37.

Goldberg, Jonathan. *Endlesse Worke: Spenser and the Structures of Discourse.* Baltimore: The Johns Hopkins University Press, 1981.

————. *James I and the Politics of Literature: Jonson, Shakespeare, Donne, and Their Contemporaries.* Baltimore: The Johns Hopkins University Press, 1983.

————. "Sodomy and Society: The Case of Christopher Marlowe." *Southwest Review* 69 (1984):371–78.

Greenblatt, Stephen. *Renaissance Self-Fashioning: From More to Shakespeare.* Chicago and London: The University of Chicago Press, 1980.

————, ed. *The Forms of Power and the Power of Forms.* Special issue of *Genre* 15, nos. 1–2 (1982).

Greene, Gayle, and Coppélia Kahn. "The Social Construction of Woman." In *Making a Difference: Feminist Literary Criticism*, edited by Gayle Greene and Coppélia Kahn. London: Methuen, 1985.

Greene, Gayle, and Carolyn Ruth Swift, eds. *Feminist Criticism of Shakespeare.* Two special issues of *Women's Studies: An Interdisciplinary Journal* 9 (1981):1–217.

Guidi, José. *Images de la femme dans la littérature italienne de la Renaissance: préjugés misogynes et aspirations nouvelles. Castiglioni, Piccolomini, Bandello.* Paris: Université de la Sorbonne nouvelle, 1980.

Hoffman, C. Fenno, Jr. "Catherine Parr as a Woman of Letters." *Huntington Library Quarterly* 23 (August 1960):349–67.

Hulse, Clark. *Metamorphic Verse: The Elizabethan Minor Epic.* Princeton: Princeton University Press, 1981.

Jardine, Lisa. *Still Harping on Daughters: Women and Drama in the Age of Shakespeare.* Sussex, England: Harvester Press, 1983.

Jondorf, Gillian. "Petrarchan Variations in Pernette du Guillet and Louise Labé." *MLR* 71 (1976):766–78.

Jones, Ann R. "Assimilation with a Difference: Renaissance Women Poets and Literary Influence." *Yale French Studies* 62 (1981):135–53.

Jones, Ann R., and Peter Stallybrass. "The Politics of *Astrophil and Stella.*" *Studies in English Literature* 24 (1984):53–68.

Jordan, Constance. "Feminism and the Humanists: The Case of Sir

Thomas Elyot's *Defence of Good Women.*" *Renaissance Quarterly* 36 (Summer 1983):181–201.

Kahn, Coppélia. "The Rape in Shakespeare's *Lucrece.*" *Shakespeare Studies* 9 (1976):45–72.

———. *Man's Estate: Masculine Identity in Shakespeare.* Berkeley: University of California Press, 1981.

———. "Excavating 'Those Dim Minoan Regions': Maternal Subtexts in Patriarchal Literature." *Diacritics* 12 (Summer 1982):32–41.

Kahn, Coppélia, and Murray M. Schwartz, eds. *Representing Shakespeare: New Psychoanalytic Essays.* Baltimore: Johns Hopkins University Press, 1980.

Kastan, David Scott. "Shakespeare and 'The Way of Womenkind.' " *Daedalus* 111 (Summer 1982):115–30.

Kinney, Arthur F., and Kirby Farrell, eds. *Women in the Renaissance.* Special issue of *English Literary Renaissance* 14 (Autumn 1984):253–439.

Lanham, Richard. "*Astrophil and Stella*: Pure and Impure Persuasion." *English Literary Renaissance* 2 (1972):100–115.

Larnac, Jean. *Histoire de la littérature féminine en France.* 11th ed. Paris: Editions Kra, 1929.

Lazard, Madeleine. *Images littéraires de la femme à la Renaissance.* Paris: Presses Universitaires de France, 1985.

Lefranc, Abel. *Grands écrivains français de la Renaissance.* Paris: Librairie Ancienne Honoré Champion, 1914.

Lenz, Carolyn Ruth, Gayle Green, and Carol Thomas Neely, eds. *The Woman's Part: Feminist Criticism of Shakespeare.* Urbana: University of Illinois Press, 1980.

McAuliffe, Denis J. "Vittoria Colonna and Renaissance Poetics, Convention and Society." In *Il Rinascimento: Aspetti e problemi attuali,* edited by Vittore Branca et al., 531–42. Florence: Olschki, 1982.

McKendrick, Melveena. *Woman and Society in the Spanish Drama of the Golden Age.* New York: Cambridge University Press, 1974.

McKewin, Carole. "Shakespeare Liberata: Shakespeare, the Nature of Women, and the New Feminist Criticism." *Mosaic* 10 (Spring 1977):157–64.

MacLean, Ian. *Woman Triumphant: Feminism in French Literature, 1610–1652.* Oxford and New York: Oxford University Press, 1977.

Marcus, Leah Sinanoglou. "The Milieu of Milton's *Comus*: Judicial Reform at Ludlow and the Problem of Sexual Assault." *Criticism* 25 (Fall 1983):293–327.

Miller, Beth, ed. *Women in Hispanic Literature: Icons and Fallen Idols.* Berkeley: University of California Press, 1983.

Montrose, Louis Adrian. "Celebration and Insinuation: Sir Philip

Sidney and the Motives of Elizabethan Courtship." *Renaissance Drama* 8 (1977):3–35.

———. " 'Eliza, Queene of Shepheardes' and the Pastoral of Power." *English Literary Renaissance* 10 (1980):153–82.

———. " 'The place of a brother' in *As You Like It*: Social Process and Comic Form." *Shakespeare Quarterly* 32 (1981):28–54.

———. " 'Shaping Fantasies': Figurations of Gender and Power in Elizabethan Culture." *Representations* 1, no. 2 (Spring 1983):61–94.

———. "The Elizabethan Subject and the Spenserian Text." In *Literary Theory and Renaissance Texts*, edited by Patricia Parker and David Quint. Baltimore: The Johns Hopkins University Press, 1985.

———. *In Mirrors More than One: Elizabeth I and the Figurations of Power.* Chicago: University of Chicago Press, 1986.

Northrup, Douglas A. "Spenser's Defence of Elizabeth." *University of Toronto Quarterly* 38 (April 1969):277–94.

Novy, Marianne. "Shakespeare and Emotional Distance in the Elizabethan Family." *Theatre Journal* 33 (October 1981):316–26.

Parten, Anne. "Masculine Adultery and Feminine Rejoinders in Shakespeare, Dekker and Sharpham." *Mosaic* 17 (1984):9–18.

Perrigaud, Martha. "The Self-Made Cuckold: Marguerite de Navarre and Parole féminine." *Chimères* (Spring 1982):55–69.

Phillips, James E., Jr. "The Background of Spenser's Attitude toward Women Rulers." *Huntington Library Quarterly* 5 (1941–42):5–32.

———. "The Woman Ruler in Spenser's *Faerie Queene.*" *Huntington Library Quarterly* 5 (1941–42):211–34.

———. *Images of a Queen: Mary Stuart in Sixteenth Century Literature.* Berkeley: University of California Press, 1964.

Quilligan, Maureen. *Milton's Spenser: The Politics of Reading.* Ithaca, N.Y.: Cornell University Press, 1983.

Richardson, Lula McDowell. *The Forerunners of Feminism in French Literature of the Renaissance from Christine of Pisa to Marie de Gournay.* Johns Hopkins Studies in Romance Literature and Languages, no. 12. Baltimore: The Johns Hopkins University Press, 1929.

Riefer, Marcia. " 'Instruments of Some More Mightier Member': The Constriction of Female Power in *Measure for Measure.*" *Shakespeare Quarterly* 35 (Summer 1984):157–69.

Rigolot, François. "Louise Labé et la redécouverte de Sappho." *Nouvelle Revue du XVIe Siècle* 1 (1983):19–31.

———. "Quel *genre* d'amour pour Louise Labé?" *Poétique* 55 (September 1983):303–17.

———. "Signature et Signification: Les Baisers de Louise Labé." *Romanic Review* 75 (January 1984):10–24.

Screech, Michael A. "The Illusion of Postel's Feminism." *Journal of the Warburg and Courtauld Institutes* 16 (1953):162–70.

————. *The Rabelaisian Marriage: Aspects of Rabelais's Religion, Ethics, and Comic Philosophy*. London: Edward Arnold, 1958.

Shepherd, Simon. *Amazons and Warrior Women: Varieties of Feminism in Seventeenth-Century Drama*. New York: St. Martin's Press, 1981.

Sims, Edna M. "Resumen de la imagen negativa de la mujer en la literatura española hasta mediados del siglo XVI." *Revista de estudios hispanicos* 11 (October 1977):433–49.

Stallybrass, Peter. "*Macbeth* and Witchcraft." In *Focus on "Macbeth,"* edited by John Russell Brown, 189–209. London: Routledge and Kegan Paul, 1982.

Thorp, Willard. *The Triumph of Realism in Elizabethan Drama, 1558–1612*. Princeton: Princeton University Press, 1928.

Tomalin, Margaret. *The Fortunes of the Warrior Heroine in Italian Literature: An Index of Emancipation*. L'Interprete, vol. 33. Ravenna: Longo Editore, 1982.

Trafton, Dain A. "Politics and the Praise of Women: Political Doctrine in the *Courtier*'s Third Book." In *Castiglione: The Ideal and the Real in Renaissance Culture*, edited by Robert Hanning and David Rosand, 29–44. New Haven and London: Yale University Press, 1983.

Vickers, Nancy J. "Diana Described: Scattered Woman and Scattered Rhyme." *Critical Inquiry* 8 (Winter 1981):265–79.

————. " 'The Blazon of Sweet Beauty's Best': Shakespeare's *Lucrece*." In *Shakespeare and the Question of Theory*, edited by Geoffrey Hartman and Patricia Parker, 96–116. London: Methuen, 1986.

————. "The Mistress in the Masterpiece." In *The Poetics of Gender*, edited by Nancy K. Miller. New York: Columbia University Press, 1986.

Waller, Marguerite. *Petrarch's Poetics and Literary History*. Amherst: University of Massachusetts Press, 1980.

Woodbridge, Linda. *Women and the English Renaissance: Literature and the Nature of Womankind, 1540–1620*. Urbana and Chicago: University of Illinois Press, 1984.

Wright, Celeste Turner. "The Amazons in Elizabethan Literature." *Studies in Philology* 37 (1940):433–56.

————. "The Elizabethan Female Worthies." *Studies in Philology* 43 (1946):628–43.

4. Art

Allen, Virginia. "The Naked Lady: A Look at Venus in the Renaissance." *Feminist Art Journal* 6 (Spring 1977):27–29.

Berger, Robert W. "Rubens's *Queen Tomyris with the Head of Cyrus*." *Bulletin of the Museum of Fine Arts* [Boston] 77 (1979):4–35.

Bissell, R. Ward. "Artemisia Gentileschi—A New Documented Chronology." *The Art Bulletin* 50 (June 1968):153–68.

Broude, Norma, and Mary D. Garrard, eds. *Feminism and Art History: Questioning the Litany*. New York: Harper and Row, 1982.

Cropper, Elizabeth. "On Beautiful Women: Parmigianino, Petrarchismo, and the Vernacular Style." *The Art Bulletin* 58 (1976):374–94.

Fine, Elsa Honig. *Women and Art: A History of Women Painters and Sculptors from the Renaissance to the Twentieth Century*. Montclair, N.J.: Allanheld and Schram. 1978.

Garrard, Mary. "Artemisia Gentileschi's *Self-Portrait as the Allegory of Painting*." *The Art Bulletin* 62 (1980):97–112.

Haraszti-Takacs, Marianna. "Nouvelles données relatives à la vie et à l'oeuvre de Sofonisba Anguissola." *Bulletin du Musée hongrois des beaux-arts* 31 (1968):53–67.

Harris, Ann Sutherland, and Linda Nochlin. *Women Artists: 1550–1950*. New York: Alfred A. Knopf, 1977.

Hofrichter, Frima Fox. "Artemisia Gentileschi's Uffizi *Judith* and a Lost Rubens." *The Rutgers Art Review* 1 (1980):9–15.

Kahr, Madlyn Millner. "Rembrandt and Delilah." *The Art Bulletin* 55 (1973):240–59.

Kühnel-Kunze, Irene. "Zur Bildniskunst der Sofonisba und Lucia Anguisciola." *Pantheon* 20 (March/April 1962):83–96.

Marrow, Deborah. *The Art Patronage of Maria de' Medeci*. Ann Arbor: UMI Research Press, 1983.

Martindale, Andrew. "The Patronage of Isabella d'Este at Mantua." *Apollo* 79 (March 1964):183–91.

Parker, Rozsika, and Griselda Pollock. *Old Mistresses: Women, Art and Ideology*. New York: Pantheon Books, 1981.

Petersen, Karen, and J. J. Wilson eds. *Women Artists: Recognition and Reappraisal from the Early Middle Ages to the Twentieth Century*. New York: New York University Press, 1976.

Ragg, Laura. *The Women Artists of Bologna*. London: Methuen, 1907.

Steinberg, Leo. *The Sexuality of Christ in Renaissance Art and Modern Oblivion*. New York: Pantheon Books, 1984.

Strong, Roy. *The Cult of Elizabeth: Elizabethan Portraiture and Pageantry*. London: Thames and Hudson, 1977.

Wirth, Jean. *La Jeune Fille et la mort: recherches sur les thèmes macabres dans l'art germanique de la Renaissance*. Geneva: Droz, 1979.

5. Education

Adamson, J. W. "The Extent of Literacy in England in the Fifteenth and Sixteenth Centuries: Notes and Conjectures." *The Library*, 4th ser., 10 (1929):163–93.

Bayne, Diane Valeri. "The Instruction of a Christian Woman: Richard

Hyrde and the Thomas More Circle." *Moreana* 12 (February 1975):5–15.

Bornstein, Diane. Introduction to *Distaves and Dames: Renaissance Treatises for and about Women*. Delmar, N.Y.: Scholars' Facsimiles and Reprints, 1978.

Brink, J. R. *Female Scholars: A Tradition of Learned Women before 1800*. Montreal: Eden Press Women's Publications, 1980.

Cannon, Mary A. *Education of Women during the Renaissance*. Washington, D.C.: National Capitol Press, 1916.

Charlton, Kenneth. *Education in Renaissance England*. London: Routledge and Kegan Paul, 1965.

Cressy, David. *Education in Tudor and Stuart England*. London: Edwin Arnold, 1975.

————. *Literacy and the Social Order: Reading and Writing in Tudor and Stuart England*. Cambridge: Cambridge University Press, 1980.

Green, Lowell C. "The Education of Women in the Reformation." *History of Education Quarterly* 19 (Spring 1979):93–116.

Hull, Suzanne W. *Chaste, Silent and Obedient: English Books for Women, 1475–1640*. San Marino: Huntington Library, 1982.

Hyrde, Richard. "A Plea for Learned Women." *Moreana* 13 (February 1967):5–24.

Kaufman, Gloria. "Juan Luis Vives on the Education of Women, 1523." *Signs* 3 (Summer 1978):891–97.

Keating, L. Clark. *Studies on the Literary Salon in France, 1550–1615*. Cambridge: Harvard University Press, 1941.

Kelso, Ruth. *Doctrine for the Lady of the Renaissance*. Urbana: University of Illinois Press, 1956.

King, Margaret Leah. "The Religious Retreat of Isotta Nogarola (1418–1466): Sexism and Its Consequences in the Fifteenth Century." *Signs* 3 (Summer 1978):807–22.

————. "Thwarted Ambitions: Six Learned Women of the Early Italian Renaissance." *Soundings* 59 (Fall 1976):280–300.

Labalme, Patricia, ed. *Beyond Their Sex: Learned Women of the European Past*. New York: New York University Press, 1980.

Murray, Lucy Hunter. *The Ideal of the Court Lady, 1561–1625*. Chicago: University of Chicago Libraries, 1938.

Quentin-Bauchart, Ernest. *Les Femmes bibliophiles de France* (XVIe, XVIIe, & XVIIIe siècles). Paris: D. Morgand, 1886.

Rabil, Albert Jr. *Laura Cereta: Quattrocento Humanist*. Medieval and Renaissance Texts and Studies, vol. 3. Binghamton, N.Y.: Center for Medieval and Early Renaissance Studies, State University of New York at Binghamton, 1981.

Rousselot, Paul. *Histoire de l'éducation des femmes en France*. Paris: Didier, 1883.

Watson, Foster, ed. *Vives and the Renascence Education of Women*. New

York: Longmans, Green and Co., 1912. Reprint. New York: Kelly, 1972.

Wright, Louis B. "The Reading of Renaissance English Women." *Studies in Philology* 28 (1931):671–88.

6. Religion

Bainton, Roland H. "The Role of Women in the Reformation." *Archiv für Reformationsgeschichte* 63 (1972):141–42.

————. *Women of the Reformation in Germany and Italy.* Minneapolis: Augsburg Publishing House, 1971. Reprint. Boston: Beacon Press, 1974.

————. *Women of the Reformation in France and England.* Minneapolis: Augsburg Publishing House, 1973. Reprint. Boston: Beacon Press, 1975.

Biéler, André. *L'Homme et la femme dans la morale calviniste: la doctrine réformée sur l'amour, le mariage, le célibat, le divorce, l'adultère et la prostitution, considérée dans son cadre historique.* Geneva: Labor et Fides, 1963.

Hanlon, Joseph Damien, Sister. "These Be But Women." In *From the Renaissance to the Counter-Reformation*, edited by Charles H. Carter, 371–400. New York: Random House, 1965.

Haugaard, William P. "Katharine Parr: The Religious Convictions of a Renaissance Queen." *Renaissance Quarterly* 22 (Winter 1969):346–59.

Inguanti, Maria. *Le Donne della Riforma in Italia.* Rome: Casa editrice battista dell'unione cristiana evangelica battista d'Italia, 1968.

Irwin, Joyce, L., ed. *Womanhood in Radical Protestantism: 1525–1675.* Studies in Women and Religion, vol. 1. Lewiston, N.Y.: Edwin Mellen Press, 1979.

Roelker, Nancy Lyman. "The Appeal of Calvinism to French Noblewomen in the Sixteenth Century." *The Journal of Interdisciplinary History* 2 (Spring 1972):391–418.

————. "The Role of Noble Women in the French Reformation." *Archiv für Reformationsgeschichte* 63 (1972):168–95.

Ruether, Rosemary Radford, ed. *Religion and Sexism: Images of Woman in the Jewish and Christian Traditions.* New York: Simon and Schuster, 1974.

Steinmetz, David C. "Theological Reflections on the Reformation and the Status of Women." *Duke Divinity School Review* 41 (Fall 1976):197–207.

Thomas, Keith. *Religion and the Decline of Magic.* London and New York: Scribner, 1971.

————. "Women and the Civil War Sects." *Past and Present* 13 (1958):42–62.

Thomson, David P. *Women of the Scottish Reformation: Their Contribution to the Protestant Cause.* Crieff, Perthshire: St. Ninian's, 1960.

7. Law

Hess, Rolf-Dieter. *Familien- und Erbrecht im württembergischen Landrecht von 1555, unter besonderer Berücksichtigung des alteren württembergischen Rechts.* Stuttgart: W. Kohlhammer, 1968.

Hogrefe, Pearl. "Legal Rights of Tudor Women and Their Circumvention." *The Sixteenth Century Journal* 3 (1972):97–105.

Perry, Mary Elizabeth. " 'Lost Women' in Early Modern Seville: The Politics of Prostitution." *Feminist Studies* 4 (February 1978):195–214.

Petot, Pierre. *Le Statut de la femme dans les pays coutumiers français du XIIIe au XVIIIe siècles.* Recueils de la Société Jean Bodin pour l'histoire comparative des institutions, vol. 12. Brussels: Editions de la Librairie Encyclopédique, 1962.

Rossiaud, Jacques. "Prostitution, Youth and Society in the Towns of Southeastern France in the Fifteenth Century." In *Deviants and the Abandoned in French Society*, edited by Robert Forster and Orest Ranum, 1–46. Baltimore: The Johns Hopkins University Press, 1978.

Ruggiero, Guido. "Sexual Criminality in the Early Renaissance: Venice 1338–1358." *Journal of Social History* 8 (Summer 1975):18–37.

Samaha, Joel. "Gleanings from Local Criminal Court Records: Sedition Amongst the 'Inarticulate' in Elizabethan Essex." *The Journal of Social History* 8 (Summer 1975):61–79.

Sharpe, J. A. "The History of Crime in Late Medieval and Early Modern England: A Review of the Field." *Social History* 7 (1982):187–203.

Weiner, Carol Z. "Sex Roles and Crime in Late Elizabethan Hertfordshire." *Journal of Social History* 8 (Summer 1975):38–60.

8. Witchcraft

Anderson, Alan, and Raymond Gordon. "Witchcraft and the Status of Women—The Case of England." *British Journal of Sociology* 29 (June 1978):171–84.

Briggs, Katherine Mary. *Pale Hecate's Team: An Examination of the Beliefs on Witchcraft and Magic among Shakespeare's Contemporaries and His Immediate Successors.* New York: Humanities Press, 1962.

Clark, Stuart. "Inversion, Misrule, and the Meaning of Witchcraft." *Past and Present* 87 (1980):98–127.

Curie, E. P. "The Control of Witchcraft in Renaissance Europe." In *The Social Organization of Law,* edited by Donald Black and Maureen Mileski, 344–67. New York: Seminar Press, 1973.

Douglas, Mary, ed. *Witchcraft Confessions and Accusations.* New York and London: Tavistock, 1970.

Kors, A. C., and E. Peters, eds. *Witchcraft in Europe 1100–1700: A Documentary History.* Philadelphia: University of Pennsylvania Press, 1972.

MacFarlane, Alan. *Witchcraft in Tudor and Stuart England.* New York: Harper and Row, 1970.

————. "Witchcraft in Tudor and Stuart Essex." In *Crime in England, 1550–1800,* edited by J. S. Cockburn, 72–89. Princeton: Princeton University Press, 1977.

Marshburn, Joseph H. *Murder and Witchcraft in England, 1550–1640.* Norman: University of Oklahoma Press, 1971.

Midelfort, Eric. *Witchhunting in Southwestern Germany, 1562–1684: The Social and Intellectual Foundations.* Stanford: Stanford University Press, 1972.

Monter, E. William. "Inflation and Witchcraft: The Case of Jean Bodin." In *Action and Conviction in Early Modern Europe,* edited by Theodore K. Rabb and Jerrold E. Siegel, 371–89. Princeton: Princeton University Press, 1969.

————. *Witchcraft in France and Switzerland: The Borderlands during the Reformation.* Ithaca, N.Y.: Cornell University Press, 1976.

Nelson, Mary. "Why Witches Were Women." In *Women: A Feminist Perspective,* edited by Jo Freeman, 451–68. Palo Alto, Ca.: Mayfield Publishing Co., 1975.

Soman, Alfred. "The Parlement of Paris and the Great Witch Hunt (1565–1640)." *Sixteenth Century Journal* 9 (July 1978):31–44.

Villette, Pierre. *La Sorcellerie et sa répression dans le nord de la France.* Paris: La Pensée Universelle, 1976.

Young, Alan R. "Elizabeth Lowys: Witch and Social Victim, 1564." *History Today* 22 (December 1972):879–85.

9. Medicine

Benedek, Thomas G. "The Changing Relationship between Midwives and Physicians during the Renaissance." *Bulletin of the History of Medicine* 51 (Winter 1977):550–64.

Boss, J. M. "The Seventeenth-Century Transformation of the Hysteric Affection, and Sydenham's Baconian Medicine." *Psychological Medicine* 9 (May 1979):221–34.

Brain, Lord Russell. "The Concept of Hysteria in the Time of William Harvey." *Proceedings of the Royal Society of Medicine* 56 (April 1963):317–24.

Donnison, Jean. *Midwives and Medical Men: A History of Inter-Professional Rivalries and Women's Rights.* New York: Schocken Books, 1977.

Eccles, A. *Obstetrics and Gynaecology in Tudor and Stuart England.* Kent, Ohio: Kent State University Press, 1982.

Flack, Isaac Harvey [Harvey Graham]. *Eternal Eve: The History of Gynaecology and Obstetrics.* Garden City, N.Y.: Doubleday, 1951.

Forbes, Thomas R. *The Midwife and the Witch.* New Haven: Yale University Press, 1966.

————. "The Regulation of English Midwives in the Sixteenth and Seventeenth Centuries." *Medical History* 8 (July 1964):235–44.

Hunter, Richard, and Ida MacAlpine, eds. *Three Hundred Years of Psychiatry, 1535–1860.* London and New York: Oxford University Press, 1963.

MacLennan, Hector. "A Gynaecologist Looks at the Tudors." *Medical History* 11 (1967):66–74.

Mead, Kate Campbell (Hurd). *A History of Women in Medicine.* Haddam, Conn.: Haddam Press, 1938.

Niccoli, Ottavia. " 'Menstruum quasi Monstruum': parti mostruosi e tabù mestruale nel '500." *Quaderni Storici* 44 (August 1980):402–28.

Schnucker, Robert V. "Elizabethan Birth Control and Puritan Attitudes." *Journal of Interdisciplinary History* 5 (Spring 1975):655–68.

Smith, Hilda. "Gynecology and Ideology in Seventeenth-Century England." In *Liberating Women's History,* edited by Berenice A. Carroll, 97–114. Urbana: University of Illinois Press, 1976.

Veith, Ilza. *Hysteria: The History of a Disease.* Chicago: University of Chicago Press, 1965.

Zilboorg, Gregory. *The Medical Man and the Witch during the Renaissance.* Baltimore: The Johns Hopkins University Press, 1935. Reprint. New York: Cooper Square Publishers, 1969.

10. Marriage and the Family

Ariès, Philippe. *Centuries of Childhood: A Social History of Family Life.* Translated by Robert Baldick. New York: Vintage Books, 1962.

Bels, Pierre. "La Formation du lien de mariage dans l'église protestante française (XVIe et XVII siècles)." *Le Droit des gens mariés* 27 (1966):331–44.

————. *Le Mariage des protestants français jusqu'en 1685.* Paris: Librairie générale de droit et de jurisprudence, 1968.

Bullard, Melissa Meriam. "Marriage Politics and the Family in Florence: The Strozzi-Medici Alliance of 1508." *American Historical Review* 84 (June 1979):668–87.

Burton, Elizabeth. *The Elizabethans at Home.* London: Secker and Warburg, 1958.

————. *The Early Tudors at Home, 1485–1558.* London: Allen Lane, 1976.

Davies, Kathleen M. "The Sacred Condition of Equality—How

Original Were Puritan Doctrines of Marriage?" *Social History* 5 (1977):563–80.

Diefendorf, Barbara B. "Widowhood and Remarriage in Sixteenth-Century Paris." *Journal of Family History* 7 (Winter 1982):379–95.

Fichtner, Paula Sutter. "Dynastic Marriage in Sixteenth-Century Habsburg Diplomacy and Statecraft: An Interdisciplinary Approach." *American Historical Review* 81 (April 1976):243–65.

Fitz, Linda. " 'What Says the Married Woman?': Marriage Theory and Feminism in the English Renaissance." *Mosaic* 13, no. 2 (Winter 1980):1–22.

Herlihy, David, and Christiane Klapisch-Zuber. *Les Toscans et leurs familles.* Paris: Ecole des hautes études en sciences sociales, 1978.

Johnson, James T. *A Society Ordained by God: English Puritan Marriage Doctrine in the First Half of the Seventeenth Century.* Nashville: Abingdon Press, 1970.

Kelly, Joan. "Family Life: A Historical Perspective." In *Household and Kin,* edited by Amy Swerdlow, 1–45. Old Westbury, N.Y.: Feminist Press, 1981.

Kirshner, Julius, and Anthony Molho. "The Dowry Fund and the Marriage Market in Early Quattrocento Florence." *Journal of Modern History* 50 (September 1978):403–38.

Lafon, J. *Régimes matrimoniaux et mutations sociales: les époux bordelais (1450–1550).* Paris: SEVPEN, 1972.

Laslett, Peter. *Family Life and Illicit Love in Earlier Generations: Essays in Historical Sociology.* Cambridge: Cambridge University Press, 1977.

Le Goff, Jacques, and Jean-Claude Schmitt, eds. *Le Charivari: actes de la table ronde organisée à Paris [25–27 avril, 1977] par L'Ecole des Hautes Etudes en Sciences Sociales et le Centre National de la Recherche Scientifique.* Paris: CNRS, 1981.

Le Roy Ladurie, Emmanuel. "Family Structures and Inheritance Customs in Sixteenth Century France." In *Family and Society,* edited by Robert Forster and Orest Ranum, 75–103. Baltimore: The Johns Hopkins University Press, 1976.

Levine, David. *Family Formation in an Age of Nascent Capitalism.* New York: Academic Press, 1977.

MacFarlane, Alan. *The Origins of English Individualism: The Family, Property and Social Transition.* Oxford: Blackwell, 1978.

Ozment, Steven. *When Fathers Ruled: Family Life in Reformation Europe.* Cambridge: Harvard University Press, 1983.

Stone, Lawrence. *The Crisis of the Aristocracy, 1558–1641.* Oxford: Oxford University Press, 1965.

————. "The Rise of the Nuclear Family in Early Modern England: The Patriarchal Stage." In *The Family in History,* edited by Charles

E. Rosenberg, 13–57. Philadelphia: University of Pennsylvania Press, 1975.

—. *The Family, Sex and Marriage in England, 1500–1800.* New York: Harper and Row, 1977.

Wyntjes, Sherrin Marshall. "Survivors and Status: Widowhood and Family in the Early Modern Netherlands." *Journal of Family History* 7 (Winter 1982):396–405.

Yost, John K. "The Value of Married Life for the Social Order in the Early English Renaissance." *Societas* 6 (Winter 1976):25–39.

11. Work

Beech, Beatrice. "Charlotte Guillard: A Sixteenth-Century Business Woman." *Renaissance Quarterly* 36 (Autumn 1983):345–67.

Brown, Judith C., and Jordan Goodman. "Women and Industry in Florence." *The Journal of Economic History* 40 (March 1980):73–80.

Clark, Alice. *The Working Life of Women in the Seventeenth Century.* New York: Harcourt Brace, 1920.

Dale, Marion K, "The London Silkwomen of the Fifteenth Century." *Economic History Review* 4 (October 1933):324–35.

Davis, Natalie Zemon. "Women in the *Arts Mécaniques* in Sixteenth-Century Lyon." In *Lyon et l'Europe, hommes et sociétés, mélanges d'histoire offerts à Richard Gascon.* 139–67. Lyon: Presses Universitaires de Lyon, 1980.

—. "Women in the Crafts in Sixteenth-Century Lyon." *Feminist Studies* 8 (Spring 1982):47–80.

Gilder, Rosamond. *Enter the Actress: The First Women in the Theatre.* Boston: Houghton Mifflin, 1931.

Hacker, Barton C. "Women and Military Institutions in Early Modern Europe: A Reconnaissance." *Signs* 6 (Summer 1981):643–71.

Henriques, Fernando. *Prostitution in Europe and the New World.* London: Macgibbon and Kee, 1963.

Herlihy, David. "Deaths, Marriage, Births, and the Tuscan Economy." In *Population Patterns in the Past,* edited by Ronald D. Lee, 135–64. New York: Academic Press, 1977.

Jacobsen, Grethe. "Women's Work and Women's Role: Ideology and Reality in Danish Urban Society, 1300–1550." *Scandinavian Economic History Review* 31 (1981):3–20.

Masson, Georgina. *Courtesans of the Italian Renaissance.* London: Secker and Warburg, 1975.

Middleton, Chris. "Peasants, Patriarchy and the Feudal Mode of Production in England: A Marxist Appraisal, Parts 1 and 2." *Sociological Review* 29 (Fall 1981):105–54.

—. "Patriarchal Exploitation and the Rise of English Capitalism." In *Gender, Class and Work,* edited by Eva Gamarnakow et al. London: Heinemann, 1983.

Roberts, Michael. "Sickles and Scythes: Women's Work and Men's Work at Harvest Time." *History Workshop: A Journal of Socialist Historians* no. 7 (Spring 1979):3–29.

Sullerot, Evelyne. *L'Histoire et sociologie du travail féminin.* Paris: Gonthier, 1968.

Wiesner, Merry E. "Paltry Peddlers or Essential Merchants? Women in the Distributive Trades in Early Modern Nuremberg." *Sixteenth Century Journal* 12, no. 2 (Summer 1981):3–13.

12. Politics

Elshtain, Jean Bethe. *Public Man, Private Woman: Women in Social and Political Thought.* Princeton: Princeton University Press, 1981.

Freeman, John F. "Louise of Savoy: A Case of Maternal Opportunism." *Sixteenth Century Journal* 3 (October 1972):77–98.

Giffin, Frederick C. " 'Good Queen Bess': The Monarch as Master Politician." *International Review of History and Political Science* 10 (February 1973):104–28.

Heisch, Allison. "Queen Elizabeth I: Parliamentary Rhetoric and the Exercise of Power." *Signs* 1 (Fall 1975):31–55.

———. "Queen Elizabeth and the Persistence of Patriarchy." *Feminist Review* 4 (1980):45–56.

Hinton, R. W. K. "Husbands, Fathers and Conquerors." *Political Studies* 15 (1967):291–30; and *Political Studies* 16 (1968):55–67.

Jensen, De Lamar. "Catherine de Medici and Her Florentine Friends." *Sixteenth Century Journal* 9 (July 1978):57–73.

MacCaffrey, Wallace T. *Queen Elizabeth and the Making of Policy, 1572–1588.* Princeton: Princeton University Press, 1981.

Neale, John E. *Elizabeth I and Her Parliaments.* 2 vols. London: Cape, 1957. Reprint. New York: Norton, 1966.

Paul, John E. *Catherine of Aragon and Her Friends.* New York: Fordham University Press, 1966.

Read, Conyers. *Lord Burghley and Queen Elizabeth.* New York: Alfred A. Knopf, 1960.

Scalingi, Paula Louise. "The Scepter or the Distaff: The Question of Female Sovereignty, 1516–1607." *The Historian* 41 (November 1978):59–75.

Schochet, Gordon J. *Patriarchalism in Political Thought: The Authoritarian Family and Political Speculation and Attitudes Especially in Seventeenth-Century England.* New York: Basic Books, 1975.

Strage, Mark. *Woman of Power: The Life and Times of Catherine de Medici.* New York: Harcourt Brace Jovanovich, 1976.

Weinstein, Minora. "Queen's Power: The Case of Katherine Parr." *History Today* 26 (December 1976):788–95.

Index

Absolutist monarchy, xix, xxiv, 227,
323n.5; connection to theories of the
"classical body," 124; domestication
of, 3–4, 11–12, 131; in *Richard III*,
164. *See also* Patriarchy
Adams, W. Howard, 374n.28
Adamson, Nancy, 223, 370n.57
Aers, David, 334n.8
Agrippa, Cornelius, 254–55, 377n.2,
379n.16, 381n.28, 383n.41, 392n.23
Alberti, Leon Battista, 175, 182, *Book of
the Family*, 206, 216–17, 322n.36,
355nn. 1, 3, 367nn. 30, 31, 37, 377n.2;
On Painting, 175
Alciati, *Emblematum liber*, 127, 345n.21
Allegory, 85, 89, 101, 103–4, 107, 113,
148, 171, 265, 269, 384n.8
Alpers, Paul, 385n.15
Alpers, Svetlana, 26
Althusser, Louis, 20, 318n.8, 324n.12
Amazons, 70–71, 76, 77–78, 79, 94,
330n.12, 331n.19, 381n.28; as male
fantasies of motherhood, 75
Anderson, Perry, xix, 320n.22
Androgyne, 146–53, 290, 348nn. 3, 12,
349n.18
Annalistes, 318n.9
Anne of Austria, 231, 374n.32
Anne of Cleves, 242, 245
Anne of Denmark, wife of James 1, 9,
12
Antifeminism. *See* Misogyny
Apelles, 175, 181
Aragona, Tullia d', 392n.21
Ardener, Shirley, 133, 346n.47
Arendt, Hannah, 341n.8
Aretino, Pietro, 304
Ariès, Philippe, xviii, 6, 319n.15
Ariosto, 189; *Orlando Furioso*, 257, 259,
294
Aristophanes, 146–48, 152
Aristotle, 8, 75, 241; misogynist tradi-
tion derived from, 217, 243, 245, 247–
51, 253–55, 380nn. 17, 18, 19, 382n.31
Arrow, Kenneth, 208, 363n.3

Artemisia, 230–41, 256, 373nn. 18, 20
Aubrey John, 276–77, 387n.13
Austin, J. L., 161, 384n.11
Axton, Marie, 332n.22
Aylmer, John, 131, 346n.43, 377n.2

Bacon, Sir Francis, 8, 80, 84–85, 275,
332n.26, 346n.46
Bakhtin, Mikhail, 123, 126–27, 153,
322n.36, 344n.4, 345n.16, 347n.67
Balibar, Etienne, 318n.8
Balint, Alice, and Michael Balint, 37
Barbaro, Francesco, 127, 299–300, 306–
7, 309, 345n.19, 377n.2
Barber, C. L., 35, 66, 326n.6, 328n.31,
329n.3
Bardone, Françoise, 372n.11
Barfield, Owen, 385n.18
Barri, 176
Battara, Pietro, 364n.13
Beard, Mary, 318n.6
Beaujour, Michel, 350n.27
Becker, Gary S., 366n.23, 368n.43
Béguin, Sylvie, 374n.29, 375n.34,
376n.49
Belges, Lemaire de, 289
Belleau, 289
Bellini, Giovanni, 182
Bembo, Bernardo, 358n.27
Bembo, Pietro, 182–83, 189, 357n.17
Benci, Ginevra de', 183, 187 (fig. 7), 188
(fig. 8), 189, 357n.16, 358n.27
Berger, Harry, 328n.5, 385n.13
Bernardino of Siena, Saint, 215–16,
367n.30
Berry, Edward I., 353n.8, 355n.25
Bettelheim, Bruno, 52
Bible, 343n.20, 351nn. 39, 40
Billon, François de, 374n.26, 377n.2
Blau, Francine, 366n.23
Blazon, 182, 276
Bloch, Marc, 318n.9
Bloom, Harold, 298
Blount, Charles, 275

Women's education, *cont.*
humanist treatises, 242–58, 377n.2, 383n.45; via Renaissance conduct books, 126–27. *See also* Humanism
Women's work, xviii–xix, xxvii–xxviii, 191–205, 206–24; and mortality rates, 370n.60; and Protestant ideology of sexual division of labor, 106–22; and seventeenth-century grain riots, 142; civic virtue of, 377n.2, 378n.6; devaluation of, 339n.3, 363n.4, 368n.42; domestication of, 367n.28, 369n.50; guild restrictions on, in German cloth industry, 194–205; in Renaissance Tuscany, 206–24, 365n.20. *See also* Labor, division of
Women's writing, xv, xxi, 287–98, 299–316, 389n.17; addressed to women, 307–9; impact of on normative lin-

guistic structures, 292; in defense of women, 313–14, 377n.2, 392n.23; privatization of, 299
Wright, Celeste Turner, 330n.12
Wright, Louis B., 340n.7
Wrightson, Keith, 331n.15
Wroth, Mary, 301
Wyatt, Thomas, 322n.37
Wunder, Heide, 193, 360n.11

Yates, Frances A., 332n.27, 373n.17, 374n.28, 376n.44

Zamaron, Fernand, 302
Zaretsky, Eli, 359n.4
Zenobia, xxix, 231, 243, 245–48, 254–58